Into Africa,
Out of Academia

Into Africa,
Out of Academia

A Doctor's Memoir

Kwan Kew Lai

McFarland & Company, Inc., Publishers
Jefferson, North Carolina

LIBRARY OF CONGRESS CATALOGUING-IN-PUBLICATION DATA

Names: Lai, Kwan Kew, author.
Title: Into Africa, out of academia : a doctor's memoir /
Kwan Kew Lai.
Description: Jefferson, North Carolina : McFarland & Company, Inc.,
Publishers, 2020. | Includes bibliographical references and index.
Identifiers: LCCN 2020033167 | ISBN 9781476679723 (paperback : acid free paper) ∞
ISBN 9781476638676 (ebook)
Subjects: LCSH: Lai, Kwan Kew—Travel—Africa. | Médecins sans frontières
(Association) | Women physicians—United States—Biography. | Medical assistance,
American—Africa. | Public health—Africa—International cooperation. |
AIDS (Disease)—Africa.
Classification: LCC RA390.A2 L3354 2020 | DDC 362.1096—dc23
LC record available at https://lccn.loc.gov/2020033167

BRITISH LIBRARY CATALOGUING DATA ARE AVAILABLE

ISBN (print) 978-1-4766-7972-3
ISBN (ebook) 978-1-4766-3867-6

Front cover, top to bottom: Zedekiah, severely malnourished, tried to feed himself
when his mother stopped feeding him; refugees from the DRC lined up at the
UNHCR administrative tent with their meagre belongings to register for a
refugee card; the women from the Mothers' Union feeding the children a meal
of githeri and beans at one of the feeding programs in Maseno, Kenya;
the author cares for a sick child under the Bieh tree in Mirmir, South Sudan

Printed in the United States of America

*McFarland & Company, Inc., Publishers
Box 611, Jefferson, North Carolina 28640
www.mcfarlandpub.com*

To my husband, Scott,
and my children, Tim, Cara, and Charles,
who tolerate my long periods of absence and still remain
my ever faithful and enthusiastic cheerleaders,
and to all those living with HIV/AIDS,
the internally displaced people,
and the refugees of Africa who touched my life.

What counts in life is not the mere fact that we have lived. It is what difference we have made to the lives of others that will determine the significance of the life we lead.

—Nelson Mandela. *Nelson Mandela by Himself: The Authorized Book of Quotations* (New York: Macmillan, 2011).

Table of Contents

Acknowledgments

First of all, I would like to thank the many non-governmental organizations (NGOs) which took me on a wild ride with them in so many volunteering missions and allowed me to play a small role in helping my fellow human beings in times of need. In return, the people I came in touch with taught me humility, hope, persistent trust in humanity, and to always count my blessings. Despite the unbelievable hardship, insurmountable problems, inconsolable and heartbreaking tragedies they had been through and still face, they continue to show tremendous courage and resilience in overcoming them and always harboring hopes for a better future. Throughout all these years, I have received more than I have given.

Above all I want to express my deepest thanks to my family who stood by me and gave me their unconditional support when I went off again and again to challenging and perilous places which would worry any loved ones. In my book debut, *Lest We Forget: A Doctor's Experience with Life and Death during the Ebola Outbreak*, I mentioned my son and husband, Charles and Scott FitzGibbon, staying with me during the quarantine, but I failed to remember that both my daughter, Cara Sibelle Lai, and James Sibelle, her dear friend then and now her husband, were there with me as well. I want to apologize to Cara and James who traveled specially from Burlington, Vermont, to welcome me back from my first Ebola volunteering in Liberia in 2014 during my quarantine period. They were not afraid of the possibility of contracting the deadly infection, while the people from the Massachusetts Department of Public Health were cautious and kept their distance from me. They were obviously and understandably worried about my dangerous mission and being there with me when I reached home meant a great deal to me. If I were incubating Ebola, they would be at risk as well, and it would also mean that there would be a danger of them spreading it to their respective school and workplace: The University of Vermont and the Hole in the Wall Gang Camp in Connecticut. The implications could be huge. I was thankful to be home safely.

List of Abbreviations

AC—air conditioning

ACTION—AIDS Care and Treatment in Nigeria

AFREC—Africa Emergency Committee

ANC—antenatal clinic

ART—antiretroviral treatment

ARC—AIDS-Related Complex

ARV—antiretroviral

BBC—British Broadcasting Corporation

BCA—British Central Africa

BOMA—British Office for Management Administration

BPRM—Bureau of Population, Refugees, and Migration

CD4—cluster of differentiation 4

CHAI—Clinton HIV/AIDS Initiative

CHN—community health nurse

CNDP—National Congress for the Defense of the People

CNN—Cable News Network

CDC—Centers for Disease Control and Prevention

CTC—Clinical Treatment and Care Center

DfID—Department for International Development

DHO—District Health Officer

DMO—District Medical Officer

DNO—District Nurse Officer

DRC—Democratic Republic of Congo

ECHO—European Commission Humanitarian Aid

EID—Early Infant Diagnosis

FHI—Family Health International

FPD—Foundation of Professional Development

GAM—Global Acute Malnutrition

GMF—Global Medic Force

HIV/AIDS—Human Immunodeficiency Virus/Acquired Immunodeficiency Syndrome

ICEHA—International Center for Equal Healthcare Access

ICTR—International Criminal Tribunal for Rwanda

IDI—Infectious Disease Institute

IDP—internally displaced people

IEHK—International Emergency Health Kits

IHVN—Institute of Human Virology Nigeria

IMC—International Medical Corps

IMF—International Monetary Fund

KSh—Kenyan shillings

MAF—Mission Aviation Fellowship

MOH—Ministry of Health

MP—Member of Parliament

MSF—Médecins Sans Frontières

MTI—Medical Teams International

NACA—National Action Committee on AIDS

NATO—North Atlantic Treaty Organization

NEPA—National Electric Power Authority

NGO—Non-Governmental Organization

OCHA—Office of Coordination of Human Affairs

OPD—outpatient department

OPM—Office of the Prime Minister

ORS—oral rehydration solution

PEPFAR—President's Emergency Plan For AIDS Relief

PrEP—Pre-Exposure Prophylaxis

PHCC—Primary Health Care Center

PMTCT—Prevention of Mother to Child Transmission

RMO—Regional Medical Officer

SPLA—Sudanese People's Liberation Army

SPLM—Sudan People's Liberation Movement

TASO—The AIDS Support Organization

TB—tuberculosis

UN—United Nations

UNAIDS—Joint United Nations Program on HIV/AIDS

UNDP—United Nations Development Program

UNESCO—United Nations Educational, Scientific and Cultural Organization

UNHAS—United Nations Humanitarian Air Service

UNHCR—United Nations High Commissioner for Refugees

UNICEF—United Nations International Children's Emergency Fund

UNIDO—Upper Nile Initiative and Development Organization

USA—United States of America

USAID—United States Agency for International Development

VCT—voluntary counseling testing

VETA—Vocational and Education Training Authority

WC—World Concern

WFP—World Food Program

WHO—World Health Organization

WR—World Relief

Preface

At the end of 2004, the Asian tsunami hit Indonesia, Thailand, India, and Sri Lanka.[1] The unforgettable tragic images continued to tug at my heartstrings until I found an NGO to take me to the devastated villages of South India where I launched my first medical humanitarian volunteering mission. My experience there reminded me that that was what I had always wanted to do but had put it on the back-burner until my children had grown. After that profound personal involvement, I left my position as a full-time professor of medicine in the safe haven of academia where I spent eighteen years of my life, and I plunged into the unknown and at times insecure arena of medical volunteering in the developing world, including Africa.

In the ensuing years, I divided my time between practicing clinical medicine part-time in the Boston area in the United States and volunteering in epidemic and disaster response relief efforts in various parts of the world organized by different humanitarian organizations including *Médecins Sans Frontières* (MSF) or Doctors Without Borders. I had offered my services in the HIV/AIDS epidemic; after natural disasters such as the earthquakes in Haiti and Nepal and the typhoon in the Philippines; the drought and famine of East Africa; during the war and conflicts in Libya and the Democratic Republic of Congo (DRC); in South Sudan after the civil wars; during the outbreaks of cholera in Haiti; the greatest and deadliest Ebola outbreak in history in West Africa; and in several refugee camps, including the camps in Greece for refugees from Syria, Afghanistan, Iran, and the countries of sub-Saharan Africa, and in the largest refugee camp in the world for the Rohingya in Cox's Bazar, Bangladesh.

When I first landed in Africa, I traveled to rural Mtwara, Tanzania, to provide education and hands-on care of HIV/AIDS patients with the Clinton HIV/AIDS Initiative (CHAI). I was immediately struck by the stark contrast between the situation of the hospitals and medical care there and what I was used to in the United States of America. It was my first encounter with the infrastructure and personnel of the healthcare system in a developing country. There were numerous obstacles to optimal care: the overcrowding of the hospitals, almost always without running water; the lack of availability of handwashing facilities, hand sanitizers, gloves, isolation rooms; the behavior of personnel defying infection control practices in situations when handwashing facilities were available; the sheer overwhelming volume of the patients waiting to be seen in any given day; the lack of laboratory diagnostic testing; the shortage of medicine; and few or non-existent therapeutic choices. These conditions not only floored me, but I had to learn quickly to adjust and improvise to come up with a care plan that was most expedient for the patients.

Into the African Bush and Out of Academia: A Doctor's Memoir is divided into two parts. The first part proposes to examine the HIV/AIDS epidemic in parts of Africa where I volunteered and to recount my experiences providing care in resource-limited regions in times of uncertainty. The second part looks at the seemingly constant and relentless problems faced by several African countries due to man-made and natural disasters which caused inordinate hardship among the populace in terms of insecurity of basic human needs of food, shelter, sanitation, and healthcare. The focus here is on the healthcare needs of the displaced people and the refugees.

Interspersed with the recounting, I will share with and hope to transport the reader to areas of Africa with their unspeakable beauty and awe, places not frequently explored by the usual tourists.

The limitations of the book are that it concentrates on the HIV/AIDS epidemic in a few countries: Tanzania, Uganda, Kenya, South Africa, Nigeria, and Malawi. I was there a few years after the President's Emergency Plan for AIDS Relief (PEPFAR), the United States governmental initiative to address the global HIV/AIDS epidemic and to help save the lives of those suffering from the disease, primarily in Africa, began in 2003.[2] It provides a snapshot rather than following progress over a period of time. However, this snapshot touches on the treatment and prevention efforts, the Prevention of Mother to Child Transmission (PMTCT), and the social impact of the infection as I weave in my personal experiences and observations while mentoring in the various hospitals and clinics. All of these countries were also confronted by similar issues of denial of the infection, the social stigma, the slow acceptance of HIV/AIDS treatment and care by the people, and the plight of the children who were orphaned by the epidemic. I attempt to summarize the progress these countries have made to date towards the goals of ending the epidemic.

The book also discusses the provision of medical care for the internally displaced people and the refugees during war, conflict, unrest, and famine. This includes my experiences as a volunteer during the Arab Spring in Libya; in South Sudan which, after nearly two decades of civil war, in 2011 became the newest nation in Africa; in the Horn of Africa when it was troubled by famine and drought; and in the refugee camps in Uganda as a result of the conflict in its neighboring country of the Democratic Republic of Congo (DRC), resulting in the pouring of refugees across its border in a short period of time.

This account covers the period of my volunteering from 2006 through 2013. At the end of 2013, a puzzling but deadly epidemic began in West Africa which later became known as the greatest Ebola outbreak in history.[3] I volunteered to help with the outbreak twice, once in Liberia and the second time in Sierra Leone in 2014 and 2015, and that dark time has been published in my previous book, *Lest We Forget: A Doctor's Experience with Life and Death during the Ebola Outbreak*.[4] I was glad I went and was even gladder when the epidemic ended, and I came home safely not once but twice.

Besides my involvement in the Ebola outbreak, I spent time from 2014 through 2018 volunteering in various parts of the world other than Africa. In 2014, shortly after returning from Malawi, I flew to Tacloban, Philippines, to do relief work after Typhoon Haiyan devastated that part of the world.[5] When I completed my quarantine after returning from the Ebola outbreak in Sierra Leone in 2015, I went to Nepal after the 7.8 magnitude earthquake[6] and to Puerto Rico in 2017 after Hurricane Maria.[7] From 2017 through 2018, I spent time in Haiti to provide primary care, then traveled to various refugee camps: mainland Greece and the Greek Island of Lesvos caring for refugees from Syria, Afghanistan, Iran, and the countries of sub-Saharan Africa,[8] and in the world's biggest refugee camp for the Rohingya in Cox's Bazar, Bangladesh.[9]

Increasingly the world has become more like a "global village" with rapid globalization, complex economic and social interdependence, and connectedness. As I volunteered in different clinical settings in different countries in Africa, I became convinced that the recounting of such existing conditions and experiences in a book, pointing out the huge gulf of disparity in the healthcare system, could only serve to prepare personnel interested to contribute to and improve the overall global health and the students of global health as they launch their visits to resource-limited regions in the course of their training in their public health career.

Diseases know no borders, and our world is so interconnected that the more we are aware of and understand its shortcomings and the needs of our neighbors, the better we will be in a position to help.

Introduction

2005, The South Asian Tsunami, My First Mission in Medical Volunteering

> *"Life comes to a point only in those moments when the self dissolves into some task. The purpose in life is not to find yourself. It's to lose yourself."*
> —*David Brooks*[1]

Africa intrigued me. I had always wanted to go there to see it for myself, to experience the different countries, the climate, the terrain, the myriad tribes, and their customs and cultures, the wildlife… Africa conveyed to me a sense of the unknowns, mysteries, and adventures. It is a land filled with the wonders of natural beauty and natural resources as well as poverty, struggles, wars and conflicts, natural disasters, tales of political intrigues, and corruption.

I recalled a photograph on the front page of a local newspaper during the famine of East Africa of 1984 showing an emaciated goat caught up among the branches of a tree totally devoid of leaves save one. The desolate, parched landscape with a few stark, naked trees stretched far into the vast distance, not a soul in sight. The goat died on the tree while seemingly going after that single leaf waving enticingly at the end of a bare branch. The fierce desire to survive despite the utter hopelessness of the situation struck a poignant chord deep in my heart and left an indelible impression in my mind.

In the ensuing days, pictures of the crisis filled the pages of the newspapers and media.[2] Images of skeletal and malnourished children: parched lips stretched over their protruding teeth, eyes hollow with a haunting stare, rib cage showing. They sat listlessly, some leaning against their equally thin, exhausted mothers, though the mothers' bodies were obscured by the folds of their wrappers which draped over their heads against the fierce sun. My firstborn was then two years old—robust and healthy, never knowing a day of hunger—a stark contrast to the gaunt look of starving children thousands of miles away.

Christmas at my home has always been a special family time. Christmas 2004 was like all past Christmases: beautiful, warm, safe, secure, and lovely. I remembered being shell-shocked when I came downstairs the morning after Christmas and turned on the television; news of the tsunami in South Asia filled the television screen twenty-four seven with horrific pictures of enormous waves sweeping people, animals, buildings, trees, and vehicles that were in their way.[3] Glued to the set, I watched with disbelief at the helplessness of humanity against Mother Nature. All day long, something tugged at my heart and that feeling refused to dissipate or leave me alone. I knew I had to go there to help.

There followed a lengthy search on the internet for an NGO that would take me as a medical volunteer on its team. By the time I found one and was prepared to leave for Banda Aceh, Indonesia, the Indonesian government stopped volunteers from coming to that devastated village. Instead, I landed on Singarathopu in Cuddolore, a tiny village on the southeastern part of the Indian subcontinent.

I was one of five volunteers from different parts of the U.S. who converged on the airport in Frankfurt, Germany. I arrived before everyone else and spent part of the night sleeping on the stiff, uncomfortable chairs. Scott, the field coordinator of the Cooperative Baptist Fellowship, met us at the airport in Chennai, India, shortly past midnight. He was curt and somewhat impatient; perhaps it had been a long day for him, or perhaps he had been in the field far too long and found us greenhorns somewhat naive and wearing for him. Far away, the night-lights of Chennai shimmered. A rare breeze gave slight relief from the humid air. This was my first time in India; the India of Kipling, the India of the British East India Company I read about in my history book, and the India that was the homeland of all my Tamil secondary school friends in Malaysia.

I roomed with Rosie, one of the nurses, in a guesthouse in Chennai. A droning ceiling fan moved around the hot, stale air in our bedroom. All too soon after my shower, I was sweating quite profusely, but fatigue finally took over and I fell fast asleep. In the morning, we spotted a coconut tree right outside our window, its fruits temptingly within reach.

We were to set up a clinic in Cuddolore, an impoverished village in the south of India devastated by the tsunami. In the big city of Chennai, we had a better chance of getting the things needed for the clinic. We wandered through the dusty and winding streets of the market in the hazy morning heat and squeezed ourselves flat against the sides of buildings for passing bullock carts. Solomon, the local national ground coordinator, led the way to shop for sheets, clothespins, ropes, and most importantly, to a local pharmacy to buy medicines.

After lunch, we spent the next four hours careening down the road that headed south through Pondicherry. The road was a one-lane roadway with fast-moving traffic. The driver weaved his way along, recklessly overtaking slower vehicles while pointing our van head on with oncoming ones, many times narrowly missing being hit. Wreckage of buildings and uprooted trees were scattered along the shoreline. A few tall, majestic, plush, whitewashed mansions had withstood the tsunami and remained standing unharmed and undefiled on the beach. A small, unassuming shrine of flimsy thatched construction housing a Hindu god stood in isolation in the vast expanse of bare sand, miraculously untouched by the wind and deluge. The locals believed their god was protected from the natural disaster. Colonies of tent camps with the logos of the hosting nations—England, Germany, Switzerland, Japan, Canada, USA—cropped up here and there with rows of latrines lining the periphery of the settlements, standing guard.

Before our team arrived, the Cooperative Baptist Fellowship had been running their clinics in various schools. The Indian government agreed to let us use an abandoned, old birthing unit in the village as our clinic. The equipment and medical supplies from the school clinics had been packed up and transferred to the new venue. Late in the afternoon, Cuddolore loomed into view across the Kedilam River; the concrete bridge leading to it remained standing. Many fishing boats lifted and swept by the tsunami were left lying helter-skelter on the dirt road that wound through the village, looking out of place but surprisingly undamaged. The van weaved around them. The slanting rays of the setting sun shimmered gently through the leaves of the trees and coconut palms. The van finally pulled up in front of an old building. We got out, stretching our tired bodies after such a long ride.

Old incubators and rusty bed frames had been cleared out of the birthing building and left outside in a forlorn pile. The unit, with one private examination room, a pharmacy, and a huge room that we used sheets to divide into three examination areas, had been swept. There were only two stretchers: one in the private examination room, and the second one in one of the makeshift exam rooms which we used as our emergency triage area. A waiting room was hastily rigged up with a tarp slung over some poles on the dirt ground in front of the building. Gracious neighbors loaned a few plastic chairs to place under the tarp. We stocked the shelves with medications, organizing them according to the ailments we were expecting to see: eye ointment, ear drops, cough medicines, pain killers, antibiotics, vitamins… while Scott purified some water for all of us to use.

The village of Singarathopu had about 2,500 people; there were two other villages flanking it with about 1,000 people each.[4] Early the next day a crowd of villagers gathered to be registered. Someone had already gone around the village using a bullhorn to announce the opening of the clinic. Moses, the Indian doctor who had been working with the Cooperative Baptist Fellowship since the disaster, held court in the only private room. Our volunteer corps consisted of one doctor, two nurses, a physiotherapist, and two technical persons. Our obstetrician, who was also our team leader, was turned back at the airport for the lack of a visa. I had use of one of the makeshift rooms equipped with a desk and three chairs. Moses' and my assistants cum translators were aptly named Mercy and Grace. With no examination table, I had to get used to examining my patients sitting on a chair fully clothed.

As we were not the first team to arrive right after the tsunami, we were mostly seeing patients with festering wounds sustained during the disaster, various aches and pains, "giddiness," and total body ache. As the days went on, people with respiratory infections, diarrhea, fever, and more chronic problems such as hypertension, asthma, diabetes, and heart disease appeared. This was my first experience working in the field; it was difficult for me to prescribe only a few days' worth of medicine for such chronic illnesses. The villagers were told to go to the government clinics to get their future supply of medicines.

The tsunami had destroyed most of the houses in the village. World Vision built a windowless one-room tin shed, essentially a sweatbox, for each family. During one of my lunch breaks, a woman beckoned me into her shed. It took a while for me to get used to the dark interior, having just walked in from the bright sun. Near the entrance was a set of three stones serving as a tripod for cooking; oftentimes the fumes from the cooking fire built up in the badly ventilated shed. A tiny, single floor mat sat on the sandy floor. The owner had her meager belongings tucked in a dark corner. Most villagers chose to sleep outside since it was boiling hot under the crackling corrugated tin roof even at night.

Twice a week, a water truck came to deliver much needed water for the villagers. NGOs provided staples such as rice, salt, and cooking oil. The villagers lined up their containers and jerry cans, their ingenious way of forming a queue long before the food trucks arrived so they did not have to wait in the hot sun.

One morning towards the end of our stay, a rumor of another tsunami coming the way of the village quickly circulated. The memory of the devastating tsunami was still fresh in the minds of the villagers, and fearing the worst, they rushed to the bridge, the only exit. Later in the morning, a middle-aged woman walked in with a badly scalded arm. She had been boiling water on the three stones in her little store where she cooked breakfast for some paying customers. When she heard that another big wave was coming, in her haste to escape, she overturned her pot and burned her arm.

The Indians in the south were mainly Tamils. Despite the disaster, the women were surprisingly well dressed, not in tatters. The most amazing thing was they were universally barefoot even as they were all fully decked from head to toe. Grace, my translator, wondered why I wore no jewelry, declaring that even the poorest Indian woman wore a costume bangle with rings adorning the toes which peeked from below the hem of her sari.

We treated around a hundred patients a day, and by the end of two weeks, close to a thousand people, but we were unable to care for a few patients with serious illnesses. One day the distraught parents of a young man with stomach cancer carried him into the clinic. Having exhausted their funds to arrive at the diagnosis via a biopsy executed in a general hospital, they could no longer pursue treatment in the big city. Without treatment, he would surely die. For the first time in my life, I was confronted with a situation that probably was more commonplace in the developing world than I realized; the enormity of the hopelessness and the helplessness of this young man's medical condition left me speechless. In the end, Scott promised to find funds to see to his care; I had the feeling that he was just appeasing us, the volunteers who just came for a few weeks and thought they could change the world.

At the end of our mission, I traveled to Sri Lanka to see the devastation the tsunami inflicted on this teardrop island. Tents set far away from the ocean as temporary shelters for the displaced Sri Lankans dotted the southwestern coast, and stood alongside stretches of destroyed homes; only rubble and foundations remained. After the debris had been picked up, the beaches looked peaceful with graceful palms swaying as though nothing ever happened. Already there were signs of rebuilding.

In Thelwata, the wreckage of the displaced train stood eerily off its track, bent and broken in many places but emptied of its passengers who did not know that it would be their last journey that fateful day.

Providing humanitarian medical aid had been a life-long dream of mine. Growing up in Malaysia, I read about Dr. Thomas Dooley and his humanitarian work in Vietnam and Laos and was moved and inspired by his selflessness and compassion.[5] I heard about Dr. Albert Schweitzer who went to Africa to set up a hospital for the people in Gabon.[6] Even at that age, I thought it would be fulfilling to care for people who would otherwise not be able to receive medical care. My India tsunami experience reaffirmed that desire.

A full-time academic career in medicine could not accommodate time for volunteering. To volunteer for three weeks in India, I had to produce a letter from the India Ministry of Health to give to the clinical chief of infectious diseases where I was a professor to prove that I was truly going to India to volunteer. As a member of the faculty, I could only take two weeks off at a time and only after making sure my colleagues were caring for my patients and covering my teaching responsibilities while I was away. To wish to volunteer for an extended period was not tenable. In the end, I left my full-time position as a Professor of Medicine, stepped out of my comfort zone, and embarked on the next stage of my career. Not many healthcare facilities would consider hiring a doctor who could not provide any promise of long-term stability, so I floundered around for a few years trying to mix clinical practice with a big dose of medical volunteering. I opted to cover hospital and clinic practices on a per diem basis, keeping myself open to respond to disasters whenever and wherever they occurred.

After a long search for NGOs that offer opportunities for volunteering, MSF and International Center for Equal Healthcare Access (ICEHA) came to my attention. MSF required a commitment of three to six months, which was too long for me; I still had a child that was of high school age. ICHEHA asked for a six-week assignment, a more acceptable length of time. They were involved in the mentoring of healthcare personnel in the treatment of HIV/AIDS patients in resource-poor countries of Africa and Asia. I signed up to volunteer with them.

In late 2006, ICHEHA found me an assignment with their partner, Family Health International (FHI), which works with the world's most vulnerable people. I was hoping to be sent to Africa, but my assignment was in Ho Chi Minh City in Vietnam. My dream of going to Africa would have to wait a little longer.

Part I

HIV/AIDS Epidemic and Medical Care in Africa, 2006–2013

1

Tanzania

2006, Mentoring in Rural Mtwara with the Clinton HIV/AIDS Initiative (CHAI)

"AIDS is no longer a death sentence for those who can get the medicines. Now it's up to the politicians to create the 'comprehensive strategies' to better treat the disease."

—Bill Clinton[1]

Congratulations, you are now at Uhuru, Tanzania, 5859 m. Africa's highest point!

Bleary-eyed, I struggled to touch the lopsided wooden signpost on the top of Kilimanjaro. It had taken John and me six days with the help of our guides, Moses and Peter, to reach this point. Moments ago, I scrambled over Stella Point just as dawn broke over the blue glaciers, majestic and cold. Dragging my tired body over the crater rim, I almost stumbled over a tall body covered by a white sheet, his hiking boots sticking out; the body was already in rigor mortis, a life taken by Kili. Moses told me he was the man who said "hello" to me on our way up the summit the night before, the man I met at Shira Caves, hiking Kili to bond with his daughter, only to be parted from her forever.

Right after I came home from Vietnam, ICHEHA did not have any volunteering opportunities and specifically nothing for Africa. I found out that the CHAI had ongoing HIV/AIDS programs in the urban areas of Tanzania and just started such programs in the rural areas. They would need clinicians like myself to volunteer as mentors. After many weeks of completing paperwork and checking my credentials, I was to report to Dar es Salaam in March of 2006.

It was in the evening in February 2006 when I arrived at the airport of Tanzania, tired from my many hours of flight from Boston via Amsterdam. I finally touched the soil of Africa. The atmosphere had changed in Amsterdam when I noticed that the majority of the passengers were Africans, perhaps returning to their homeland for a visit or for a long stay, and a spattering of excited foreigners in khakis and hats ready to embark on their respective safaris.

Even though I had always wanted to go to Africa, I truly had very little geographical knowledge of the continent. In secondary school, I had the options of studying the geography of the United States of America or Europe, but Africa was not one of them.

While perusing the map of the African continent, I had no idea that its highest mountain, Kilimanjaro, was in Tanzania, but it instantly beckoned me to hike it. The first thing I intended to do in Africa was to climb to its highest point. With only five weeks left before my departure, I hiked around my neighborhood with a loaded backpack, and ran up and down a snow-covered slope with my dog, Cosmo. I bought a pair of good hiking boots and borrowed the rest of my gear from my children. My hiking pole was the broken, collapsible handle of a ceiling duster.

After going through immigration and retrieving my baggage—a bag for my volunteering assignment and another just for my hiking expedition—I stepped into a confusing sea of people holding placards with names of the passengers they were meeting. I had booked a hike for Kilimanjaro with the Good Earth, and it was a relief to see that my ride was waiting for me. After all, this was my first time in Africa, and since I was arriving after dark, it was comforting to have someone to deliver me safely to my lodge. As it turned out my transport was a big, old, yellow school bus, and it was picking up a number of passengers either hiking Kilimanjaro or going on a safari.

The non-air-conditioned bus lumbered through a dark city with inconsistently lit streetlights; it was as if the government was attempting to save electricity. A brisk breeze blew through the open windows. After what seemed like a long time, we finally left the city and drove through grassland with scattered trees lit by the sheen of the moonlight. Then the bus sputtered, coughed, slowly limped over to the side, and stopped. Immediately the heat and humidity built up in the bus. The driver told us that there was some engine trouble, and we would be cooler outside the bus while he tried to fix it. We got off. A man looked under the hood, and another slid under the bus while the driver was busy talking on his cell phone.

The moon peered through the clouds. It suddenly dawned on me that we could be in the midst of predatory animals, especially the nocturnal ones. Some passengers wandered off into the bushes to relieve themselves. After a spell, the driver informed us that another bus would come to take us to the lodge. When it finally arrived, there was a bustle of activity transferring our luggage, and soon we were on our way to Arusha.

The secluded lodge was expansive. Paintings of wild African animals adorned the enclosing walls. My room was off in a far corner of the courtyard of lush garden. I was thankful to get a shower, even though the water came through the showerhead in a cold trickle. With the ceiling fan droning overhead, I snuggled in the cozy bed and slowly drifted off into a deep sleep, dreaming of Africa.

At the time of my departure for Africa, CHAI had not decided where to send me, but they knew it would not be Dar es Salaam. I had e-mailed them that I would likely not be reachable for three weeks prior to my reporting date, but I did not tell them where I would be. I was sure that out on the slopes of Kilimanjaro and in the wide wild open plains of the Serengeti and Ngorongoro Crater, there would not be any internet access.

In the morning, I awoke to the chirping of birds. Many of the occupants were getting ready for their hike or safari. I had one free day to explore Arusha with a guide and another tourist. Narrow slivers of broken concrete sidewalk or red dirt riddled with hazardous holes created by the eroding rain flanked the paved street. As we passed the International Criminal Tribunal for Rwanda (ICTR), an international court established in November 1994 by the United Nations Security Council to judge the people responsible for the Rwanda genocide and other serious violations of international law in Rwanda,[2] our guide warned us to refrain from taking any pictures.

Being foreigners, we drew quite a bit of attention, locals calling from across the street to say hello. We saw a number of tall Maasai men wearing colorful beads, braided hair dyed ochre with henna, dark bodies draped in cloth colored deep blood red or indigo. They stood on one leg while leaning against their spears or herding sticks, some leisurely cleaning their teeth with a twig. At a busy outdoor market, vendors sold household items and brightly colored Tanzanian *kanga* with proverbs inscribed on the borders. At another market, the Maasai were selling their animals: goats, sheep, and cows. Sensing some hostility, we wandered along the periphery, as our guide was reluctant to take us deep into the market, warning us not to take pictures without permission.

When I had contacted the Good Earth to arrange for my hike, I wanted to take the easiest route—the Marangu or the Coca Cola Route—but Mr. Narry persuaded me to take the Machame Route, also known as the Whiskey Route. According to him, the Japanese loved the easier Coca Cola Route because it was of a gradual incline and provided hut accommodation, but the longer and steeper Whiskey Route was more scenic, provided impressive views and habitats, and was the route of choice for most seasoned climbers even though they had to sleep in tents. I chose the Machame Route with some trepidation as it was for the physically fit with some hiking experience, and this would be my first serious hike. Just before I left for Africa, a Kilimanjaro hiker from the U.S. was killed while sleeping by loose rocks falling down onto his tent, giving me some pause for this upcoming adventure.

I was the only hiker who signed up for this particular hike with the Good Earth tour. When my mountain guide, Moses, came to brief me on the eve of the climb, he told me two men, John from America and Doug from South Africa, would be joining me. I was glad to have their company but at the same time was a little worried that I would slow them down.

After breakfast, Moses took me to the hotel where John and Doug stayed. We waited for them to finish their breakfast only to be driven back to my lodge. African time seeped in while the men took some time to rent gaiters and hiking boots. Moses was completely relaxed and looked as though for all the world, time had stood still for him. It took an hour to drive to the Mount Kilimanjaro National Park, with tantalizing glimpses of the peak of Kilimanjaro raising our excitement. However, it did not look like the classic snow-capped mountain of yore, rather only scanty trails of snow graced its top. Still, it looked awesome and majestic.

Children waved as we drove on a narrow red dirt road, passing through the village of Machame on the lower slope of Kilimanjaro with lush vegetation and mud huts. At the gate, Moses checked us in with our passports. Villagers congregated near the gate selling straw hats. Our porters were already waiting for us, packing tents and food, and now securing our duffel bags. All these had to be weighed as each porter was only allowed to carry a certain amount of weight.

Off to one side of the trail were copious signs warning hikers not to climb if they had a cold, sore throat, or breathing problems, and to descend quickly if they experienced signs of mountain sickness.

Finally, we were ready to go. Moses asked us to follow Peter, his second-in-command, and he would catch up with us. We had no doubt he would, seeing that he must have climbed Kili innumerable times. Peter kidded that Moses was off to the pub for a stiff drink. Many of our porters—some carrying their packs strapped from their shoulders or their foreheads and some with their packs sitting atop their heads—passed us and left us very quickly in the dust. Carrying our daypacks, we joined several other groups. The rainforest trail was muddy and slippery, lined with ferns with gigantic leaves as big as I was. A few colobus monkeys, with their distinctive black and white faces, were swinging in the towering trees. On the trail was a middle-aged couple; the man with a protruding paunch trekked along with their guide. Though he appeared physically unfit, he kept up a good pace. A huge group of enthusiastic hikers sponsored by Dasani overtook us; they faced a triple threat challenge of first hiking to the peak of Kilimanjaro followed by biking and a marathon!

On our first day as we approached Machame Camp, trekking from around five thousand feet to over nine thousand feet, the trees became shorter and heather appeared. Misty rain began to fall. Spanish mosses sparkled with the raindrops, looking like old men with dreary beards hanging from their droopy chins. In the distance, the snowy peak of Kilimanjaro beckoned.

At the checkpoint, a sign said, "No high heels allowed!" Our porters had arrived long before us and had already set up our tents, including a big tent for us to dine in. A white-necked raven sat on a tree branch right outside my tent, watching as I struggled for breath while putting on my hiking boots. Even at a height of just shy of ten thousand feet, I was already feeling the effects of the high altitude. Dinner was especially delicious after a hard day's climb. It turned out that John and Doug were good friends, and they had been preparing for this hike by climbing their local mountains, more than what I had done.

After breakfast, we left the glades of rain forest and continued on an ascending path through increasingly sparse trees and bushes into moorlands covered by ethereal mist mingled with large plumes of white clouds blowing across the slopes. Many species of flowers grew and thrived along the rocky ledges: pink, yellow, and a spattering of bright orange. A group of college students from Brown University overtook us, practically running. Moses shook his head and muttered, "*Pole pole*, slowly, slowly" in Swahili. He said they were being foolish and climbing Kili was not a race. This suited me fine since I was probably the slowest of the three hikers.

Perching on big boulders, we stopped to have our lunch. Moses pointed out a group of hikers several hundred feet from us, belonging to a luxurious tour group that cost many times what we were paying. They were usually men from some rich corporate groups; each hiker had his own mountain guide who even carried the daypack for him. They ate at actual tables complete with tablecloth and chairs and used portable toilets enclosed in pristine white tents; these items were carried by the porters up and down the mountains.

We finished our day at Shira Camp on a small plateau in the high rocky and barren moorlands. In the distance Mount Meru peered through the clouds; the scene was at once both beautiful and desolate.

After setting up my sleeping bag in my tent set near a big boulder with lots of heather and smaller boulders scattered around, I went exploring a set of caves called Shira Caves, stopping every few feet to catch my breath. I ran into a father, probably in his sixties, and his daughter exploring the caves with their guide. I could not help but wonder whether he might have a heart condition that would make hiking Kilimanjaro a great gamble. One of the caves showed evidence of being used as a campsite with old ashes on the dirt floor. Indeed, in the old days, the porters used the caves as their sleeping quarters. As night fell, Moshi town beckoned with its lights shimmering and blinking far down below; civilization was a long way away. Tonight we decided to take acetazolamide to prevent mountain sickness.

The outhouses were quite a way downhill from our campsite; they were just holes in the ground with walls on three sides. I found myself having to pee in the middle of the night after taking acetazolamide; this I did conveniently behind the boulder surrounded by shadowy heathers with the moon shining at me. My fingers tingled and a slight headache crept into my temple; I could not tell whether this was a sign of mountain sickness or my migraine. My migraine pill took it away.

On our third day, we hiked along a ridge through the alpine desert strewn with rocks, with barely any trees, towards the Lava Tower or Shark's Tooth. The highest point of our hike on this day was at sixteen thousand feet. A hiker from the luxurious tour was resting on a rock while his personal guide gave him a talk on the flora in the area. A few energetic hikers climbed up to the top of the Lava Tower, but Moses said we should conserve our energy for Uhuru Peak, the highest point of Kilimanjaro. A snow squall fell as we rounded the base of Lava Tower.

From here we tracked down a trail into the Barranco Valley with the sounds of a brook gurgling nearby. More and more vegetation appeared as we passed the Garden of the Senecios with gigantic, impressive senecio plants. The lobelia, though smaller, still seemed to tower above me. The senecio had a cylindrical base of a couple of feet of light brown scraggly dead leaves from which sprouted two to six smaller but darker brown trunks, again covered with dead-looking leaves. These were crowned with tufts of large green leaves. A few of these tufts would give rise to flowers. Lobelia, on the other hand, seemed to arise from a huge tuft of green leaves that looked similar to the tufts that crowned the senecio, followed by a cylinder of scraggly brown leaves reaching up into the sky. They did not look like any plants I had seen before. All day the mist blew across our path, enshrouding the alien forest.

On day three we hiked up to sixteen thousand feet and then returned to sleep at Barranco Camp at thirteen thousand feet for acclimatization. Looming behind our campsite was a one-thousand-foot rocky cliff, the so-called Barranco Wall. This was the challenging, steep ascent that awaited us. The mist continued to blow throughout the evening, now and then allowing fleeting glimpses of the peak of Kilimanjaro. During the night I was awakened several times by wheezing and coughing from Doug's tent.

Morning came. Some teams had already begun tackling the Barranco Wall. The rocky ridges were so steep in some spots that we were forced to scramble on all fours. We made way for a tall man carrying a stack of plastic chairs on his shoulders, evidently for the luxurious tour group, walking upright effortlessly. After scaling the steep portion of the trail, we trekked up and down, crossing small, bubbling, cool streams and rivulets where melting snow from the glaciers flowed. Sitting at the edge of a mountain ridge looking down at the fluffy clouds far below my feet, I felt like I was floating high up in the heavens. Moses leaned against a giant boulder speaking on his cell phone. Not far away from him another mountain guide sat on a rock, pensively enjoying a smoke while most of us were puffing and huffing. The desolate landscape was devoid of vegetation, grey and brown shale rocks strewn everywhere. We ran into the man with the paunch and his wife resting on the lonely trail. Impressed by his ability so far, I had great hope that I should be able to reach Uhuru Peak. From a high ridge we could see the steep drop to the Karanga Valley, followed by a trail up another steep slope on the other side towards Barafu Camp. The creek at Karanga Valley was the last chance to get water before the summit. Porters backtracked and scrambled down the creek to collect water and up again to the campsite before nightfall, with their jerry cans strapped to their backs.

Moses pointed out the highest out-house at the campsite; it sat alone right at the edge of a cliff. Another outhouse not too far from it had fallen on its side as strong winds swept through this elevation. I located my tent, surrounded on all three sides by rocks, sheltered from the wind. Snow was falling silently; it was getting quite cold.

We had a much-needed tea break and rested before dinner. The cook continued to amaze us with his skills of different offerings. While our appetite decreased with the high elevation, we were told to eat to store the energy we would need for our final assault on the peak. We were quiet at dinner knowing that we had to get up around ten in the evening to get ready for our summit. It was difficult to relax and sleep. Again, more wheezing and moaning emanated from Doug's tent.

Ten o'clock rolled along sooner than we wanted. We had a drink of hot tea and a bite of biscuit. Many teams had already started on the ascent, marked by a long string of lights snaking along the slope of the mountain. Doug took a while to get out of his tent and to put on his gaiters. We started on the rocky trail with me right at the heels of Moses, who led the way, and Peter bringing up the rear. The night was cold. We had on our winter gear. The wind blew the clouds over the moon, decreasing the visibility of our path. We all had our headlamps on except Peter, who was using a flashlight. After about twenty minutes, coughing and breathing heavily, Doug requested to have a rest. Many teams passed as we waited. His requests for stops became more frequent and came at shorter intervals. Moses gently asked him whether he thought it was best for him to go back to base camp. Doug was adamant about continuing on, seeing that his goal of summiting was so close. Another big team passed us. A man said "Hello" to me. I could not see him clearly because of the glare of the headlamp. He said, "We met at Shira Caves." Then I knew who he was. Soon we were the last team on the trail. Doug was clearly having difficulty keeping up. Moses persuaded John to talk to his friend, to put some sense into him that there would be a next time. The mountain would still be there, and he should not risk his life trying to summit it. After a long while, Doug reluctantly agreed to descend with Peter.

Moses, John, and I continued, and without the frequent stops, we made a steady, albeit slow, ascent. I concentrated on following Moses' footsteps, through heavy scree. Now and then I looked up, only to see a lone rock or two scattered on the slopes. Peter helped Doug descend to base camp and soon caught up with us. Around two in the morning I switched off my headlamp as the moonlight was good enough to allow me to see the well-worn trail along sheets of gravel. Only my heavy breathing broke the engulfing, profound silence. The peaceful scene was indescribably beautiful. Despite wrapping my water bottle with my wool socks, it froze. We stopped several times to get a drink of hot tea from Peter's thermos and a bite of energy bar. Once I went behind a big boulder to relieve myself, baring my bottom to the cold air.

It was a long night. As we approached Stella Point on the crater rim, we passed a few guides hastily bringing down the limp bodies of some young hikers. Were they the students from Brown University who were racing on the second day of our hike? One of them brushed by me, white breath steaming through pursed, purplish-blue lips. The wife of the man with the paunch passed us on her descent. She had reached Stella Point but decided that was as far as she would go. Her husband had to descend from base camp the night before because of high altitude sickness.

Dawn arrived as we approached Stella Point. With a great effort, I raised my heavy legs one after another and climbed over the crater rim, where I almost ran into the man I had met at Shira Caves. Moses waited there for me and said, "Welcome to Stella Point!"

Through the dawn light the glaciers appeared, majestic and cold. A few hikers had gone down to the bottom of the crater to look at the glaciers at close range. I was too exhausted to attempt that.

John and I were elated to reach this point, but Moses reminded us that we still had another thirty minutes of hiking before reaching the highest point at Uhuru Peak. We could see a trail flanked by rocks snaking upwards. The terrain was rocky with confection-like snow lightly covering the surface and huge glaciers silently standing guard down below to our left. John and I plodded on with Moses and Peter trailing us. Earlier, John said to Moses that no matter what happened, he would summit. He would be willing to crawl to Uhuru if he had to.

At Uhuru Peak the sun had already risen. Moses and Peter congratulated us. We savored this moment and wanted to engrave this memory into our minds forever.

Moses and John paired up to descend, leaving Peter and me trekking together. Peter and Moses did not follow the trail; instead they "scree slid" hastily and efficiently, skidding and sliding through the loose gravel at quite a rapid rate. I was more tentative but imitated Peter's slippery descent. Gaiters would have come in handy, but I had not rented them. Below us I saw Moses turning around and looking at me. Later John told me that he repeatedly said, "That is one strong woman."

The bright sun reflected off the white snow, blinding me and making me sweat. I stripped down to my fleece. Two porters alternately carried and threw a home-made stretcher up the slope with the goal of bringing a body down. It took us a much shorter time to get back to Barafu Camp, the base camp where our porters eagerly waited for us with their congratulations. Doug felt greatly improved when he reached base camp and was glad he did not attempt to summit.

After some food, we began our long day of hiking down in great spirits through alpine desert and then moorlands to Mweka Hut Camp at ten thousand feet. That evening we had our final meal together followed by a long sleep. In the morning we had our pictures with our porters, cook, and guides. Since they would be fast on their descent, we would not be seeing them again as they headed on their separate ways towards home.

At the Mweka Gate, we received our certificates and saw some of our porters washing up at the sinks. It was a seven-day hike, but we felt as though we had been gone a long time. I gave my hiking pole to Moses, who told me his father would use it as a walking stick. It was sad to say good-bye to all the people who helped us summit Kilimanjaro. Without them, it would have been impossible for us to reach the top.

The next day Mike joined me for a week of safari in the Serengeti Plain and Ngorongoro Crater. He became quite ill on his second day attempting the hike up Kili and had to be carried down from the mountain. At Lake Manyara National Park, there were a number of curious-looking trees with sausage-like fruits hanging from their branches. In this small park, we saw baboons, blue monkeys, zebras, wildebeest, giraffes, elephants, and many species of birds. Then, right among the trees, we spotted a few tree-climbing lions; the lionesses rested regally on the tree branches while a lion was just posing atop a tall cement block, yawning.

Mike and I wanted to rough it. We were on the so-called budget safari. Instead of luxurious lodges, we slept in tents and ate what the cook prepared for us and not in the restaurants. The next morning after breakfast, we drove to Serengeti.

On the way we paid to visit a Maasai village while our driver waited in the cruiser. A number of tall Maasai men in their red and indigo wrappers holding their long staffs greeted us, while women with colorful beads around their necks entreated us to buy the necklaces. The men did a dance for us, jumping straight up into the air, almost half a meter high. A young man who claimed to be the son of the chief took us to a dwelling: a round mound of stick covered with mud, where we sat on low stools. After we got used to the dim interior, a couple of beds came into view and three stones for cooking. The young man asked for more money if we wanted to visit the rest of the compound. We refused and got up to leave, all the while wishing that our guide was here to bail us out.

In the center of the compound was a corral of thorny acacia branches for the cattle to settle at night, safeguarding them from predators. We walked into a schoolhouse with a blackboard covered with letters and numbers while a group of children rattled them off. As we left we saw the chief's son whipping up a thick wad of green U.S. bills in front of the rest of the men. This all seemed like a tourist trap to us, a very lucrative business for the Maasai whose simple livelihood it was to herd the cattle in the Serengeti Plain with the animals supplying all the meat, milk, and blood they needed.

It was a long, hard, dry, bumpy, dusty, and hot drive in the Serengeti. A wake of vultures, their naked necks exposed to the sun, hovered over the carcass of a waterbuck, clawing and pecking with their powerful beaks. In the distance, we saw a male and female ostrich bouncing away like a pair of ballerinas dancing on the steamy grassland, and a lone hyena slinking in the vast plain. The Serengeti was truly endless.

As we rounded a *kopi*, a few prides of lions were resting at the entrance of their dens and some were on top of the rocks, taking their siesta. Their meals were waiting for them down below: wildebeest, zebras, waterbucks, Thompson gazelles, elands…

At night, we camped on an open campground with no fence around us. A sign hammered onto a tree trunk warned us: *Caution: do not get out of the campsite, animal may attact* (spelled with a t instead of a k) *human being.* Our eating area was fenced in to prevent the baboons from stealing our food. No food was allowed in the tents for fear of attracting unwanted visitors at night. In the evening there was a murmuring of excitement as some campers spotted a lion sitting on top of a *kopi* close to the campground. We had to use the latrine by ten o'clock at night and after that, no one was to get out of their tents until dawn. I congratulated myself for not being in one of the tents out in the periphery of the campsite. I figured that if a lion were to take a prey, it would choose a victim right at the edge.

At four-thirty in the morning, I rose and waited in the tent, listening for the engine of a cruiser and looking for its light to pierce the pitch black of Serengeti; I had signed up for a hot-air balloon flight. A few nocturnal animals were startled and froze in mid-track, eyes glowing in the glare of the headlights in the chilly morning. I was deposited in a plain where I could discern the dark shapes of a few deflated balloons against a grey dawn. The balloons were slowly blown up, rising like giant shadows. Soon we were up in the basket, and the warmth from the hot air took the chill from us. Up into the sky we went. The sun was rising over the Serengeti as it has done for millions of years. A profound silence and serenity cloaked the great Serengeti despite it being teaming with lives. We flew very close to the tops of some acacia trees but spotted few animals. Towards the end of our flight, we neared a river. Two hippopotami ran frantically from the fast landing balloon, returning from their nighttime forage only to be disturbed and intruded upon by us aliens. A sumptuous breakfast awaited us at a long table covered with a white tablecloth and set with real china under a giant acacia tree. What a lovely ending to a great morning.

One day we went looking for hippopotami and crocodiles near a river. The big, googly eyes and snouts of the hippopotami peered and bobbed above the brown, glistening water; occasionally they surfaced, snorted water, and plopped down under the water again. Crocodiles lay lazily in the sun, some on the beach and some half in and half out of the muddy water.

Over the next few days, we saw many more herds of buffaloes, impalas, and the funny warthogs with their short curly tails, frisking about on their short legs, rooting for food on bended knees. The giraffes with their lumbering walk, heads and long graceful necks stuck out of the tops of trees, delicately wrapped their tongues around the thorny acacia leaves.

We watched as one giraffe bent down on its front legs to reach a puddle on the dirt path right in front of our cruiser for a drink. One day after a drenching rain, a whole flock of rather mournful-looking marabou storks huddled by a lake, looking like closed dark umbrellas on a rainy day; a few more were on the tops of the acacia trees, all facing the same direction!

Cheetahs and leopards eluded us. Once we saw a kill high up on a tree branch, but no leopard. On our way out of Serengeti, two lionesses, well hidden in the tall grass, stalked the wildebeests with a great deal of patience.

At the Ngorongoro Crater, we set up camp near the crater rim, where some elephants had been spotted. That night I heard stomping just right outside my tent, but I was too afraid to peek. Soon the stomping faded away. In the morning I stalked a marabou stork milling around my tent. It was almost as tall as I was.

After breakfast, we rolled down the path along the slope of the crater to the bottom. Ngorongoro was well known for its rhinoceroses. We saw the usual suspects: zebras, wildebeests with their young (some nursing), buffaloes, elephants, but no rhinoceroses. Once our guide thought he saw a rhino in the distance, but it was just a buffalo. Near a lake we saw many waterfowls and a pride of lions. I wondered how long it took the elephants to wander all the way down to the crater and how they were going to get out of it again or would they? Perhaps not. They might very well be content to stay all their lives in the Ngorongoro Crater.

On our long drive back to Arusha, we stopped by the roadside to admire a gigantic baobab tree. It would probably take close to fifty persons to surround it. The drought had been plaguing Tanzania before I arrived. A heavy rainstorm pelted down, and very quickly, the rainwater became rivulets racing to the gorges that had been bone dry. The parched ground allowed no surface water to seep deeper into it. The cool air from the rain was a welcoming relief.

Back in Arusha, I hand washed most of my dirty clothes and hung them all around the room to dry. I was able to access my e-mail via the very slow internet in the cramped office of the hotel reception. CHAI informed me that there was no spare driver and vehicle to fetch me from the airport and so I was to catch a taxi. Since I had been in Africa for almost three weeks now, albeit in the mountain and the wilderness, I was sure I could handle it.

Before leaving Arusha, I paid a visit to the ICTR for the Rwanda genocide. I was surprised to be let in rather easily after passing through security. I sat in an anteroom next to the courtroom proper, separated only by huge glass windows. A row of judges sat in the background while a lawyer questioned a witness. Since I walked into the middle of the interrogation, I had no idea what was going on. The process of questioning was also rather slow. Still I was glad that I did witness a piece of history.

My departure from Arusha to the airport was via a public bus. The driver made sure I got on after I watched my bags being hoisted onto the roof. After retrieving my bags at the airport in Dar, I walked out, only to be bombarded by many frantic offers for a taxi ride. It was rush hour and the taxi was not air-conditioned. As we approached the center of the city, we were stuck in traffic for some time. All of a sudden, my driver crossed the median strip to the other side and took a less congested side street to CHAI headquarters.

I met the coordinator for the rural programs, Dr. Ipuge, in his office where a large map of the southeastern part of Tanzania took center stage. CHAI had programs on HIV/AIDS in Dar es Salaam and Zanzibar, and about eight months prior to my arrival, they started several programs in the rural areas. One of these places was Mtwara, in the southeast part of Tanzania, close to the border of Mozambique. Three Clinical Treatment and Care Centers

(CTCs) were set up in the Mtwara region: one in urban Masasi, a second in rural Masasi, and a third in Ligula Hospital; they planned to open two more in Newala and Tandahimba. The plan was to have 400,000 HIV-infected Tanzanians receiving antiretroviral drugs by 2008 and another 1.2 million enrolled in care. I was the first mentor for the doctors and nurses to arrive.

In Dar, I stayed in a very lovely hotel with a view of the city, and the food was sumptuous. In some ways, I felt guilty that I should live so well when I was supposed to be helping people who were so needy. Dar had plenty of non-descript concrete buildings with flat rooftops; many were adorned with laundry lines with clothes hanging to dry. Most of the walls on the topmost floors of the buildings were streaked with black mildew nurtured by the rain over time. A white mosque and its minarets appeared prominently among the buildings. Islam is very much a part of Tanzania, and dressing modestly was prudent. On the other side of the hotel, the harbor was close by where one could board a boat to go to Zanzibar, the spice island.

Joe and Dr. Katenga boarded Precision Air with me, and the flight from Dar to Mtwara took just a little over an hour. As we approached Mtwara, the bright red earth roads weaved their way through the lush green of the Tanzanian terrain; lush now but a few weeks ago this area had been deep in the throes of a drought. We had left the busy city for rural Tanzania.

Situated near the Makonde Plateau, Mtwara area was one of the more remote locations in Tanzania. After the First World War, the British took over control of what was then German East Africa from the Germans and renamed it Tanganyika.[3] It was slated to be a center for a vast agriculture scheme that involved plantations growing groundnuts to make up for post-war food shortages in the United Kingdom and to export the rest to Europe. The plantations eventually failed, but the town of Mtwara remained.[4] Because the blueprint was that of a plantation, houses in Mtwara were spaced far apart. To get from place to place, the Mtwarans walked, biked, or boarded the *dalla dalla* or minibuses on unpaved roads; thus a trip to the CTC could be both time-consuming and costly.

In 2003, between 1.2 and 2.3 million people in Tanzania were living with HIV/AIDS with the prevalence rate of between 6.4 to 11.9 percent,[5] higher than that of the sub-Saharan African region of 7.2 percent and the global rate of 1.1 percent. In sub-Saharan Africa, women accounted for more than half (57 percent) of adults estimated to be living with HIV/AIDS.[6]

We met with the Regional Medical Officer (RMO) who was like a medical director of the hospital, and Dr. Kivo, the District Medical Officer (DMO). The RMO's office was filled with furniture; most prominent were his huge desk and the conference table, and we had to squeeze ourselves into chairs that were pushed snugly against the wall. As in all our meetings or visits to an institution in Africa, the signing of our names in a visitor's book was a requirement. The meeting was quite formal, and we all sat at the long rectangular table while the RMO presided. There was a distinct hierarchy in the medical establishment; everyone listened respectfully to the RMO with very little discussion. To get any project started here, the RMO would have to be kept informed.

Poverty abounded in Mtwara. This was very much evident in the hospital and clinics. Ligula Hospital was built in 1964, and it probably had not changed a great deal from when it first opened. The CTC shared space with the regular outpatient clinic and only opened on Wednesday and Thursday. HIV patients mingled with the regular patients and were not singled out. The waiting rooms were always crowded with patients sitting on benches or lying on the floor, waiting patiently. Flies swarmed around open wounds, settled on the eyes and

Ligula Hospital in Mtwara, Tanzania, built in 1964.

lips of the patients. During the rainy season, the ceiling leaked onto the floor, and patients waded through ankle-deep water to see their doctors.

When I arrived in March of 2006, the CTC had been open for eight months. It had enrolled four hundred HIV patients, two-thirds being women, and half of those enrolled had started on treatment. There were only sixteen children.[7] I met Dr. Mdoe, whom I would be mentoring, and the staff: Clara Mbatiya, the clinical nurse; Perpetua Bernard, the counselor; and Shabia, the voluntary counseling testing (VCT) nurse. Mama Salum, the home-based nurse, was on duty in the hospital.

The next order of business was to find a place for me to stay as I was the first volunteer there, and nothing had been set up ahead of time. Our driver drove us from tarmac roads onto red-earthed paths, lined by cashew trees. We visited a deserted lodge where the bar, restaurant, and rondavel were devoid of tourists and activities; the outdoor pool was scummy and abandoned, and the grounds overgrown with tall grass and bushes. I silently prayed that this would not be where I ended; it was too lonely and forsaken. We drove to another lodging run by a church, but the rooms were dingy even in broad daylight. Dr. Katenga took a quick look and shook his head. The last place was the old Boma Hotel in Mikindani, a national monument and an old fort over a hundred years old. It was built by the Germans in 1895, but during the First World War, the British took over control, hence the name BOMA (British Office for Management Administration).[8] Painted all white, it was beautifully restored into a hotel with nine rooms, run jointly by a British charity organization, and the Tanzanian government; the proceeds from running it and other activities went into helping the village of Mikindani. Situated on the side of a hill overlooking the Indian

Ocean, it commanded breathtaking views, especially during sunrise. This was to be my temporary abode until a more suitable place was located. The Boma was excessively expensive for a two-month stay and too far from Ligula Hospital where I would be working.

In the late afternoon, I took a walk into the village where the houses were mainly made of sticks and mud with thatched roofs. There were a few stucco ones with mud-stained bases, but all were in dire need of repair. The interior of the huts with their dirt floor was dark with filthy curtains hanging from the small windows. Children followed me around, many barefoot, and some in their school uniforms. An old slave market that looked like a church, painted sage green and white, set apart from the village; it was peaceful and quiet now but must have an unspeakable past. Not too far from it was a dilapidated building with a plaque on its broken wall announcing it as "THE REPUTED DWELLING PLACE OF DR. DAVID LIVINGSTONE FROM 24TH MARCH TO 7TH APRIL 1866 FROM HERE HE BEGAN HIS LAST JOURNEY."

The setting sun painted the sky over the Indian Ocean with colors of orange, yellow, blue, and purple. I settled into the Zanzibar bed shrouded by a mosquito net, the bed frame brightly painted with indigenous flora and fauna as well as the fruits of the sea. I could not wait to start my mentoring at the CTC of Ligula Hospital of Mtwara, a regional referral hospital for the surrounding district hospitals.

Joe, a laboratory consultant, had come to check on the laboratory equipment that ran chemistries, complete cell count, and most importantly CD4 count—the enumeration of the immune cells in one's body that helped to determine the eligibility of HIV-infected individuals for starting treatment and gauge the response of the immune system to treatment. The equipment sat in an air-conditioned room, the most comfortable place in this humid sticky environment. CD4 counts were run daily, and each of the outlying clinics was given a certain day of the week in which to collect blood which was then transported to Mtwara via a courier. A limited number of CD4 counts were run each day. As the number of HIV/AIDS patients increased, the demand for it would increase, running the risk of overwhelming the system. Already many patients traveled long distances to have their CD4 counts done, and they had to be turned away during the late morning hours when the quota for the day was reached.

For the first two weeks, Dr. Mdoe, whom I was to mentor, had left for Dar for some personal issues, so I worked with Dr. Aloyce Mshana. He ran the program for the PMTCT and referred HIV mothers to the CTC after they delivered their babies. There was no system to track if these women followed through with their instructions. Most mothers did not show up simply because they feared the stigma associated with HIV for their infants. Husbands of women who tested positive for HIV refused to come forward for testing, assuming that their wives had become infected from some other source. Their own families often shunned these women; convincing the men to come forward to get HIV testing was a tall order. The stigma of HIV infection drove many patients to travel a whole day to be seen at another district, incurring traveling and lodging expenses and losing one or two days of work. They were only given a month's supply of medications, forcing them to make such a journey every month.

An aunt of a five-year-old child brought her in because she was tired all the time and not thriving, and she was tested positive for HIV. Both her parents had died of AIDS, and she was never tested until now. Miraculously she survived all her five years. She stared at me the whole time, for I must be the first *mzungu* on whom she had laid her eyes.

Perpetua and Clara were the counselor and nurse clinician who refilled and explained the side effects of the HIV medications and counseled the patients on medication adherence. The goal for my two-month stay was to mentor the physician, Dr. Mdoe, who had attended a course in HIV care in Dar and had worked at the CTC in Ligula Hospital since its inception in June of 2005. Then I was to travel to Newala and Tandahimba, several hours away over potholed dirt roads to help set up two new CTCs and to provide continuing medical education at the hospitals.

Wearing a white coat tinged a faint brown, Dr. Mdoe came to work without a stethoscope. For him caring for patients entailed a brief history and then writing a prescription; there was no physical examination to help with the clinical decision making. Because of inattention to basic examination, many conditions were often missed and not diagnosed. Sensing subtle resistance to some of my suggestions, I was careful not to lean on him too hard, mindful of the fact he might feel intimidated to be mentored by a woman. After a week or so of observing him, I decided to make my move. One morning he prescribed a cough medicine for a patient who came in coughing without listening to his lungs. I asked him how he knew the patient did not have pneumonia or lung infection if he did not listen to his lungs.

"I just know after so many years of taking care of patients," he answered.

I rose to listen to the patient's lungs and heard some extraneous sounds suggesting a possible lung infection. To prove my point, I ordered a chest x-ray. Viewing the x-ray against the light from the window, indeed there was a patch of pneumonia.

A gaunt man with AIDS lost nine kilograms in one week, just before he was to start on antiretroviral agents (ARVs or medications for the treatment of HIV infection). His chest x-ray showed possible tuberculosis (TB). TB infection in an HIV patient often had unusual presentations. For him, he rarely had a cough but the overall wasting, which was made worse by his HIV infection, left him looking ravaged and utterly devastated; he had hardly any fighting chance to combat these two killers.

ARVs not only improved the immune system, they also resulted in increased appetite. A fifty-one-year-old woman began treatment in 2004, and her immune cells had returned to normal. She complained of being hungry all the time. It turned out that she frequently ate only one meal a day; she had tea and bread in the morning, more tea at lunch, then rice and beans for dinner. It was rare for anyone here to be able to afford meat. She blamed her hunger on the ARVs and threatened to stop taking them, imploring us to find her some food; it was quite a dilemma as many of the people here were poor. This was my first mission into an AIDS riddled African country. I was sure that this problem must be obvious for organizations like the Clinton Foundation when they started their HIV treatment program. Was the issue of food security ever raised, confronted, and a solution found?

In the ensuing days I showed Dr. Mdoe oral candidiasis (yeast infection of the mouth), and oral hairy leukoplakia (white patches usually found along the sides of the mouth or tongue thought to be caused by the Epstein-Barr virus). The presence of either of these infections connotes immune deficiency. With limited resources, looking into the mouth was actually the cheapest and easiest way to gauge the immune state of the patients.

One day a quiet man walked into the clinic while Dr. Mdoe was rounding in the hospital. Christine, the new HIV clinical director, translated for me. For quite some time now, he had observed the swelling of his private area. Despite my gender, he was not shy to get undressed for me to take a look. His scrota were swollen, and his thighs and legs were peppered with the bluish-red and purple bumps of Kaposi sarcoma (cancer of the lymph nodes and blood vessels). On his hard palate, he had globs of deep purple Kaposi lesions. He had repeatedly mentioned his problem to the doctor during his previous visits, but no one asked him to disrobe. With such extensive disease, he would need chemotherapy in addition to the treatment of AIDS. Dar was a whole day's journey from Mtwara; not many patients could afford the trip, let alone the treatment. I was left not knowing how to solve his problem, a difficult situation without an easy or obvious answer in a resource-poor country.

A mother finally brought in her seven-month-old baby for HIV testing. She herself was infected and was on treatment but refused to believe that her baby might be infected until she failed to gain weight. It was a fiasco to get the baby weighed. We had to send her to the pediatric unit to use the only baby scale there. The baby, with sunken eyes and ribs poking through her chest, weighed a

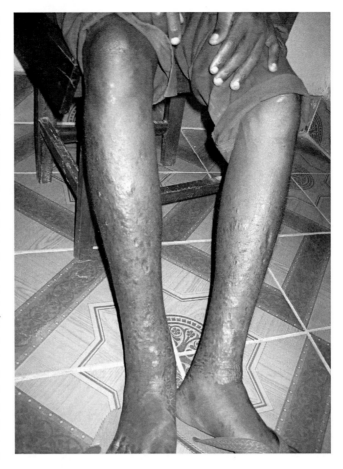

A young man with myriad purplish lesions of Kaposi's sarcoma, cancer of the lymph nodes and blood vessels.

mere 4.4 kilograms. She did not cry when examined. I held her light body, looking into her unfocused, lifeless, and joyless eyes.

One morning Dr. Mdoe and I took a long walk along a corridor crowded with many waiting relatives, almost all women, to make rounds in the hospital. He pointed out a rotunda in the hospital compound where the women cooked. The hospital did not provide food for the patients; relatives cooked for them and provided ninety percent of the nursing care. The ward was a long building lined on both sides with wrought-iron beds with peeling white paint, placed only a few feet apart from each other. Blue or hunter green mosquito nets, tied up for the day, hung from the ceiling. The patients brought in their own sheets, and when all of the beds were full, two patients shared a bed, their heads resting at different ends.

A nurse followed us with a cart of charts as we moved from patient to patient. Dr. Mdoe spoke briefly to them but did not touch or examine them. Out of curiosity, I decided to look into the mouth of each and every one of the patients with my flashlight. To my surprise, at least a third of the patients had yeast infection and/or hairy oral leukoplakia. None had been tested for HIV, and they needed it. I asked Dr. Mdoe whether we could offer testing. Apparently before HIV testing, every patient had to be counseled, and there were not enough HIV counselors and no room for private counseling. I lamented missing this golden opportunity to diagnose HIV in this captive audience and to offer treatment and prevent transmission.

Two patients lay next to each other: one a seven-year-old girl, and the other a thirty-year-old woman. Both of them had been admitted overnight with a diagnosis of meningitis; neither had been started on antibiotics. The staff was waiting for their relatives to buy the intravenous lines and the antibiotics. In America, we are taught that meningitis is a life-threatening infection, and patients suspected of having such an infection would be started on antibiotics within thirty minutes of arrival in the emergency room. For both patients, Dr. Mdoe prescribed crystalline penicillin and chloramphenicol for bacterial meningitis, antibiotics that we no longer use in the U.S. For good measure he prescribed quinine for cerebral malaria. There was one nurse for the whole ward of seventeen patients. There was no telling when the relatives could raise enough money to buy the antibiotics, and when the nurse would have time to administer them.

Further along an old woman had an infected wound in her thigh; a stench emanated from the dressing, soaked through with a green ooze. The dressing had not been changed since she came in two days ago; her relatives had yet to bring in new dressings from the pharmacy, so the patient would just have to live with the old malodorous ones, never mind the antibiotics.

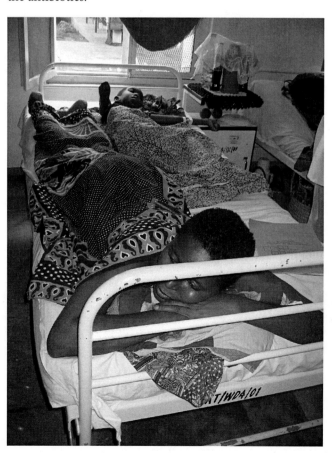

Patients sharing a bed when the ward was full.

Patients did not automatically get diagnostic studies even if they were deemed necessary by the doctors. If a patient presented with signs of meningitis, no spinal tap was done. To do so, the patient's relatives had to buy the lumbar puncture tray, so the diagnosis was made clinically. The hospital did not have the capacity to do all the laboratory tests; the equipment owned by the Clinton Foundation was solely for the use of the CTC. Even if an inpatient were in need of a test, it could not be done via the state-of-the-art equipment. The fees charged were different if a patient were seen by a clinical officer versus a doctor, and the medications prescribed when filled in the hospital pharmacy also cost less if the patient were seen by a clinical officer. In Ligula Hospital, where limited resources were the rule, patients' ability to pay took precedence over the saving of their lives.

In the isolation ward, there were a few patients with diarrhea. Flies swarmed around the caps of water thermoses. There were no functioning taps. Indeed, it was rare to find a working tap in the hospital. We washed our hands with soap and water from a tank when the sink stopped working. Dr. Mdoe wiped his hands on the already graying window curtain or on his white coat when the roll of reusable cloth was all used. I just air-dried my hands.

At lunch break, I sat on an outside bench ready to enjoy my egg sandwich while shooing away hordes of flies descending on my food. Slowly, I became aware of children sitting on the ground, creeping ever so quietly and stealthily closer to me, eyes watching me eat. I lost my appetite and gave up eating lunch for the duration of my stay in Mtwara. When the HIV project director, Christine, came later in the month, she took me to the hospital cafeteria. The ubiquitous flies were there, but more disconcertingly, the rag that was used to wipe the table was grimy and gray. I had the terrible fear that the young girl waiting on us could just as well use it to wipe the clean dishes. I did not order any food and never stepped in there again.

Perpetua and Clara's lunch was just a thermos of tea, coffee, or cocoa; occasionally they had fish. They survived on two meals a day because they had no money for lunch. I could not see myself eating lunch when they drank tea to fill their stomachs. So like them, I ate two meals a day.

Dr. Mdoe took Christine and me to the "Frelimo," the maternity ward used to house exiled Mozambicans who formed Frelimo or the Mozambique Liberation Front in 1962 seeking to overthrow the Portuguese colonial rule in their country to gain independence.[9] At the reception, a very pregnant woman lay on a bed covered with a dirty brown sheet. This room opened into a ward with three beds, each equipped with a pair of large, bloodstained canvas stirrups. A pregnant woman occupied a soiled vinyl bed with no sheet, and another arrived on her own two feet, alone and unescorted; she was led to an empty vinyl bed. Off to one side was the delivery room with three beds equipped with rusty steel stirrups, lending an air of austerity and reminiscent of the butchery of medieval times. Delivery beds purportedly scrubbed clean looked ominously bloodstained. Beside one of the delivery beds, a wooden tray lined with a bloodstained rubber sheet, a giant bulb syringe lying forlornly near it, was ready to receive an innocent newborn into the world. The old bloodstains from numerous previous deliveries had set permanently into the rubber sheet; no amount of washing could ever remove them. There were three other wards: one for women post C-section, a second for women after vaginal delivery, and a third holding women in labor. The hallway led to a small room for premature babies, with three bassinets each holding up to four preemies, covered with mosquito netting. Naked light bulbs hung low over each bassinet giving out feeble heat. There were no intravenous lines or respirators. Nine preemies snuggled against each other, no nurses around, only a lone mother hovering over her baby.

After a few days of staying at the Boma, I moved to the hostel of the Vocational and Education Training Authority or VETA. My room had a lovely view of the Indian Ocean but there were no beaches, only sharp coral rocks. Disappointingly the refrigerator in my room did not work. There was no hot water, and I learned to save a bucket of water in the bathroom because the trickle of the shower often stopped flowing at the crucial moment when I was covered with shampoo and lather. Occasionally the tap surprised me by spilling out dark brown water, staining my white clothes chocolate brown as I hand washed them.

I could take my meals in the canteen, but despite its full menu, on a given day, only one or two choices were available, and I had to order two hours ahead of time. Fish was not frequently available even though the Indian Ocean was just a stone's throw away, and fresh fish could be bought directly from the fishermen in the early morning on the beaches two miles away.

Tanzania had just come off a drought when I arrived; the rain made everything look green and lush. It was slim pickings in the market in terms of fresh produce: some measly bruised bananas, anemic-looking onions, and corn. Towards the end of my stay, the produce became more plentiful, but it did not translate into more varieties in the canteen.

The proper sandy beach was about a mile away from VETA, next to a restaurant and lodge frequented by expats and rich Tanzanians. The water was warm, and the beach had soft white sand. I went to the beach one weekend and observed that the boys were in the ocean while the girls huddled together on the shore, not venturing into the water at all. When I finally went in to swim, they shyly followed and surrounded me, splashing happily away.

Tagged to the bulletin board at the nursing station in the ward were two sheets of paper listing the top ten diseases and top ten commonly used drugs. The diseases and conditions were malaria, anemia, hypertension, ARC (AIDS-Related Complex), bronchitis, pneumonia, pulmonary tuberculosis, asthma, congestive cardiac failure, and hypoglycemia. The top ten drugs were quinine, injectable penicillin, injectable chloramphenicol, panadol, nifedipine, vitamin B complex, lasix, diclofenac, injectable hydrocortisone, and 5 percent dextrose. Eighty-five percent of the patients were there for malaria.

Many newly diagnosed patients with HIV/AIDS had been infected with the virus for an unknown period and came in with wasting syndrome or slim disease, which in 2006 was rarely seen in the U.S. but still common here. In Africa, the medications used to treat HIV/AIDS were ones that western countries were just beginning to associate with some intolerable side effects, and were no longer using them. In Mtwara, some patients came in with long-term side effects of Zerit or D4T such as lipodystrophy, which manifested as abnormal truncal fat accumulation, a buffalo hump over the back of the neck, and loss of fat tissue in the limbs. They started HIV medications, buying them with their own money even before the opening of the CTC. Then, slowly, they noticed the changes in their appearance, the hollowing of their cheeks and thinning of their legs with the appearance of prominent veins. Unfortunately, there were no alternative medications available through CHAI.

Most of the married patients came without their spouses. One morning a Muslim couple attended clinic together. The man's immune cells were low, and he required treatment while the woman's were still high. It was very likely that he had infected her. A young mother who had recently delivered her baby was abandoned by her husband once he learned that she was HIV positive. She looked a picture of health despite her infection. Walking barefoot with the baby strapped on her back, she came to the clinic to get her medication refilled.

Around VETA there was farmland planted with corn and potatoes. Women and children did almost all the farming, tilling, and weeding. The men congregated in the town center, drinking in the cafe or bar, some sleeping under the spreading cashew trees, and a few begging for money when I passed by so they could buy cooked cassava from a vendor. The town center was a collection of restaurants, bars, and stores selling produce and various sundry things. One day I spotted a can of Danish cookies in a store. After dinner that night, I opened the can with a great deal of anticipation, only to be disappointed by a bunch of stale cookies. The can must have sat on the store way past its shelf life.

One weekend while wading in the shallow water at low tide, I met two women, Myema and Tafuta, collecting small shellfish stranded by the receding water. They told me that they could get two hundred and fifty shillings, about twenty U.S. cents, for a kilogram. Their catch barely covered the bottoms of their buckets. There were quite a number of sea anemones, but these did not seem to interest them.

"It takes three stones to support a cooking pot. It takes three men to support a woman." A Tanzanian healthcare worker explained to me why HIV was spreading rapidly among women. Women were economically dependent on men for their livelihood. When a married woman lost support from her husband, she might be forced to strike up other extramarital relationships in order to survive and feed her children, oftentimes exchanging sex for money. Some male HIV patients acknowledged offering money for unprotected sex, despite knowing their HIV status. When a woman became HIV-infected, her husband's family often blamed her as the source of the infection. Here, husband and wife abstained from sex throughout a pregnancy and sometimes for a few months afterwards, so often the man sought extra-marital relationships. In this Islamic community, a husband could divorce his wife with a stroke of a pen by writing a letter to his wife's father, and he could have up to four wives. A billboard on the hospital grounds ironically emphasized the importance of family, but with the practice of polygamy and having multiple sexual partners, HIV could run rampant.

I had several discussions with the Clinton laboratory director asking him to run more CD4 samples a day, but he demanded extra duty pay. I later learned from Joe, the laboratory consultant from Dar, that each machine could run more samples than the twenty that the director stipulated without additional work. I only wanted more samples to make it easy for the patients, especially those who had to travel long distances. I was unable to convince him, and he did not seem to care. Without a strong dictum from the authority in Dar, nothing had changed by the time I left.

The rotund Mama Salum was the CTC's part-time home visit nurse. She was usually quite busy with her other nursing duties, and

Sign in the hospital compound in Swahili: VITA DHIDI YA UKIMWI TUBADILI TABIA ZETUJUUYA NGONO. **Fight against AIDS. We change our sexual behavior.**

the lack of transportation meant that she rarely made home visits. While waiting for her in the nursing office to go for home visits, I noticed that the calendar on the wall was a few years out of date, and the nursing schedule posted was a few months old; everything seemed obsolete. How did this place run without a current timetable for nursing?

I spent the day with Mama Salum on her only home visit during my stay in Mtwara. The hospital cruiser dropped us off at a village. We walked through a small outdoor market before reaching a stone house. Our first patient was a middle-aged woman, a grandmother, all wrapped up in her colorful *kanga*. She had just come back from visiting another HIV patient with shingles. She had been on ARVs since 2004 and was doing well. Because of her experience with treatment, she acted as a support system for the other patients in the village. Her husband died and left her with a very nice home. She grew some crops on the land around her house, but money was always scarce. When she first learned of her HIV infection, the villagers shunned her, but now they were more accepting of her condition.

Mama Salum's daughter-in-law lived close by, and we stopped for some chai and chapatti. Swarms of flies covered the dirty dishes in one corner of the floor. I gingerly took a very small piece of the chapatti, hoping that the flies had not touched it. Mama Salum checked on a young man and a woman who ran a pharmacy and queried them on the manner in which they took their medicines. The woman was trying to set up a support group for HIV-infected patients; the stigma attached to HIV remained enormous and burdensome.

Mama Salum wished for a bicycle that she could use to save her from all the walking, and I could see why. We walked in the searing heat of the sun to the main road to wait for the *dalla dalla*. A bug van lumbered towards us, already crammed with people, yet the conductor jammed us into its airless interior smelling of stale sweat from yesterday. I stood close to the door with my torso bent under the ceiling, grateful for the air that wafted through the partially open door from which the conductor was hanging. After what seemed like an eternity, a seat was finally freed up for me. The *dalla dalla* was not considered full until a few passengers were dangling out of the door. I counted thirty passengers that day in the *dalla dalla* at one time. We got off at another village close to the Indian Ocean. That day we walked quite a long way, crisscrossing through the villages, avoiding puddles, walking along embankments of vegetable patches and the sandy beaches. Some patients were not home, and we found one at a stall selling salted fish; he had elephantiasis. We visited the young woman abandoned by her husband shortly after the birth of their third child. She was lucky to have a half-finished home and some money left to her by her father. She lived with her mother and her three children and planned to finish building her house and open a small business. Her dwelling was made of concrete blocks while the village was filled with mud and stick houses. A little girl sat in front of a hut sorting through a basket of small fish. Mama Salum said the villagers lived a very hard life and made do with whatever they could find for food. They were lucky to live by the sea.

It started to rain, and we took shelter in the front porch of a mud house. When it eased up, we walked back to the main road to catch the *dalla dalla* back to the hospital. The bus stop was next to a shed with a table filled with old shoes that should have been thrown away, but the owners wanted them salvaged. I could see why Mama Salum did not make too many home visits. In fact, when I asked her when her next home visit was, she became evasive. That evening the frogs in the marsh were croaking joyously in loud chorus, rejoicing in their mating season.

The hospital closed its clinic for the Easter weekend, so I flew to Dar and went north to visit the Kaole ruins near the center of Bagamoyo.[10] Kaole was believed to be the first settlement of the Arabs from Persia. The ruins consisted of two mosques and several tombs of coral stones and were considered one of the oldest mosques in East Africa. Bagamoyo, "lay down your heart" in Swahili, was the major slave trading post in East Africa and the last place the slaves would stay in Tanzania before being shipped to Zanzibar, and then off to the distant shores of the Arab countries, never to see their homeland again.[11] A nearby museum chronicled the slave trade in Tanganyika. The slaves were captured in the western part of Tanganyika or purchased from other Africans. They were made to carry ivory from Kigoma and Ujiji and walked for about nine months to Bagamoyo, chained at the necks and legs to each other, with children in tow. Many died, and many more were shot when they were too weak to walk. Although the slave trade officially ended in 1873, it went on secretly until the end of the nineteenth century. Bagamoyo also was the starting point for many renowned European explorers including John Hanning Speke and Henry Morton Stanley.[12] The church where Dr. Livingstone's body rested while waiting for high tide so it could be shipped to England remained standing. His two slaves took out his heart and buried it in western Tanzania when he died. They then preserved his body and carried it all the way to Bagamoyo.

Transportation in Mtwara was always an issue. The CHAI driver and van were busy with the rural coordinator, Stephen Kisakaye, outside of Mtwara. The hospital driver drove Dr. Mdoe, Christine, and me to and from the hospital. There were several rusty cruisers parked in the hospital ground; all of them sat on flat tires and were badly in need of major repair. Early on, the RMO suggested that I could drive one of the hospital cruisers. I cringed at the idea since I was not familiar with the roads and imagined myself stuck in the rutted red-earth roads badly eroded by the heavy rain. Later I learned that he meant to have me drive one of the broken cruisers if the Clinton Foundation would agree to fix it. The plan to have me help with the start-up of the programs in Newala and Tadahimba never took place. The Clinton vehicle was always busy with one thing or another and was never in Mtwara until my last week.

Towards the end of my stay, the regional coordinator, Dr. Ipuge, came to pay us a visit. Our vehicle finally appeared to take all of us to a grand tour of the other sites. At first we were traveling along decent tarmac road, but soon we were on unpaved red-earth roads. Almost all Africans walked, and a few lucky ones rode on bicycles. I could not help but wonder if they ever encountered wild animals. Dr. Ipuge said most animals were displaced to more remote areas as humans took over their natural habitat.

That day the rain fell steadily, transforming the red-earth roads into gushing, red, muddy rivers. We traveled over a bridge that was completely submerged in water. It did not have any guardrails to prevent vehicles from tumbling into the raging water, so the driver tried to steer it right in the center or what he thought was the center of the bridge. It slid on the mud towards the edge where the muddy water plunged into the rushing river below. I thought perhaps we should have gotten out of the vehicle and walked. We held our collective breath as it slithered its way safely onto the other side. At both ends of the bridge, curious villagers lined up to watch the dangerous crossing. Vehicles on both sides waited to take turns to cross the bridge including a big passenger bus. I was glad I was not in it.

Dr. Renate, an expat from Germany, told me about a German volunteer whose vehicle tumbled into a ditch while traveling in the dark. Instead of providing help, the passers-by robbed him of his cell phone, his lifeline to the outside world, and all his belongings, including the sneakers on his feet. Shoes were treasured here as most people went barefoot, and they did have to walk a great deal. He lay there in the ditch with a broken pelvis until daybreak, when he finally received help. He was flown to Germany, and a year later, he returned to resume his work. Since his horrendous experience, the German NGO made a firm rule that no one was ever to travel alone after dark.

Finally, after what seemed like ages, we ended our journey in a comfortable rest house, Kyalema Kyaro. It had a small restaurant, and as in all Mtwara regions, the menu was pretty much the same: fish, beef, or chicken, all cooked in the same kind of sauce, and served with a choice of rice, *ugali* (mashed maize), and chips.

In the morning the sun shone so brightly that the rain of the previous day was all but forgotten. Eggs cooked in different ways were the breakfast fare. The menu offered Toomatohomelet, Homeyhomeletlet, Vanshomelet (I was puzzled about this one; was it Vanishing omelet or Spanish omelet?), Fryeggs, Boiledeggs, Poteggs, and Scrapeggs. Eggs were also served every morning at the VETA along with a watered-down fruit juice, a cup of coffee or tea, and two pieces of bread with a dash of margarine and jam. There was not much variation in the breakfast offerings, so they had to be ingenious with the egg preparation. Sometimes they even ran out of eggs; the hens protested and stopped laying. Every morning I half expected the canteen staff to ask me, "Would you like green eggs? And oh, I'm sorry, ma'am we ran out of ham." Of course, they did not eat ham in this Islamic region.

After breakfast we made our way to Mkomaindo Hospital in Masasi. There Dr. Ipuge met with the hospital chief and staff for briefing and debriefing. Tanzanians reveled in this kind of exercise. As always we signed the big guest book. Mkomaindo Hospital was smaller and less sprawling than Ligula. The lab looked old, dirty, and dingy. Old brown bottles lined the dusty shelves, and the chemistry machine had not worked for months. Later we visited the clinic, a big room with no sink, and we briefly saw a woman affected by elephantiasis. A very emaciated and tired man had traveled a long way for days to Masasi to start a business, but fell ill and ran out of money. He landed in Mkomaindo Hospital, just skin and bone, and severely afflicted with scabies. He tested positive for HIV and was admitted for possible TB. I was concerned that being alone and far away from home, he would not have relatives to cook or care for him. Dr. Mrope reassured me that they would work something out for him. Behind the hospital were some huge, impressive outcroppings of granite rocks inviting hikers to climb them, but Steven warned there were lions, leopards, and cheetahs around the boulders.

Dr. Mrope rode with us over a very bad road to Ngaga Health Center twenty-five kilometers away. He traveled there twice a week to mentor the clinical officers. Around twenty patients waited in the veranda; almost all of them were in the late stage of HIV infection. A ten-year-old orphaned girl had survived an undiagnosed HIV infection without treatment. Small for her age, she had a mouth full of thrush or yeast infection, signifying that her immune system was extremely deficient. We gave her nystatin to treat her thrush, septrin to protect her from *Pneumocystic jiroveci* pneumonia (a fungal lung infection), and ARVs for her HIV infection. Shaking his head in despair, Dr. Ipuge commented that without a proper education, her future was bleak.

From here we traveled to Newala over winding, bumpy, and muddy roads, through villages with mud houses, and maize growing around them. In the distance we caught glimpses of the Makonde Plateau, the Ruvuji River, and Mozambique. Newala Hospital was a small district hospital. The CTC had opened a few weeks ago, and already it had registered a number of sick patients. Again more briefing and debriefing. Christine and I wanted to use the bathroom there, but someone had gone home with the key.

We left Newala and headed towards Tandahimba. Dr. Ipuge bought some roasted maize and *korosho* (cashew nuts) for us to munch since we did not have time for lunch. We went on the bumpy road again, looking for a good spot to go to the bushes. When we did find a place, Steven jumped out and immediately headed for the woods while Christine and I went the opposite direction towards a mango tree. Steven warned us not to go too deep because he saw a snake, so we went under some low bushes instead. Just as soon as we were done, it started to drizzle, and then the rain came in torrents.

It was dusk when we reached Thandahimba. We waited a while for the DMO to appear. There was a power outage after the storm, and I could hardly see his face in the gathering gloom. The CTC had finished seeing all the patients and was closed for the day. The books showed it would be a busy center; the clinic had opened in March and had already enrolled about eighteen patients. Outside the building was a forlorn, disabled ambulance, hood opened, tires completely deflated, rusted for who knew how long.

We were on a mission to travel all the way back to Mtwara that evening over wet, puddle-riddled, and rugged dirt roads, passing small villages with mud houses with no electricity. Dim light from lanterns and candles flickered in some houses, and occasionally fluorescent lighting here and there from merchants who could afford a generator. Shadowy figures huddled in the doors enjoying the cool evening air. Each town only consisted of a few shops, and it took us just less than a minute or a wink of the eye to pass through. Several owls flew by. After three excruciating hours, we arrived at Mtwara, and it sure looked a lot larger than those towns we visited. We had called the Korosho Restaurant in Mtwara a few hours ahead of time to order our dinner. Even so, we waited for another hour before our food was ready. We needed the restroom badly. Riding on a bumpy road with a full bladder was not a fun thing. The next day, I woke up achy all over.

Tanzania was the first African country I visited, and I realized very quickly that Tanzanians had a different sense of time. Punctuality was not their strong suit. I had often been left waiting for hours for a ride or an appointment. When they did show up, there was never any word of apologies. Once I waited for a whole morning for a ride from Mama Salum who was organizing a beach outing; no one showed. Finally, I called her on her cell phone only to find out that the outing was not going to take place because she could not arrange for a ride. There was no phone call from her to let me know. I later learned from the staff in Dar that Africans did not like to disappoint, and even if they knew they could not fulfill a promise, they would keep on saying, "I'm coming!" so be prepared to wait and wait and wait. An expat once told me "*kesho*" did not mean tomorrow; it really meant "stay awake and wait." I was not to take it literally when someone said he was coming or he would be there in a few minutes (*bado kidogo*); it would be more like half an hour or a couple of hours. Whether it was going to happen in the next minute, hour, day, week, month, year, or never, was anyone's guesses. However, at times to me, it seemed like an everlasting wait.

Dr. Renate came to Mtwara with her husband from Germany. She was on a two-year contract working on an AIDS prevention program. At first she had all sorts of innovative ideas and plans, but she was stymied at every turn, so much so that after the first month she was wondering whether she should pack up and leave. No one showed up for meetings when they were arranged, and if they showed up, they were ill prepared. Her superior was often absent from work and reports from her never materialized, and oftentimes, Dr. Renate ended up doing them for her. Where was she? In Africa, there was a huge incentive to go for continuing education. Traditionally NGOs paid the attendees a stipend for each day of attendance in addition to an all-expense-paid trip. Whenever there was such a conference, most Africans would grab the opportunity to go. In this case her superior was often gone here and there for conferences, leaving her work unfinished or to be completed by the expats. Dr. Renate told me in the beginning she cried "bitter tears" every night. After a while she learned to be more patient and accepting of the African way.

Dr. Ipuge met with the powers that be at Ligula Hospital to bring them up to speed regarding the HIV program in Mtwara and CHAI's vision for expansion. In Tanzania everything moved like molasses; I had to learn to be extremely patient. This was hard since my time there to effect a change was limited. For Dr. Renate, she had two long years.

During my last week, I finally had a CHAI driver and cruiser at my disposal, or so I was told by Dr. Ipuge before he flew back to Dar. David, the driver, was supposed to come to fetch me at VETA the following morning. At the end of clinic, I waited for him at the designated place, but he did not show. When I finally reached him by cell phone, he was extremely apologetic. He told me that the RMO asked him to fetch his guests from the airport, and he was not sure when he would be able to take me back to VETA. The CHAI cruiser was well kept compared to the hospital cruiser, so the RMO used it for his guests. In the end I went home with Kula Bali, the hospital driver, in the old beat-up cruiser. For the rest of my last week, the CHAI cruiser was always in the service of the RMO, and I was hardly the beneficiary.

On my last day at the Ligula Hospital, Dr. Mdoe asked me to leave my pocket flashlight for him. I wanted to think that I had succeeded in convincing him that performing a physical examination was important in the evaluation of the patients, and he was going to at least look into their mouths. This was 2006, but the HIV-infected patients we saw here were like the patients we saw at the beginning of the HIV epidemic in the U.S. in the 1980s, wasted, severely anemic, and extremely immune-deficient.

Christine would be staying in Mtwara to oversee the start-up of a few more CTCs, and future volunteers would continue with the mentoring program. Another issue that became quickly apparent in the patients attending the CTC was the lack of food for proper nutrition. CHAI could consider food aid to the patients and their families for a period until their health improved to such an extent that they were able to get gainful employment; this would also improve their adherence to taking their medications. After I sent in my reports and recommendations for future volunteers, I boarded the plane to Dar.

In December 2013, the UNAIDS Program Coordinating Board called on UNAIDS (Joint United Nations Program on HIV/AIDS) to establish new targets for HIV treatment scale-up beyond 2015 globally.[13] The result was 90–90–90, an ambitious treatment target to help end the AIDS epidemic. The targets are as follows: by 2020, 90 percent of all people living with HIV will know their HIV status, 90 percent of all people with diagnosed HIV infection will receive sustained antiretroviral therapy, and 90 percent of all people receiving antiretroviral therapy will have viral suppression. Modeling shows that achieving these goals will enable the end of the AIDS epidemic by 2030. The 2018 Tanzania's 90–90–90 progress report showed no data available for what percent of people living with HIV knew their status, 66 percent of people living with HIV were on treatment, and 73 percent on treatment were virally suppressed.[14] Gender inequality, stigma against people with HIV, and shortage of human resources remain barriers to progress.

My next stop in Tanzania was Zanzibar, the spice island. I arrived in the evening by plane, and my driver took me to a gigantic beachside barbecue of seafood; it was as though the whole of Stone Town inhabitants had turned up to have their evening meal. Numerous stray cats scavenged for food under the tables. Over the following days I explored Stone Town, marveling at the arabesque architecture with beautiful arches and wooden balconies, some of which loomed over the streets. I visited the Sultanate Palace, the House of Wonders, and a dusty museum that was touted to have the skeletal remains of the extinct dodo; for that I had to scout around looking for the gatekeeper to open the door for me. Evidently, very few tourists came to visit the museum. While inside I tried to sign to him what I was looking for. He showed me the wonderful collection of shells, but I kept on flapping my arms imitating a bird. Eventually I spotted it locked unpretentiously in a glass case. I felt like Alice in Wonderland.

I took a spice tour through a few villages hunting for various spices: nutmeg, vanilla, cloves, cinnamon, and lemon grass, and to Nungwi, a fishermen's village located at the northernmost tip of the island. The sea was a brilliant blue under an azure sky; being here felt like the summer was endless. Here on the beaches, there were still men making dhows as in the old days.

I went back to Dar via ferry, and from there I took a three-hour flight to Kigoma in the western part of Tanzania. Upon my arrival, there was no one to receive me. I waited until dusk, and finally Abashi came with a driver in a pick-up truck. He took me to a seedy rest house at the edge of Lake Tanganyika, surrounded by dense vegetation. The room was dark and lit only by a dim naked light bulb dangling from the ceiling; mosquitoes swarmed over us, and we escaped their onslaught only when we ducked inside the room. Abashi was leaving me for the evening, but before he could hop on the pick-up truck, I ran out to argue with him that I was supposed to stay in the Kigoma Hill Top Hotel, which I could see from where he dropped me. There followed phone conversations in Swahili, as he made a call to Dar to check on the accuracy of my information. In the end we lugged my suitcase uphill towards the Hill Top, a clean, upscale hotel with lodges scattered on a manicured ground and no mosquitoes. The vast expanse of Lake Tanganyika lay in front of me as the sun's rays colored it in various orange hues.

In the morning I explored the lake by the hotel and took a brief swim. The manager of the hotel, an Indian man, was at the beach with his two children and took me for a spin in his speedboat. Abashi came to transport me in a wooden boat equipped with a motor for our thirty-five-minute ride over the lake to Gombe Stream National Park. The boatman and his helper were on board with a frightened chicken tied by its legs, and Abashi said this was to be my dinner. Lake Tanganyika was enormous with deep blue water. A few boats ferried passengers across the lake, about thirty passengers in each boat, many sitting with their legs dangling over the sides of the vessels. We stopped at a fishing village with mud-bricked houses and thatched roofs, and immediately women and children surrounded me and looked at me with inquisitive eyes. Tiny fish were drying on mats in the hot sun, and many wooden fishing boats were scattered on the beach while men were busy repairing their nets.

A *"habari"* sign, welcome in Swahili, was displayed on the landing dock of Gombe Stream National Park. I was told that my abode was Jane Goodall's first lodging, not posh by any means but spacious: it had a kitchen, a sitting room overlooking the lake, a bedroom, and another room off the kitchen for dining. The outhouse was several yards away. Purportedly there was a shower next to it, but there was no water. When it came time to clean myself, I was shown the lake, and so I took a swim, risking contracting bilharzia. Further down the beach was Jane Goodall's old laboratory with creepers climbing all over it, trying to pry their way inside. We ate dinner by candlelight, but since I did not want to eat the chicken, Abashi, the boatman, his helper, and my chimpanzee guide ate heartily.

My guide took me to trek the chimpanzees the next day after showing me their family tree and names on a chart. In the forest among the branches, we saw several groups, mainly mothers and infants. My guide could tell them apart, but to me they looked so similar, it was impossible to know who was who.

On our way back to Kigoma, we visited Ujiji, a slave trade town settled by the Arabs, and the oldest town in western Tanzania. This was also where Burton and Stanley reached Lake Tanganyika in 1858 and where Stanley met Livingstone. In 1869 the *New York Herald* sent Henry Morton Stanley to find the missing missionary and explorer David Livingstone. He found him in Ujiji on the shore of Lake Tanganyika in 1871, apparently greeting him with the now famous question, "Dr. Livingstone, I presume?"[15] A memorial was built where they met; the old mango tree was no longer there, and a new mango tree had been planted in its place. At the site there was a small museum holding the most rudimentary artifacts of daily life and newspaper cuttings about the Livingstone expeditions; there were none of Livingstone's original artifacts, however. One had the distinct feeling that the termites were slowly but surely making a meal out of those fragile papers in this moldy, musty building. The museum gatekeeper looked just as decrepit as the place and asked to be compensated as the museum guide.

At the Dar International Airport, Moses came to deliver my duffel bag that held my climbing gear. I had left it at the Clinton office with Dr. Ipuge when I first arrived at Dar. It was good to see a familiar face. My first trip to Africa was a fantastic experience; I went up to the highest point of Africa and experienced its natural wonders of scenery and wildlife. Most importantly, I knew through my very first voluntary effort in Africa that I would be returning.

I had been away for three months. When I reached home, spring had sprung. I truly appreciated the newness of life that seemed to be impatient about manifesting itself. The new tender buds, the young leaves, the vulnerable but brave flowers that pushed through the earth, all harbingers of spring, lifted my spirits. The scene at home was in great contrast to the endless plains of Serengeti dotted with acacia trees, the timeless, peaceful, brown, and green depression of the Ngorongoro Crater, and the silent majestic presence of Kilimanjaro. I was glad to be home, but Africa had also stolen a piece of my heart.

2

Uganda

2006, Teaching at the Infectious Disease Institute, Makerere University in Kampala, Uganda

"Education, awareness and prevention are the key, but stigmatization and exclusion from family is what makes people suffer most."
—*Ralph Fiennes*[1]

A wiry Ugandan man, his wet body glistening in the bright sun while his muscular arms wrapped tightly around a yellow jerry can, looked pensive but resigned as he jumped into the raging waters of the Nile, giving himself up to its power. Moments ago a tourist had handed him a few shillings and challenged him to ride the Nile rapids. The rapids roared as he quickly disappeared into the foaming water; now and then a black and yellow object bobbed up and down helplessly, narrowly missing boulders, and soon that too vanished.

To celebrate the end of our training course, the whole class had traveled to Jinja to the source of the Nile to marvel at its power. We watched this daring Ugandan man earning his living riding the raging rapids on a puny jerry can for a bit of money from tourists. I felt complicit watching him. Every year there were fatalities.

Despite that I went white water rafting in the Nile one weekend; along with other rafters we rode out ten rapids with four of them at grade five. Our guide warned that every single one of us would be thrown overboard by one of the rapids. Indeed, our dinghy flipped over twice. Water swirled all around me and rushed into my nostrils and for what seemed like an eternity; I could not tell whether I was up or down until finally I bobbed up to the surface.

In the summer of 2006, shortly after returning from Tanzania, I applied and was accepted as one of the trainers to represent the Infectious Disease Society of America to teach in the HIV/AIDS program at the Infectious Disease Institute (IDI) of Makerere University in Kampala, Uganda.[2] The goal of the training program, which consisted of lectures, skill building, and clinical mentoring, was to improve the ability of healthcare workers in Africa to provide high-quality HIV/AIDS care and preventive services in Uganda and other African countries. After completion of their training, the trainees had access to the AIDS Training Information Center with a call-in/e-mail service where they would receive specialist guidance on treatment-related issues and became trainers for other trainees when they returned to their home country. By 2006, since its inception, the IDI of Makerere University in Kampala had trained over 1000 healthcare workers from over twenty countries in Africa.[3]

In November 2006, I took my second trip to Africa, this time to Uganda. I arrived a week early to trek the endangered mountain gorillas at the Bwindi Impenetrable National Park. The road from Kampala to the southwestern part of Uganda was littered with potholes, and vehicles from both sides hoarded the better part of the road, endangering oncoming vehicles that had to swerve to avoid a collision. A few big trucks lay helplessly on their sides on the dirt shoulders, likely there for a while before they could be righted. We passed through fields of papyrus and busy towns with hawkers swarming our vehicle whenever we made a brief stop, selling roasted corn on the cobs, barbecued rodents, and pigeons on sticks, cold bottled water, soft drinks, and pineapples. At the equator, for a shilling, one could flush an outdoor toilet to see which way the water swirled. Ankole cattle, with their show-stopping, fantastic, symmetrically shaped horns, stood patiently in the fields while ugly, grey and white marabou storks hovered over garbage for a morsel of food. The noisy, yellow weaverbirds made their nests on the branches of trees that no longer looked like trees; their leaves were mostly gone and replaced with dangling nests. Green mountains with carefully terraced slopes and elegant crown crested cranes, the national bird of Uganda, graced the distant fields. Children in dirty, oversized T-shirts waved frantically at passing vehicles trying to sell guava. I stayed in a lodge not too far from where a few years ago a number of tourists were killed by the rebels.[4] There was no light in my room, and the outhouse was in the woods.

In the morning we were organized into groups for the trekking. In the beginning, the path was gradual but very quickly gave way to steep slopes with dense growths and hanging creepers. It had rained recently, so the path was muddy and slippery; guards with guns escorted us in case the gorillas became aggressive. Then the leader put his index finger to his lips, pointed quietly ahead of him, and there among the bushes sat a regal silverback. Further up was a cluster of juveniles digging termites from a rotten fallen tree trunk and eating them. One juvenile was on a branch eating some fruits while a mother with an infant clinging to her belly climbed up a tree. An audible hush descended on us at this special moment of witnessing this family of gorillas.

Despite the relative peace here, our group contained three United Nations peacekeepers from Australia and Germany who had taken a break from their duties in Khartoum in Sudan, a grim reminder that somewhere in Africa, on-going conflicts were still a reality of life. In the village many people, including children, were carving wooden gorillas for sale; tourism played a big part in their livelihood.

The students for the November course were mostly from Uganda, with one each from Ethiopia, Botswana, and Nigeria. They were doctors, nurses, laboratory personnel, and a dentist; therefore, their experiences on HIV/AIDS were quite varied. Some were already actively caring for HIV/AIDS patients and quite familiar with the use of ARVs. The core course covered topics on the basic biology of HIV, epidemiology, diagnosis of HIV in adults and children, when and how to start ARV, adherence, drug toxicities and interactions, switching therapy, opportunistic infections, TB, malaria, prevention of mother to child transmission, counseling, post-exposure prophylaxis, and data management. The students had the opportunity to prepare and lead journal discussions on studies pertinent to Africa and were taught how to critically read and appraise an article. They proved to be quick learners, and quite a few of them presented their discussions with the use of Power Point slides, quite an accomplishment in a span of a few weeks as for some of them it was their first experience with the use of a computer. They presented cases from their own clinics highlighting problems relating to adherence, drug reactions, limited resources particularly in the area of laboratory testing, and limitations of second-line regimen for HIV treatment. Not all trainees enjoyed access to the enumeration of the immune cells or CD4 counts in

Students and faculty of the HIV/AIDS program at the Infectious Disease Institute (IDI) of Makerere University in Kampala, Uganda, supported by the Infectious Diseases Society of America.

their own laboratories; therefore quite a few had to resort to the use of lymphocyte counts using the WHO guidelines to stage the HIV infection. No one had access to viral load with the exception of one student from Botswana who seemed to have access to state-of-the-art laboratory testing including viral load (a test looking at the number of viruses present in the patient's blood, and genotyping, a test to look at the resistance of the virus to a particular HIV drug). The ARVs available to the trainees were also quite varied. The basic triomune—three HIV drugs in one pill: lamivudine, stavudine, and nevirapine—was the first line regimen available to all trainees. Then the second line regimen was different depending upon what was made available to each clinic. Lipodystrophy had begun to rear its ugly head with widespread and long-term use of stavudine in Africa. As in Tanzania, patients began to notice a change in their appearance, and that soon became the new stigma for AIDS in resource-limited countries, making some patients reluctant to take their medications.

IDI was next to Mulago Hospital in Kampala.[5] While the institute had a state of the art research laboratory run by Johns Hopkins University, the hospital, the national referral hospital of Uganda, was old, dirty, dark, and over-crowded. The wards were filled with iron beds with chipped paints and ripped vinyl mattresses mostly without sheets unless patients' relatives brought them. Under and in between the beds and in the hallways were more patients sprawling on mattresses placed on the floors, looking sick and listless, with their relatives hovering over them. Unlike in the U.S. where the attending physicians (physicians responsible for a group of interns and residents) make rounds daily, here they might appear every three days or not at all. The clinical officers under training were often forced to make decisions on their own. The attending who took us around barked at them for not following his orders from a few days ago to give intravenous fluids to a patient who was then dehydrated; he was now groaning audibly and seemingly confused because he was even more severely dehydrated. In America, the relatives would be up in arms but here his relative sat by his side quietly, not questioning his care. With a ward overflowing with so many patients, how could all of them be cared for?

Author with students in front of the Infectious Disease Institute in Kampala, Uganda.

Mulago is one of the best national referral hospitals in Uganda, but even the best does not seem to measure up to the western standard. Patients struggled to get better under circumstances that were absolutely unconducive to healing. Outside on the lawn, in contrast to the drab wards, colorful laundry was laid out by the patients' relatives, to dry under the sun.

Ashley, my housemate at Kira guesthouse, and I spent a weekend in Ngamba Island, a sanctuary for chimpanzees by Lake Victoria. Some juvenile chimps hopped on our backs as though we were their mothers; they were rather heavy and clingy. We hiked along the lake, careful not to touch the water as it was heavily infested with bilharzia, a parasitic worm that could cause schistosomiasis or snail fever.

In addition to the core course, the trainees received

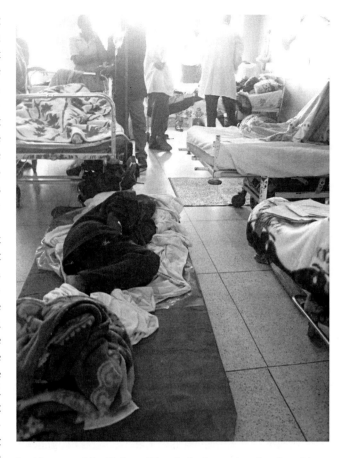

Inside a ward in Mulago Hospital, the national referral hospital of Uganda. Overflow patients slept on mattresses on the floor.

about eighteen hours of hands-on experience in a variety of clinical models of HIV care in Kampala. They visited the Adult and Pediatric Infectious Disease Clinics at the IDI; medical wards at Mulago Hospital; Mildmay International,[6] a faith-based charity providing HIV/ AIDS care, education and training; Reach Out Mbuya, community-based HIV care facilities;[7] the AIDS Support Organization (TASO)[8] and Uganda Cares.[9] At the Pediatric Infectious Disease Clinic, the HIV pediatric patients and their families were given a ration of protein-rich food while the children were being treated. The food incentive was instrumental in enticing the parents to bring their children back to the clinic. Reach Out Mbuya was a faith-based program offering holistic HIV care encompassing body, mind, family, and community. It provided HIV testing and counseling, HIV and TB treatment, home visits, alcohol treatment, food aid, a micro-credit program, school fees, and family and community support. The clinic at St. Balikuddembe Market, under the sponsorship of Uganda Cares in Kampala, used an innovative approach to reach HIV-positive vendors, bringing care right where the patients were. The clinic was on the second floor over the bustling market, convenient for the merchants who could avoid traveling long distances and missing a full day of work. It was so successful that it had outgrown its capacity to care for the large number of patients with over 1,300 clients as of August 2006.[10]

In 2005, the HIV/AIDS epidemic in sub-Saharan Africa left about twelve million children orphaned.[11] In the clinics in Uganda, parents or relatives elected not to reveal to their children their HIV status and why they were taking medications. Healthcare workers had to be careful not to mention HIV/AIDS in their presence. The stigma of HIV infection continued to be a barrier for disclosure, and the timing of disclosure remained a delicate issue.

One trainee presented a poignant story of a ten-year-old boy whose mother, before she died, urged him to take all his medicines daily because if he did not, he would die. He was not told he had HIV. After his mother's death, he moved to another village to live with his grandmother. Mindful of his mother's caution, once he ran out medications, he sold his rooster to get a bicycle to ride to a hospital clinic. While there he was tested for HIV, and the boy was informed of his HIV status. This was the first time that he knew he was HIV infected. One could debate whether he should have been told of his status without the presence of an adult or whether he could truly give informed consent for testing. In the clinics that we visited, it was not unusual for children, after they have been on treatment, to walk unaccompanied many miles to the clinics for follow-ups. This presented quite a challenge for the healthcare workers regarding giving instructions to a young patient with no adult present.

As of 2018 in Uganda, 81 percent of the people living with HIV knew their status, 89 percent of people with HIV infection received antiretroviral treatment, of which 78 percent achieved viral suppression.[12] The barriers in achieving the UNAIDS' 90–90–90 targets to end the HIV/AIDS epidemic by 2030 included implementing "the Test and Start approach" of initiating early treatment of HIV, developing strong policies against stigma and discrimination, increasing domestic healthcare financing, healthcare staff delivering HIV/AIDS services, and increasing access to viral load testing by decentralizing viral load testing services.[13]

The third annual marathon and 10K races happened one weekend in Kampala. Ashley, Dylan and I decided, on the spur of the moment, to run the 10K, joining four thousand runners on the streets of Kampala. We each brought along a bottle of water, not knowing for sure whether there would be water stations. Indeed, after half an hour of running in the heat in a city of seven hills, many Africans were yelling for water, but we did not see a water station until almost forty-five minutes into our run. All of us finished the race; I completed my first 10K in one hour and ten minutes.

At the end of November, the swarming of the grasshoppers began. All over town, there was a continuous droning as grasshoppers flew hither and yon, darkening the sky and covering the walls and vegetation. On the university campus, marabou storks were busy picking them out of the air and from the bushes. Children captured them and placed them in plastic bags to be eaten later. The locals set up walls of slippery tarp to trap them as they flew into the tarp, slipped, and fell into the nets below. Outdoor markets sold bushels of cooked and uncooked grasshoppers. In Kira House we had fried grasshoppers one evening before dinner as an appetizer; they tasted like anchovies.

After I finished teaching, I joined three Italians, Luca, Marco, and Giovanni, and traveled to Kasese, west of Uganda. We were to begin a nine-day climb up the Rwenzori Mountains, or Mountains of the Moon, as Ptolemy named them in the second century A.D. Margherita, at 5,109 meters, is the highest peak in the Rwenzori, first summited by Prince Luigi Amedeo, Duke of the Abruzzi, and his party in 1906.[14] 2006 was the one hundredth anniversary of the summit; this was the main reason these Italians were climbing the mountains. Luca and Marco were in their thirties, and Gionny, a retired cardiologist, was seventy-three. Luca and Gionny had previous mountaineering experience. Luca was the only one who spoke some English. Rwenzori means "the rain may come," and in fact this is an apt name. It rained or snowed, depending on the elevation, every day when we were there; the terrain in the lower elevations was so muddy that we had to wear Wellingtons almost every day except on the day of the summit. That day we climbed over steep rocks and then traversed over glaciers in harness, hiking boots, and crampons. It was so wet that below the snowline, the trees, rocks, and mountain surfaces were covered with weeping moss dripping with droplets of water. In the muddy areas, we hopped from tussock to tussock, trying to avoid landing in the thick mud that would rapidly suck our boots up to the knees. Because of the rain, we crossed raging rivers several times, and once we had to be roped together to avoid being washed away.

On the morning of the third day, the cook gave us the bad news that we were running out of food. Justus, the chief guide, sent some porters down to get more food. We could not understand why this happened. Sunday the coordinator, who brought me to Rwenzori, had done all of the purchasing of food, and I imagined he knew how much food was required. On the other hand, when we arrived at the foothills, there were more porters than he had anticipated. From that day on, we were limited to two cubes of chocolate and biscuits for lunch. Peter, the second guide, had nothing except his thermos of tea so I shared my meager food with him. The Italians came prepared with their cheeses, prosciutto, and salami... They were set.

Every night I got up to look at the mountains standing in profound silence, keeping their secrets to themselves; and one night the moon came out of the clouds. Then I thought the name "The Mountains of the Moon" was a beautiful description for this range of mountains, majestic and forbidding. Surrounded on all sides by this everlasting mountain range with their several peaks and the moon shining down on the bog, one felt awfully small and insignificant, but the beauty and peace were indescribable.

We slept in our sleeping bags in huts. At base camp before the summit, our hut was perched precariously on the side of a steep rocky cliff. Its zinc sidings sang with the howling wind, and it was bitterly cold. The outhouse was perched at another small hill. To get there one had to climb down some rickety wooden ladder to a small ravine, and then climb up another ladder to make it into the wind-swept outhouse whose door was being whipped back and forth as the last person who was there forgot to latch it. It was hazardous to attempt the route to the outhouse during the day; imagine doing that in the dark. During the night, I bared my bottom to the cold and ease myself outside the cabin.

The fifth day was our day of summit, and at six in the morning, the day dawned clear and cold. Justus told us to hurry because the unpredictable weather could change quickly. After downing a cup of tea and two pieces of bread with jam, it took us a tedious two and a half hours of hard climbing over very rocky and jagged terrain before we finally caught a glimpse of Margherita. Reaching the snowline, we hurriedly attached our crampons onto our boots, took out our ice axes, and roped ourselves together with our harnesses. I quickly ate the two cubes of chocolate before commencing my climb up the glaciers, struggling to breathe in the thin air. Justus pointed to a crevasse several feet away from us. The wind was whipping the snow, and the blinding white drift blended steeply into the whiteness of the sky, and they became one. For a while one could not tell which way was up or down. We negotiated the climb down a steep incline and then along a narrow ledge hugging the side of a cliff; the whiteout obliterated the bottom of the abyss, falling eternally into the vast whiteness. There was such an unbroken expanse of whiteness that the marker for the sum-

On our way to the summit of Mt. Margherita of the Rwenzori Mountain range in Uganda.

mit was almost buried in the snow. Peter grinned at me and said I had reached the summit. I thought he was pulling my leg. It took us a grueling six and half hours. We spent about twenty minutes there, and the Italians took a video of themselves for their mountaineering club.

Unlike Kilimanjaro, the descent from Margherita was slow and arduous. The wind was blowing the snow all around us, blinding us. The Italians and Justus had gone ahead. I was quite tired and had long ago finished my two liters of water. My thirst drove me to suck on icicles and eat some snow. When we finally reached the rocky parts of the climb, the moisture on the rocks had become frozen and icy. Peter and I were tied to each other via our harness for safety. Once he slipped and fell a few feet ahead of me over a slippery rock, and I hit the ground in a hurry; fortunately, he stopped slipping. Daylight disappeared and I used my headlamp, but Peter thought he could see with the moonlight. Eventually he used his flashlight as well.

We reached camp at nine that night after a fifteen-hour hike on two pieces of bread, two cubes of chocolate, and no bathroom break. I had a mouthful of warm tea, but my stomach rebelled and I promptly rejected it. I could not see myself eating the same mush that was given us nightly and went to sleep without dinner. That night the temperature dropped, and we could hear the wind whipping the metal walls; I was freezing in my sleeping bag. I got up and put on all the clothes I had to keep warm.

After the summit, we had three more days of hiking. During one of the days, we had to climb up six hundred feet to Freshfield Pass before descending to our next camp. It snowed and we were not dressed for it. The whole mountain range was a winter wonderland; we were wet and cold, and my left hand became swollen; I had not brought my gloves that day. Below the snowline, the rain was persistent every day; we had to contend with raging rivers, once crossing the same river four times. Water got into my Wellingtons. My rented boots were big for me, and my toes were numb. We tracked through miles and miles of mud until we were quite tired of it. Because of the rainy season, our hikes were seven and eight hours long each day except for the summit, which was a crushing fifteen hours. The cook rationed our lunch to biscuits and chocolate, and eventually we were down to half a bar of chocolate for lunch one day. We literally burned our body fat for fuel. The food supply finally arrived on our last night during our descent, and we had the best dinner. It had taken the porters five days to get us more food, a little bit too late for our climb. They gathered at the bottom of a slope to cheer us as we descended a steep rocky slope, utterly exhausted. At the bottom of the mountains, weighing ourselves on the scale used by the porters, we all had lost a few kilograms.

During my last night in Kira House, I was low on Ugandan shillings. My best bet for dinner was to go across the street into the slum, scouring the local outdoor barbecue as I did not have the cash to go to a restaurant. While one expat told me he ate there regularly without getting sick, I certainly did not want to get ill as I was leaving for home on the plane late that night. The aroma of fried chicken and the enticing sales pitch convinced me that all that grilling should kill off the lurking and harmful germs. I bought and ate a delicious piece of chicken with some money left over for tips for the housekeeper and the driver.

In the evening we drove from Kampala to the airport in Entebbe. Like Dar es Salaam in Tanzania, the street lights were not on, and hordes of people walked the street with vendors occupying yardage of the tarmac without much regard to oncoming traffic. It was as though there was an endless, outdoor party in the haze of the lights powered by generators. The van hit one of the numerous potholes in the road and woke me up from my reverie. Unbeknownst to me, I would be making the same trip on this road to and from Kampala and Entebbe a few more times in the coming years.

3

Kenya

Following the 2007 Presidential Election

"A single, ordinary person still can make a difference—and single, ordinary people are doing precisely that every day."
—*Chris Bohjalian*[1]

In 2007 and 2008, though I was looking very hard for a placement through ICEHA, nothing panned out. I decided to strike out to Kenya on my own to volunteer in the Maseno Mission Hospital, a small hospital under the auspices of the Anglican Church.[2] From the end of 2007 and through periods of 2008, Kenya had emerged from a crisis after the alleged rigged election of President Mwai Kibaki on December 27, 2007.[3] Widespread, violent ethnic riots erupted, and many were killed. Expats including those in Maseno and Peace Corps volunteers were hurriedly dispatched home. On February 28, 2008, Kibaki and Raila Amolo Odinga signed a power-sharing agreement; the National Accord and Reconciliation Act established the office of the prime minister, and a coalition of governments was created.[4] Another two months passed before the power-sharing cabinet was formed.

It was in front of this backdrop that I visited Kenya at the end of October 2008. Nairobi looked peaceful enough; business seemed to be going on as usual, but I did not go into the Kibera slum, the largest slum in Nairobi, only passing by it. However, I was impressed by the huge mounds of rubbish collected there, choking a stream. As we approached the house run by the Catholic mission where I would stay for a few days, I saw a prominent sign in front of a government building that proudly announced, "This is a Corruption Free Zone!"

Before going to Maseno Hospital, I did a four and half-day hike up to Lenana Point of Mt. Kenya, at 4,985 meters, the second highest mountain in Africa. Two British men joined me for the first three days of our hike. It was a three-hour gentle hike on our first day to Old Moses Hut at 3,300 meters. We had a guide, Robin, a cook, and a porter, a far smaller entourage than my hike up Margherita. It was a pleasant surprise to see a flush toilet in the hut with bunk beds. When darkness fell I came out into the cold, crisp night to peer at the Milky Way; the millions of stars striding across the vast sky never ceased to amaze me with how beautiful and spectacular nature could be.

On day two, our goal was Shipton's Hut at 4,200 meters, a seven-hour hike through heather with brave red-hot pokers scattered here and there; water from spongy tussock grass seeped into our boots. The jagged shards of Mt. Kenya shimmered in the distance. Chilly, damp mist obscured our way, a blessing in disguise, as we could not see how steep our path was going to be. Soon cabbage-like senecio and ostrich-plume lobelia took over. After we scaled a particularly steep ridge, the three jagged peaks flecked with snow loomed.

The highest peak was Batian, and next came Nelion, but we were climbing to Lenana Point, the least technical climb of Mt. Kenya. The local Kikuyu believe that Mt. Kenya is the home of the god Ngai, and they will not climb to the summit for fear of him. Shipton's Hut faced directly toward the fearsome peaks of Batian and Nelion. By the time we reached the hut, the temperature had dropped quite precipitously.

For most climbers, the summiting would start at two-thirty in the morning of the third day; it meant that they would go to bed early and then start hiking early in the morning. I chose to spend an extra day hiking around to acclimatize. Robin took John up the summit that night; his partner stayed behind because of a cold. The next morning Peter and I climbed close to 4,500 meters, battling the cold and the fierce wind. The valley stretched far below us and right behind rose the awesome peaks of Batian and Nelion. Skirting the base of Batian, we came upon a reflective pool surrounded by lobelias and senecios with hydraxes scampering in and around the rocks. The two hikers who left in the morning to summit Batian came back, having failed to do so because the rock surfaces were too slippery.

Around three in the morning of October 28, Robin and I began to summit against a strong cold wind, climbing up the steep, slippery scree; it was a long, seemingly endless slog which eventually changed from gravel to snow and ice. The sun rose, myriads of orange, yellow, and red rays piercing through the clouds and slowly emerging above them. From the summit, Lewis Glacier appeared on the north side of the mountain. A plaque commemorating the death of a hiker read,

> *Go safely friend*
> *For here is high*
> *Go daringly*
> *where eagles fly*
> *Go eternally*
> *with Jesus nigh*

The weather and icy path made conditions unsafe for us to attempt the descent on the other side of Lenana, so we hiked down the same way on the slippery, graveled scree that caused me to slip and land on my behind ungracefully. We made it down to base camp in time for breakfast and then hiked 5 kilometers and 1000 meters down to Old Moses' Camp. With this hike I had now climbed all three of the highest mountains of Africa: Kilimanjaro, Mt. Kenya, and Mt. Margherita of the Rwenzori Mountains.

That afternoon we drove back to Nairobi. This time I stayed in a hotel in the center of town. The room was simple and clean. In the evening, I went to Carnivore for dinner, hoping to have a taste of impala, but there was none. I did have a bite of crocodile, which was sinewy as opposed to the tender ostrich.

The following day I joined two men, Robert from Germany and John from Ireland, for a two-day safari in the Maasai Mara. Robert had been traveling around the world for almost a year, starting his journey in China, moving through the Middle East, and now through Africa. John lived in Australia, having transplanted himself from Ireland. The road to the Maasai Mara was extremely bad, full of potholes. Workers were working on the expansion of the existing road; perhaps it would be better in the future.

At the Maasai Mara, the lodge was eerily quiet; we were the only people there with at least four to five people waiting on us. We felt a little guilty at getting so much attention. Tourism had suffered since the riots after the election. The next day very early on in our game drive, we saw a pride of lions feasting on a freshly killed wildebeest while the lionesses and their cubs waited patiently on the sideline for their turn. The guide told us that the lions did not hunt unless it became necessary; the lionesses did the hunting. The lions would eat first, and the lionesses and their cubs waited until the lions were satiated. Finally, the lions had their fill, and one of them walked slowly, with his head held high and his mane waving gently in the breeze, to a water hole for a drink. A wake of vultures hovered above, waiting for their turn at the carcass. During our game drive, we saw many buffaloes, wildebeest, elephants, Thomson's gazelles, zebras, impalas, and giraffes.

It was the tail end of the great wildebeest migration. A stench emanated from the numerous bloated carcasses of wildebeests; many perished trampling over each other scrambling up the steep slopes of the riverbank. On the opposite shore, crocodiles were sunbathing on the beaches while hippopotami were bobbing up and down in the water oblivious of them. The pride of lions we saw in the morning was sitting peacefully on the plain, satiated at last; it was the patient vultures' turn to pick away on the remains of the carcass.

I chose to camp out, and the campsite was a distance away from the lodge. Lolkerra, the caretaker of the campsite, draped in his bright red Maasai *shaku,* leaned on his staff as he informed me that he would prepare hot water for my shower. He started a fire to heat a big cauldron of water connected to a tank, and by pulling on a rope, he caused trickles of hot water mixed with the cold to come through the showerhead. While waiting for the water to get hot, we sat down in the shade, and he told me with a certain degree of pride that he was taking a second wife soon. He had two children with his first wife; his daughter was studying law in Nairobi, and his son was still in school in the bush. When asked if his wife was agreeable to the second marriage, he simply said that his wives would be friends. His second wife was the same age as his daughter, and he said she would be a great companion for his first wife. He owned close to one hundred goats; he modestly said they were not that many by Maasai standards, and for his future wife he paid a dowry of twenty goats. The feasting and celebration would last a week. From the glint in his eyes, I could see that he was looking forward to it.

After my evening meal in the lodge, one of the hotel helpers led me to the camp. It was pitch black, and he carried no light but nimbly picked his way on the path while I followed with my headlamp. In the middle of the night I heard snoring; someone, perhaps a guard, came and slept in one of the tents a few yards away.

I left Robert and John and went my separate way to Lake Nakuru. My driver took me first to a seedy rest house, which thankfully turned out to be full. Then he drove through the town to another rest house. My itinerary clearly stated that I would be staying in a lodge in the park, not in a rest house in town. A call to Nairobi confirmed what I told the driver. By then we had only fifteen minutes to get to the park before it closed. I was glad that I stood my ground. I wondered how many tourists were unlucky enough to let the tour agency get away with this practice of switching to a lesser accommodation. The lodge in the park was clean and luxurious, and the food was fantastic. A few warthogs and a buffalo roamed just outside my window. Unlike Maasai Mara, this place was teeming with tourists. My insistence on staying in the park also benefited my driver; he had never seen so many varieties of delicious food, and I bet his abode was not too shabby either.

In the morning, our cruiser had a flat, but the driver fixed it in no time. Lake Nakuru is famous for its numerous bird species, notably the pink flamingos that formed a pink border along the shore of the lake. Pelicans mingled among the thousands of flamingos; I was so enthralled I did not notice a herd of buffalo slowly making its way towards me. My driver asked me to get into the cruiser at a steady pace but not to run in a panic. He had been watching my back.

Foreigners packed Kenyan Air to Kisumu. I only realized that they were from CNN when I saw the equipment stamped with the name. Ralph, a fourth-year medical student, came on the same plane to volunteer at Maseno Hospital. Dianne, Sue, and Chilemba, the driver, met us. Dianne, a nurse, came to volunteer for a year with the support of her local church. Sue, a pre-med student, wanted to volunteer before going to medical school. We stopped in Kisumu, the city in Nyanza where riots were rampant right after the election in 2007, to change some money. Right at the roundabout, CNN had already set up their audio-visual equipment, ready for their reporting of the upcoming U.S. presidential election. A giant poster of Obama with the caption "Change we can believe in" looked down at the square. Obama's paternal grandmother had lived in Saiya, not too far from Maseno.

The tarmac road to Maseno was surprisingly well paved with stretches of farmland on both sides. After passing the equator marked by a sign courtesy of the Rotary Club, the cruiser turned into a dirt road where many *boda bodas* and *piki pikis*, local bicycle and motorcycle taxis, traveled. After about fifteen minutes, we made a sharp turn onto another dirt road flanked by stores and beer pots, or the local bars, and arrived in front of the wrought iron gate of the hospital. Chilemba honked, and the gatekeeper ran quickly to roll it open.

A smooth red-earth road ran through the shady hospital compound; the cruiser went further up the road and ran over a lawn before stopping in front of a beige stucco house. Emmah, the somewhat rotund housekeeper, came running out to welcome us. An open veranda with a couple of homemade rattan rocking chairs graced the front of the house. Then we walked into the sitting room with two sofas; this room also served as the dining room, and in one corner was a television. There were five bedrooms; the biggest one had a double bed, which was Dianne's room. The other rooms all had from one to four bunk beds. I shared a room with Sue. There were two toilets and a shower. The kitchen was at the back, with a tiny room with a sink right across from it. We had no shortage of unwanted visitors; besides scurrying cockroaches, a frog croaked all night long under my bed, and slugs peeked at me from the toilets and sink at unpredictable and disconcerting times. The lawn in front and on one side of the house was kept short by the neighbors' cows. Emmah nurtured maize and groundnuts on the other side.

Maseno Hospital started as a small Anglican mission hospital in 1906 under a fig tree.[5] Maseno was a westernized word from the Luhya word for a fig tree, *omasena*. From the 1930s to the 1980s, Maseno Hospital gained a reputation as a model hospital for the western province, but it met with difficult times in the 1990s. At that time, the Swedish Rotary began funding the hospital, and the physicians provided inpatient care, surgery, and mobile outreach to the surrounding communities. This funding ended in 1999. In December 2001, Nan and Gerry Hardison came here from the United States under the auspices of the Episcopal Church of USA Volunteers for Mission for Service in the Anglican Church of Kenya Diocese of Maseno North; they had been here for seven years. Gerry ran the hospital; his wife ran the Saint Philip's Theological College, as well as helping with the women in the communities in the Orphan Feeding and the micro-lending programs.

Maseno Hospital had four inpatient wards: men, women, pediatrics, and maternity with about sixteen beds each. It also had an outpatient department, a maternal/child health clinic, a Comprehensive Care Clinic (CCC) for HIV/AIDS, a medical laboratory, a pharmacy, an x-ray department, and an operating theater. It provided training for healthcare workers and was in the process of revitalizing the Maseno Mission Hospital School of Nursing with the help of Dianne.

The women's ward was often filled to capacity, spilling over to the veranda; the men's

Maseno Hospital in Maseno, Kenya, built in 1906 by the Anglicans.

was usually about half full, while the pediatric ward was variably occupied, ranging from no patients to about three to five patients. Maseno Hospital did not have any surgeons on site, When there was a need for a C-section or other elective surgeries, surgeons from outside Maseno came to perform them.

On the hospital grounds was the CCC for HIV/AIDS, which was partially funded by PEPFAR. It provided testing, counseling, treatment, follow-ups for over 1,200 patients, and clinical and community outreach.[6] At Maseno Hospital, the patients paid a deposit of 2,000 KSh (Kenyan shillings, about 25 U.S. dollars) for a medical admission and 3,000 KSh for a surgical admission. The hospital charged 500 KSh per day for hospitalization. Once they recovered, patients' payments had to be settled before they could be discharged. The hospital continued to charge their daily stay at half the cost while their relatives scrambled to look for the money to pay their hospital bill.

We made rounds in the hospital twice a day, seven days a week, starting with the pediatric ward. Malaria was the most common infection; other infectious diseases were TB, HIV/AIDS, dysentery, and tungiasis. Tungiasis is caused by a sand flea also known as jigger, or chigoe, which lives in the soil or sand.[7] Most children are victims of this infection which affects their feet, fingers, mouths, elbows, and backs as they walk barefoot, play in the soil, and sleep on the bare dirt floors. Over the years, the irritation results in continuous infections with swollen, thickened, and deformed legs and hands filled with oozing sores.

Kenya is famous for its long-distance runners, but every morning during my six-mile run on the potholed tarmac roads through the University of Maseno and on the unpaved muddy clay roads, I did not encounter a single runner. However, chants of "Obama" often greeted me, especially in front of the campus. I arrived a few days before the US presidential election. Our black and white television set chose an inopportune time to break down, on the day of the election, disappointing us greatly. Without internet access, we had a news blackout. Instead, we spent a quiet evening reading with our headlamps as the single naked ceiling light bulb in the sitting room did not emit enough light for us to read.

At rounds the next day, we heard rumors about the results of the election, and it was not until a day or two later we saw the results splashed on the front pages of the local newspapers. The vendor promptly doubled the price of the newspapers for the *azungus*. After the election, President Kibaki declared a National Obama Day, a holiday for most people except the villagers who needed to work every day for their living. Throughout Kenya, many newborns bore the names of Michelle or Barrack Obama.

Ralph joined me in some of my runs. We lived just south of the equator so for every run, we crossed into the northern hemisphere and then re-crossed the equator back to the southern hemisphere. One evening we decided to cut across the yards of some houses in a village to the Agriculture School of Maseno. Ralph was leading, running on a narrow dirt path. In the gathering gloom, a mother hen with two chicks crossed our way, Ralph ran by them without mishap while my left foot landed squarely on one of the chicks. I thought for sure I had crushed it, but miraculously as I lifted my foot, it got up and shook its head in a daze and wobbled away, seemingly unharmed while the mother hen clucked furiously at our retreating figures. We later traced our steps back through the village to see if the chicks were all right, but they were long gone.

Behind our house was a hill with numerous gigantic boulders that seemed to have been randomly dropped by Almighty on the slopes and the top of the hill. Some lay helter-skelter while others seemed to have been carefully and neatly arranged like Lego blocks. Yet a few others seemed to have been placed on top of each other very precariously, as though a tiny push would topple them and send them hurtling down the slope to the valley below. From there, on a clear day, one could see the sunset over Maseno with Lake Victoria faintly in the distance.

Power failure was both unpredictable and frequent; once we had no power for two and a half days, and there was no storm to explain the failure. Despite the rain, there was a shortage of water. It was not unusual to turn on the faucet, and all one got was thick, brown, muddy water. One had to resort to using bottled water for emergency. Once in the middle of my shower, the water turned to mud, matting my hair. Emmah kept a barrel of water in the shower for such an unexpected and surprising occasion. In the hospital wards, there had not been any running water for the past three months. On the hospital ground, there was a water pump where village children and women gathered to fetch water. The children took turns at the pump and sprayed water at one another; water droplets sparkled in the sunlight, and for a brief moment, the children seemed gloriously happy.

Various shops lined the village dirt street that led from the hospital to the university, and women ran many of them. There was a particularly entrepreneurial woman who ran a telephone service, as not everyone owned a cell phone. In the morning, women sat on stools and made pancakes on frying pans or deep-fried bread dough in pots placed on three stones or a simple stove fashioned from a big tin can. Men owned the bigger sundry stores and the beer pots.

A teacher, a Rotarian who organized the jiggers treatment program at a school in Kwilhiba Parish, brought in Philip. She had heard about him through his neighbors. Philip was twenty years old but looked more like a teenager, stunted and shy with eyes perpetually downcast as though he was not used to so much attention being bestowed on him. When he did raise his eyes to steal a fleeting glance, they were deep pools of sadness, loneliness, loss, and bewilderment. His body was caked with mud, and patches of skin that were not covered with mud were scaly, as he suffered from a skin condition called ichthyosis. Having spent most of his life sleeping on the dirt floor of the one-room mud house which he shared with his grandmother, almost his entire body was infested with jiggers; the worst infection was in his legs which were swollen and covered with scabrous and open sores. Philip was an orphan; his father died before he was born, and his mother shortly after his birth. His grandmother, who raised him, became increasingly demented as she aged. Philip earned a living by cutting and selling firewood but that was not enough to maintain the house, which was in a dilapidated condition. He was alone after his grandmother died. Dianne bathed him gingerly and sponged him with chemicals which would have to be repeated daily to kill the jiggers; his body would not be returned to normal, but at least the infection would be arrested. He changed into clean clothes after Dianne slathered him with petroleum jelly to soothe his scaly skins and open sores. After a hot meal of *ugali* and beans, he was put into a hospital bed, probably the first bed that he ever slept in.

Quietly Dr. Hardison whispered under his breath, "He is our starfish." He was referring to the widely adapted starfish story by Loren Eiseley.[8] It recounted a discourse between a wise old man and a child on a beach where the child was busy throwing starfish into the sea, arguing that they would surely die under the hot sun while the tide was going out. Bewildered, the man reminded him that there were so many starfish stranded on the beach that he could not possibly save them all. Whereupon the child picked up one starfish

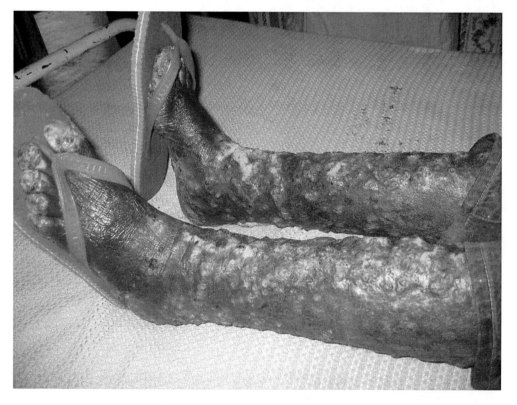

Philip's legs infested with tungiasis, caused by a sand flea also known as jigger.

with care and threw it into the sea and said with a firm conviction, "It made a difference for that one."

All of us would meet many more Philips in this world in our lifetime. To some, changing a few lives at a time might not make a huge difference, but it would surely change their lives and ours.

Fatuma had been lying patiently in the hospital bed for several days now with loss of appetite, a distended belly, and abdominal pain, waiting for a surgeon to come from Kisumu to do an exploratory laparotomy. Her husband came to see her a few times, seemingly feeling out of place among the many female visitors. Finally, one morning she was taken to the operating theater, and sure enough, she had widespread ovarian cancer. The surgeon removed as much of the tumor as he could for palliation of her condition, returning her to the ward with tubes protruding from her belly. Her relatives did not want her to know her real diagnosis and prognosis. Strangely, she did not ask; she was just glad that she had the surgery and was feeling much better with a smaller belly. Fatuma was discharged back to her village with a grim augury of death hanging over her.

We struggled with how to share the only clunky oxygen tank between three patients requiring oxygen at the same time. All afternoon and night, the tank was shuttled from patient to patient. Miraculously they all survived their ordeal, and all that remained was an empty tank with no immediate prospect for being filled. In the course of my stay at Maseno, we saw a young woman slowly dying of heart failure, a heart that had been ravaged by rheumatic fever, and another woman dying from kidney failure with worsening kidney functions but no dialysis machine to remove the toxins. Eventually both of them slipped into a coma and died quietly.

In the nursing station, someone wrote in bold letters with a red marker on a piece of paper taped to the wall, THE FIRST RIGHT OF A HUMAN BEING IS TO BE ALIVE. Outside the operating theater, a couple of thriving periwinkles bravely grew from a crack in the wall high above the ground. Nothing seemed to snuff out their desire to live.

Phoebe, a sad, emaciated twenty-eight-year-old mother came in with her two-year-old son, Zedekiah both wasted by AIDS; she weighed thirty-five kilograms and he a mere seven kilograms. Zedekiah's fleece top and pants were too big for him; the sleeves and pant legs had to be rolled up. Phoebe had three children: the oldest was seven years old, healthy and not HIV-infected; the second child died three years ago; and Zedekiah her third, had AIDS. Both Phoebe and Zedekiah were turned out of the house by her mother-in-law and her HIV-positive husband, who later took a second wife. Her mother-in-law kept the healthy seven-year-old with her, separating him from his mother. Phoebe and Zedekiah lived in a hut sharing whatever meal given to them, she being too ill to work. Phoebe had oral thrush and Kaposi sarcoma on her legs, and Zedekiah had profound developmental delay, too weak and ill to stand, walk, talk, or smile. He did not even cry or struggle when the nurse gave him a shot. In the hospital, Phoebe and Zedekiah slept in a private room and received a carton of milk. Zedekiah was fed rice and beans for dinner. He was eager to eat; no sooner had he finished swallowing his morsel of food, he opened his mouth for more while mama ate with little interest and appetite. After a while, she settled her baby and plate on the floor and lay down on the bed, curled up in a fetal position facing the wall in a state of deep despair. Zedekiah, left alone on the cement floor, looked lost but managed to scoot on his bottom towards the plate of food. Slowly he dipped his fingers into his food, scooped it into his mouth, and fed himself. Mama seemed to have given up on eating. Zedekiah's older brother came to visit; he was playful, robust, and helped his mother to feed the little brother,

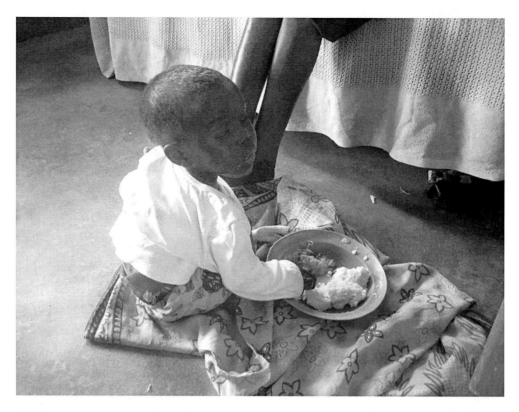

Zedekiah, severely malnourished, tried to feed himself when his mother stopped feeding him.

piggybacked him and played with him. Phoebe asked for a spare change of clothing, communicating her wish to me via hand gesturing, I gave her some of my clothes. When Zedekiah was given a small stuffed animal, he did not know what to do with it, but he had no such trouble with food. She and her child needed an HIV treatment and, most of all, a safe place to stay and food security.

One afternoon, a mother brought in her mute, feverish ten-year-old boy, Benson. His blood test showed he had pancytopenia: all his red blood cell, white blood cell, and platelet counts were low. His father was deceased. Suspicious of possible HIV infection, we advised testing, and he was positive. It took many days of persuasion for the mother and her two other children to get HIV testing, and they were all infected. The stigma of the infection worried the mother so much that she was not desirous of knowing their HIV status. With treatment through the CCC, we hoped the family would somehow be made somewhat whole again.

The Maseno HIV/AIDS Awareness and Development Organization built the Bailey/Whaley Health Clinic in 2005 in celebration of the 100th anniversary of Rotary International. Women ran most programs in Maseno, and women and children attended the clinics. Very few men got involved or attended the clinics; if they came at all, they usually came at the end of the afternoon, looking apprehensive. This clinic provided "First Food" for weaning infants and children: a precooked porridge blend of whole maize, millet, sorghum, soya, oil, and sugar with added vitamins and minerals.

A craft shop was kept alive by a group of village women, a HIV support group meeting in a little shed close to the hospital grounds. It had been organized by a Peace Corps volunteer before she was evacuated when the riots broke up after the election of 2007. They took turns using the single Singer sewing machine, teaching each other crafts, stringing paper beads, and churning out items for sale.

HIV/AIDS left behind a legion of orphans often taken care of by their grandmothers. Nan Hardison, Dr. Hardison's wife, helped the women set up a Mothers' Union to feed these orphans a nutritious meal every Saturday in their parishes. There were thirty-eight parishes in the Diocese of Maseno North, but there were enough funds donated from churches in the U.S. for only sixteen parishes, feeding about five hundred children per site at $4,000 a year. The meal was crunchy hot corn and beans or *githeri* prepared in big cauldrons started the night before in fume-filled sooty rooms.

Dr. Hardison and the Maseno staff provided care in five mobile clinic sites on Saturdays, again supported by donations from the U.S. at a cost of $5,000 per year per site. One Saturday we traveled to Ekwanda with our medical supply to such a clinic set up in a school. A few classrooms were set up as examination rooms with curtains as dividers. The patients' charts were spread out on the desks outside. We saw mainly children with respiratory sickness, aches and pains. Outside was a family of five: a thin, malnourished mother with her four even more malnourished boys, one of whom was just a baby of a few months old. Her three older boys had a haunting, gaunt, and haggard look, the skin tightly stretched across

their cheeks and prominent, white teeth protruding through their lips. They wore oversized adult clothes with limbs sticking out like sticks on knobby knees, fingers and toes infested with jiggers. They soaked their infected feet in a big communal basin filled with chemicals to kill the fleas. The oldest boy had fleas burrowing in his lips, and a villager carefully pried them out with a needle. They were all so thin and wasted that it would not be a surprise if they were also HIV-infected. Their mother, nursing her baby, expressed her fervent wish to have a fifth child because she wanted a girl. How could she have the reserve to have a fifth child? What would happen to all these children with ill health and very likely no opportunity for an education? Where was her husband? All around them, many more children

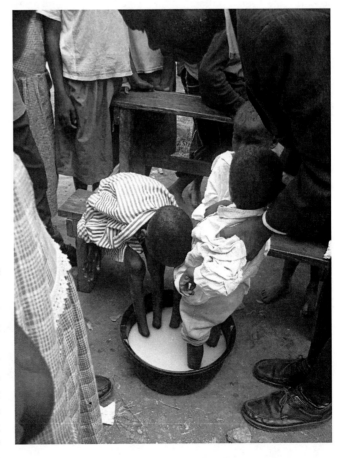

Children infested with tungiasis soaked their legs in a communal basin of chemicals during a mobile clinic in Ekwanda, Kenya.

with jiggers were sitting on benches, waiting patiently for their turn at the communal basin of chemicals.

After the clinic, the women of the Mothers' Union served the *githeri* meal. Children lined up in a very orderly fashion holding plates, mugs, or plastic bags. Most were barefoot, and some were wearing their school uniforms, probably the only decent clothes they owned. Voluminous billows of smoke enveloped the women bending over buckets of warm *githeri,* scooping up portions with a mug for the eagerly waiting, hungry children. A very well-dressed boy, in baby-blue silk pants with pink and purple hearts sewn on the pant legs and topped by a gold Nehru shirt, looked strangely regal even though the top was missing a gold button, and he was barefoot. Hungry children, balancing their food carefully, sat down on the lawn or on the cement floor or leaned against walls of huts, and scooped up the beans and corn with their bare hands; only a few brought along a spoon. A little girl carefully divided a portion of her food into a plastic bag and then tied a knot on it before she abstemiously ate the remaining *githeri* from her bowl.

The Mothers' Union held weekly meetings when Nan Hardison helped the women to complete their applications for micro-loans ranging from 20,000 KSh ($250 U.S.) to 50,000 KSh ($625 U.S.). The proposed business projects included farming of grains, sales of paraffin/kerosene for cooking within the community, and sewing, using the loan to purchase fabric and sewing machines.

Thunderclouds threatened one evening when we went to a church for the inauguration of the new micro-lending program supported by the Jubilee Ministry of the Diocese of

The women from the Mothers' Union feeding the children a meal of *githeri* and beans at one of the feeding programs in Maseno, Kenya.

Massachusetts. The loan applicants were women of all ages, including many grandmothers in long blue dresses with puffed sleeves, their hair wrapped in blue or white head-kerchiefs. Some hitched a ride with us, chattering excitedly and animatedly in Swahili. Not a single man applied because they considered the loans too small for their grand schemes of business. We waited patiently for Bishop Simon Oketch and his entourage of men. When they finally arrived, they were immediately ushered into a private room and served tea. Bishop Oketch made his appearance amidst applause. Nan very likely spearheaded this program, but she wisely gave credit to him. He asked the women to praise the Lord for graciously lending them a hand and reminded them that they needed to be responsible for the loans. There were loud, enthusiastic singing and clapping, "Let us rejoice and be glad," interspersed with chants of "Obama" and Nan's enthusiastic "You go, girls." As though wanting to participate in this celebration, outside a strong wind blew, dark clouds gathered, and distant thunder rolled.

In front of the church, a group of children elbowed each other as they hunkered over small holes in the ground, catching termites flying out of their nests into the waiting traps of plastic bags anchored with rocks over the exits. As they lifted the bags, numerous little hands flew wildly into the pile of termites and delivered these straight into their mouths, spitting out the wings as they munched on them. Some more circumspect connoisseurs pulled out the wings first before delivering the struggling live morsels into their hungry mouths. During the days that followed, there were many more swarms of termites appearing from nests around the hospital grounds, mainly in the evenings. Children and monkeys alike feasted on these live snacks.

Children in the village often played with a *panga* or machete without adult supervision as though it were a toy, slashing away on bushes or chopping nuts held by their little hands. Joab, a nine-year-old boy, came to the outpatient department after he had all but severed his baby finger with a *panga* while cutting grass. Holding bravely onto his hand, he quietly walked to the minor operating theater for a tetanus shot, an amputation, and then was discharged—a day in the life of a Kenyan boy.

Friday nights seemed to be for funerals. Singing, wailing, and drumming could be heard all through the night, making sleep elusive. Often villagers waited for such nights to avenge their grievances. At the funeral, many became inebriated, and the avengers came with *pangas* under the cover of darkness, slashing away at their enemies with impunity. On Saturday mornings, casualties arrived at the operating theater, some minor, and some major. Once a surgeon was called in urgently to stitch up a man with many *panga* injuries: a deep gash running from his left eye across his cheek to his mouth, numerous slashes on his arms, and a big cut across his knee narrowly missing his joint. It took the surgeon all morning to make the man whole again, almost. The perpetrators were never apprehended. For every Friday night of mourning, we braced for the next day's casualties.

Sue and I took an outing with the VCT nurse on the land cruiser, which took us as far as it could go and dropped us at a village to seek out people who were willing to have a quick HIV testing. We walked to various houses and knocked on the doors. The counselor proceeded to counsel the occupants, and some were willing to submit to testing. When they tested negative, she counseled them on how to prevent HIV infection. Many homes were made of mud bricks covered with cement, topped with a tin or thatched roof, and the tinsel-framed photographs of family members and posters of politicians decorated the walls. Streamers made from papers torn from used notebooks hung from the ceiling. There was always a sitting room with a big sofa, dimly lit by light filtering through small apertures for windows. Some houses had dirt floors often frequented by chickens, pecking away and leaving their droppings along the way. Bright rows of canna lilies or other flowering bushes graced the front of the houses with a few cows grazing on the lawn.

Praxedes, a single HIV positive mother, took Dianne and me for home visits one day. The land cruiser again took us on the red dirt road as far as it could go and left us to go on foot, seeking out the widowed mother of two who had volunteered to be our guide. The widow's children were dressed in dirty, tattered clothes. She tended the land around her house and grew maize, struggling to make ends meet. We spent the day hiking up and down that hilly farming village in search of patients of the CCC of Maseno.

It was a hot sunny day. We first visited a couple of girls aged eight and ten who were orphaned and lived with their aunt. Praxedes asked them to show her how they took their medicines. This was important because their aunt worked, and they were on their own as far as taking medicine was concerned. In HIV treatment, taking medicine as close to ninety percent of the time was important in achieving a virus burden that was undetectable in the body, thus improving the chances of the immune system to reach normality. The girls lined up their medications on the coffee table and enumerated the number of pills they had to take and how frequently through the day. We hiked through farmlands of maize, sweet potatoes, and bananas. We waited for the farmers to return from their fields, for it was after all their working day. Red and white beans were drying on mats under the sun while chickens milled around trying to get some free feeding. In the afternoon, we finally made a circuit back to the red dirt road, joining many villagers who were walking to or from the market. Praxedes told us that many patients walked for more than two hours to and from the CCC for their clinic visits, as they did not have the money to take the *boda* or the *piki*.

At the tarmac road, clinic was over for a prenatal and maternity unit which also offered free VCT. On the walls were several signs and posters. One showed a couple at the top with the question: "Why is HIV spreading fastest in marriages?" This was followed by a picture of the original couple with their partners outside their marriage: "It's because husbands and wives have spare wheels." The last picture depicted each partner having multiple partners and so on and so forth, thus spreading the infection. The caption read: "It's because spare wheels have spare wheels too." Beside this poster was an equally big poster with a handwritten quote from Martin Luther King, Jr., "In the end we will remember not the words of our enemies, but the silence of our friends."

Praxedes did not remain silent but acted with magnanimity and kindness. She herself was living with AIDS and bringing up two children of her own as a single parent. She had met Sophie, an orphan, sick and wasted with HIV-related complications, when she was brought to Maseno Hospital by her relatives in July 2008 and left to die. Remarkably, Praxedes took her into her home and adopted her as her own; Sophie thrived with the love from a woman who had ample room in her heart to bring up yet another abandoned soul. On December 1, 2008, World AIDS Day was celebrated at the CCC with food, singing, and dancing. Many clinic patients walked for miles to get there to join in the celebration, and after that, they would walk home for hours but with joy, love, and hope in their hearts. On that day Sophie wrote and recited a poem in Kiswahili as she lit the "HOPE" candle.

> AIDS is a killer disease[9]
> *It killed my mother.*
> *It killed my father.*
> *It killed my grandmother.*
> *It killed my grandfather.*

Why are we so ashamed?
We cannot hide in the forest.
We need to fight this killer disease.
We need to live with hope.

This came from the heart of a little girl, living with AIDS, haunting and wrenching. Now she indeed was given hope from a woman who cared.

In 2017, Kenya had a total of 1.5 million people living with HIV with a prevalence of 4.5 percent among people ages 15 to 49 years. For the WHO's 90–90–90 target of ending HIV in 2030, USAIDS data of 2018 showed that Kenya had no data for the percent of people who knew their HIV status, 75 percent of people living with HIV were on treatment, and 84 percent were virally suppressed.[10] Barriers to HIV response included stigma and discrimination. Homosexuality is still criminalized, and this deters men who are having sex with men from seeking diagnosis and treatment. Between 2010–2014, the Kenyan government prosecuted 595 cases of homosexuality.[11]

We had Thanksgiving early at the Hardisons' home the weekend before the real Thanksgiving: chicken in place of turkey, mashed potatoes, gravy, *sukuma wiki* (braised collard greens flavored with spices), cranberry sauce, baked pumpkin, and a mango cobbler. Ralph figured out how to use the oven and baked the delicious mango cobbler, but he was off to Maasai Mara for a safari and missed Thanksgiving dinner. Even the two dogs at the Hardisons, Simba and Little Brown had some chicken bones for their dinner. We had many things to be thankful for when we looked around the village where harvest was poor and prices of food, notably maize, the main staple, had increased.

The Monday after Thanksgiving, eighty boisterous thirteen-year-old boys came into Maseno Hospital. They would be there for five days for AIDS education and circumcision, a pilot project funded by an NGO and organized by the CCC. Circumcision has been shown to decrease AIDS risk.[12] Three more waves of eighty adolescents would follow this first group in the following three weeks. The children had their meals, and officials made speeches in a large candy-cane striped tent erected on the hospital lawn. Colorful mattresses covered with plastic were strewn wall-to-wall on the floor of the pediatrics ward, replacing the beds. Most children came with their belongings tied up in a basin; only a few had bags. The grown-ups came with them but left them on their own in the hospital for the next five days. The next morning and throughout the day, the boys lined up for their circumcision, which had to be done over several days. Woe to those boys who were scheduled to have their circumcision close to the end of the week, for by then they had heard from the other boys what kind of experience they had. Some timid ones resisted fiercely to the bitter end, much to the consternation of the clinical officers and their helpers who were involved in this "foreskin follies" as Dianne, the volunteer nurse, called their busy week of nearing one hundred circumcisions. Before their circumcision, the boys wore their shorts and pants and were quite rambunctious, but after their surgery, all the boys abandoned the wearing of trousers and shorts. Instead, they wrapped themselves with colorful *kanga* or *kikoi*, wearing it like a *sarong* and walking gingerly with their legs spread apart; they were more subdued then. In the mornings as I returned from my run, they hailed me with a loud chorus of "*mzungu*." I mercilessly answered back "*maumivu*" (pain in Kiswahili). At the end of the week, they packed up their belongings in a basin, wrapped and tied it up with their *kanga*, and returned home. The hospital was quiet again at least for the weekend, waiting to be besieged by another group and another round of the foreskin follies.

One early morning we arrived at the women's ward to find a young couple hovering over their daughter who was in and out of consciousness. The young girl was brought in overnight delirious with a high fever, having been sick for a few days. When the parents decided to bring her in, it was too late. She had cerebral malaria. They sat patiently and quietly by her and sometimes picked up her limp body and wiped her forehead, waiting for the inevitable. There was no rebuke or blame, just sadness and resignation. We watched silently, feeling completely helpless. The father just said as if trying to console us, "The Lord made her and was ready to take her away." There were no tears in his eyes.

In the afternoon when we returned for our rounds, the bed was empty.

I took a walk around the hospital ground for the last time, saying my silent good-bye to Maseno. Nurse Salome sat on a bench sharing an intimate moment with her daughter. The cat left behind by the Peace Corps volunteer prowled among the maize stalks; she was lucky as the volunteer continued to send money for her care. Two young sisters sprawled on the lawn in front of the guesthouse playing with their blonde-haired, slender but busty Barbie dolls. Someone from America must have donated these. In my short time here I observed that in one of the impoverished regions of Kenya, despite their daily struggles to live, the people were happy in their own way and accepted the fate that was dealt to them in a manner that was hard to comprehend.

I flew from Kisumu to Nairobi and then to Mombasa and spent a few days wondering in Fort Jesus and the old town. The fort looked weather-beaten with patches of mildew on its crumbling walls. An arch of gigantic elephant tasks crowned the main road of Mombasa for the visit of Queen Elizabeth many years ago. A very thin mother begged while sitting on the dusty pavement under a patch of skimpy shade with her emaciated, hollowed-eyed baby pulling and suckling ineffectively on her withered breast. Did their loved ones abandon them to struggle for an existence that was without joy, hope, or love? Traffic roared by, and pedestrians in smart-looking office attire walked by them as though they were invisible. Perhaps she was such a frequent sight on this stretch of the road that the onlookers were numb and oblivious to her plight.

From Mombasa, I took the Likoni Ferry to pick up a bus that headed south to one of the beach resorts. As in Maasai Mara, the resort was deserted; the owner graciously gave me one of the many empty rooms instead of setting a tent on the lawn for me. In the evening, he commiserated with me how business had declined since the riots, and if it did not pick up soon, he was not sure how he was going to survive. On the beach, there were camel owners trying to sell camel rides to a few wandering tourists. A young well-built Kenyan man, a so-called "beach boy," was tending to an older Western woman, swimming, drying her, and walking with her.[13] Several Kenyan men approached me, seemingly wanting to accompany me on my walks, but I told them firmly "No." In the evening, I saw the beach boy and his Western lady in one of the bigger lodges in the resort, having a drink. Sex tourism in Kenya was alive and well. Older Western women often came to Kenya to have a fling with younger Kenyan men. The fear of HIV/AIDS must have receded into the back of their minds.

Walking up the ramp from the ferry on my way back to Mombasa, someone tried to unzip my backpack. A young, off-duty police officer who had just come back from visiting his family tried to get a *matatu* for me without success, but eventually, he insisted on paying for a pedicab, and saw to it that I arrived safely back at my hotel. As I stepped out of the pedicab he handed me his business card and asked me to call him if I should run into trouble. In my travels, I was often approached by strangers who offered their help, which might or might not be wanted, with the ultimate goal of getting something back from me. I did not feel that with this police officer.

I flew back to Nairobi and stayed at the Flora Hostel Consolata Sisters where I left my climbing gear five weeks ago. My next destination was Mt. Kenya Hospital near Kerugoya. John, a driver recommended by Dr. Wangai of the hospital, turned out to be the same driver used by the Hardisons for airport transfer. I avoided using him when I first arrived at Nairobi because I learned that he charged the *azungus* a higher fare. I did not discuss fare with him, thinking naively that Dr. Wangai would have negotiated a fair price for the ride. It took more than two hours to get to the hospital, and on the way, John discussed the cost of the ride, which was far more expensive than I expected. I did not have enough money to pay him, so he made a stop at a bank suggesting that I go to get some money, which I refused. We arrived at the hospital in mid-afternoon, and Dr. Wangai was not there, only Peter his second in command who gave me a tour of the hospital where Dr. Wangai had arranged for me to volunteer for two weeks. The hours passed and despite several phone calls to him, he did not appear. So we went to his house, where he met us in his undershorts on the front porch. John wanted to return to Nairobi before it got too dark, so we finally negotiated a fair price for the trip, which apparently also included payment for his return trip to Nairobi. I did not want to engage his service for my return trip to Nairobi, sensing that he charged an exorbitant fee.

Mt. Kenya Hospital was in central Kenya and was supported by the Anglican Church of Kenya through the development department of the Christian Community Services of Mt. Kenya East. My e-mail communications with Dr. Wangai before my arrival seemed to indicate that I could volunteer there without any problem, but he told me that a recent incident involving the breaching of confidentiality made the hospital a little skittish about having volunteers at the site. After a lengthy discussion, while standing on his front porch, as did not invite me into his house, I concluded that my volunteering there was untenable. Disappointed, I climbed into John's car and left Dr. Wangai standing by his iron gate in his undershorts.

There was no guesthouse in the hospital, so I stayed in a hotel with a view of Mt. Kenya in the distance; despite a deep sense of loneliness with Mt. Kenya looking down, I felt a kinship with it since I started my adventure in Kenya in the mountains. Dr. Wangai did not make any further appearance to say good-bye. In the morning, Peter took me to the bustling bus station to catch a *matatu* to Nairobi; I decided to travel cheaply like the locals. I could not afford to pay John for another round trip fare to Nairobi. Peter admonished the conductor to make sure I arrived in Nairobi safely or else he had to answer to him when he returned.

At Nairobi, I packed a small bag and flew to the island of Lamu two weeks early. Lamu is one of Africa's most historic and picturesque villages, situated about sixty miles south of the precarious and volatile Kenya-Somalia border. From the airport, I took a boat to the island. Eighteenth-century architecture lined the shore, beautifully weathered by centuries of wind and salt; a few whitewashed mosques with green and blue turrets and green minarets stood out among the buildings. The call to prayer was a fixture on the island and woke everyone up at an unearthly hour. Many veiled women walked the narrow streets or worked near their houses. Garbage clogged a number of wells, rendering them unusable, and water pumps had since replaced them. Along the narrow streets, there were no cars, only hard-working donkeys. In the evenings the tired donkeys were let loose to forage for food; the only blades of grass grew in the enclosed courtyards of some mosques where they had no access. They walked forlornly, looking, and sniffing for any abandoned left-overs.

On my first day in Lamu, I was besieged by a Captain Ali to take a dhow trip to the other islands with two other tourists who did not materialize. When asked where those tourists were, he told me one was sick and the other had to take him to see the doctor. Unfortunately, I had been cheated since he did not take me on the itinerary he promised or serve me the delicious seafood lunch for which I had already paid him. Returning to Lamu early from the failed dhow trip, I offered to pay him half of the cost of the trip, which he reluctantly accepted after I threatened not to give him any money at all. Then I reported him to the tourist police, who told me that Captain Ali was up to his old tricks again. I counted myself lucky for declining his invitation to his home for a home-cooked Swahili meal.

Further along the island in the north were the pristine white beaches of Shela, where foreigners came to build expensive homes, eateries, and hotels. The houses were better maintained, and the beaches were not used for defecation. However, the old Lamu town retained its old character; the labyrinth of narrow back alleys enticed tourists to wander and get lost in them, and the beaches were busy with daily activities of fishing, net repairing, and dhow building. Sunrise and sunset did not discriminate; they displayed their splendor and glory equally on the disparate parts of the island.

I flew back to Nairobi one final time. While there I visited Karen Blixen's home, trying to imagine her struggle with her failed coffee plantation and the David Sheldrick Wildlife Sanctuary where orphaned baby elephants were being bottled fed and raised tenderly and, when ready, released into the wild. There I got to pet a blind rhinoceros in his pen. My final destination for my day in Nairobi was the Langata Giraffe Centre, run by the African Fund for Endangered Wildlife, a sanctuary for the rare Rothschilds giraffes. Like many tourists, I hand-fed and kissed a friendly giraffe from a raised circular wooden structure; rather it stuck out its rough tongue and rubbed it against my cheek. To me, giraffes are one of the most graceful and gentle creatures in this world. They are one of my favorite wild creatures in Africa besides the elephants, which rank high for me because of their intelligence and uncanny memory.

The taxi driver I met at Wilson Airport came to take me to Jomo Kenyatta International Airport. Upon my arrival in Europe, I could now safely drink water from a drinking fountain. It took me a few minutes to get used to something that I had always taken for granted. I could also rinse my mouth with tap water after brushing my teeth without fear of swallowing any contaminated water or that brown muddy water would spill from the faucets. I could not help but noticed the larger sizes of Westerners compared to the Africans. CNN announcers were blabbering away with rare pauses at a rate that seemed unnaturally fast. All of a sudden, I became nostalgic for the slower pace of life that I just left behind.

Like it or not, I knew I was finally home!

4

South Africa

2009

"AIDS is no longer just a disease, it is a human rights issue."
—Nelson Mandela[1]

Lonely Planet described Musina in South Africa as "a hot, dusty little town with a frontier feel to it."

Thuso took me to Musina Hospital, which still bore its old name, Messina. Two enormous tents, set up by the Red Cross as rehydration centers to care for the cholera-stricken patients, still remained prominently on the front lawn of the hospital, empty now. The cholera outbreak started in Zimbabwe in August of 2008 and by the end of July 2009, there were over 98,000 cases with 4,000 deaths.[2] In April 2009, in South Africa, there were over 12,000 cases with 65 deaths, while in the Limpopo Province where Musina was, there were over 5,000 cases with 26 deaths.[3]

In the period following the cholera outbreak, many more Zimbabwean refugees found their way to South Africa to escape political unrest, economic collapse, and to seek a better life. In 2000, Robert Mugabe of Zimbabwe, the longest-serving ruler of any African country, instituted the resettlement program of the land reform. Between June 2000 and February 2001, a total of 2,706 farms were listed for compulsory acquisition,[4] thus beginning the process of the takeovers of white-owned commercial farms, leading to economic collapse and runaway inflation. The bustling town of Musina was about seventeen kilometers from Zimbabwe and became the first port of call for these refugees. Near the border a towering sign showed flames engulfing the word "ZIMBABWE" and "Zimbabwe democracy now"; the caption further warned: Your neighbor's house is burning, help us put out the flames of hatred and violence before they reach you.

After close to a year of looking for a volunteer position with Global Medic Force (GMF), previously known as International Center for Equal Healthcare Access (ICEHA), I finally was given a mentoring position in South Africa. I was to fly into Johannesburg. I remembered hearing about this notoriously dangerous city from the Scotsman traveling with me in the Maasai Mara, with its rampant pick-pocketing, and deadly carjacking. In some parts of the city, the crime rate was so high that even the locals avoided going there.

Through Lonely Planet, I found a backpacker hostel right on the outskirts of Jo'burg. Fortunately, the hostel arranged for someone to pick me up at the airport as I arrived in the evening. This was a private, family-owned dwelling with a well-tended garden, an outdoor patio, and a wading pool. My housemates were three men from South Africa, Brazil, and Lebanon. The Brazilian was an engineer for some project in Johannesburg, and he took all of us out for a seafood dinner after which he wanted to have a go at the casino. The Lebanese slept in his tent on the lawn. He had been traveling alone for close to three years, beating the German whom I met at the Mara in the duration of travel. His marriage had ended a few years ago and taking advantage of his unencumbered state, he traveled the world. He had grown a long beard, and his hair was in dreadlocks. Was he truly happy or was he running away from facing his problems at home? The South African, like many South Africans during the time of apartheid, left his country many years ago and immigrated to Australia; he merely returned to look for species of aloes. I felt I was among friends. When I left Johannesburg a few days later, the South African gave me his cell number just in case I ran into problems in Musina where I would be volunteering. His parting words were, "You are heading into the bush!"

I arrived a week before the start of my volunteering, so on a bleak rainy day I visited Constitution Hill, depicting the turbulent past and the transition to democracy of South Africa.[5] The overcast sky echoed the sad and dismal past: the Constitution Court; the prison "Number Four" with its depressing and oppressive rows of dimly-lit cells; the women's jail; and the white-washed fort, a prison for "Whites-only" with the exception of Nelson Mandela, who was jailed there for a time. My guide was edgy entering Jo'burg, taking me to Carlton Center, the tallest building, pointing out Mahatma Gandhi Square way below us. We hardly spent any time in the notorious streets of Jo'burg.

As we approached Soweto, just below the highway was a collection of shabby, dilapidated tin sheds, sprawling in the wet grassland, with rocks and bricks scattered on the roof-tops holding the roof down from a windy storm; moist smoke oozed slowly and lazily from small chimneys. The older section of Soweto seemed more settled and residential, not at all like a shantytown. The Hector Peterson Memorial, where the now-famous image of a young man, holding a dying schoolboy in his arms as his hysterical sister ran beside him screaming, commemorated the Saturday, June 16, 1976, Soweto Uprising, when South Africa's black youth challenged the white apartheid government.[6] The events were a turning point in South Africa's political history and are now marked with a public holiday, Youth Day. In the Mustwaledi Shantytown of Soweto, houses looked more like temporary shelters with corrugated tin of various sizes, shapes, and colors. Outhouses in the yard were cordoned off with barbed wire or fences made of discarded metals and appliances.

I met up with a group of fourteen other travelers from Germany, Denmark, Switzerland, and the United States, and we went on a seven-day Kruger Swaziland tour organized by the Nomad Group Tour. Our tour guide and driver were Brian and Mike, both from Zimbabwe. This was summer for South Africa with brilliant blue sky dotted with puffy white clouds. As the clunky bus drove out of the city towards Mpumalanga, the landscape transformed into a lush countryside with green mountain ranges and eucalyptus trees. The Panorama Route took us to the Blyde River Canyon with the "Three Rondavels" promontory of the Drakensberg escarpment: three cylindrical blocks of mountains of red sandstone with green conical tops, reminiscent of the houses or huts of the indigenous people here. We followed the escarpment and through what was called God's Window, the lowveld came in and out of view from the fog, tantalizing us with the magical views of canyons, gorges, mountains, and river. The Blyde River Canyon formed the northern part of the Drakensberg escarpment. Through countless eons, the swirling whirlpools formed by the Treur River plunging into the Blyde River caused waterborne sand and rock to grind huge, cylindrical potholes into the bedrock of the river, creating the Bourke's Luck Potholes.

The Moholoholo Wildlife Rehabilitation Centre rehabilitated injured or lost animals—lions, cheetahs, hyenas, and birds—and then released them back into the wild. Some badly injured animals became long-term residents, as they would fall prey quickly to stronger creatures in the wild. We tried our skill at feeding the vultures, powerful birds that descended on our leather-padded arm as they snatched a piece of raw meat from the caretaker. We took turns petting a pair of baby rhinoceroses, tamed and friendly, almost to the point of soporific stupor.

In the afternoon, we entered the world-famous Kruger Park, spotting elephants, giraffes, zebras, impalas, and a single wildebeest. The tall grass of summer made it difficult to detect the animals. Before dinner I squeezed in my training run with my headlamp; I was training for the 2009 Boston Marathon.

The next day was a full day's game drive viewed from the commanding height of our truck, sighting a few hippos bathing in the river and many kudus, many more elephants, and a lone buffalo. As the warm slanting glow of the sun hit the tall grass, it revealed a couple of rhinoceroses, and an adolescent rhinoceros crossed the dirt road clumsily. High above, threatening black clouds covered the sky with spears of sunlight coming over the mountain ranges; patches of yellow, red, orange and purple set the silhouettes of the trees ablaze. Soon the lights disappeared and darkness engulfed us save for the headlights, which shone on a hyena caught by surprise in the grass. We were then stopped dead in our track as a lioness lay languorously on the road drawing warmth from the tarmac, and a lioness and a lion in the thicket both eyed us with disinterest.

The following day we departed Kruger via Malelane Gate and traveled to Swaziland, a landlocked country bordered by South Africa and Mozambique. Recently King Mswati III changed its name to eSwatini or "the land of the Swazis" to commemorate its 50th anniversary of independence from Britain and to celebrate his 50th birthday.[7] Swaziland has one of the highest AIDS incidences in Africa, with a rate of 26 percent among people 15 to 49 years of age,[8] and is one of the poorest countries with 39.7 percent of the population estimated to have been living under the international $1.90 poverty line in 2016 and 2017.[9]

We spent the next two days in the Mlilwane Nature Reserve, exploring the area on foot and on mountain bikes. Nyalas and warthogs wandered freely around our domed huts. In the morning, I crisscrossed the park, running through a thick eucalyptus forest drinking in its deep scent. As I scaled a slope on a winding path, I was so intent on looking on the road surface that when I looked up momentarily, I was startled by a tall, dignified kudu atop a mount next to the path. It evidently had been following me from this vantage point. When our gazes locked, it turned abruptly, probably wondering from whom I was running away. In the evening, the crescent moon looked down serenely on our campsite. It had been a very restful two days in Swaziland.

We said good-bye to Swaziland and took a scenic drive towards the warm coast of the Indian Ocean, re-entering South Africa. Soon after our arrival at iSimangaliso Wetland Park, we boarded a boat for a sunset cruise on the lagoon for some bird and hippo viewing. The next day we drove to the Hluhluwe-iMfolozi Park, a game reserve and the only state-run park in the province of KwaZulu-Natal where all the Big Five lived. We only detected three: the elephants, the buffalo, and the white rhinoceroses. Due to the conservation efforts, the park had the largest population of white rhinos in the world. Our guide spotted a kill on a high branch of a tree with a few hyenas circling at the bottom, but no leopard in sight.

In the late afternoon, we arrived at Durban, South Africa's largest marine port and a well-known surfing destination. Here I had my last dinner with the group and bade them farewell as they were going to Drakensberg, Lesotho, Port Elizabeth, and beyond.

I had scheduled a tandem sky diving after leaving the group, but because of the rain, it was canceled. I quickly arranged a trip to Sani Pass in Lesotho, the highest pass in that country that linked it to South Africa. The 4 × 4 truck took us up a gentle path that quickly became steeper and narrower near the top. The gentle, rolling mountains, covered with soft, mossy green vegetation, were intermittently obscured by a heavy mist carrying with it damp and cold air and then reappeared when the sun broke through the clouds. Higher up, the mountains became rockier and undulations of mountains upon mountains running into one another formed an endless range stretching far into the distance. Halfway up at immigration, hordes of Basothos made their way to South Africa for work or marketing, stopping to have their passports checked. When we reached the top at 9,400 feet, the mists rolled in thickly, engulfing the edges of the cliffs. Ghostly shadows of men wrapped in blankets on horseback, grazing horses, donkeys, and sheep appeared and disappeared as the mist thinned and thickened, blown around by the chilly wind.

We reached the village at the top, and Basothos wrapped in thick woolen blankets were selling local crafts; many more were just sitting on rocks or on the ground, some wearing their traditional *mokorotlo*, the Basotho conical straw hat. The houses were rondavels made of stones with a thatched roof, as stones were abundant, and wood was scarce in this region. We had lunch at the highest pub there.

On our way down, a man appeared through the mist with a bundle of firewood, probably collected from a distance for this area was devoid of trees. Some pranksters had staged a huge boulder by the side of the road as though it had fallen on top of a mannequin; only his rubber boots stuck out from underneath the boulder. A few of us laughed nervously.

I spent the night at the Khotso Backpackers lodge in the southern Drakensberg with its endless series of undulating mountain ranges. The next day I went for a short hike to a small waterfall to see the cave paintings by ancient Bushmen. In the afternoon, a guide took me horseback riding up to a mountain top. On a long stretch of grassland, my horse began to canter; it felt very beautiful, but the guide stopped all of a sudden. After that we only trotted. Since much of the terrain was rocky and uneven, trotting was not such a fun thing.

In the cool afternoon, I went running the two resident dogs were delighted and started to follow me, but I was told not to let them. I had to fool them by deviously and surreptitiously sneaking away. I took a different route, and lo and behold after about a mile, I heard panting behind me; the dogs somehow found me, and I had to lead them home again. The owner of the backpacker hotel was away, training for the Two Ocean Ultra-Marathon. At the back of his house, painted on some planks of wood were these words: "The pain of giving up far outlasts the pain of finishing." The roly-poly grey cat lorded over us in the kitchen; surprisingly this cat could jump despite being so fat. When I was ready to leave, the horse groomer showed me where the cat was sleeping, on top of the kitchen cabinets near the ceiling.

Back in Durban, I went running in the morning on the beach, the so-called Golden Mile. It was still dark, but a few anglers were already fishing. The sun struggled to peep through the clouds. I dipped into the surging ocean twice before heading back to shower. Unfortunately, the weather did not cooperate for skydiving yet a second time. The local bus took me into the center of Durban to Victoria Street Market where African crafts, animal hides, saris, and spices (hot-hot peri peri, father-in-law curry powder, mother-in-law exterminator) were sold and then the City Hall. Late in the day, I flew back to Johannesburg to begin my volunteering.

Thuso, the local coordinator, drove Bjorn, my fellow volunteer, and me to the office of the Foundation of Professional Development (FPD) in Pretoria for our orientation. In 2008, sub-Saharan Africa remained the region most heavily affected by HIV worldwide, accounting for over two-thirds of all people living with HIV and for nearly three-quarters of AIDS-related deaths worldwide. South Africa was and still is one of the countries most severely affected by the AIDS epidemic. In 2007, South Africa had close to six million people living with HIV/AIDS and one and half million orphans as a result of the disease.[10] The 2008 national HIV prevalence amongst all age groups in the Limpopo Province where we would be going was seven percent; KwaZulu-Natal had the highest rate, eighteen percent, with the South African national prevalence rate of ten percent.[11] However, the HIV prevalence levels in pregnant women attending public antenatal clinics were much higher: 40 percent in KwaZulu-Natal and 20 percent in Limpopo. The Limpopo Province had the fourth largest population, and it was the poorest. Eighty-nine percent of the population lived in the rural areas, half of whom were under the age of twenty. The unemployment rate was the highest in the country, standing at over 30 percent.[12]

South Africa was relatively slow in setting up its HIV/AIDS program because of the government's embrace of HIV/AIDS denials under the presidency of Thabo Mbeki. The belief was that HIV did not cause AIDS, and the cause "was poverty, bad nourishment, and general ill-health. The solution was not expensive western medicine, but the alleviation of poverty in Africa."[13] In 2006, Jacob Zuma, who was then president of South Africa, claimed publicly that his risk of contracting HIV after having sex with an HIV-infected partner was low because he was a healthy man and that he took a shower afterwards[14]; this claim dealt a blow to the progress made by NGOs to raise awareness of HIV/AIDS. Fake AIDS cures such as uBhejane were sold in South African pharmacies.[15] Zeblon Gwala concocted this herbal mixture and pitched it as the sole cure for AIDS, not to be taken with other HIV medications. South Africa has one of the highest estimated TB incidence rates per capita and corresponding incidence rates of HIV-positive TB cases.[16] In July 2004, at the International AIDS Conference in Bangkok, Thailand, Nelson Mandela made this statement: "Today we are calling on the world to recognize that we can't fight AIDS unless we do much more to fight TB as well."[17]

We were also blasted with statistics on murder, rape, assault with grievous bodily harm, and aggravated robbery in South Africa, leaving us feeling uneasy. The little bit on crime prevention did not diminish my anxiety.

Bjorn, a pediatrician from California, was assigned to Sashego, not far from Polokwane, the capital of Limpopo Province and two and a half hours north of Pretoria. My assignment was another two hours' drive north of Polokwane, in Musina, the closest town to the Zimbabwe border at Beitbridge over the Limpopo River.

The next day, Thuso drove us to Polokwane and took us to a car rental agency; because of the long distance of our assignment sites, we would have our own vehicles. After saying good-bye to Bjorn at Polokwane, I found myself at the wheel for the first time in Africa. Driving on the left side of the road and having to switch gears with my left hand confused me; the signal was on the wrong side of the steering wheel and each time I signaled, I turned on the wiper instead. The drivers here drove furiously fast. The slow drivers were supposed to pull closer to the breakdown lane to allow the fast drivers to pass, but I did not know that. Several times cars whipped by so close to my car that I was horrified. Unlike East Africa, South African highways were wide and smooth with no potholes to steer around. South Africa was widening the roads to Polokwane from Durban for the 2010 World Cup, which seemed to send the country into a frenzy. I followed Thuso's car for over two hours of the nerve-wracking drive, passing by long stretches of lands with low shrubs and thorny trees, over mountains, and through a tunnel.

At Maseno, I met briefly with the clinic staff and the interim medical director of the hospital, Dr. Mohakhan, who until recently was the medical director of the Fountain of Hope Clinic-the HIV/AIDS Clinic. Thuso asked me whether I noticed groups of Zimbabwean refugees congregating under the shades of trees as we approached Musina. I was concentrating so hard on my driving that I did not. At the garage where Thuso took me to fix a flat in my tire, there was a scuffle between two boys; apparently, a refugee had taken something from a store, and the boy from the store was trying to get it back. The garage owner gave both a severe scolding, adding that the young South African boy should show some gesture of kindness towards the refugee. Thuso said crimes had increased with the arrival of the refugees.

We drove to the lodge where I would be staying for the next six weeks, leaving behind the dusty frontier town as soon as we walked into the green, lush, cool but still humid grounds filled with tropical trees, a few old baobabs, and flowers. My room was in a quiet spot, and I shared a refrigerator with three other tenants. Right by the bar, the kitchen, and eatery was a small pool that would be good for cooling off in the hot afternoons. Deep in the garden nestled an outdoor rotunda for reading, drinking, and relaxing, an oasis in Musina.

On my first day, I was to report to the clinic promptly at seven-thirty in the morning. Many patients had already been waiting outside, sitting on benches since six-thirty. They had traveled long distances, as far as ninety kilometers, while others who had missed their turns to be seen in the clinic the day before slept overnight on the hospital grounds, hoping to be seen early the next day. The last bus home for many who lived far away was at one in the afternoon, and around noon, there was always a flurry of activity to get these patients seen. Two nurses were triaging the patients, handing out cards with numbers to see the pharmacist, nurses, and the doctor. Since Dr. Mohakhan had been recruited to be the acting medical director for the hospital, Dr. Phaladi was the only doctor in the clinic. She had been seeing all the patients who had been recently handled by two physicians. The clinic borrowed the hospital pharmacist to dispense medications, which meant the patients had to wait for him to be free.

The Fountain of Hope Clinic was in a container with a shotgun central corridor and rooms branching off on either side. It was on the hospital grounds located next to three other containers: clinics for TB/outpatient service, the laboratory, and a mobile dental clinic. It had ten offices/consultation rooms, a filing room, an administrative office, a data center, a waiting room, and an over-flow waiting room in a sheltered area outside the clinic, a storeroom, a staff/tea room, a pharmacy, a staff bathroom, and two patient bathrooms. There were UV lights and air-conditioning, however, the windows in the waiting room were always open to improve ventilation; as a result, it remained hot and humid. The personnel included the FDP project coordinator, the project manager, one doctor, four nurses, three social workers, a dietitian, a data entry person, a data manager, a counselor, two administrative clerks, and a cleaner.

The clinic started about a year and a half ago, partially funded by USAIDS and PEPFAR, and had already outgrown its capacity. The services offered were quite comprehensive: HIV testing, counseling on adherence to ARV medicines and their side effects, social services, and dietary advice with offerings of limited food aid, general medical care, diagnosis of TB and opportunistic infections related to HIV with sputum culture and sensitivities, and access to radiology. The National Laboratory was in the next container and offered a whole slew of laboratory testing with complete blood count, electrolytes, lactate, renal and liver functions, hepatitis A and B serologies, and pregnancy tests. The doctor was also able to perform lumbar punctures to rule out cryptococcal meningitis, which was one of the more common types of meningitis seen in AIDS patients. In many cases, the results were available in a matter of hours. The immune cell count or CD4 and HIV viral load were sent to Polokwane, two hours away; the results could then be reviewed with the patients within a month. The laboratory services offered here rivaled those at the IDI in Kampala.

By eight-thirty, there were still no signs of the doctor or nurses; one of the staff members led the patients in prayer, followed by rousing and enthusiastic singing, diaphragms pressing on empty stomachs. Just as in all the African countries I have been, long-suffering waiting seemed to be the norm; there were no raised voices of complaints, impatience, or demands. The doctor finally appeared around ten, and she, along with the other personnel, had a leisurely breakfast in the common room for another half hour before they were ready to call in their first patient. By this time, many patients had been waiting for three to four hours.

Since its inception, the clinic had about 2,500 HIV/AIDS patients with half of these on treatment. Three-quarters of these were women, and only six percent were children. There were around one hundred patients at the clinic a day, and the sole doctor, who used to see ten patients a day, now saw between thirty to forty patients a day; the remainder of the patients were triaged to see other healthcare personnel.[18] Despite approaching a clinic census of 3,000 patients with over 90 percent of the women attending the clinic of childbearing age, there was no effort on the part of the healthcare personnel to ask these women whether all their children had HIV testing. Many of these women had been on treatment for a while and had seen its benefits. Some HIV-infected mothers stopped taking ARVs after delivery, believing incorrectly that they no longer needed them. One mother thought that she could transmit HIV to her daughter by sleeping next to her or sharing a toilet, and some did not know a baby could get HIV via transmission from a mother while in the womb or at delivery.

At least three out of the five days of the week, the doctors including Dr. Phaladi started in the hospital, ward rounding, operating in the theatre for emergency C-sections, attending morbidity and mortality conferences, and general medical meetings. These meetings/rounds were to start at seven-thirty in the morning, but they never started on time. They routinely ran half an hour to forty-five minutes late; the tardiness delayed the starting of the clinic to around ten or ten-thirty.

One morning, Dr. Mohakhan requested my attendance at the mortality and morbidity conference at his office at seven-thirty. I arrived at quarter past seven, waiting patiently outside his office. At seven-thirty, I knocked on the door and received no answer. When it was well past seven-thirty and not a single soul had shown up, I began to doubt if I were at the right office. The front desk assured me I was, except that I should know Dr. Mohakhan usually showed up around eight-thirty. A few minutes past eight Dr. Omitogun, the presenter at this conference, leisurely sauntered in; more doctors showed up including the Dr. Mohakhan. I had forgotten that I was in Africa.

The main goal of my assignment was to mentor the doctor and the nurses at the Fountain of Hope Clinic. I was also to visit the referral clinics and offer advice on scaling up testing and treatment, take part in ward rounds, present formal talks for the doctors and nurses in the clinic as well as at the hospital, and conduct seminars for FPD medical staff in the Limpopo Province.

As soon as one entered the southern edge of the town of Musina, there were refugees sitting or lying listlessly under the flame or baobab trees. Thousands of refugees from Zimbabwe flocked to the showgrounds in Musina seeking refuge from deportation. With the influx, cholera spread to Musina in 2008 and overwhelmed the capacity of Musina Hospital to care for them.[19] That was when Red Cross intervened and set up tents on the hospital grounds as rehydration centers.

In 2008, Zimbabwe had one of the world's fastest shrinking economies and also one of the world's highest rates of inflation. The International Monetary Fund (IMF) put the annual inflation rate in September 2008 at 489 billion percent.[20] Since 2005, Human Rights Watch estimated that between 1 to 1.5 million Zimbabweans fled across the border into South Africa, the region's economic power.[21]

The healthcare system in Zimbabwe deteriorated, and many Zimbabweans crossed the border to neighboring countries to visit the clinics for HIV care.[22] About five to ten percent of the patients seen each day at the Fountain of Hope Clinic were Zimbabweans. Some traveled for days to reach the clinic to receive a one-month supply of ARVs and had to make their way back again. Some arrived hungry and dehydrated, too weak to make the return journey home, and wished to be admitted to the hospital. However, the hospital was full most days. They were usually given some intravenous hydration in the clinic and sent on their way. The TB Clinic next door saw similar numbers of TB patients from Zimbabwe seeking medications. Pregnant Zimbabwean women came to Musina Hospital for the delivery of their babies when they were close to term. Almost all of them received no prenatal care, and many ended up having emergency C-sections. Many came to find employment in South Africa, leaving their family behind. Many more could not afford to get a passport; hence they crossed the one-kilometer wide, crocodile-infested Limpopo River to try to enter South Africa illegally. In doing so some drowned, others lost limbs or lives to the crocodiles or contracted bilharzia. In the dry season, the river was narrower, making crossing easier. After crossing the river, they had to go through a gauntlet of barriers and obstacles, cutting through or scaling a double wall of razor wire and avoiding border patrol. In addition to these obstacles, they risked being attacked by roaming bandits who would rob them of their meager belongings, and women risked being raped.[23]

The refugees congregated on the showgrounds of Musina. Normally used for the exhibition of agricultural produce, it became the site for a makeshift refugee camp.[24] It was a barren, dusty area with few trees, about the size of a football field and enclosed by a broken barbed wire fence. Some refugees used the fence to rig up a tent with large plastic sheets, but most used pieces of fabric, cardboard, or blankets, which provided some shade; hardly materials to stave off heavy downpours or hot sun with temperature reaching into the mid-ninety degrees Fahrenheit during the day. Some just spread their mats under a few scanty acacia and flame trees around the area, surrounded by their meager belongings. When I visited, the refugees quickly surrounded me and asked if I were a journalist. Many wanted me to find them a job, any job at all; they were willing to work. A man proudly showed me his humble tent made of pieces of straw sacks strung together with strips torn from the sacks draped over a short stumpy tree as all the choice trees had been taken. Pieces of cardboard lined the dirt floor. In the tent were a bar of soap, some clothes, and a big bottle of water. This man was very lanky and the tent was small; he would have to sleep in a fetal position in order to fit in it. Outside his tent sat another young man, bending his head and wrapping his forehead in his hand in utter despair.

At the peak of the refugee migration, the camp catered to about 4,000 people, most of

A makeshift refugee camp for the Zimbabweans on the showgrounds in Musina, South Africa.

A tent made of sheets of plastic and strings rigged up against a tree stump in the showgrounds in Musina, South Africa.

them young men, but there were some women with young children. Almost all of the refugees were Zimbabweans with a spattering of Ethiopians, Somalis, Nigerians, Congolese, and Mozambicans; they walked or hitched their way from their countries to the camp. There were no adequate sanitation facilities, with only nine portable toilets and four taps for a few thousand people who drank and washed their clothes and themselves in the open with no privacy. The place looked like the aftermath of a natural disaster, strewn with trash and small pieces of plastic not big enough to piece together for a tent. There was no UNHCR; only local churches and NGOs came on weekdays to the camp to dish up a supply of sugar, corn flour, canned fish, and oil. On weekends, the refugees were left high and dry. All over the showgrounds, young men gathered around makeshift stoves of three stones, cooking *pap*, or *mieliepap*, a traditional porridge made from mielie-meal or ground maize in big tin cans, stirring the sticky meal with a stick, using branches and twigs found around the camp for firewood. Most looked listless and spent their afternoons lazing in the tents or under shades. Clothes were hung over fences and trees to dry.

Outside the showgrounds, locals set up cartons filled with fried ears of corn and popcorn for sale. It was a wonder that the cholera outbreak did not continue. MSF provided basic medical care on site including voluntary counseling and testing for HIV. Patients who tested positive for HIV were referred to the Fountain of Hope Clinic, and those who were too sick to be cared for as outpatients came to Musina for hospitalization. They were the lucky ones because they had proper shelter and food at least for a few days.

The Zimbabweans were seeking political asylum as well as to escape the economic downturn in their country. The Home Affairs officials of South Africa processed about three to four hundred of the refugees a day and issued permits for only twenty percent of these people, denying permits to most of them who came to South Africa for economic reasons. Some had to wait for months for their papers to be processed allowing them a three- to six-month stay before they had to go through the process of reapplication. There were rumors of bribery and sexual favors from the refugees if they wanted to be in the front of the queue.[25]

In the first week of March of 2009, the Department of Home Affairs began evicting the refugees from the showgrounds to the consternation of relief organizations, fearing that there would be a greater humanitarian crisis when the refugees were driven underground.[26] They were either deported or repatriated to various parts of South Africa. In the weeks following the eviction, the nightly news covered the overflow of refugees sleeping on the sidewalk outside the Central Methodist Church in Johannesburg.

By the end of March of 2009, the Department of Home Affairs changed their tune and introduced a temporary permit granting thousands of Zimbabweans the right to live and work in South Africa, and access to healthcare and education for an initial period of at least six months, thus halting the mass deportation of undocumented immigrants.[27] Previous policies had rejected up to eighty percent of applicants on the grounds that they did not meet the requirements of the Refugee Act; it did not accommodate economic migrants, which formed the majority of the applicants. As refugees with no status or status in legal limbo, they could easily be exploited as cheap labor and suffer human rights abuses such as assault and eviction. The new policy offered some form of protection. On the sides of the vans of Home Affairs was written the slogan "Bringing services closer to the people." South Africa belongs to all who live in it. After the xenophobic clashes in the refugee camps in the outskirts of Johannesburg in May of 2008, when many refugees from various countries, most of them Zimbabweans, were killed and injured, the South African government was trying hard to accommodate the millions of refugees arriving in their land.[28]

Many Zimbabwean refugees I spoke to did not have much faith in the new unity government of Robert Mugabe and Morgan Tsvangirai. Most adopted a "wait and see" attitude before their decision to go back. Despite their deplorable situation, many of the refugees were hopeful of a new beginning. All they wished for was the opportunity for basic human needs: a job and a place to call home. They were not looking for a handout; they were willing to work for a living. Their resilience, patience, and desire to live in the setting of unrelenting waves of disappointment and harsh circumstances were truly inspirational.

One weekend I went to visit the camp in the mid-afternoon. Many refugees were lying on mats taking shelter from the heat. Three young men followed me around, two Zimbabweans and a Mozambican; they had not eaten because the relief agencies did not come on the weekends. I gave them some rands, and they entreated me to give them a ride to the supermarket. I was hesitant but eventually relented. When I dropped them off at the market, they could not contain their delight and requested that I came by again the next day so they could eat.

Lateness was pervasive. For morning hospital rounds, I continued to be the only person on time at seven-thirty; other doctors would arrive half an hour later. I learned to bring a book with me to read while sitting on a bench waiting. A few of the white South African nurses, who spoke Afrikaans, upon seeing me waiting complained that "the black South Africans" were never on time. It was true that all the doctors I had been rounding with happened to be black Africans. One day well after eight, the medical director who headed rounds still had not appeared. Tired of waiting, a nurse called him, but he had turned off his cell phone. Around eight-thirty, Dr. Phaladi's cell phone rang. The delinquent director had finally called to cancel rounds; he offered no reason, and none was demanded by the team. The doctors all went on their own rounds, which they could have started in a timelier fashion if the director had chosen to call earlier. Later in the morning, he came to our clinic and did not offer any apologies for his lateness or cancellation of rounds. The lateness in starting rounds in the hospital ultimately affected the proper functioning of the clinic. It also caused immeasurable suffering of the patients, especially those with young children and long distances to travel, with loss of wages and income. Much to the credit of the clinical staff, some stayed beyond the official closing time to ensure all the patients were seen.

When I raised the issue of lateness with Dr. Mohakhan, he laughed and said, "This is Africa. This is how Africans normally operate. In America, you are paid higher wages and so you come to work on time." Later a few doctors pulled me aside and told me privately that they were grateful I confronted him with this issue, as it was not their place to criticize him. When he asked me to give a lecture, I demanded that everyone had to be on time; otherwise, I would pack up and leave the lecture hall. This worked. Evidently being on time was possible.

Musina Hospital wards were a lot cleaner than the hospitals I had seen in Mtwara and Kampala. Patients' beds were still close together, and sinks were not abundant. Healthcare workers did not wash their hands in between patients, and in the TB ward, only the nurses wore masks, while the doctors did not. Did they think that they were immune to contracting TB?

A stack of billions and trillions of Zimbabwean notes sat on a bedside table of a Zimbabwean man hospitalized for pneumonia. Upon noticing my interest, he said weakly, "You could take them; they are not worth anything."

A young woman was blind in her left eye, caused by a herpes zoster infection. She came in too late for the doctor to save her eyesight. Her scars healed, and she was ready to go home. The most striking thing was she seemed to have accepted her fate that she was blind in one eye for the rest of her life; there was no sign of sadness or grieving, just quiet resignation. I could not imagine a young woman in the U.S. being so calm about this personal tragedy. There were malnourished children and children with malaria and TB, a young man with a swollen arm from a snakebite, and another with a chronic infection of the shinbone that showed through his infected flesh.

Sister Johanna, the program manager, and I went to visit a village clinic in Madimbo, eighty-nine kilometers from Musina. This clinic referred patients to the Fountain of Hope Clinic when they were ready for ARVs. The problem for them was transportation. Sister Johanna expressed the hope that one day a month, the doctor and pharmacist from the Fountain of Hope Clinic could travel to this clinic and see the patients there instead. Outside the clinic was an empty UNHCR tent that had been rigged up as a rehydration center during the peak of the cholera outbreak.

One day I joined the hospital team to visit an outreach program at the Hope Primary School in Doreen, about forty kilometers away. Surprisingly the school was well equipped with a number of computers. Our dietitian gave an education session on nutrition. The school provided a luncheon of corn, beans, and rice, which the children ate with their fingers while sitting on the ground. They were wearing white shirts and grey skirts or pants, and about half of them were barefoot. I gave a pair of sandals to a young girl, thinking that she would put them on right away; instead, she ran home to give them to her mother. A distraught mother brought in her teenage daughter who had suffered for several days with diarrhea, leaving her quite dehydrated. She refused to drink the rehydration fluid, so we called for an ambulance. Algae and trash filled the canal from which the villagers drew their water.

The outreach team walked to a village and spoke to a group of women sitting under a tree with their children about condom use and VCT, but they said their husbands had the final say; they were more interested in the free sacks of maize flour. After trekking for quite some time under the hot sun, we stopped at a brick factory. Kenneth obtained permission from the factory owner to speak to the men, discussing at length HIV testing and prevention. There was no model to demonstrate the use of condom, so I offered Kenneth the banana from my lunch bag.

Having a car allowed me to travel around Musina more conveniently on the weekends. One such weekend, I rose at four-thirty in the morning and drove for more than two hours, watching the brilliant sunrise before finally reaching the Pafuri Gate of the north side of Kruger Park. As I headed south into the park, I could see the border post to Mozambique to my left, with long stretches of high, probably electrified fences lined with lamps along a lonely gravel road. Baobab trees gave way to acacia trees growing in the tall grass. Springbucks, kudus, and zebras grazed in the savannah, elephants lumbered in the distance, and giraffes arched their necks to get the choicest morsels from the trees. A stately buffalo crossed the road leisurely, ignoring me completely.

After lunch at a restaurant by a body of muddy water, I drove along a dirt road that Lonely Planet recommended as a place for leopard sighting. As I turned a corner at a T-junction, a huge elephant with broken tusks lumbered ahead of me, with the blue sky and a few puffy white clouds as its background. Surprised by its appearance, I squeezed my car against the bushes and cut my engine, hoping that it did not notice me. Indeed, its gait was so purposeful as it was making a beeline for its destination that it paid no heed to me. Disappointed that I did not find any leopards, I looped back and followed a narrow road. As I went over a bump, I spotted a buffalo resting in the shade of a short tree, eyes closed and all four legs tucked underneath its body, looking majestic with the perfectly symmetric curving horns framing its drowsy and contented face. The dirt road led to a partially submerged bridge where a blue crane stood in the water. I crossed slowly, spraying the water back into the river. The sun was getting hot; I drove back to the tarmac road and ran into a herd of elephants. In the distance, a family of warthogs milled around a watering hole, a few of them with heads raised, looking briefly in my direction.

I headed home on the long track of tarmac road, having decided to bypass a gas station close to the park; I was flooded with worries all the way as my gas gauge sank lower and lower in this endless stretch of deserted grassland with scattered red stony hills. Finally, before I took a sharp turn towards Musina, I spotted a gas station surrounded by palm trees studded with many weaverbirds' nests. For the rest of my journey home, the landscape changed to one adorned with baobab trees.

It was well past noon when I arrived at the Mapungubwe National Park, a UNESCO World Heritage Site. The Limpopo River shimmered in the distance, across the mopane woodlands and sandstone formations. At the entrance of the tree top walk, a sign said, "At last he came to the banks of the great grey-green greasy Limpopo River, all set about with fever trees…"—Rudyard Kipling's *The Elephant's Child: Just So Stories.*[29] A gate led to a set of wooden stairs to the tree top walk perched among the fever or acacia trees, peaceful and serene. The confluence of the legendary Limpopo and Shashe Rivers demarcated the boundaries of South Africa, Botswana, and Zimbabwe, and a few eagles soared over the sky. The Limpopo River was grey-green all right as described by Kipling. However, high up on the raised platform, I was safe from the bi-colored snakes and the crocodiles, neither of which was spotted by me; perhaps they were taking a siesta.

On my way home I stopped at a gas station to get some petrol; I did not have enough cash for a full tank. The attendant took an inordinate amount of time to pump the gas. I became worried that she was going to overfill, and I would not be able to pay her. I reached in my bag, took out my wallet, and stepped out of the car, forgetting that my window was down a third of the way. I also forgot the cardinal rule of not leaving my belongings on the passenger seat in plain sight. In the few seconds that I went around to talk to her, someone reached into the driver's side, pulled out my bag, and snatched my camera lying beside it. The attendant saw it but waited for the two boys to run away before letting me know I had been robbed. By then they had melted into the crowded street. I was more distraught that they took my passport. Unbeknownst to them, my bag had no money in it since I had taken out my wallet. I would rather they had my money than my passport. At first, I thought that the attendant might be in cahoots with them, but she said they would go after her if she had brought my attention to them when they were stealing. I wandered into town and by the open market, hoping to spot my bright red sling bag. The vendors all sympathized with my loss and clucked, "That's a shame!"

I drove to the seedy local police station, where a few sad and unsavory characters were milling around, to report the theft. I waited for a while to get the attention of a police officer. Finally, a senior police officer came, sat across from me at the counter, and leaned towards me. With his face inches from mine, he said thefts were common here, and I would never see my possessions again, so why bother filing a report. However, I told him that I needed a police report to apply for another passport. Eventually, a young police officer came with a pen and paper and started to take down my statement. He wrote laboriously and with a great deal of effort. Soon he made a mistake, tore up the report, and went to fetch a fresh piece of paper. He listed the contents of my bag: passport, *Gorillas in the Mist* by Dian

Fossey, my car rental contract, and camera. I signed the statement and asked for a copy. He went to the back of the office and disappeared for a long time, only to return to tell me the printer was broken; I would have to come back the next day to get a copy. For a minute the cynic in me wondered if he wanted a bribe.

The following morning, I went to the police station again. At an outdoor-canopied office in the yard, several officers were gathered, including a white South African woman who immediately took notice of me. She waved to me to come to her, and hearing that I needed a copy of the police report, she immediately dispatched an officer to get it for me. That was that. She was in command; the other officers seemed to be standing at attention, and the malaise of the night before dissipated.

I drove to Polokwane to meet Thuso, who took me to the U.S. Consulate in Jo'burg to apply for a new passport; it would be ready in four weeks. I was hoping to leave by three in the afternoon so I would not have to drive for four hours through the winding mountainous regions towards Musina alone in the dark. It turned out we did not leave Jo'burg until well after five. As we approached Polokwane, it was past seven in the evening. Peering through the headlights on the roads filled with trucks, Thuso described how I should first drive to a roundabout then take the first right aiming to take the highway towards Zimbabwe. He said he would call me to make sure I was all right.

In our hurry to leave, we did not have time for dinner; my late lunch was long gone. I heaved a sigh of relief when I found the highway towards Zimbabwe. Soon I was on the outskirts of Polokwane, and there were no lights save for the headlights from the trucks on the highway heading north. GMF, the NGO that had sent me, forbid volunteers to drive at night. My heart jumped when my cell phone rang. I fumbled for it in the dark; it was Thuso. I drove on, settling down emotionally the longer I was on the road. Thuso called me a second time, evidently worrying a little bit. The night was silent and dark, and often I found myself alone for long stretches of time on the highway.

Finally, I was out of the mountainous area. Through my window, millions of stars in the sky beckoned. I pulled my car over the grassy bank, turned off the light, and walked around to the other side. Completely shrouded in darkness, alone in the wilderness, I stood there for a long time, drinking in the beauty, taking in the mysterious starry sky, silent, majestic, and awe-inspiring. Creeping slowly in the back of my mind was the thought of wild animals in this region. What if such an animal confronted and attacked me? I hastened to walk around the car to the driver's side and slip into the safety of its interior. Through the back-view mirror, I detected a glimmer of light in the distance, the headlights of an approaching vehicle. By half past ten, I finally drove into Musina, exhausted, and hungry. I went into the restaurant in the lodge looking for something to eat.

Beitbridge, named after Alfred Beit, founder of the De Beers diamond mining company, spanned the Limpopo River and connected South Africa and Zimbabwe. I wandered close to it one day, attempting to go to Harare in Zimbabwe. When I walked into the immigration office at the border, I realized that with no passport and no proof that I rented the vehicle, even if I were able to cross the border, my return to South Africa would not be a sure thing. My vehicle could be impounded since I had no proof that I rented it, having lost the rental document along with my passport. I let the idea of visiting Harare die.

Day-migrants crossed the border daily to Musina, to buy commodities that were scarce in Zimbabwe. Only pedestrians used the original bridge since a new bridge for vehicles had been built. On both sides of the Limpopo River on no-man's land were coils of barbed wire to deter illegal immigrants from crossing. Despite that, many did cross over, cutting through the wires and braving crocodiles in the river. On the South African side, the barbed wire was once electrified. When there were fatalities, an outcry made the government switch off the electricity. Desperation drove many Zimbabweans to brave all these obstacles to cross to South Africa.

On my final day, the clinic gave me a rousing send-off with food, singing, clapping, and they presented me with a stone giraffe spreading its legs and lowering its neck to get a drink of water. FDP canceled Bjorn and my debriefing sessions, so we just submitted a report about our assignment in the Limpopo Province. In 2017, eight years after I left South Africa, it still had the biggest HIV epidemic in the world with 7.1 million people infected at a prevalence of 18.8 percent among adults aged 19 to 49 years.[30] In 2018, it made huge progress towards reaching the 90–90–90 UNAIDS targets for 2020; it reached its first goal target with 90 percent of people aware of their HIV status, 68 percent on treatment, and 78 percent achieved viral suppression. It is the first country in sub-Saharan Africa to fully approve pre-exposure prophylaxis (PrEP) and made available to people at risk for HIV. People at very high risk for HIV infection who are on PrEP, taking daily HIV medications, reduce their chances of infection; it has been shown to reduce the risk by 90 percent through sex and by 70 percent among people injecting drugs.[31]

Before I left Musina heading back to Pretoria at the end of my assignment, I drove by the refugee camp; it was almost empty. Charred remains of stones and wood from cooking, pieces of cardboard, and plastic blew gently and desolately in the sultry breeze. The stumpy tree against which one of the refugees built his tent was partially burnt; its trunk had partly turned into charcoal, its leaves brown and shriveled with a few green leaves fortunate to escape being burnt. The occupant was long gone, to where I would never know. Hanging on the barbed wire fence were abandoned clothes and blankets, and on the ground well-worn sneakers. One wondered why anyone would abandon such valuable items unless the leaving was rushed and in the confusion, precious belongings were left behind. A handful of women, men, and children formed two lines under the scorching sun behind the vans of Home Affairs to be registered. The Home Affairs Office was closing down the refugee camp in the showgrounds. The evening news broadcast that many of the Zimbabwean refugees ended in Jo'burg near the Methodist Central Church which was filled to the gills, leaving a number of refugees spilling into the streets and sleeping on the pavement.[32]

On my way to Polokwane to meet Bjorn, whom I did not even see in the span of six weeks in the Limpopo Province, I drove through the beautiful mountain area of Zoutpansberg, stopping at the monument marking the site of the Cape of Capricorn. At Polokwane, we returned one of the rented cars and Bjorn and I then drove to Pretoria. As we watched the sun set over Pretoria, Bjorn poignantly said at his age of seventy, there were fewer sunsets left for him, and he tried not to miss any of them.

In the morning, we parted company. I was off to Zimbabwe to visit the great Victoria Falls, *Mosi-oa-Tunya* as the Kololo tribe named it—literally "the cloud that thunders." On my first evening in Zimbabwe, I took a boat down the Zambezi River. In the distance, the misty water of the falls rose gently like smoke into the sky. As the sun, looking like a fireball, set in the distance, its rays reflected off the smoking particles of the fall waters, bright orange, and yellow. As it finally made its disappearance, the water spray became wispy, plummy black smoke rising above the silhouette of the trees. From my lodge, I could feel the filmy water spray on my face even though I was a distance from the falls. At night, I could hear its roaring thunder as I sat in front of my lodge. Unfortunately, the mosquitoes did not allow me to linger too long in the open; I had to quickly retreat into my chamber.

Early the next morning a mini-bus came to take me to Chobe National Park in Botswana. A pack of hyenas ran across the road hunting for food. Just when we were close to the border of Botswana, a heavily loaded truck jackknifed across the road, blocking our way. Another truck, while trying to circle around it, was stuck in the drainage area, stretching itself towards the bushes and stopping any vehicle attempting to go around it. There was a real threat that I would miss my safari in the national park. Our resourceful driver drove gingerly around the jackknifed truck onto the sloping side of the road. Miraculously we did not overturn and succeeded in circling the huge obstacle and proceeded to drive towards the Kazungula border post.

As we cruised along the inky blue Chobe River, families of hippos were having their morning swim, spraying water through their nostrils. Crocodiles were harder to find; their heads, nostrils, and sinister eyes barely made it out of the water, looking more like rotten logs floating lazily. An alert giant monitor stuck its head among the tall grass. A cormorant stood on a log with its wings open to dry them in the sun with a whole array of water birds: Egyptian geese, kingfisher, the sacred ibis, and storks. A family of elephants splashed in the river, bathing, and spraying water with their trunks while a couple of kudus came to the water edge to get a drink. Life seemed to be idyllic.

After a delicious lunch, we boarded an open safari truck. Unlike the closed safari vans in East Africa, the open truck made one feel vulnerable to the outside world of wild animals. The very first creature we saw was a warthog, which ran quickly into the bush and then turned around to look at us; the top of its face just above its snout was covered with dirt from rooting in the soil for food. A kudu was reaching out to some tender leaves on a bush, picking the choicest morsel for its lunch. A pair of Rothschild giraffes was doing a slow graceful dance around each other, entwining their necks. In the distance, the sun shone on some brightly colored, shimmering and fluttering creatures, which turned out to be a swarm of yellow, white, and brown butterflies feeding happily on a pile of elephant dung. Many elephants congregated around a water hole; some were wallowing in the shallow parts while a few were bathing and spraying water. Baby elephants toddled behind their mothers. Once the driver drove through a herd of elephants crossing our path, separating a baby from its mother; the mother whipped around, looking rather frantic, coming dangerously close to our truck. Once baby and mother were reunited, the mother came looking for us, and then proceeded to charge; the driver beat a hasty retreat. We spotted a giraffe bending its long front legs awkwardly to get a drink of water collected on the road. Towards the end of the afternoon, a family of elephants walked through the bushes from the direction of the Chobe River; they were all wet from their bath. While we waited for them to cross, one of the elephants collected a load of dirt in its trunk and sprayed it all over its back. Evidently going to the river to bathe was for cooling off and not for any personal hygiene.

Outside the lodge, Zimbabweans were looking for T-shirts or anything that the tourists could give them. The inflation was so high that the Zimbabwean currency was worthless. Many were trying to sell their currency for U.S. dollars. A Zimbabwean offered me a bill of a trillion Zimbabwean dollars for a U.S. dollar. The grocery store was closed. Through the windows, I could see the empty shelves. Only a small store that sold cold drinks, fruits, and sweets, shops for tours for the falls, stalls with art and crafts, and hotels remained open.

At Victoria Falls, the statue of Livingstone, erected at the hundredth anniversary of the discovery of Victoria Falls, looked fondly at the two tall basalt cliffs shrouded in mist. The tumultuous water rushed around the Cataract and Livingstone Islands in the Zambezi River before its inevitable plunge into the abyss with a deafening roar and a radiant double rainbow rising from the depths of the gorge. The mist fell on me like rain. In the distance, the ecstatically symmetric Victoria Falls Bridge spanned the gorge, and beyond it, an attendant was helping a bungee jumper at the end of his jump. A brilliant rainbow spanned the bridge on the Zimbabwean side.

As I sat quietly in the open restaurant having my dinner, listening to the roar of the falls and catching the mist when the direction of the wind sent the moisture to my camp, I remembered the Zimbabwean refugees in South Africa who wished to return to their country if and when it settled into peace and economic stability. It might not come as quickly as they liked. The Zimbabweans in Victoria Falls survived because of tourism. Without it, it would be difficult to imagine how the locals here would have made ends meet.

The next morning, I was taken to the heliport to take the flight of the angels. The helicopter flew to the upper reaches of the Zambezi River on which were scattered several islands including the Cataract and Livingstone Islands. Immediately beyond these were plumes of white clouds created by the water plunging hundreds of meters into the chasm. The silver, placid sheen of the river came to an abrupt end, meeting with the white clouds created by the plunging water—the Smoke that Thunders. Far in the distance, the Zambezi River reappeared, flowing below the Victoria Falls Bridge.

Flying back to South Africa, my last stop was Cape Town with its iconic Table Mountain often shrouded in clouds as its backdrop. On misty mornings, Table Mountain looked like a bowl brimming with hot soup and over its rim, a profusion of steam issued. At Robben Island, Ahmed Kathrada, anti-apartheid activist and a former prisoner on the island said, "We would want Robben Island to reflect the triumph of freedom and human dignity over oppression and humiliation, of courage and determination over weakness, of a new South Africa over the old."[33] Nelson Mandela spent eighteen of his twenty-seven years of imprisonment there, working at the quarry breaking small pieces of stones from large boulders, his eyesight ruined by the bright light reflected off the rocks. His Spartan cell had a roll-up mattress and blankets, a platter on a table, and a trash can. It was lit by faint light filtering through a high small barred window. The waves came crashing on the boulders bordering parts of the island. On the pebbly beach, rows upon rows of black and white African penguins mingled with black cormorants. A couple of African penguins, who mated for life, waddled under the low bushes, nestling against each other. From here, Cape Town seemed so close and yet so far. To survive such lengthy periods of solitary confinement, the prisoners had to harbor hopes for freedom from oppression. They had to hold fast to Langston Hughes' "Dreams." As barren as Robben Island was, they had to remain hopeful and dream of freedom and not let their spirit die.[34]

One could not visit Cape Town without paying a visit to District Six, which used to be a vibrant inner city of mixed residential areas located in the bowl of Cape Town and linked to its port. Its residents were mainly black: Cape Malays, black Xhosa, Indians with some Afrikaans, and whites. In 1966, the government declared District Six as a whites-only area using the Group Areas Act,[35] and over 60,000 residents were forcibly removed by the apartheid regime. The old houses were bulldozed, and the displaced people were relocated to the barren, outlying, sandy area of the city now famously known as the Cape Flats. I spent an afternoon in one of the townships in Cape Flats, a mixture of one story-homes, two to three story-flats, tin sheds, and rows of communal outhouses lining its periphery. Newcomers squatted on the sidelines in lean-to sheds. One big living space filled the inside of the smaller homes, beds rolled up during the day to make space for eating and cooking; sleeping took place in the same tight quarters. Clothes fluttered from the clotheslines in the

Lean-to sheds in Cape Flats, Cape Town, South Africa.

common courtyards with scattered outhouses. Children ran around barefoot and stayed out of the hot container homes.

The District Museum in District Six portrayed the history of apartheid and its effects on the ordinary people through an intimate look at their personal stories, belongings, and interiors of their homes. On the ground floor was a large map where residents could leave their comments. There were old street signs, the bench with its "Whites Only" plaque, and countless memories, moving stories retold by the people who had their lives torn apart.

The most moving story of all was the story "A Homing Pigeon's View of Forced Removal," narrated by Noor Ebrahim, one of the founders of District Six Museum.[36] During one of the meetings of the District Six Land Restitution Case, he stood up and told his poignant story of his fifty prized homing pigeons, for which he built a loft using the wood from his home in District Six in his new home at Athlone. After a three-month stay in the new home, he felt it was time for his homing pigeons to learn to fly back to their new home. He let them fly away. In the evening, he waited apprehensively, but there was no sign of his pigeons. The next day when he drove by his old home in District Six, "I saw a sight that shook me to the core; my pigeons, all fifty of them, were congregated on the empty plot where our home had stood. Getting out of my car, I walked over to where the pigeons were. Very surprisingly, they did not fly away, but looked into my eyes as if to ask, 'Where is our home?'"

I, for one, was ready to go home.

5

Nigeria
2009

"HIV & AIDS: If you're not infected, you're affected."
—*Vanguard Nigerian News*[1]

In June of 2010, GMF contacted me the second time to go to Nigeria. It was in the summer of 2009 when they first asked me; I was unable to go then. This time around, I was traveling in Turkey. I scrambled to find colleagues to cover my hospital shifts, but before I could arrange anything, another physician beat me to it and signed up to go. A day or two later, GMF contacted me again. Apparently, the Nigerians wanted someone with clinical experience. I would depart for Nigeria in the first week of August 2010.

I kissed my cat, Marshmallow, profusely as she basked in the sun in the foyer on the dog bed. She tolerated me briefly and promptly found a comfortable place for her head, curled up, and went back to dozing again, not realizing that I would be away for a long while.

From the airplane, the landscape near Abuja was dotted with numerous blocks of mountains, seemingly randomly dropped like cookie dough onto the vast, flat, green plain. A prominent sign on the wall of the immigration hall at the airport asserted the seriousness of the Nigerian government against internet defrauding. The immigration officer only gave me a four-week stay, despite the fact that my invitation letter from the Institute of Human Virology Nigeria (IVHN) clearly stated I would be in Abuja for six weeks and I had paid for a three-month visa. He told me I had to go to the immigration office in Abuja for an extension. When asked whether I had to pay an additional fee, he adamantly told me no. I rather doubted it. My fellow volunteers from the United Kingdom and Gambia were given a six-week stay, but those of us from the U.S. were given four. The U.S. government had applied strict immigration rules on Nigerian nationals, and the Nigerian government had retaliated.

Segim met me at the airport. The road from the airport to the city was well paved, but as in most African countries, there were no disabled lanes; only sloping strips of red earth with deep grooves carved into them by the rain flanked the road. Bush taxis often tried to circumvent traffic jams by driving along these strips, precariously tipping severely to one side towards the ditch. This was in the midst of the rainy season. As we approached the capital, the gigantic whitewashed Gateway of Abuja welcomed us.

Austin, the night housekeeper, took one look at me and appeared dismayed and confused. He fumbled with his paper, stared at me again, and then gestured for me to wait at the porch. The guesthouse had six apartments on three floors. He traipsed up and down and looked at several rooms, shaking his head vigorously. I thought perhaps the rooms had not been cleaned, and he was not expecting me. After what seemed like a long time, he ushered me to a ground floor apartment; immediately a strong damp musty odor invaded my nose. He turned on the switch, but the light did not come on. Floundering his way in the dark, he found another switch. When he flipped it, a dim ceiling light came on. There were several empty, gaping sockets in the ceiling and two standing lamps with no light bulbs. It was as though someone had come and taken all the light bulbs away. A hallway from the living room led to three bedrooms.

Austin showed me the smallest and darkest of the three, wedged between the two end rooms. A single dim, naked light bulb hung from the ceiling revealing a bed, which took up almost the entire room. There was a desk placed at one end, and in between them, a desk chair was wedged tightly. To get to the cupboard or the bathroom on the far side of the room, I had to move the desk chair and squeezed my way between the bed and the desk. Besides the head of the bed, an armchair sat in a U-shaped corner facing the wall, leaving just about enough legroom for someone to sit staring at the wall. There was no place for the night table; it was simply left next to the desk right outside the bathroom. I switched on the desk lamp, but there was no light; it was missing a light bulb. Despondent, I asked Austin if I could have the bigger and brighter first room, but he told me it had been assigned to another doctor, who turned out to be Bjorn with whom I volunteered in South Africa; he was not due for another two days. The third room was occupied. I requested another light bulb, but Austin said I had to talk to the day housekeeper. As I unpacked to put my clothes in the cupboard, a few cockroaches scurried across the floor towards the darker recesses.

I went up to the second floor to visit Marie, one of the three nurses volunteering with us. She had been the first to arrive and had a palatial room facing the front with two large windows and a spacious ensuite bathroom. There were two other, equally large rooms in her apartment, and she suggested that I moved into one of them, as the other nurses would not be in for a while. When I inquired of Austin, he would not agree as they had been spoken for. Unlike my living room, here there was no musty smell, and all the light fixtures had their bulbs. The couch and the floor seemed to be brand new, and the television worked, whereas ours just showed snowflakes of static. The kitchen was clean and well equipped, and both the stove and refrigerator worked.

Later I learned that someone had mistaken me as a man from my gender-neutral name and placed me in the men's apartment; that was why Austin was flustered and gave me a double look. Unfortunately, as the men in the apartment seldom cooked, any functional equipment was taken to the nurses' apartment. Nobody knew that the stove and refrigerator did not work since no one ever used them. However, it was hard for me to understand why they tolerated the fact that there was only one working light bulb in the dining room, and the television only showed static on the screen. It took a few more days for more light bulbs to be ordered and the stove to be fixed, and many more days for the refrigerator to be marginally functional. However, the mustiness in the living room did not go away. It did not help matters that we frequently had heavy rainstorms, and the rain splashed and leaked through the windowsills onto the floor. Soon it seeped through the ceiling, leaving additional wet and moldy markings and the pervasive mustiness lingered in the air.

By the end of the week, the full complement of volunteers consisting of three doctors and three nurses had arrived. We were three teams, each consisting of a doctor and a nurse. I was on Team One with Fiona, a Nigerian nurse educator who immigrated to the United Kingdom when she was a teenager. We were to concentrate our mentoring efforts on the adult services at the National Hospital and Asokoro District Hospital. Team Two consisted of Oliver, an HIV doctor from Zambia, and Jennette, an African American nurse, and they were to go to the University of Calabar Teaching Hospital in the southwestern part of Nigeria, near Port Harcourt, the oil capital of Nigeria. This was the place we were warned not to go near because of the high incidence of kidnapping. Team Three, Bjorn, a pediatric doctor, and Marie, a pediatric nurse, was to mentor at the pediatric services at the National Hospital, the Federal Medical Centre in Keffi, Asokoro District Hospital, and the University of Abuja Teaching Hospital. In the end, Fiona and Oliver were the only volunteers whom the Nigerian immigration office graced with a six-week stay. With the passports of the U.S. contingent still held in the immigration office for the extension, Fiona and Oliver went to Calabar instead.

Our first week was spent in orientation by the IHVN at Maina Court in Abuja, learning about the different services provided. We met Dr. Patrick Dakum, the head of IHVN, and Dr. Mary Ann Etiebet, Senior Clinical Technical Advisor, who gave an overview of IHVN and the HIV/AIDS status in Nigeria.[2]

In 1999, President Olusegun Obasanjo set up the President's Committee on AIDS and the National Action Committee on AIDS (NACA) for HIV prevention, treatment, and care.[3] In 2008, the HIV prevalence rate in Nigeria was 4.6 percent. By 2009, HIV prevalence rose, and it accounted for around nine percent of the global HIV burden, the second largest incidence of HIV/AIDS in the world with 2.6 million people of the 33.4 million living with HIV/AIDS worldwide. In 2016, Nigeria continued to have the second largest HIV disease burden in the world with 3.2 million, after South Africa which had 6.8 million though prevalence had been stable at 3.4 percent.[4] Of the HIV-infected persons, 55 percent were women, and there were around 56,000 new antenatal infections per year. Of those infected, 750,000 adults and 103,000 children were eligible for treatment; only 35 percent were on ARVs. Despite being the largest oil producer in the world, Nigeria ranked 159 out of 177 on the United Nations Development Program (UNDP) Human Poverty Index. This poor Human Poverty Index, along with the rising HIV prevalence, meant that Nigeria faced huge challenges in fighting the HIV and AIDS epidemic. The Nigerian government contributed only around five percent of the funds for the antiretroviral treatment program; much of the funding came from PEPFAR and the World Bank.[5]

In 2004, IHVN began a collaboration with the University of Maryland with funding from PEPFAR. Along with the NACA and AIDS Care and Treatment in Nigeria (ACTION), an estimated 139 care and treatment sites and 42 community sites were established.[6] Other members of IHVN gave a brief overview of pediatric care, HIV/TB, PMTCT, community-based care and support, adherence support, laboratory, HIV testing and counseling, pharmacy services, documentation practices, quality of care initiatives, and training activities.

We toured the various places where we would be mentoring, with the exception of Calabar, which would require flying to the southwestern part of Nigeria. The pediatric and adult HIV/AIDS clinical areas of the Federal Medical Centre at Keffi were quite crowded, and the waiting room was filled with patients both young and old. The National Hospital of Abuja was quite impressive as regards open space, lighting, ventilation, and cleanliness, unlike most of the hospitals I have seen in Africa.

Since its inception roughly six years ago, the adult HIV/AIDS special treatment center has been housed in what looked like a temporary mobile unit at the periphery of the hospital; it quickly outgrew its capacity for the immense number of patients it served. The congested place with its dimly lit interior had an overall impression of age and decay; some of the fixtures were defunct, and the roof leaked. The patients in the waiting area, however, seemed to be accepting of such crowded conditions, a tribute to their patience and forbearance. Ventilation was not particularly good, and there was no separate area for patients who were coughing and potentially might be infected with TB. The space issue extended to all areas of patient care: waiting room, triaging area, adherence counseling room, pharmacy, consulting rooms, and the medical record room. At least five counselors occupied the crowded adherence/counseling room, and in their busiest time, they might be counseling five patients simultaneously, while trying to overcome the awful din. In such a small room, it would be highly improbable that the patients would be forthcoming with some of their answers regarding safe sexual behavior, social issues, and adherence, not to mention the difficulty of paying attention with so many people talking at the same time. There was absolutely no privacy, and confidentiality was out of the question. In the pharmacy, there were three to four people dispensing medications, wading through numerous empty bottles strewn about the floor, a scene of chaos and mayhem.

There were four consulting rooms; two clinicians shared a room, rendering it rather useless as regards confidentiality for history taking and examination. Every inch of the surfaces of the rooms was cluttered with furniture, notes, buckets, and computers waiting to be hooked up. Most of the sinks had long stopped working.

Patients arrived at the clinic around six in the morning, and it opened between seven and seven-thirty. They were seen in order of arrival. At eight, a staff member provided an education session that lasted for two hours, along with prayers and singing. Topics covered included medication adherence, transmission, and home-based care. One patient wanted to

The adult HIV/AIDS special treatment center of the National Hospital of Abuja, Nigeria.

know how to take his medications during the fasting month of Ramadan. Another morning a hat was passed around for donations for the funeral of a fellow patient; many had so little, and yet they were generous in their giving. The doctors did not start clinic until around ten after rounding in the hospital or attending conferences. A visit to the HIV clinic in Africa for a patient was a whole day affair; waiting was the rule: to be seen, to get counseling, laboratory or diagnostic testing, and to collect medications. I marveled at their patience. In all my stay in Africa, only once did I encounter a patient who vented his frustration. This patient had spent some time in Ireland and received his HIV care there. When he was finally ushered in to see us, he was utterly beside himself with the waiting that he had been through so far.

At Asokoro District Hospital, space was even more acute. There were two adult HIV/AIDS clinics: one in the hospital, and a second one in an apartment building right outside the hospital. The hospital clinic had three consulting rooms; two doctors shared two of the three consulting rooms, but the only room that had an exam table was in the consulting room for the chief. All the rooms were cluttered with papers, and there were no sinks for handwashing. The small, dark medical record room was filled to capacity, from floor to ceiling; many of the files spilled out into the hallway and onto the floor despite big letters that said "CONFIDENTIAL" on the front covers. VCT and adherence counseling was conducted nearby. Patients were then sent to the hospital laboratory and pharmacy where there was more waiting.

The second HIV clinic was less congested as it sat farther from the main thoroughfare. The waiting and triage areas were in the lobby, and the patients spilled onto the front lawn. This clinic had three consultation rooms; two healthcare personnel shared a room with an examination table rigged with a mobile screen for privacy.

The University of Abuja Teaching Hospital was in Gwagwalada, an hour away; here only the pediatric team would mentor. The waiting area was in a wide-open, well-ventilated space. The clinic space for the nurses and counselors was tiny and in open cubicles, affording little privacy. The pediatric ward was virtually empty because of the recent doctors' strike.

The medical house staff in the HIV clinic spent one to two weeks of classroom training at the Institute of Virology, followed by several weeks of shadowing with a senior doctor before they began to see patients on their own. The Nigerian government required all university graduates to spend a year as a member of the youth service corps, "Corpers" they called themselves. Dr. Garba, my mentee, was spending an entire year of her youth service on the care of HIV patients. Because of the sheer number of patients to be seen in a day, she could not perform physical examinations for all of them. The exception was if they were new patients or old patients with specific problems. However, she spent so much time having a patient describe her itchy rash in the genital area, it would have been more expedient to have one quick look. Similarly, examining the mouth looking for thrush, the telltale sign of deficient immunity, only took seconds, but most African doctors seemed averse to doing such simple tasks. Dr. Anga, a family practice consultant, saw a patient with Kaposi lesions on the arms and legs for two months but did not convey such complaints to Dr. Garba, who saw him a couple of weeks later. The patient complained to Dr. Anga about his hoarseness, and upon examination, the doctor discovered he had a Kaposi lesion in his palate and a few in the conjunctivae. The take-home lesson was a quick look into the mouth and an overview of the skin seemed to be useful, even if one was pressed for time.

Piles of papers covered all the exam tables in the clinic, a telltale sign that no one had

Patients waiting outside an apartment building that housed the adult HIV/AIDS Clinic of Asokoro District Hospital in Abuja, Nigeria.

used them for the right purpose in a long time. A fifty-two-year-old HIV positive woman who had been attending the clinic for the last two years complained that each time she told her doctor about feeling "something coming out of her private area," she was told that with time, her ARVs would take care of her problem. No one had once done a genital exam. One day while waiting to see her doctor, a research assistant recruited her for a research study on "Screening for Cervical Cancer" and she was finally examined; her vagina was lying in between her thighs; she had a vaginal prolapse. She looked over to me and said, "When I left home this morning, I prayed that I would meet with the right doctor. Now I can go home and thank God." It had taken two years for this woman to have her diagnosis.

In the wards, many of the patients were HIV positive, and some had active TB. There was no isolation ward for TB patients, and patients with active disease were in the same ward as non–TB patients. No one bothered to wear masks!

In my short tenure here, I saw a number of patients with wasting diseases mainly due to co-infection with TB; that seemed to be the biggest problem. Others presented with opportunistic infections besetting HIV patients with very poor immune systems such as toxoplasma encephalitis, cytomegalovirus retinitis, Kaposi sarcoma, esophageal candidiasis, pruritic papular skin eruption, and chronic diarrhea, reminiscent of the AIDS era in the late eighties in the United States.

In 2018, data for Nigeria's progress toward 90–90–90 targets of ending HIV/AIDS in 2030 showed that only 43 percent of people living with HIV knew their status, 87 percent were on HIV treatment, but there were no data on what percent was suppressed.[7] Despite advances in the scaling-up of HIV clinics in the country, Nigeria was still burdened with similar problems encountered in other African countries. There were cultural issues in Nigeria that served as barriers to achieving the 90–90–90 targets, such as the practice of female genital mutilation, denial of women's access to inheritance, widowhood rites, encouragement of multiple sexual partners for males, and marriage of young girls to much older men. The practice of polygamy in some communities fanned the spread of HIV.[8] Women overwhelmingly attended the clinics; most husbands refused to be tested. Stigma remained a major issue. Often husbands left their wives to marry a younger woman, thus potentially continuing to be the spreader of HIV if they were HIV positive. A few years later, they would have become so debilitated that they showed up in the clinic with end-stage infection. In the clinic, we encountered instances of non-disclosure to the respective partners resulting in tragic instances of discontinuation of antiretroviral therapy for fear their spouses would find out. This inevitably led to the advancement of HIV infection and transmission of infection to the unsuspecting partners. Legal barriers of discrimination against people living with HIV and with different sexual orientation and same-sex relations in Nigeria exist. LGBT people could be punished with 14 years of imprisonment.[9]

The scaling up of programs quickly outgrows the clinical space and overwhelms the manpower to care for these patients. There is a lack of sites that deliver HIV services including testing sites, PMTCT sites, and treatment. The shortage of trained healthcare providers in Nigeria, especially at the state and community levels, remains a huge obstacle to the country in meeting its scale-up targets. Making treatment of HIV accessible to the rural areas continues to plague advances in HIV treatment.[10]

Our guesthouse was in "embassy row"; just a few steps from us were the embassies of Mexico, Portugal, and Indonesia. Most of the private homes procured the help of gun-toting security guards in front of the gate and fences were topped with barbed wire and broken glass. Before our arrival we received reams of instructions warning us not to go out in the streets alone; the security guards were to accompany us. On my first morning run, I asked the security guard whether it was safe to run around the neighborhood; he answered in the affirmative. For the duration of my stay, I ran without incidence. Some mornings I encountered groups of Nigerian men in loud animated discussion, but I gave them a wide berth. In the evenings, many Muslims performed a ritualistic ablution by the sidewalks, rolled out their prayer rugs, and prayed. It was Ramadan.

Noisy weaverbirds made their nests on the row of palm trees right across from us, weaving the palm leaves into nests and slowing robbing the trees of their photosynthetic ability. They were extremely shrill early in the morning and at dusk. Threatening afternoon thunderstorms and early morning rain seemed to be the rule at this time of the year. In a short period, the torrential rain flooded the roads and rivulets formed; momentarily the temperature cooled off. Invariably during the rainstorms, the electricity was cut off, although it did go out at some other unexplained periods. The generator situated right outside my back window kicked in, creating such loud noises that sleep was hard to attain. Under the National Electric Power Authority (NEPA), power outages had been the standard for the Nigerian populace like many of the African nations where I had been.

Earlier on in our assignment, we went to visit our friends in Calabar. The risk of the kidnapping of foreigners for ransom out in the southeastern part of Nigeria was foremost in our minds, and lately, even Nigerians were not immune, especially the well-to-do. Here we were, four Americans making our way to Calabar; we were easy targets. We left at different times for the airport. Sunday, my driver, drove me by the iconic "Welcome to Nigeria" Arch on my way to the airport. I attempted to take a picture of it but was not able to. Despite my protestations, Sunday pulled over to one side and got out to take a better picture. A man in civilian clothes shot out of nowhere and yelled at him. In a flash, a soldier with an AK-47 hanging from his shoulder appeared at my window. Banging on it, he barked in a stentorian voice, "Give me the camera and get out!" Sunday gripped the steering wheel and swallowed hard. The soldier ordered him to drive across the road through a stream of rushing, oncoming cars to a grassy knoll where a small office sat. Off to the side of the office was a tin shed, and through its dim light I could make out four soldiers sitting or lying on an old, dirty mattress playing cards.

The gun-toting soldier asked for our identification cards. I handed my driver's license rather than my U.S. passport, in case he treated me more harshly when he found out I was from the U.S. He also confiscated Sunday's car keys and ordered me to sit down. There was a plastic chair and a bench made from a plank placed on some iron frame. I made space for Sunday on the bench, but he remained standing. With my camera in his hands, the plainclothes man asked me why I took the picture of the arch and what I intended to do with it. I did not see what all the fuss was about as the welcoming arch of Abuja was in the public domain available on the internet. I asked him to delete it from my camera and send us on our way. He did not reply but took down our names and asked Sunday for the name and phone number of his boss.

While we were being rudely interrogated, the same soldier with the AK-47 shouted at another driver who strayed to the side of the road to pull into the lot. A well-dressed man emerged from the car. Then my interrogator deliberately stood in front of me, cutting my view of the man. Later the man drove away. When Sunday and I were alone, he whispered in my ear that the driver had quietly bribed the soldier.

The plainclothes man asked Sunday to call his boss, but he told him he had no time left on his cell phone. I offered my cell phone, but Sunday shook his head. The man insisted that he could not let us go until Sunday's boss came. He made the call, and when I asked when Sunday's boss was coming, he replied, "Soon." This did not reassure me as I had a plane to catch in two hours. Turning to me, he asked me whether I had money; he could put me in a taxi as his problem was with Sunday. I objected to him keeping Sunday, and Sunday in turn did not want me to leave in a taxi. Finally, I called William, the man in charge of transport at the Institute of Virology; he promised to dispatch another driver to take me to the airport. The soldier toting the AK-47 read loudly and haltingly the writing at the back of Sunday's T-shirt—"To Serve the People of Nigeria"—which was more than he was doing now.

Sunday finally sat down beside me and whispered, "They want money."

"A lot of money?" I asked.

"I would not give them any. I work for the government."

"Don't they too?" I thought to myself.

William and another man named Frederick arrived with Alfred, the older driver. From a distance, I noticed that the plainclothes man was talking less aggressively with William and Frederick. We could not hear what they were discussing. Walking over to me, the plainclothes man asked me to erase the picture of the arch from my camera. Then William asked Alfred to take me to the airport. Later I called Sunday and learned that Frederick gave the man 500 nairas, about 3 USD, a pittance for such a show of force and aggression, and a waste of so many people's time. Corruption still abounded and was alive and well in Nigeria.

My fellow volunteers had already arrived at the airport; the plane to Calabar was delayed by three hours. So much for trying to reach the airport on time. It must be the Nigerian way as there was no announcement or explanation for the delay. Periodically one of us walked to the reception to ask when the plane was leaving, only to be told it would be SOON. When we finally were on board, we waited in the plane on the tarmac for another hour. This time we had an explanation; President Goodluck Jonathan was landing in the Calabar Airport.

The next day was Saturday, and it turned out to be the day for a local election in Calabar. Many roads were closed, and only official cars or taxis in the outlying areas were allowed on them. On my morning run, I saw a man taking a bath by soaping himself in a pool of water that had collected in a blocked drain.

After breakfast, we walked to a Drill Ranch run by an American couple—a conservatory for rescued animals, mainly primates, which lived in a big cage. There were other animals: bushbucks, crocodiles, and parrots. A nyala kept as a pet walked freely and followed us around, occasionally attempting to nibble at my heels or butting my legs with its tiny horns. Later we took a taxi to the National and Slave Museums, paid the entrance fee, and waited for the museum operator to show up, but no one did. Evidently, everything was closed for the election.

After losing an entire day which we were supposed to spend at the Obudu Ranch, we woke up around four in the morning and rented a van leaving the hotel at five-thirty. All too soon we ran into a roadblock. A soldier toting an AK-47 approached our van menacingly and peered inside. It was still dark. To our relief, he waved us on.

As it got lighter, more pedestrians and vehicles appeared on the road. The condition of the road was surprisingly good until we reached the outskirts; there it became riddled with potholes and ruts. At the second roadblock, a soldier peered into the van and shouted, "They're free." And let us go. Our driver told us he was looking for kidnapped victims. We went through at least a dozen such roadblocks made from bundles of wood, branches, tires, and sandbags and manned by soldiers and police; our van had to weave its way through the obstacles.

Entrepreneurial children and boys filled the big potholes in the roads with branches and sand, and when we slowed down, they asked for money. There were so many of them it was impossible for us to compensate them all. The boys threw stones at us when we passed without paying our "tolls." The towns looked like any other African towns: stalls with local goods for sales; ugly dilapidated shops selling clothes, car parts, and shoes; farmers' markets with goats, sheep, and chickens roaming about. Women had on wrappers of various designs and colors, expertly balancing buckets of their wares on their heads; some had babies on their backs, heading for the markets.

The drive that was to take five to six hours took nine hours before we arrived at the entrance of the Obudu Cattle Ranch and Mountain Resort. It was already three in the afternoon. A car arrived at the same time with its trunk open where a big bull was squeezed tightly, apparently heading for the top of the plateau. From the cable car, the mountains were shrouded in dense fog, green, quiet, and peaceful. The serpentine road coiled its way up with twenty hairpin turns. At the top of the Obudu Plateau was the mountain resort; the mist rolled in and the grazing cattle loomed in and out of view. The Obudu Mountain Run or OMR, an 11 K mountain race started in 2005, began at the entrance and ended at the top. An Australian won the first race, but after that, the Ethiopians took the lead. There were cash prizes for the race: 50,000 USD for the runner who came in first place.

After checking in, we went to a "facility tour"; a nature walk that was hard to appreciate considering the dense fog that just came into the plateau, a canopy walk, the conference center, and the presidential suite where the president and foreign dignitaries stayed. In the dairy farm, we met Donald the Bull, only five years old but already weighing 1900kg. The rain started to fall. We had some yogurt, remembering that we had not eaten all day since a scone and an egg roll early in the morning.

Dinner was delicious, though a little pricy for our volunteers' pockets. A heavy mist rolled in and through our headlamps, we could hardly find our way back to the lodge. There were spare beds in our spacious lodge, and we tried to persuade our driver to sleep there. He was insistent on sleeping in the van, so Oliver threw him a blanket. Cognizant of the fact that we had to leave at five in the morning for the seven-hour drive back to the Calabar Airport, we settled in; we had actually spent less than fourteen hours at the ranch. The next day at the airport, Arik Airline was delayed yet again.

None of the other volunteers were interested in going to Lagos, a city notorious for chaos and crimes. Armed with the Lonely Planet West Africa guidebook, I planned my trip. Fortunately, Dr. Mendes suggested that I got in touch with Peace, who could arrange for me to stay in the IDI guesthouse. After work on Friday, my plan was still in flux. Alfred took me to the Sheraton Hotel to change some money to purchase my ticket and gave me the name of his friend who worked at the Lagos airport to arrange for ground transport when I arrived.

On the way to the airport, we ran into a horrendous traffic jam. Simeon expressed his frustration with the liberal use of expletives, very unlike his quiet personality. Oftentimes he drove like the bus drivers in Nigeria, careening down the red-earth shoulders overtaking numerous vehicles. We finally weaved our way to the domestic entrance only to be caught behind a hesitant driver who stopped abruptly right in front of us twice. Finally, Simeon passed him, whereupon he overtook us and stopped in front of us, opening his car door and charging towards Simeon. He turned out to be a soldier strutting about in his uniform, wielding his authority, and asking Simeon in a loud and angry voice why he overtook him. Simeon told him he had to swerve around him since he stopped so abruptly, but he would not take that as an answer and yelled, "Get out!"

Simeon did not get out but said he was sorry. I interjected and asked him politely to kindly let us go since I had a plane to catch. To my surprise, he relented and walked away. I had fifteen minutes until departure time when Simeon pulled into the parking lot.

There was a mob in front of the IRIS Airline check-in counter. I approached an airport official and told him my dilemma. He took me to the desk just right behind a tall Swede who happened to be going to Lagos. The kind Swede took my ticket along with his and waved them in front of the ticket person at the check-in. We got our boarding passes, checked through security, and had time to visit the bathroom before heading out on the tarmac to board the plane.

Peace finally texted me the number of the driver who would pick me up at the Lagos airport. I spent an hour fending off numerous taxi drivers at the arrival hall before my IHVN driver arrived, accompanied by another man. Even when they approached me, I could not tell whether they were official, as they came in an old taxi not an IHVN van. The man who greeted me at the arrival hall said he would come with me, but after about one hundred yards, he quickly got out and told me the driver knew how to get me to the guesthouse in Ikeja. At Ikeja the security guards did not have any instructions to let me in, and I did not have an IHVN ID. After a few phone calls, we finally drove down a long driveway to a two-story guesthouse with a colonial façade. At the door, Sonbu, dressed in a bright yellow eyelet traditional dress, greeted me. She spoke and moved with grace and promptly showed me my room, clean and well lit. She told me she was there to do anything I wanted, so I asked her to get me some jolloff rice, fish, a salad, and a Fanta. I was hungry after my travels.

Early the next morning, the sky opened up, and the rain poured. Sonbu and her boyfriend, Dermi, joined me in a hired taxi for 12,000 nairas for a day jaunt to Lagos. Crossing the long bridge onto Lagos Island, houses on stilts in the canals appeared through sheets of rain.

One would never mistake the National Museum for a building of national stature with its modest and unassuming yellow ochre façade with green trimmings. Thin metal statues adorned its front. The ticket office was not manned; we paid our entrance fees to a woman who was found wandering about, and she switched the light on in the museum for us. We were the only visitors. The museum was divided into three sections: religious life, political dealings, and military power and might. The three main tribes, Yoruba, Igbo, and Hausa, were heavily represented. The dusty artifacts were not dated; the labels were brown and curled at the edges, tired and worn. Under the Benin brass artifacts, a bold caption stated that the British looted a large portion of the Benin brass, and they are now on display in the British Museum.

At the back of the museum, in a little hut-like building was housed the infamous bullet-riddled Mercedes Benz in which Murtala Muhammad, the military ruler of Nigeria from 1975–1976, was assassinated. Around the walls were depicted the rules of the pre-colonial, colonial, and post-colonial eras. The post-colonial era was filled with coups and military rules with such names as Abasangio, Sani Abache, Babandinga ... and finally the current president, Goodluck Elele Jonathan.

The rain continued to pour as we drove over a bridge spanning a lagoon to Victoria Island with its many posh hotels. We strolled along the empty, wind-swept, sandy Bar Beach where hordes of plastic chairs and tables were strewn around, and trash formed a wavy line on the beach where the waves had pushed it. The enormous waves came crashing to shores, probably with dangerous undertow. Some young touts came asking for a parking fee; the driver waved them away. At Ikoyi Island, he drove us into the residential areas to gawk at the big mansions there.

We backtracked to Lagos Island to the Balogun market. The rain had eased a little. Stores and stalls lined the streets selling a myriad of things: textiles, hats, shoes, blouses, jewelry, cow's stomach, skin, tongue, beef... Wading through mud puddles, Sonbu bought a dress, a blouse, and some towels. Our driver drove by the National Theater, and we visited the somewhat run-down National Stadium which had been replaced by another one in Abuja that was not even used very often. We made our way back to Ikeji, stopping at Sweet Sensations for a late lunch: fried rice and fish. It was a fun-filled day despite the rain.

On Sunday, Sonbu made omelets. I went to Redeemer Church next door for a very rousing evangelical service; most of the men and women wore their traditional clothes with the women wearing fantastic headdresses, perhaps even more majestic than Queen Elizabeth's hats. The women's dresses showed off their curvy figures in the most flattering way. Only in West Africa could men wear shocking pink eyelet outfits and still looked dignified. Sonbu accompanied me to the airport. At the Abuja Airport, Alfred came to fetch me. It was good to see a familiar face and to be back in Abuja.

Back at our clinic, Fiona and I saw a young woman abandoned by her husband when she was found to be infected with HIV. Her ten-month-old-baby had not been tested. The clinic gave her "Action Meal"—a bag of protein-rich food. We heaved the heavy box onto her head and watched her petite, slender frame carrying the weight in her ramrod fashion while piggybacking her baby. After a few steps, she turned around, looked at us, and gave us a big bright smile.

Ramadan was coming to an end. Dr. Gebi was arranging for Marie, Fiona, and me to go to Kano in the northern part of Nigeria to celebrate Eid al-Fitr, marking the end of Ramadan. He had obtained tickets for us to attend the Durbar at the Emir's Palace, and he sat down with us to discuss cultural issues as Kano is heavily Islamic. Alfred took us to the airport; he would be going home to Bauchi, and this would be the last time we would see him as we would have finished our volunteering by the time he came back. He had been a solid rock for us, someone we felt safe with while traveling in Nigeria.

At the airport, Fiona gave our tickets to an Arik Air attendant whom she had befriended on her frequent trips to Calabar to get our boarding passes. While waiting Fiona received a call from Dr. Jemini from Kano, wanting to know whether we had obtained "clearance" from Dr. Mensah, the head of the IHVN, to travel. Fiona took it upon herself to call Dr. Mensah, and he advised against traveling to the north. After the conversation, she miraculously obtained a refund for our tickets, without asking us whether we still wanted to proceed with our travel. She thrust 30,000 nairas into my hand, telling us the travel to Kano

was off. Marie was visibly relieved. For days she had been worried about the reactions of the Muslims to the threats to burn the Koran by Pastor Jerry Jones in Gainsborough, Florida, on September 11. She feared retaliation on Americans, pointing to her blond hair, blue eyes, and fair skin. She had said that if she were asked where she was from, she would say Canada.

Fiona called for Alfred to come and fetch us back to the guesthouse. I was very disappointed, having looked forward to the Durbar and to visiting Kano. Then I made a firm decision to go to Kano alone and called Dr. Jemini in Kano to tell him I was still coming. To my surprise, he did not object and thought that nothing would happen. He would arrange for a driver to fetch me at the airport in Kano.

A young mother carrying a box of "Action Meal," protein-rich food provided by the HIV/AIDS treatment center, on top of her head while piggybacking her baby; her husband abandoned her after she tested positive for HIV.

With my decision made, I traipsed over the Arik ticket counter to re-purchase my ticket, only to be told that all tickets to Kano had been sold, including those just turned in by us; this was a big holiday for many Muslims to go home to be with their families. I inquired about a later flight but was told to wait. My mouth was getting dry. The man at the counter took some time to book my flight after I filled out some forms. I finally bought a ticket for the same flight, but it was another five and a half hours before our plane took off. I often marveled at the patience displayed by the Africans. This time, however, while waiting on the tarmac, a tall well-dressed Nigerian man berated the poor Arik attendant about the long delay and that Arik had no regard for the customers' time. It was Eid al-Fitr, and he wanted to be home to spend more time with his family; he asked if Arik would compensate him for the loss of his time. The plane had come from Sokoto, and the pilot who flew it to Abuja was supposed to be off, but he now had to fly us to Kano. Just before take-off, he made an announcement about our impending, exciting journey because of a thunderstorm, but he would do his best to avoid the rough patches to give us a safe trip.

Bulus waited at the Kano Airport for hours for me. I had called him just before take-off to tell him I was finally leaving the airport in Abuja. To his credit, he remained cheerful and welcomed me to Kano with a big smile. He was surprised to see me alone and quickly reassured me that Kano was safe. On our way to the hotel, a car and a truck were stuck on Murtala Muhammad Road, which was in such disrepair that the tarmac had disappeared, giving way to deep sticky mud. Most cars and *okadas* used the other lane, which still had some remnants of tarmac, but they were all traveling in the wrong direction. It was close to eleven o'clock when I arrived at the Tahir Guest Palace.

I had a peaceful night, but the next day Mary Ann from IHVN called from Abuja. She asked me with a great deal of concern whether I knew there was a travel advisory to northern Nigeria and urged me to leave at any inkling of trouble. Unbeknownst to me, there had been an incident in Bauchi the day before I left Abuja. Gunmen suspected to be from Boko Haram, a terrorist group that opposes non–Islamic education in Nigeria, attacked a prison, releasing hundreds of prisoners who were awaiting trial for sectarian violence.[11]

Bulus and Awwal came to take me around Kano. We first visited the 250-year-old Gidan Dan Hausa or "The Son of the Hausa Residence," which trumpeted the beauty of Kano's mud-walled architecture. The original owner was a local chief who managed the Emir's farmland, and later it became home to Hanns Vischer in 1908, the first British Director of Education of Northern Nigeria.[12] Vischer ran a school and taught English to all the young princes of the Kano Emirate. He was given the traditional title Dan Hausa, or the "Son of Hausa." Thus Kano became the birthplace of western education in northern Nigeria.

The gate, festooned with blooming bougainvillea, led us into what was once a very grandiose garden, sadly overgrown with weeds; four symmetrical sets of stone benches built into the side of the main path remained. The Hausa was a dark brown, fortress-like structure with pointed, pale brown pillars adorned with curlicue designs along the walls. Around the house and scattered about in the garden were huge clay pots and iron cauldrons planted with flowering bushes; Awwal said the containers were about fifty years old.

The hall took us into a living room decorated with distinctive black and red curlicues, and some artifacts on display included a horse decorated with the paraphernalia for the celebration of the Durbar. A stone staircase led to a flush toilet, then Vischer's bedroom, but it was locked and the absent keeper had the key. The house with its flat roof was refreshingly cool in the heat of mid-afternoon.

We headed into the old city, passing through one of the several gates of the city wall. The tarmac road filled with fume-generating noisy *okadas* soon gave way to small dirt roads lined with mud-brick houses and children playing barefoot. At the foot of the red-stoned Dala Hill, broken steps, apparently 999 of them, led to the top, and children playing around the foothills came scrambling up with us where we were rewarded with a panoramic view of Kano. The tin, flat roofs of the old city lay below us, and the green domes of mosques were far away.

We plunged back into the heavy traffic and passed by the Emir's Palace, whose walls were also the same dark brown as Vischer's house. Horses cantered along the walls ahead of the Durbar.

Our next stop was the Kofar Mata Dye Pit, where indigo cloth had been dyed for hundreds of years, or so Bulus informed me. There were numerous pits; some were in active use, while others were filled with dirt or garbage and had not been used for a long time. Awwal said the pits belong to specific families, and only those families could use them. Each narrow pit was six meters deep. It was first filled with 100kg of indigo which was left to sit in the pit for three days. Then thirty buckets of ash were mixed in and again left for three days. The last ingredient was five buckets of potassium, and after stirring, left to sit for three more days. The final concoction was ready after fifteen days of sitting and was used for a whole year. The color depended on how long the cloth was left in the pit; the longer it was left, the darker it would be. An old man draped in a loincloth bent over and dipped a tied beige cloth into a pit to dye. Then all at once, I was besieged by a group of men who whipped out several swatches of indigo cloth showing different patterns: stars, moon, sun, sunshine, Hausa. The most spectacular of all was the Emir and his people: a swirling circular pattern of small circles spinning off from a central pattern which represented the Emir. I picked sunshine for Fiona, Emir and his people for Marie, and a smaller piece which showed the sun and moon for my son, Charles, who was a Peace Corps volunteer in Sierra Leone at that time.

We drove out of the gate of the old city and caught a glimpse of the pavilion in front of the palace parade ground where the Durbar would be held on Saturday. The Gidan Makama Museum, which used to be the old palace, was across from the new palace. Its front resembled that of the Hanns House, typical of the Hausa architecture. I was rather disappointed when Awwal said it was too late to pay it a visit.

The next day was the beginning of Salat al-Eid celebration; many Nigerians had already attended mosque and were on their way home. Men, boys, and girls filled the streets, resplendent in their colorful national garbs—white, powder blue, citron, pink, peach—all walking hurriedly. There was a conspicuous absence of women. A few fortunate Nigerians rode in cars, and an entire family of six crammed onto the seat of a motorcycle taxi called an *okada*: an adult driver, two little ones in front straddling the gas tank, and three older kids on the back in their shinny outfits with their legs dangling. A group of young boys in long flowing robes over long trousers, spotting sunglasses and felt hats in this hot sweltering climate, posed for my camera. One of them had his colorful prayer rug casually draped over his shoulder. The young girls, attractively dressed in satiny blouses over long, sarong-like skirts, their heads covered with colorful, lacy shawls, were adorned with gold and silver necklaces, bangles, rings, and earrings. A green Arabic sign along the road with an English translation read, "There is no diety worthy of worship except Allah." Deity was misspelled as diety.

September 11th happened to be the day of the Durbar. I got up early, intending to go to the museum. The hotel proprietor suggested that I should get a taxi; the driver wanted 5000 nairas or 32 USD for a two to three-hour hire. I had bargained it down to 3000 nairas when one of the storekeepers at the gate informed me that he could get me an *okada* for a few hundred naira. I waited and waited, but none appeared. In the end, I decide to walk, using a bad copy of a map of Kano from *Lonely Planet of West Africa* as my guide. I got lost once but was able to find my way back to the right track to the dusty old town. There was a pregnant excitement in the air; people were dressed up, horses with beautifully decorated saddles were fed generously, and a few trumpeters and drummers marched by.

After passing through the gate of the old city, I got tired of dodging traffic and walking on uneven, broken, or non-existent sidewalks. Very few people spoke English; a kind woman tried to get me an *okada,* but when the owner asked for a high fare, she impatiently waved him away. I kept on walking while keeping an eye out for *okada* drivers to flag. By the time a second driver came along, I had spotted the museum a hundred meters away. As I looked, I realized that the Emir's Palace was indeed right across from it.

The reception area was the oldest part of the museum and had survived for over six hundred years. The original iron gate of the old city was on display there. The museum depicted the colonial era, the period of independence with its succession of Emirs, and a whole section devoted to Islam. It was quarter to one, and I had to be back at the hotel by two to meet up with Bulus for the Durbar. I tried to board a bus to Alu Avenue, only to be told that the bus did not go there and was advised to take an *okada.* I had promised myself not to venture onto one because of the potential danger of accidents, but I had not much choice given the time constraint. I pressed the young driver to drive carefully. At a roundabout while we stopped for the traffic to pass, an old man riding on an *okada* next to me gestured to me and spoke animatedly in Hausa. Somehow, I immediately understood him to mean that I should not put my arms around my driver's waist; rather he reached behind himself to show me where I should place my hands. I did in fact find a rack behind me to hold, and he showed his approval with a big smile as we pulled into the roundabout traffic. I had to close my eyes several times, as we had a few narrow escapes. My driver and I posed for a shot on his *okada,* a shot that I would keep as a souvenir.

Bulus arrived in his sea-green *agbada* topped with a *fila,* his robe and cap; Myima and her niece were given Marie and Fiona's tickets. They wore black head coverings with black *abaya* modestly covering their beautifully embroidered dresses, which peeked between the folds of the *abaya.* I had on my Nigerian dress a tailor had made for me in Abuja; it was so tight that I had to hike it way up to scale the high steps of the van.

The police opened the palace gate after Bulus showed them the invitation letter. We drove along the path leading towards another gate. Once through the second gate, Myima led the way to the staircase leading to the pavilion filled with many expats while Bulus went to park. We hurried up and squeezed into the third row; unfortunately, there was not enough space for Bulus, who ended sitting quite far from us.

Far away on the road outside the fence of the palace, horseback riders mingled with *okada* riders. A commotion in the crowd announced the arrival of the governor of Kano.

Around four-thirty in the afternoon, a procession of horseback riders began to stream into the parade grounds. Riders and horses alike were dressed in opulence; along with them drummers, longhorn blowers, warriors wielding spears and other weapons, marched in. Each province with its unique regalia was represented. Spectators lined the fence of the palace; some brave ones perched dangerously on the top of lamp posts while others sat on the top of billboards and high walls with legs dangling. The Emir's children and grandchildren, wearing white headdresses, rode smartly and regally, some carrying long staffs while others donned dark glasses. The littlest ones had headdresses with what looked to me to be two pointy bunny ears. The Emir followed behind his entourage, dressed in white with

During the Durbar at the end of Ramadan, horsemen from different provinces with their distinctive regalia marched in front of the Emir at his palace parade ground, Kano, Nigeria.

green trimming and a helmet-like, silver hat trimmed in gold. In his right hand, he held a short scepter. He was shielded from the sun with a huge umbrella trimmed with red fringes; white gauze veiled his face. Surrounded by courtiers dressed in green and bright red headdresses, he sat in one corner of the parade grounds while various horsemen paid homage to him by galloping from a far corner and stopping short in front of him, showing off their horsemanship.

All of a sudden and without warning, Myima hustled us out of the pavilion and down the stairs, timing our exit with the appearance of the Emir as he exited the palace grounds through the gate. Then it was a mad scramble to our van as we weaved our way through the sea of people to the palace gate down the long drive to the main gate. It was pandemonium with the police directing traffic. The fumes were intense. Bulus took several detours before arriving at the Tahir Guest Hotel. In the evening, I wandered outside the hotel and bought myself some *suya* wrapped in a newspaper for my dinner.

On Sunday, I walked into a village to go to church. Huge piles of garbage covered the sides of a large deep pond with a few goats picking away. The pond was actually created when the red earth was dug and used for bricks for some construction elsewhere. Children sat outside their homes: rows of houses of mud blocks partially covered with stucco lined the winding dirt roads. At the church, congregants walked in and out constantly. I did not stay long as I could not understand the service.

Bulus took me to the Kurmi Market, largely closed because of the festival. Muhammad Rumfa (1463–99), the greatest of Kano's Hausa kings, established this market.[13] For centuries, camel caravans brought traders from all over West Africa using the Trans-Sahara trade route to trade, including the sale of slaves. Slavery existed even before the Europeans arrived. The building where slaves were traded still stood. Nowadays, merchants sold beads, traditional clothes, leather goods, and what appeared to be rocks, which Bulus said were used by the villagers to soften meat and for medicinal purposes.

In the afternoon, I ventured to the Emir's Palace on my own. Bulus had said that women were allowed to wander in the palace grounds with no questions asked. A handsome and regal horseman was resplendent in his outfit of gold, orange, and blue stripes with ropes made of the same color scheme. He was wearing a black turban with white embroidery and had a white sash wrapped around his waist with dangling tassels of gold, brown, and green. He rode a horse decked in gold regalia and tassels with hardly any space for its eyes to peer through. This nameless horseman proudly posed for me, holding his staff in one hand and smiling. Along the palace wall were tattered horses stripped of their regalia, waiting forlornly for their food. Outside the back palace gate gathered groups of boys who were not allowed into the palace grounds, while hordes of women and girls squeezed past them. One young woman took my hand and led me through the crowd by the gate into the relative calm of the palace grounds. The walls were dark brown with geometric figures carved into their surfaces. A sign on the wall commemorated the Emir Ado Bayero's forty years on the throne, 13th of October 1963 to 13th October 2003. Carpets covered the cool tiles of the rooms where leather cushions were scattered. The women probably hid in the back rooms, as there were no signs of anyone around. I walked the length of the palace grounds and ended up at the front gate where the viewing pavilion was.

In the afternoon, Bulus took me to the airport to fly back to Abuja. As always Arik Air was behind schedule; mysteriously the passengers seemed to know when the flight to Abuja was ready, even though I did not hear any announcement and almost missed my flight. Marie and Fiona loved their indigo fabric. They spent their four-day weekend lying next to the swimming pool of the Hilton Hotel. Abuja was deserted for the end of Ramadan.

We all went to Blake's for a fish dinner for our last night in Abuja. A few days after my departure from Nigeria, while the people celebrated the 50th Anniversary of the Independence of Nigeria, a bomb blast in Abuja left eight people dead and three injured.[14] A few months later another bomb attack, in Abacha barracks in the capital, left at least four people dead and many critically injured.[15] We were indeed fortunate to be volunteering in a tenuous period of relative calm.

6

Malawi

2013, My First Mission with Médecins Sans Frontières

"Every minute of every day, a child under 15 is infected with HIV—the over-whelming majority of children under 15 who are HIV-positive get infected through their mothers at birth. Without treatment, half of these children die before they reach their second birthday.

"I still cannot fathom how difficult it was for the women I met to find out that they were HIV-positive. It is such a courageous undertaking in countries where there is still considerable stigma about the disease. They got tested to ensure that their unborn babies would have a chance of life by being born free of the virus."

—Gabriel Byrne[1]

It was a long journey for my first mission with MSF. It took me a while to arrive in Nsanje, Malawi.

My first inquiry with MSF was right after my tsunami experience in 2005. I went to New York to attend a one-night information session where I learned that MSF required at least a three-month commitment. Since my last child was still in high school, I did not feel the time was right for me. And so my second foray into MSF was in March of 2012 when I finally had my long interview with MSF and was then invited to their three-day information session in New York. Their selection process was quite stringent, and they only invited ten percent of the interviewees to attend. By then the time commitment in the field had length-ened to at least nine months but was most often a year.

In January of 2013 when I finally signaled to MSF that I was available to volunteer, they sent me a number of programs for consideration. The first was Myanmar, which was quickly taken off the table as that was not for a first missioner. This was followed by sev-eral programs in Uzbekistan for HIV/TB but for a period of a year. However, I preferred six months which I was told would not be a likely scenario; the minimum length of the mission was for nine to twelve months. Then quickly in succession came an HIV project in Zimbabwe for a period of a year, an Ethiopian program in kala-azar or leishmaniasis, and a program in South Sudan in general medical care. Even before I could wade through the information that kept on piling up electronically, the Malawian project in HIV/AIDS was presented to me as perhaps the most suitable given my training and mentorship experience in HIV/AIDS in Africa. This was to be for a period of nine months, despite my wish to be there for six.

I was asked to send in my notarized diplomas and a police report and to be ready to leave by mid–April while they applied for my work permit that might take up to two months. In late May, I received permission from the immigration office in Malawi to stay in their country for six months while waiting for a work permit. My departure date, which was slated to be June 1, was further delayed by my illness shortly after returning from South Sudan. I had contracted dengue fever. And so another two months would pass before I left for Malawi. MSF agreed to let me go to Malawi for seven months, closer to my original request of six months. I had to be medically cleared for a second time, this time by my infectious disease doctor, Dr. Cam Ashbaugh.

On July 26, I finally boarded an early train to MSF in Manhattan for my briefing. New York City is not one of my favorite cities, perhaps because I do not know it well despite having run through all five boroughs in the 2009 NYC Marathon. It looks rather imposing and impersonal compared to Boston. That evening, I flew to Lilongwe, Malawi, via Charles de Gaulle and Nairobi. Unfortunately, because of a delayed departure in Charles de Gaulle, I missed my plane for Lilongwe, which meant staying overnight in Nairobi. My luggage did not arrive in Lilongwe, and after two days of waiting for it, Kenya Airway informed me that it had been left in Paris. Perhaps my luggage had rebelled and was strongly hinting that I was meant to be in Paris.

The temperature in Lilongwe, the capital of Malawi, was cool and not at all humid; this was their winter. Malawi, formerly Nyasaland, is nicknamed "the warm heart of Africa," probably because it has been a relatively peaceful place. From the little I saw, it was a big sprawling city. The tarmac road was smooth and not pot-holed, surprisingly for an African country. However, like most African countries, there was a conspicuous absence of sidewalks so that the edges of the tarmac road were slowly being eroded. Soon a two-lane road would become a one-lane one, and opposing traffic would have to dodge each other while traveling on it.

We rose early the next day to drive to Blantyre, named after Dr. Livingstone's birthplace in Scotland, a five-hour journey. It was cold, probably around fifty degrees Fahrenheit. Clusters of men in warm winter jackets huddled over an open fire that they had made from dry leaves and trash. Women were hurrying in the early dawn to the market. In the distance, layers upon layers of mountains were shrouded in a purplish-blue hue with whisks of mist gracing their peaks. Now and then in the vast flat plain rose isolated globs of mountains, as though God was tired of making mountain ranges and just simply dropped earth and rocks on the plain; they appeared out of place. The orange-red sun rose over the mountain ranges, slowly dissipating the mist. Calvin and Hakim, my traveling companions, stopped at the market to haggle over potatoes, onions, okra, and tangerines. Men and women stood in the middle of the road with arms outstretched, holding onto full-grown, live chickens by their legs to passing vehicles, hoping to make a sale. Frequently we were overtaken by minibuses which started here in the 1990s; the locals called them "*mdula moyo*," which meant literally "cut your life" in Chichewa. They sped on the motorway and got involved in fatal accidents resulting in senseless loss of life. One minibus passed by with the slogan "HARD TIMES NEVER KILL" printed on the back.

Baobab trees, my favorite trees in Africa, stood stark naked, looking rather pregnant with their bulbous trunks. This being winter, they had shed all their leaves. At one point between Dedza and Ntoheu, the motorway ran along the border of Mozambique; one could literally step off the vehicle and walk right over to it.

At the MSF office in Limbe, not too far from Blantyre, I had two days of briefings while fighting off jet lag and trying to keep awake. On the bulletin board was a news release: "Somalia: Kidnapped MSF staff released after 644 days." Two MSF volunteers had been

The author arriving at Médecins Sans Frontières office in Limbe, Malawi, to begin her volunteer work in HIV/AIDS in Nsanje.

kidnapped in October 2011, at Dadaab, Kenya, where I went a month later to do medical relief in the drought stricken area by the Kenya/Somalia border. They were just released in July 2013.[2]

Five days after I left New York, I was finally on my way to Nsanje, leaving the cool, almost wintry weather in Blantyre in the highlands for the lowlands. I was freezing without my warm clothes, as my suitcase still had not made its appearance. As we descended into the lowlands, the Shire River, that flowed out of Lake Malombe and Lake Malawi and eventually joined the Zambezi River, could be seen basking in the valley in Nsanje, slithering like a silver snake. Half of the trip to Nsanje was on tarmac road with the rest of the road under construction. This part of the Rift Valley where Nsanje nestled was flat, and the temperature was surprisingly pleasant, at least for now. I had finally arrived.

Nsanje sat on the tip of Malawi at its southernmost region, remote and isolated, and only a few hundred meters above sea level, which explained the hot and humid weather. Its temperature could top forty-five to fifty degrees Centigrade in October and November. Just days before I left, a neighbor suggested that I read *The Lower River* by Paul Theroux.[3] It is a novel about a former Peace Corps volunteer returning to this area hoping to relive his happy times forty years ago, only to be greatly disappointed by the lack of progress and to see the crumbling structures, including the school he helped build. Almost all the people he knew had died and the inhabitants could not care less about education. They were manipulative, almost hostile to him, and were more interested in fleecing him. The hot and uncomfortably humid days blended together, making him listless and helpless, unable to rescue himself from sinking further into a morose state. It was so despairingly dark that I regretted having read it, wondering what I had gotten myself into. In his *Dark Star Safari,* Theroux described Nsanje this way: "Once known as Port Herald, Nsanje was so buggy and malarial it had been Malawi's Siberia for decades, a penal colony for political dissidents. Undesirables were sent to the southern region to rot."[4]

The Shire House where we lived nestled deep in the village, looking plush and incongruous compared to the smaller houses. MSF rented it from the owner who had recently built the house. The spacious house had a screened front porch with rattan chairs to lounge in, a large living room, a dining room, and a kitchen with a spacious pantry. From the screened porch at the back, one could see the mountains in the distance. There were six bedrooms; all had ensuite bathrooms except three, one of which was mine as I was the last one of the team to arrive. We were two doctors, a nurse, a health promoter, a laboratorian, and a logistician. It was an all-woman, international team: Philippines, Belgium, Australia, and the U.S.

The most wonderful thing was the kitten; she had just arrived the week before me from Blantyre, playful and cute, and instantly she made this place feel like a home. She was to catch the mice in the house, but for now she was too little. On my first night in Shire House, she spent the entire night with me, snuggling and occasionally nibbling on my earrings, necklace, and bangle. A few names had been floated around for her: Scruffy, Mimi, and Engine, the latter for her loud purring. I gave her a Chichewa name, Kuyvina, which meant to dance, which she seemed to do a lot of, being quite frisky. Roger, the young black dog, was our security dog, but his situation was appalling. He was cooped up all day and at night, let out but tied to a short leash by the gate with no time to run around and be free.

At the MSF office in Nsanje, I had a few more days of briefings. I was completely overwhelmed and saturated with so much information, new faces, and names. My role here was as an MD mentor in HIV/AIDS for fourteen health facilities, working in conjunction with the Ministry of Health (MOH).

Over the weekend I took a three-hour walk into the town; people were mostly friendly whenever they were greeted: *muli bwanji* (how are you), *ndilibwino* (I am fine), *zikomo kwambiri* (thank you very much). An imposing shell of a church, half-finished, looking almost like a cathedral and too grandiose for Nsanje, stood quietly at the entrance to our village. It had been under construction for roughly twenty years but ran out of funds. Apparently someone had siphoned off a large amount of the funding. Market day was Wednesday, so there were fewer sellers of tomatoes, roasted corn, fried pork… The little shops, however, were open, selling soda, chips, sweets, salt, pepper, sugar, lotions… A bicycle tire repairman set up his shop under a baobab tree.

Along the Shire River, young men congregated on the graveled beach, howling at me to come and take their pictures. A couple of them went to a more secluded area to bathe, soaping their glistening, naked, black bodies, and dipping into the water to wash. This was the Nsanje World Inland Port; three boats, which looked more like pleasure boats than cargo ships, were anchored there. The locals could not help me to understand the nature of the port. Later I learned that the previous president, Bingu wa Mutharika, went ahead and built this inland port in Nsanje despite the Mozambican president's insistence on further studies on the impact on the environment and other feasibility studies before its construction.[5] The port was to link this landlocked country through the Shire-Zambezi River to Chinde in Mozambique, thus reducing the cost of overland transport of goods from Blantyre to Beira, Mozambique. On October 27, 2010, the president of Malawi, along with those of Zambia and Zimbabwe and the townspeople attended the opening of the port, but they waited in vain for the large barge from Mozambique to appear. This six-billion-dollar defunct project stood like an eyesore in Nsanje. Many locals lost their lands to the development and apparently had not been compensated. The Shire River was slowly being hemmed in by islands of water hyacinth on deposited silt, making it impossible for large ships to navigate.

My suitcase finally arrived after almost a week of being missing. It had at least five tags on the handle; it had spent five days in Paris and then several rush tags to Nairobi, Lilongwe, and finally expedited via Ethiopian Airway to Blantyre.

On Sunday morning I ran through villages, crossing two dry riverbeds and finally connected to the only tarmac road to Nsanje; a sign said "Chididi" at the T-junction, pointing to the dirt road I came from. Before this road was built a few years ago, the last forty-six kilometers to Nsanje used to take three hours; it was now about a half-hour. The houses in the village were of red bricks, some plastered, with tin or thatched roofs, and many had outhouses. One could have electricity or running water basing on one's financial means. Otherwise, there were boreholes scattered in the villages. Retracing my way since there were no true landmarks here to prevent me from getting lost, a group of bare-footed, laughing children followed me. I felt like the Pied Piper of Hamelin.

Malawi is a narrow, landlocked country bordered on the eastern side by Lake Malawi. It is the most resource-limited country in southern Africa and the most densely populated in the whole of Africa with a fertility rate of 5.7 per female.[6] The population of Malawi is now at eighteen million. It was at fourteen million in 2000 with 40 percent of the population living below the poverty level, and over 85 percent were subsistence farmers in the rural areas.[7] Foreign aid from the IMF and the World Bank and countries like USA, Britain, and Germany constituted about 40 percent of the entire government budget and paid the bills for over 90 percent of its investment and development projects. An economy that depends on subsistence farming and some exportable cash crops will find it difficult to be rid of foreign aid dependency.[8]

Life expectancy is among the lowest in the world because of HIV/AIDS, malaria, and TB, and the lack of healthcare system, but in recent years it has risen to 64 years in 2018, up from 46 years in 2000.[9] In healthcare, donors contributed at least 60 percent of the expenditure during the 2006 to 2009 cycle. One of the more acute problems is the persistent shortage of healthcare workers. In 2014, the country was operating on 33 percent of the required healthcare workers as stipulated by WHO, and of those only 35 percent of them served in the rural areas where 80 percent of the population resided.[10]

In 2010, Malawi had one of the highest HIV prevalence with the national rate of 10.6 percent. The highest was in the southern region, the most populated region where Nsanje is, at 14.5 percent, twice the rates for northern and central regions.[11] In the same year, 65 percent of new HIV infections among adults were estimated to occur in the southern region.[12] Most recent data for HV and AIDS in Malawi were from 2017; it continued to have one of the highest HIV prevalence in the world, at 9.2 percent among the adult population (aged 19 to 49 years). The mode of transmission was unprotected heterosexual sex, with mother to child transmission being second, accounting for 25 percent.[13] In 2016, Malawi had made some progress towards the WHO 90–90–90 targets of ending HIV/AIDS epidemic in 2030. Fifty-three percent of the people were aware of their HV status, 73 percent were on treatment, and 78 percent were virally suppressed.[14] The barriers to achieving the goal were many and included cultural barriers of initiation ceremonies and rituals leading to unprotected sex with girls most often affected. One of the positive moves was when Malawi outlawed child marriage in 2017, raising the age to eighteen.[15] Multiple and concurrent sexual partners, with polygamy still remaining legal, put women at risk for HIV. Like most African countries, stigma and discrimination remain significant barriers. Data including electronic data records are only available in a few sites. There is also the lack of healthcare infrastructure, HIV testing sites and kits, and ready access to testing and healthcare centers. One of the most critical barriers is that Malawi has one of the most severe health workforce crises in Africa, with the lowest physician-to-population ratio at 2:100,000 and second lowest nurse to population ratio at 28:100,000. It would not be easy for it to achieve the targets.[16]

MSF has been in Malawi since 1997, with the aim to reduce the morbidity and mortality of HIV and TB. In 2003, it started the treatment of HIV/AIDS and its associated infections in Thyolo.[17] Since 2011 it has been involved in Nsanje to support the MOH in a mentorship program in the provision of quality HIV care. It also introduced targeted health systems to test and treat serodiscordante couples, sex workers, non-surgical male circumcision, and all HIV positive pregnant women, as well as the integration of HIV/TB services. My main role was to run the mentorship program with my MOH counterparts and help with the integration of other services with the help of two MSF mentors and MOH healthcare personnel as mentors. The hope was to pass the baton to them so they could take over the program when MSF ended this portion of their greater scheme. This was slated to happen at the end of 2013, close to the end of my assignment with MSF.

A headline in the July 31, 2013, issue of the newspaper, *The Nation*, ominously announced: "Food Insecurity to Rise in Malawi."[18] The population growth in Malawi, which was predicted to be at 3.3 percent per year over the next decade, 2013 to 2023, compared to that of the rest of the sub-Saharan Africa of 2.8 percent, posed a threat to food security. The three countries that were predicted to have the most significant increase in food insecurity were Malawi, Uganda, and Chad. Other countries such as the Central African Republic, the DRC, Burundi, Eritrea, Somalia, and Zambia were not far behind. A native here testified to the fact that for at least the last thirty years, he could not remember a year in which some form of food distribution was not given to Nsanje district.

I have been to Africa so many times and still cannot understand why so many of the countries in the continent are always in perpetual need of foreign aid. Relief agencies have been in Africa for years, and yet poverty, hunger, famine, lack of education, healthcare, and water and sanitation problems persist; the agencies do not seem to be able to make a dent in these confounding problems plaguing Africa despite tons of money being poured into it. Some Africans think aid agencies are the problem and that they trigger the cycle of dependency. However, without them, many of the impoverished inhabitants in regions that have been forgotten by their government will be left to suffer. I remember seeing a map of the areas around Dadaab in Kenya completely taken over by different relief agencies; the government seemed to take little interest in providing any services for the people there. A cynic would argue that the government had no reason to provide care, as their own people would be taken care of by the relief agencies. There lies the argument for the cycle of dependency. If, on the other hand, relief agencies pulled out now, the whole fabric of the African society that depended on them would collapse.

An election outcome of an African nation has virtually no impact on the lives of the people in the remote areas, as the leaders have totally neglected them for years. Corruption may be partly to blame for the lack of progress in many of the African nations. Many leaders have enriched themselves and their cronies through their powerful position and contrive to stay in power for as long as they can to continue to benefit from their ill-gotten gains.

A few years ago the Kenyan parliament voted to tax the Members of Parliament (MPs).[19] Apparently, unlike the regular citizens, MPs were exempt from paying taxes, and when it came close to the time when they had to pay their due, they voted against having taxes levied on them. They enjoyed many perks as politicians and shouldering a fair share of the tax burden was distasteful to them. Was it greed that drove them to vote against being taxed? On my second visit to Kampala, the roads were just as bad as the first time I went there. I commented to a Ugandan that if I were the President of Uganda and had been in power for such a long time, I would be ashamed of the poor condition of the roads. He said facetiously that the president would reply that he did not have the money to improve them and would need some foreign aid.

Food insecurity in Malawi has been a perpetual problem due to drought and flooding. The flat area in Nasanje is prone to flooding by the Shire River during the rainy season. I am not an engineer, but I wonder why a more permanent solution has not been sought, such as an irrigation system and some kind of flood control. In the countryside, there is no large-scale agriculture, and the people still stick to subsistence farming for their day-to-day survival. If their crop fails, they have no other recourse but to hope for foreign food distribution.

The other evening on my run, I was pestered by a few kids yelling, "*Mzungu*, give me money!" I am not a European white, but just the same, I am a foreigner to them, and foreigners have money. Just about the only place I seldom heard kids asking for money was deep in the bush of South Sudan. In Ethiopia the kids put out their palms asking for birr; they thought it was hilarious when I in turn put out mine and asked them for birr. Here I said, "You have to work for it." Later I learned a few words of Chichewa—*ndilibe ndalama*, I have no money; *maluzi*, I am broke—to arm myself against such verbal assaults. Sometimes I just sprinted and left them in the dust.

For my first field day, I traveled to Ndamera with a group of MSF staffers including my MSF mentors and a MOH mentor. Half of Malawi was engulfed by Mozambique in the southern region. Ndamera and Lulwe were two regions that were southernmost of Nsanje. As soon as we left Nsanje town, the tarmac road disappeared to be replaced by compact dirt road, bumpy at times, crossing several dry riverbeds. There were scattered redbrick or stucco houses with tin or thatched roofing. After about fifteen minutes, we reached Mbenji health facility and dropped off some staff. The center of town had a short tarmac road, narrow to begin with and bordered by thin slivers of dirt sidewalks which were all occupied by sellers of produce: tomatoes, sweet potatoes, second-hand clothing or *kaunjika* mainly from America, and new clothes of different African and European football teams, all spilling onto the sides of the road, making it even narrower.

We were besieged by a herd of cows which looked a little bewildered trying to maneuver around the cruiser. Their big, wide, innocent eyes looked around patiently. The land was dry but not as dry as in South Sudan; they could still find some meager pickings in the lowlands.

We crossed a defunct railway track, and the driver who was from this region could not tell me when it was last functioning. The land was overgrown with weeds. I could discern no crops, at least from the road. I was told tomatoes were grown in the hills. Mango trees were bearing small fruits now, and soon there would be a mango harvest. Baobabs, though naked, somehow managed to look dignified as they stood prominently among nondescript trees covered with green leaves.

Ndamera health center was funded by UNHCR, but I could not ascertain when it was built. It looked old and decrepit. Two taps had handwritten labels next to them, stating they were not functional. One was bone dry, and the other dripped water continuously; someone had tied it with rubber tubing to try in vain to stop the drip. The maternity section was on one side with antenatal, labor and delivery, and postnatal care units. The TB clinic and laboratory were in the center, with the HIV counseling room, public health office, and other rooms crammed with broken equipment on the other side. At the back was a huge tent set up a couple of years ago for the cholera outbreak, which happens periodically when the river floods.

The Antiretroviral Treatment (ART) or HIV treatment room was in a new building with many rooms. Only one large room was being used to see patients, and an adjoining room was used to weigh and register them. The patients waited outside in the hall in the entryway. A medical assistant and a nurse were seeing patients, mostly women and babies; only a few men attended the clinic. Many patients came from Mozambique being only five kilometers away. Patients were dressed quite warmly from head to ankles, but most had no shoes. As the temperature soared, it must be hard on their bare feet to walk on the baked roads. We drove back towards the town of Nsanje in the hot early afternoon; a baobab tree looked fried in its naked state against the hazy mountains in the distance.

Here darkness fell quite quickly and without much warning; the whole village was plunged into a dark void. I did not see any other houses with electricity, but Shire House was brightly lit with the porch lights on all night, making it difficult for me to enjoy the Milky Way. At dusk, bats living in the rafters of the house flapped their wings and flew in groups into the evening sky ready to begin their nocturnal hunting. Roger, our guard dog, was finally allowed to come out for the night.

My team went to Tengani, about half an hour north, passing through grasslands with scattered, tall trees fortunate enough to escape being chopped down for firewood; the rest were tiny bushes which suffered periodic chopping and never were able to grow any bigger. Their trunks were knobby with clumps of new shoots desperately struggling to grow into a tree. The mango trees fared a little better, as they bore fruits that could be eaten or sold, but they too suffered a period of slashing. The baobab trees with their thick trunks challenged anyone to use an ax to chop them down. They were attacked only when the hollow ones fell during a storm, and the locals had a slow burn of the trunks to turn them into charcoal for sale.

About a hundred meters from the tarmac road ran the defunct railway track that started in Lilongwe and went all the way south to Mozambique, the same one that went through Ndamera. Over a dry riverbed, part of the track floated in the air with all its trestles washed away. A vandalized train station with no roof, only broken and mildewed walls, stood forlornly by the track. Trains used to travel from Limbe to Nsanje, but they stopped years ago because the Shire River flooded and destroyed the track. The driver assured me that "they" were ready to fix the tracks soon... I took this with a large grain of salt.

In the hot sun, some villagers sat or stood by the roadsides selling small amounts of produce, a few papayas or a cluster of tomatoes; on the opposite side of the road, someone just left a small basin of beans with a scooper, hoping to attract some passing buyers. Vehicles were few and far between; I wondered how many kwachas they were able to collect selling such small quantities of goods.

At the sign of Tengani, we turned off from the tarmac to a dirt road and soon passed a cluster of buildings marked "Nsanje District, Agriculture Office, Resource Center." The windows and doors were broken, and some windows had been literally ripped off the buildings; it was obvious that no one worked there anymore. In the afternoon when we passed by again, a truck had just delivered forty to fifty sacks of something stacked neatly on the veranda of one of the buildings.

Tengani health center was in an enclosed compound. One huge chunk of the eaves was missing and another was hanging precariously from the roof. It was only prevented from falling by the support of a vertical drainpipe. There were two rows of buildings; one housed the men and women wards, which were no longer working as wards, and the outpatient department (OPD), and the other, the antenatal clinic (ANC), the maternity ward with the antenatal, labor and delivery, and the postnatal wards. A broken roof beam in the waiting room of the OPD was splinted together with metal bars from parts of a wheelchair and dangled dangerously over where the patients sat.

The six rusty beds in the antenatal ward were without mattresses; the midwife told us they no longer used that ward. On the floor was a sterilizer looking somewhat abandoned, but it was actually used for sterilizing instruments with a hotplate to heat up the water. She dragged out the one-year-old, brand-new, unused sterilizer from a dark storage room; there was no light bulb there, just a gaping socket. The donated sterilizer had a plug that did not fit the wall socket, and so it was put back in the box and stored. When she pulled it out of the box to show me, the hands on the temperature gauge were already broken. Six pairs of fluorescent light fixtures hung from a crossbeam, but only one lamp remained; some fixtures had wires sticking out. When a lamp from one of the other wards burned out, the lamps from the antenatal ward had been systematically stripped, leaving it with one last lamp. The counter of the two sinks in the labor and delivery room was cluttered with a baby scale, rags, and basins filled with used instruments. It had two beds that did not look like it was ready for the next birth. On the wall of one of the cabinets was a hand-written note on "How to deliver a baby," a notation about providing a clean, warm, and well-lit space for the newborn… In contrast, the postnatal ward was sparklingly clean with four beds with mattresses and bed nets.

The midwife's crowded exam room had a fluorescent light that did not work. She used a water tank with a spigot for handwashing. When I asked her whether things had improved or deteriorated for the three years she had been there, she paused and said, "Things have been changing."

"Are they for the better or for the worse?"

"It's better."

"In what ways?"

She paused again and answered, "We didn't use to have mattresses on the beds. A local politician bought mattresses for the postnatal ward and the labor and delivery room. The women are more comfortable now."

"But you don't have mattresses for the antenatal ward."

"We don't use it."

Apparently a request had been made for more fluorescent lights, but this had been on hold because of a plan to eventually switch to energy-saving light bulbs.

I asked, "What happened when your last light went out?"

"We ask the patient's guardian to bring candles."

"You deliver by candlelight then?"

She laughed. I peered at this patient, long-suffering nurse who worked under such distressed condition and yet survived each day on the last leg of a fluorescent lamp.

My MSF mentor Chibali said, "Maintenance is a big problem." This is not unique to

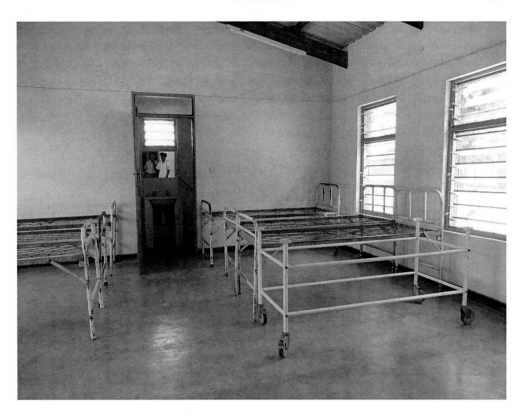

Six rusty beds with no mattresses in the antenatal ward at the Tengani health center in Nsanje, Malawi.

Malawi; it is a common and chronic problem in Africa. He continued, "It will drain the whole budget of the district if funds are given to maintain this place." We observed the midwife taking meticulous care of each and every one of her pregnant women, unhurried, even way past the lunch hour.

Outside the midwife's room, her patients sat on a bench, on the floor, or lay on *chitenje* waiting patiently for their turn to see her. Every single one of them had been tested for HIV. In any other country, patients would be up in arms to have to wait so long to see a healthcare worker. Here in Africa waiting for a long time was the norm.

Mozambique was to the east of Tengani; Mozambicans crossed the Shire River in dugout canoes and walked about five kilometers to the health center. Here the Sena people lived in Malawi and Mozambique, and they spoke a mixture of Chichewa and Sena. The boundary between the two countries blurred.

Nyamithuthu was about thirty kilometers north of Nsanje, five to seven kilometers from Tengani, near the border of Mozambique. It sat on the side of a dirt road after we turned off from the tarmac. Like Ndamera, it was built by UNHCR for the Mozambican refugees as a result of decades of civil war, first the FRELIMO, the Mozambique Liberation Front[20] against the Portuguese, and then the anti–FRELIMO movement, the RENAMO, the Mozambican National Resistance (Portuguese: Resistência Nacional Moçambicana) when millions of people were killed or displaced. The buildings were solidly built of red bricks, but because of the lack of maintenance, the wooden beams holding the roof were rotten in many places, eaten away by the termites. Before long this would not be a safe place for anyone.

The first section of the building was used by the OPD with a consultation room, an exam/dressing room, a pharmacy, a public health room, and an open waiting area. The second building housed the HIV testing room, HIV consultation room, an open waiting room, and the ANC which was also the antenatal, labor and delivery, and postnatal ward with a total of three beds. Like Tengani, the light fixtures were mostly gone; each room ran on one single fluorescent lamp. The sinks suffered from the absence of a faucet or drainpipe, with a bucket placed strategically to catch the wastewater. All the windows had broken screens, and some had missing windowpanes. Outside the clinic the walls of the latrines were broken with the doors hanging askew by their hinges; they were no longer in use.

The maternity ward was being fixed, and the business of the maternity unit was being conducted in the ANC. The roof and the beam supports of the maternity ward were rotten and infested with snakes, and its roof had been recently replaced. Unfortunately work on the ward was halted, and for the moment the ANC was filled with beds for all maternity care.

The nurse was the sole healthcare worker for ANC, OPD, and HIV clinic on the day of our visit. The medical assistant was out for some kind of training. Because this was a follow-up visit day for the pregnant women, she was able to quickly see them all. She then had to run to the OPD, leaving the HIV patients waiting. My mentors began to see patients at the HIV clinic. It was not ideal, but we were able to have her back for mentoring after she finished with the OPD.

A goat wandered in and out of a large tent funded by UNICEF and used for a cholera outbreak two years ago. It remained standing, and inside there were still remnants of the makeshift cholera beds, with a hole in the center, and instructions for fluid resuscitation. On the outside wall of the health center, precious water streamed out of a leaky faucet at a furious pace, forming a large stream that overflowed the drain and spilled over to the ground. Again Chibali could not help but comment as we were leaving Nyamithuthu, "Maintenance is always the big problem with most health centers. MSF can't fix everything."

Mbenji health center, like all the other health centers, was basically an H-shaped structure with two rows of clinic rooms connected by a corridor. One row had the OPD, ANC, and the maternity ward, and the other row the HIV Clinic and the nutrition education unit with two big cooking grills and hoods, no longer in use. The local women had set up their more familiar, traditional, three-stoned stoves next to the perfectly good grills to cook dried fish for a woman who had just given birth.

Mbenje suffered the same fate as the other health centers regarding light fixtures, rusty beds with no mattresses, clutter, and poor maintenance. It had gone without water for several months, which had only recently been restored. The whole building seemed sound structurally, however.

Women and children packed the waiting room of the HIV Clinic; only two men sat quietly among them. Like most HIV clinics, men were in the minority. Most of the women were widowed; some were divorced, which just meant that a husband left his wife to take a second or a third wife. There was no legal proceeding. It was customary for a man to abstain from having sex with his wife from when she was six or seven months pregnant till six to nine months post-partum. That was too long a period for many men, so they just took up with another woman, leaving their wives to fend for themselves. A distraught twenty-five-year-old woman had been left with her two-year-old girl, surviving by selling what she grew. She was in such an emotional state that she had to excuse herself and walk out for a while to regain her composure before coming back in to resume her visit. Often women, accompanied by their little ones, sat or lay by the roadside with a few heads of cabbage, a cluster of tomatoes or potatoes, a stack of wood, or a small basket of beans, trying to sell them to get a few kwachas to get by. Almost all the women who came to the clinic wore no shoes; all the kwachas they earned went to feed their children.

A little boy caught sight of me and ran away crying, terrified; it was probably his first time seeing a light-skinned person. In the safe embrace of his grandmother, he hesitantly reached out to touch my hand and was surprised to find that nothing untoward happened to him after all.

On Saturday, I had time for a long run towards Chididi. The locals had been slashing and burning their land in preparation for the growing season. Sinister forest fires cropped up on the slopes in the evenings and burned all night. In the morning, ashes covered our porches; the air smelled smoky, and the smog hid the mountains. For about a mile, the route to Chididi was all uphill, and on a steep stretch, a group of girls waited at the top, cheering me on. They probably climbed this hill every day carrying a heavy load or a baby and knew how hard it was to scale it. I only had myself to carry. On my run another morning, a big black mommy pig grunted twice as she crossed my path followed very quickly by ten black cute piglets. I was not sure whether this meant good luck or a bad one.

At one point it was announced to the entire MSF staff that we would have a team building activity on a weekend at a park. The staff would be provided with transportation and entrance fees, but lunch would be potluck. At first this was met with enthusiasm, but as the days went on, there was a movement to boycott the event because someone thought that lunch should be provided as well. None of us expats knew about the displeasure among the other staff, and the event was canceled at the last minute.

Five of us including the driver decided that we would make a private trip to Nyala Park after all. It was a two-hour drive over a bumpy road, passing a few towns which were having their market days. *Kaunjika* seemed to dominate the scene. Illovo Sugar Cane Plantation spanned acres and acres of land next to the Shire River, and this private company had an elaborate system of irrigation, housing, schools, healthcare centers, and sports clubs in well-kept gardens. It was a tiny, self-sufficient kingdom within Malawi, providing many people with gainful employment.

Nyala Park was very small; one could go through it in an hour, and there were no Big Five. Two of the three buffaloes had run away during the flooding season, leaving only one in the park. There were nyalas, impalas, kudus, wildebeests, zebras, vervet monkeys, and my favorite animals, the giraffes; the two mothers had just had their babies ten days ago. A zebra followed a giraffe closely as it was loping away as though the giraffe were its mommy.

We spread our mat and had a picnic under a forest of fever trees—a perfect and lovely spot. Fever trees are a kind of acacia trees with yellow trunks. Early European explorers mistook them as the cause of malaria fever. People traveling or living in the areas where they grew contracted a bad fever, and their skin turned yellow. Associating the fever with the trees, they bestowed the name fever trees. The swampy places where fever trees grew were also ideal breeding grounds for mosquitoes, which are the actual cause of malaria.[21] Rudyard Kipling mentioned the fever trees in his story "The Elephant's Child," part of the collection of *Just So Stories*. When the Elephant's child wanted to know what a crocodile ate for dinner, "Then Kolokolo Bird said, with a mournful cry, 'Go to the banks of the great grey-green, greasy Limpopo River, all set about with fever-trees, and find out.'"[22] I had been to the banks of the great grey-green, greasy Limpopo River in South Africa, but I was high up on the platform, safe from the crocodiles.

My team headed for the East Bank of the Shire River. The Shire River divided Nsanje District into a smaller northern section and a bigger southern section. The north section sat on the East Bank which was flood prone. Despite the yearly flooding, the inhabitants were reluctant to move away from this region because of the fertile soil where they could grow crops all year-round. The rest of Nsanje only enjoyed a growing season from November or December to April during the rain; the remainder of the year the ground was fallow and dry with very little farming. An added bonus for the villagers was when the flooding came, there was an abundant supply of fish.

To reach the East Bank, we had to head west to the next district of Chikwawa to a bridge that crossed the Shire towards Blantyre. There was a shorter and more direct route to the East Bank at Bangula, but the fast-flowing Ruo River, which fed into the slower-flowing Shire River, had created a tributary of sort about sixteen years ago forming "the wash-away." It prevented vehicles and pedestrians from getting to the bridge that still spanned the Shire River leading directly to the East Bank. A trip to the East Bank that used to take a couple of hours now necessitated a detour to Chikwawa to cross the Shire on another bridge in the direction of Blantyre and took five hours. At the bridge towards Blantyre, we had to loop back to the East Bank where the tarmac road ended abruptly.

At the change in the road conditions, my team members tried to scare me, not realizing that I had traveled through the remote areas of South Sudan with similar or worse roads than here. "Dr. Kwan Kew, now here is the real beginning of our journey to the East Bank, about three hours of long, bumpy, non-tarmac road."

The East Bank was a poor and God-forsaken place, but the South Sudan I was in was even more remote and isolated. We crossed many small streams where children romped in the water while their mothers did the washing, beating the clothes vigorously on the rocks. We passed an abandoned Baptist church; the missionaries had come and gone, and now only the goats scavenged in the crumbling building. Life went on in the village.

I stayed in Zuwere Forest Lodge up the slope of a hill. The lodge had a distinct odor of bat guano. The room had large windows that let in the moonlight of an almost full moon. It was a particularly windy night, large dark clouds racing across the night sky obscuring the moon. A tabby cat meowed loudly, peering through the windows trying to get in. Electricity was available from six to nine in the evening. I took a cold, trickling shower, not knowing that one could ask for hot water, smoky water that smelled of wood fire.

In the morning I ran up the steep hill behind the lodge until I reached the top of a ridge, running into villagers, young and old, carrying heavy loads downhill to sell at the market. After my run, the rain came in torrents. The roof of the lodge leaked directly onto where I sat for breakfast, dripping water on my head. Just as quickly as it started, the rain stopped, but the road had already become muddy.

I thought nothing could top the appalling conditions that I had seen in the other health centers that I visited so far; I was dead wrong. Makhanga did not even have a sign to indicate that it was a health center. As soon as we walked into the first room that looked like an anteroom to the pharmacy, we were confronted with huge gaping holes in the ceilings, moldy and brown with water damage, and an overpowering smell of bat guano permeating the air. Water puddled on the floor from the rain. The nurse midwife showed me the cause of the ceiling damage. A tree fell on the roof a year ago; bent metal roofing with a gaping hole was the result. The district was aware of it, but this could not be fixed because of a lack of funding. In fact, the district health team came quarterly, took notes of all the deficiencies, and at the end informed the health center that there was no money for repair. Despite all that, the wall of the HIV clinic was covered by a series of awards dating back to about six years ago as a center of excellence by the MOH.

Someone stuffed a roll of paper through a hole in the ceiling while another taped a square piece of board in a gallant attempt to plug the hole, while in other areas, the staff just gave up altogether and stripped the ceiling. In the maternity ward, the sterilizer was just a container sitting atop an old hotplate with wires sticking into the plug. Like Tengani, this place had a donated sterilizer with a plug that did not fit the wall socket.

In the labor and delivery room, a woman was groaning in labor, her cervix dilated and ready to give birth to her fifth baby, and she did deliver a 3.4 kg. baby boy. Because there was no light bulb in the post-natal ward, she would be spending two nights in the dark unless her family brought in candles.

Like all the other centers, the consultation rooms were littered with trash, papers, and stacks of frayed registration books not in any orderly fashion despite ample shelf space. Empty boxes and bottles spilled on the floor. No one bothered to clean up, and there was always an excuse as to who was the person responsible for creating the disorder.

Perhaps it was the full moon or the smell of the bat guano. I just lost my patience this time around and decided to talk to the person in charge. I asked him who was responsible for tidying up the mess after an ART session. He indicated the clerks were and that I should talk to them myself. But then I said, "Aren't you the one in charge?"

He had seven cleaners for this health center, and yet the place did not seem to have been dusted or emptied of trash in a while.

The In-charge said, "We have no mops! Just give us some mops and we'll clean."

The exam table donated by MSF sat in the HIV testing room because the ART room was too small for it. There had been at least an eight-month discussion of swapping the bigger HIV testing room for the small and crammed ART room. The HIV testing counselor was reluctant, and the issue went as high up as the DMO with no resolution. The HIV testing room was also filled with trash and cluttered with old broken furniture or hoarded items that someone thought would be needed in the future. I asked to speak with the HIV testing counselor and the "In charge" at the same time. When I asked the counselor if he would be willing to swap rooms with the ART Clinic, he replied, "We could discuss again with the DMO."

"Isn't this an internal issue that could be resolved between the two of you without involving the higher-ups?" As I said that, a chunk of termite nest fell from the ceiling behind where I sat, missing me narrowly.

Miraculously, he amicably agreed with the stipulations that MSF move the shelves from the ART room, replace the broken lock, and fix the non-working sink. As we walked out, hoping to extend his wish list, he pointed out the ambulance that had not worked for a year and needed "a very small part" for its engine. I nodded but did not promise anything. As I looked up at the ceiling, there were at least three supporting beams which were either broken or just hollow shells, the inside having been completely eaten by termites. Just before we left, a morose cleaner appeared with a bucket and a mop. He began to clean the floor of the HIV testing room.

In the afternoon, I went hiking on the hills behind the lodge to clear my mind of the clutter of the day and rid my sinuses of the smell of bat guano. John the driver was talking to a villager and told me he would follow me soon. On the way, the villagers asked me in Chichewa where I was going, I pointed to the top of the hills. One could almost imagine the fall foliage of New England with the clumps of orange and green trees on the slope. After I hiked for almost three-quarters of an hour, the route sloped downwards. Cognizant of the waning sunlight, I began to head back, running downhill. I spotted John, who had given up on catching up with me and had turned around, heading home. Far below us we could see the Shire Valley.

The reputation of Trinity health center as a well-kept place preceded my visit. It was a Catholic hospital and a paying one. Because of that there were fewer patients. In fact, the female ward was closed, and the male ward was being used as both a female and male ward. The place was clean, and the pediatric ward was the least depressing of all the pediatric wards I had seen in Africa. There were also a TB isolation ward and a nursing school. The ART Clinic was in a new building, and the waiting room was full that day; it was the only clinic that was free with the exception that the patients had to pay for testing of the CD4 counts, the enumeration of the immune cells.

The consultation rooms were very spacious, but there was the absence of an exam bed. The medical assistant had two patients in his room at one time with absolutely no regard to privacy and patient confidentiality.

When there was a lull, he asked my MSF mentor, Chibali, "When is the next ART training?"

"Didn't you already attend one?"

"But I'm looking for one that will pay me a higher allowance," he replied.

"Why do you go for training?" I asked.

"To get training and allowance."

"Fair enough." I thought to myself. "What if there is no allowance; would you still go?"

He thought for a moment. "If they provide food, I'd go. But if there were no food and allowance, I would not go." He added, "I'm poor."

In general, healthcare workers were paid a low wage. NGOs paid them an allowance when they went for training as a form of supplement to their meager earnings. As a result, there was an unhealthy culture of expectation of being paid allowances to be educated, so much so that attending training courses became synonymous with getting paid at a higher level. Allowance became a bargaining chip when a meeting was convened. The mentality of "What will I get in return for showing up?" permeated the whole system. A meeting called close to lunch hour conjured up "a free lunch."

Allowances aside, this medical officer whom we mentored was so slip-shod with his patients that he hardly spoke to them. He buried his face to fill out the forms, the so-called master cards, handing the forms back to the patients with their medication refills and mentioning the next appointment date. A woman came in complained of a lump in her right groin; he probed verbally but never once asked to see her swelling. He failed to listen to the lungs of a man with a persistent cough for a month. It was as though he was afraid to touch his patients. Seeing patients seemed a very tedious and mundane job for him; somewhere along the way, he had lost his passion.

There was a blackout in the village. The women patiently sat on the dirt outside the mill with their bags and buckets of corn, waiting for the electricity to come back. When it became dark and the electricity failed to turn on, they marched back home in droves, singing. In the morning they marched back; they no longer pounded their corn at home with a mortar and pestle, as they used to. There was a scuffle at the entrance of the mill. It had become more urgent to get their corn milled after all the waiting; they had lost their patience.

In the afternoon we traveled to Mesenjere to pick up another member of our team. There the nurse midwife immediately came to ask for a ride to Trinity with a primigravida with cephalopelvic disproportion; the baby she carried was too large to pass through her pelvis. They had sent their ambulance to fetch fuel at Nsanje that morning, three to four hours away, instead of transferring the patient to Trinity, which was half an hour away. We emptied our cruiser and folded up the seats, placed a mattress in it, and backtracked to Trinity for her emergency C-section. Our driver reminded me that we could only transport patients towards where we would be traveling and not backtracking, but I made the decision to do just that. I refused to have a potential loss of life on my conscience, even if this delayed our departure from the East Bank. It was dark when we reached Nsanje. Over the Shire River, the blood red ball of an almost full moon hung watchfully.

We traveled to Tengani again to observe their ART Clinic, but it turned out it was not their ART day, so we traveled further north to Phokera to a relatively new health center built in October 2006 by the donor Press. It had the usual OPD, ANC, ART, and maternity ward. The beds in the maternity ward looked comfortable, with cranks that made the beds adjustable. Already there were signs of poor maintenance; termites had begun to build their nests in the wooden beams.

The OPD consultation room was spacious, and across from it was the exam room. I asked permission to look at it, but it was locked; a bad sign. It could only mean one thing; physical exams were not performed routinely enough to warrant it being free and open. When the medical officer finally found the key to open it, the exam table was squeezed in a corner, obviously not used very often, and there were two tables keeping it company. Boxes and papers were piled on top of these; the exam room was slowly but surely turning into a cluttered storage room.

Outside the ART room was a narrow corridor also acting as the waiting room for the patients: dark, dingy, and congested. The room itself was crammed with furniture; a humongous desk took up the center space where the medical assistant presided, with papers and bottles of ARVs on the tabletop. The table took up so much space that the exam table given by MSF sat in the ANC room next door. Like many of the health centers we visited, the medical assistant had two patients sitting in front of him to be seen at the same time, again without regard to privacy and confidentiality which was the first requirement of the dictum of the MOH of Malawi for HIV care. The chair prevented the door from closing, so the patients waiting right outside were within earshot of what was being discussed. With the medical assistant sitting behind such a big desk, it was a great deterrent for him to even reach over to touch his patients.

A donor had built a new laboratory, and more buildings would be added to make Phokera into a hospital for this area. I could not help but compare the healthcare facilities here to what little I had seen in South Sudan. Malawi had a lot of help from many donors, and they had many health centers (with maternity units, a must for a nation that tops the fertility rate of Africa) which were solidly built, but poorly maintained. South Sudan, on the other hand, at least in the places I went to, did not enjoy health facilities near the inhabitants, hence the mobile clinics that we ran. They were far behind Malawi in that respect. It would be a tremendous loss if Malawi did not keep these places up to continue providing reasonable care within a reasonable distance for their citizens. The so-called "difficult-to-reach-area of the East Bank" was difficult for us to reach because of the wash-away, but the inhabitants could still reach their health center except in severe floods. The Makhanga health center, with its bat-infested, damaged ceilings and hollow beams, would soon cease to exist, sealing the fate of the villagers to travel a long way to the next health center.

Some of the expats seemed to work all the time, in the evenings and on weekends. It was a little disheartening for me for I felt I could not disturb them. This was my longest assignment, and loneliness seeped into my life. My daughter, Cara, had lovingly compiled a book of pictures of my Belmont home so I could peruse it during such time of homesickness. There was nothing much to do in Nsanje, so I took a long walk alone along the Shire River into the farms, bringing a folded umbrella with me just in case I chanced upon a crocodile. A few words of greeting in Chichewa seemed to bring up smiles from the locals and enthusiastic responses. Many women were doing their laundry the hard way on the banks and drying it on the rocks. Water hyacinths glided swiftly with the currents.

A woman who had given birth to her ninth baby three days ago at Nsanje District Hospital, her last because she finally had her tubes tied, hitched a ride with us to Lulwe. Some of her older children were already married. She was sitting on the ground at the hospital gate, and when she learned she could ride with us, she gathered her belongings tied up in a bundle, her basin, her swaddling baby, and ran with such energy one could hardly believe she just had a baby. One wondered how she planned to make her way home up the mountains in Lulwe forty kilometers away without a ride.

Lulwe health center was to the southwest tip of Nsanje, situated high up on the mountains, also considered "a difficult to reach area." It nestled on the slope of a hill with more mountains in the distance, and Nsanje sat in the hazy, flat, hot valley. The cruiser had to climb steeply at some spots over rocky terrain. Lulwe was one of the Christian mission centers and charged a fee at the clinic. As with centers that charged a fee, it was clean and better maintained. A midwife at Makhanga at the East Bank, the health center that smelled of bat guano, wished that his center could also charge a small fee so they could use the funds for maintenance. However, he knew that none of the politicians would agree lest they be voted out of office. In Lulwe, Mozambique was just a stone's throw away. It had the necessary maternity unit where a woman had given birth just that morning. Being up in the mountains and cooler in temperature, all the babies here wore a warm knitted hat.

A thirty-year-old man started taking HIV medications a year ago, and his weight went from 42 kg. to 70 kg. in a matter of months. However, recently he developed a cough, and his weight had slowly decreased to 56 kg.; the health center treated him with some antibiotics, but he did not improve. He had one sputum sample that did not show TB, and the nearest facility that could do a chest x-ray was Nsanje District Hospital, far away from here, at least on foot. The national guidelines frowned upon empiric treatment for TB. A month or so later I heard that he was finally diagnosed with TB.

An eight-year-old boy with wide-open eyes could not take his gaze off me; evidently he had not seen a foreigner before. He was sick a few months ago with fever and diarrhea. His mother brought him to Mozambique to see an "African doctor," a traditional healer who cut his arms with a razor blade to bleed him, but he continued to do poorly. At Nsanje District Hospital he tested positive for HIV, but his mother was negative. Did he get his infection from a dirty blade? In the afternoon we left the remote but temperate Lulwe, heading to the hot valley of Nsanje.

We could go to Blantyre twice a month to get away from Nsanje. Blantyre, abloom with lovely purple jacaranda flowers, was the commercial center of Malawi with many creature comforts, and many expats lived there as the climate was cool.

I love the mountains. One weekend I entertained the idea of going to Mulange, the highest mountain in central Africa. Through the Mountain Club of Malawi, I contacted Gillian, who happened to be going to Mulange. Five of us, Gillian and Aiden from Ireland, Milan from Slovakia, and Erin and I from the U.S., left early one Saturday morning for Mulange. Gillian had already arranged for two porters and a guide. Erin and I carried our own bags; we did not bring a lot, just some food and warm clothes. Gillian, who was a logistician for Mary's Meals, brought a whole lot of food, and she also rented a sleeping bag for me. For this MSF assignment, I was only allowed to bring twenty kilograms of baggage, so I had left my hiking boots and sleeping bag at home. Aiden and Milan were aiming to climb to Sapitwa, the highest peak. Erin and I wanted to do the same, but time constraints did not allow us to do so.

Mulange is 3002 meters high, not as tall as other African mountains. At the lower reaches, there was a noticeable lack of vegetation as there seemed to be a lot of forest fires; many had been deliberately set by poachers to drive out small animals for them to hunt. The sound of the nearby crackling fire burning the bushes was quite disconcerting, and the charred landscapes made the mountains look bald. Despite that, the ever-changing hues and colors of the majestic mountain range left us in awe. Parts of the trails were quite challenging; Mulange was not an easy mountain to climb. Closer to the peaks the trail became rocky. We soon ran out of water and collected water from the cool mountain stream for drinking, hoping that it had not been contaminated.

Almost at the end of the five-hour climb, we dipped into an ice-cold pool before climbing another twenty minutes to Thuchila Hut at 2000 meters. In the evening we went down a trail and sat on a slab of rock with our wine, watching the sunset over the Plateau of the Elephant's Head—a red fireball slowly swallowed by dark grey clouds. On the distant slopes, menacing red tongues of fire began to appear, burning the forest. The planet Venus silently made its appearance.

Gillian had prepared a delicious dinner at home, brought it up the mountain, and heated it over a grate in the fireplace. When I first met her, I took an immediate liking to her. For such a large, jolly woman, she was quite an amazing hiker. She had worked in Africa for several years now, first in the Congo and then in Malawi. Aiden was a nurse working near Lake Malawi. Erin had just arrived, a student in occupation therapy, doing her internship in Blantyre. Milan, a friend of Aiden, was a computer technologist traveling internationally for Dell and had recently visited Penang, the island of my birth. He was quite a stand-up comedian and made us laugh the whole evening long. When he learned that both Erin and I were marathon runners and hikers, he said to Gillian, "Next time when you invite us to come hiking, please do not embarrass us by inviting experienced hikers."

We slept on the veranda, looking at the millions of brilliant stars of the Milky Way dotting the sky. I could spot Orion the Hunter. This was the extent of my recognition of the constellations besides the Big and Little Dippers despite many a cold wintry night I and my classmates spent with our astronomy professor at Wellesley College on the rooftop of Sage Hall, gazing at the sky and poring over the constellation chart. As we watched, a shooting star streaked across the sky.

In the morning we said good-bye to Aiden and Milan who would be spending a second day scaling Sapitwa while Erin, Gillian, and I headed downhill, stopping at a cold pool of the Likhulezi River near the bottom to have a dip. It was a weekend of peace with the mountains, nature, and great company. After a few weeks in quiet Nsanje, Blantyre seemed extremely busy, and I was glad to leave it for the mountains.

Kalemba was about forty-six kilometers north of Nsanje. It was a Catholic community hospital and like Trinity, it was better maintained than the government health centers, although it had some areas that needed some tender loving care. The wards were scattered about in the compound at some distance from each other. As a hospital, however, it only provided very rudimentary laboratory investigations, malaria Paracheck, hemoglobin, and urinalysis. The ART had to send blood for viral load tests to Nsanje District Hospital.

The waiting area of the ART Clinic was in a narrow corridor, and the clerk who checked in patients used an old bed for his desk, bending over at an uncomfortable position. The nurse mainly saw patients who were asymptomatic and counseled them on medication adherence. This being a Catholic hospital, there was no family planning, but she could refer them to other facilities. However, most women had to get their husbands' approval before they could even contemplate going there.

A woman carrying a two-month-old baby on her back, when asked if her husband had been tested for HIV, replied that he was positive. When she was one month pregnant, he left her (she was the second wife), their three children, and also his first wife, and five children to have a third wife. Now she survived by tilling the land and selling what she grew. She related all this without much emotion while the nurse bantered, "Men are cruel."

On our way home the driver took a short detour in Bangula to look at the "wash-away" of the Shire River. The government was starting to build a bridge over it, and the engineers hoped to have it done before the rain came. The workers were filling up the river with rocks and earth at its narrowest part before building the bridge. I wondered if this would create a bottleneck for the swift water to flow, and if so, it could very well destroy the bridge through the sheer force of the volume of water.

The currents were swift here; men with big muscles maneuvered wooden boats loaded to the hilt with the sterns almost level with the water, while passengers were busy bailing water out of the boats while crossing this narrow section of the "wash away" to obviate the five-hour trip. If there were indeed a bridge, the boatmen would soon lose their livelihood. The locals called this part of the river *mtaya moyo* (lose one's life) as apparently when the water level was high in the rainy season, the boats often tipped over, and many passengers drowned.

My office was in the Nsanje District Hospital with the mentors whom I supervised. Here there was no Wi-Fi. I had to wind my way for about fifteen minutes through the backyards of villagers' homes, running into guinea fowls, chickens, goats, and dogs, back to the MSF office to use the internet to check my work e-mail which seemed to inundate my mailbox all the time. Or I could call for the land cruiser to give me a ride, but I preferred to walk.

There were daily "handover rounds" or morning reports at seven-thirty at the Nsanje District Hospital except on Wednesday. Then they held "grand ward rounds," when a group of senior clinical officers, medical officers, nurses, and students, about forty to fifty of them, went around different wards to see a number of patients with diagnostic and management issues. I had started to come to these rounds, and when the District Health Officer (DHO) was in town and came to rounds, they became interminable. I often had difficulty piecing the story together because the presenters tended to speak softly and fast, and oftentimes they peppered their presentations with both Chichewa and English interchangeably.

The grand ward rounds entourage was too big for it to be an effective teaching forum. If one were out in the periphery of the circle, one would be out of luck hearing the whole presentation. A thirty-year-old man had been bitten in the left cheek by an adder, a poisonous snake. There was no anti-venom. His face was bloated like a big balloon, eyes swollen shut, lips so fat that they were everted, and he had trouble breathing. The difficult decision was whether he should be treated with steroids or intubated; since the only ventilator in the hospital was in the operating theatre, no emergency operations could be performed he was intubated. The former was chosen, and he did all right overnight. In the pediatric ward, a youngster had had seizure from cerebral malaria. A young woman had tried to kill herself by swallowing organophosphate. The x-ray machine did not work when a young man stabbed himself and punctured his lung. A severely malnourished twelve-year-old girl who looked like an eight-year-old had a spleen so big that one could see it through the thin wall of her enlarged belly across the room. She had malaria and also tested positive for HIV. If she were infected with HIV at birth, she had survived all those years with no treatment. A middle-aged woman with a chronic back pain turned out to have Pott's disease or TB of the spine. A HIV-infected young man who began treatment six months ago came in with signs of meningitis; he was started on medicines to treat bacterial and cryptococcal meningitis. No longer

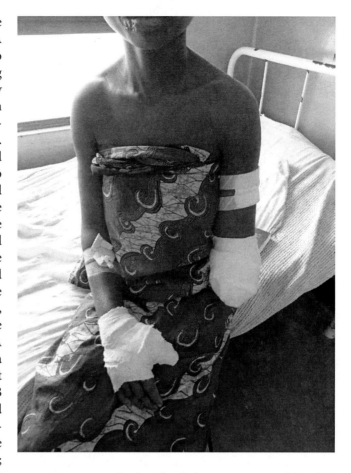

A young woman who lost her left arm to a crocodile while catching fish in the Shire River, Nsanje.

awake, he was drawing his last breath. He died shortly after we left him.

Two people were attacked by crocodiles while fishing in the Shire River. The man's arm was injured, but he was lucky not to lose it. However, the woman lost her left arm as the crocodile ripped it off when she reached into the river to catch fish. The hospital saw at least four crocodile attacks a month.

A woman from Mozambique took a local herb that acted like Pitocin to induce labor for her ninth pregnancy. When she did not progress, she consulted an "African doctor" who could not manage her, and she went to a local healthcare center, which also was unable to help her. She crossed the border to Tengani health center; by then she was bleeding heavily. At Nsanje District Hospital she underwent emergency surgery, suffered rupture of her uterus, and the baby girl was stillborn. The uterine tissues were so severely torn that the surgeon was unable to repair them; her uterus had to be removed. She had lost a great deal of blood, and unfortunately there was no blood in the blood bank. Pale and in shock but still conscious, she was transferred to Queen Elizabeth Central Hospital in Blantyre, four hours away.

There was a severe shortage of blood in Nsanje. A few nights ago, a woman had presented with severe anemia. Her relatives were asked to donate blood; one of them had HIV, malaria, and syphilis, and a second had malaria. The clinician chose to transfuse her with the malarial blood after the patient received a dose of quinine in an attempt to eradicate the parasites and prevent the recipient from getting malaria.

I was cut off from any current happenings in the world except what was being delivered to my e-mail: the conflict in Congo, occasional news about the war in Syria, and frequent updates of Red Sox's standing in the American League East. At this point they were ahead of the Yankees, and if all the stars were aligned correctly, perhaps heading for the play-offs.

One morning I spotted the mother pig with her ten piglets, which had grown three times as big since I last saw them. They were busy rooting around a giant mound of anthill. A little girl ran along with me for almost half a mile, coughing part of the way. The sun, a glowing red ball, hovered over the rooftops promising to bring us another searing hot day.

A couple of kilometers from Nsanje District Hospital on the M1 Highway was a sign pointing in the direction to Chididi. It was fourteen kilometers from the tarmac road, high up on the slope of the mountains. and could only be reached after driving over many stretches of winding, rocky, gully-filled roads. It was even harder to get to than Lulwe. The slopes showed ravages of the fires set randomly; bushes and lower branches of tall trees were charred, and grass was scorched with clumps of ashes here and there.

The African Evangelical Church ran the Chididi health center, and it charged the patients a fee to be seen. It was right across from a primary school where jacaranda trees showed off their small, lovely, purple trumpet flowers. It had a cluster of three buildings: OPD, a dispensary, and a public health office in one building, with the male ward, the HIV testing center, and clinic in another. The last one was the ubiquitous maternity unit with the postnatal unit also serving as a female ward.

The register for the Early Infant Diagnosis (EID) for HIV showed that many of the mothers and infants failed to return because they were from Mozambique. Happily, many of the infants tested negative for HIV by PCR-DNA (polymerase chain reaction, a test for detecting HIV DNA), thanks to the Prevention of Mother to Child Transmission B+ Program (PMTCT-B+). In September 2015, WHO released guidelines recommending that all pregnant women living with HIV be immediately provided with lifelong treatment with antiretroviral therapy, regardless of CD4 count. This approach was called Option B+.[23] Malawian women had a high fertility rate of 5.7, and it would seem that universal treatment of HIV-infected pregnant women could prevent transmission of HIV infection to the babies.

On our way down a steep section of the road from Chididi, a couple struggled to handle a bundle of firewood loaded on a bicycle. The man was holding the handlebar and bundle while the woman pulled the bike from behind to prevent it from tumbling down the slope. Mchacha, the nurse traveling with me, commented that when they reached home, the man would promptly go to rest or take a nap, while the woman would fetch water, cook him a meal, and if she had time, sell the firewood to get some money for food. Indeed, a woman's work never seemed to end, but some of the men's work here was not even from sun to sun; it was whenever and whatever they pleased to do. The responsibilities seemed to rest squarely on the women's shoulders.

I asked her how she was sure that would happen. She replied, "I live in a village; my father was like that, and many men are still like that."

"Why would the women want to get married then?"

"They want a partner."

There was a bright ray of hope here; Mchacha and James the driver tried to have an equal partnership with their spouses.

It was hard for me to imagine walking the many kilometers to the Boma with heavy loads to sell and then to lug a large and heavy bundle of food up the steep road for hours to feed the family, repeating this many times a week; the sheer physical labor in this heat would defeat even the fittest.

As the heat built up in Nsanje, blackouts became more common, so there was no respite from the heat using either the fan or air-conditioning. In the afternoon, Peter in our office was lamenting the fact that the crocodiles were not willing to share the Shire River with us humans. I bet the crocodiles with their crocodiles' tears welling up in their eyes would simply reply, "Oh, cry me a river!"

Sorgin was at least fifty kilometers away from Nsanje proper, a health center built in 1999 with a set-up exactly like Tengani or Mbenje. It was, however, a lot cleaner, and the structure of the building was sound. The woman who cleaned the maternity unit wanted me to know that they had run out of soap, chlorine, or any kind of cleaning agents. Their sterilizer was broken, and she sterilized the instruments outdoors in boiling water for two hours over a wood fire. In the maternity unit, a baby was just born. Outside the unit, a baby goat was sucking on its mother's teat with a violent jerking motion. By lunchtime when the heat was getting fierce, the mother goat was lying in the shade chewing its cud while the baby goat gamboled on the dry grass.

The ART Clinic was crowded, with the registration clerk and the nurse attending to the patients in the same room. The clerk spread the charts all over the table making it difficult for the clinician to function. He did not take kindly to our suggestion that he registered the patients outside the room to enable the medical officer or the nurse to have more space to see the patients.

Sterilizing instruments using firewood to heat water in a pan at Sorgin health center.

Erin and I headed towards Zomba Plateau one weekend. Parts of the road to Zomba were under construction, and our driver, Hassan, took a number of detours over rocky and bumpy dirt roads, passing the notorious Zomba Central Prison, the largest prison in Malawi. It was meant to be for about 800 prisoners, but it was so overcrowded that it was housing three times the number of inmates with prisoners packed like sardines in their sleeping arrangement. The prevalence of HIV and TB was believed to be high.

We did not stop at Zomba but instead drove up to the plateau. The day was hot and hazy. Just before we went up the plateau, we saw a sign painted on a huge boulder that said, "Welcome to Casa Blanca." Many women, girls, and some boys were carrying heavy bundles of firewood from the plateau to the town to sell. Because of the distance they had to travel, a piece of wood could fetch 50 to 100 kwacha (15 to 30 cents). Again, we rarely saw any man doing this kind of heavy work. Hassan said it was cultural. Most of the heavy work was designated for women including tilling the land, and if a man was seen doing the chores, he was not considered manly enough. If a man earned any kwacha, most of it went to drinks not to the family. Unlike the men, the women had their families foremost in their minds, while the boys sold wood for their own spending. As we drove higher along the roadside, we stopped to buy colorful wild berries: strawberries, blackberries, mulberries, gooseberries, raspberries, and passion fruits. Being *azungus*, we were charged *mzungu* prices.

We asked Hassan if a woman went to the market to sell wood, who would take care of her children? Hassan said the older children or the grandmother. But I had seen women carrying a baby on their back with a bundle of goods to sell atop their heads. Erin thought the women here needed "women's lib." Again we asked why they even bothered to get married, whereupon Hassan answered with a hearty laugh, "They want what the men can work at night." And after a pause he chuckled, "They don't know that they can have it any time of the day."

I said, "They work too hard during the day."

Ku Chawe Hotel, a posh hotel, sat at the very top of the plateau. The plateau was several kilometers across, windy and cool. Queen Elizabeth and Emperor Haile Selassie came to Zomba Plateau by helicopters and both had viewpoints named after them, but the best one yet was an unnamed viewpoint that Hassan took us to, too rocky for a helicopter landing. The day was hazy mostly from the burning of the mountains so we could not see too clearly, but we imagined Mulange in the indistinct distance.

On Monday after a weekend stay in Limbe, I traveled south to the East Bank to meet my team who traveled north from Nsanje. Unlike the last time we were at the East Bank, this time we traveled for an additional eighteen kilometers on a very narrow and bumpy road up the mountains to Thekerani in Thyolo to stay in an MSF guesthouse. The owner of Zuwere Forest Lodge had hiked up his rate, seeing that we favored his accommodation when we visited the East Bank. At the guesthouse, there was no running water, and the strong woman housekeeper fetched water starting around four in the morning, filling several barrels. I had a mortal fear of latrines, but the latrine here was surprisingly free of odor.

In the morning I ran up to the peak; the morning sun came up around five, much earlier than in Nsanje. However, from the wee hours of the morning until five, persistent and annoying calls for bus passengers to Limbe kept me awake. By then it was so bright that any hope of dozing off to sleep evaporated. Already many of the villagers were up and about, women fetching water from the borehole, and men firing up their kilns to make their tower of red bricks.

Sankhulani had an ornate globe as its water tank sitting prominently on top of its building. Ironically, this health center had functioned without water for three years. There was light in the maternity unit, but no water since the solar panel for the engine that powered the pump for the water did not work. If a woman came in to have a baby, her guardian would have to fetch water from the borehole.

A bed was prominently placed in the room for the ART clinic where the patients' files were strewn. The office had a medicine cabinet, a non-working sink, and two chairs donated by GOAL, an NGO in Ireland; a very Spartan set-up. MSF donated an exam bed that languished in the ANC because there was not enough space in the ART room. Yet this clinic in the last quarter was deemed in the graduation phase of the site assessment of the mentorship program. How on earth did that happen? Sankhulani meant choice, but the healthcare personnel running this clinic did not have many choices.

Part of my team was visiting Makhanga, the bat-infested healthcare center. I visited it last month and at that time, they agreed to switch the ART room to the more spacious HIV testing room. Unfortunately, no progress was made; it had been a contest between the MOH maintenance department and our logistics to see who blinked first, while I suggested that MSF should just go ahead and move the shelves as requested before anyone had time to change their minds. Change their minds they did, and now it seemed that the higher-ups in the MOH were involved and were against the switch, arguing that HIV testing also needed a big room. The MOH and MSF loved to end a meeting by asking for the way forward; this felt like the way backwards as this problem was listed a priority to be solved at the annual report of 2012, the year before I came. This issue resolved eventually with the switching of the rooms eleven months after it appeared in the annual report.

A small woman with a baby swaddled in a *chitenje* sat bolt upright, waiting patiently to be seen; she just had her fourth baby at home. Despite that, she did not look tired. At the ANC, all mothers-to-be were taught to have a new razor and a clean thread handy at home in case of home delivery. The women here not only had to earn a living the hard way but also to be able to deliver their own babies.

Earnest came to talk to me while we were waiting for our transport. He volunteered at the center two to three times a week as an HIV tester and counselor and helped his wife at the farm two days a week. His wife, as he put it, was a farmer working six days a week in the field. He married when he was twenty-two and his wife was seventeen; her parents took her out of standard three to work as a domestic help, a common practice for young girls. He went to school until Form Four but failed his Malawian Certificate of Education and did not have money to repeat the two years to retake his exam. They had four children; the youngest was two months old, and he said he had done "his work." They were considering family planning and surprisingly he said he was considering *kuseka* (vasectomy) as he thought his wife should not be the one to undergo any procedure.

In the afternoon, we visited the Ruo River, crossing four railway tracks, one of which was still working; a train ran from Limbe to Makhanga once a week. In the distance, a herd of cattle crossed the tracks returning from the Ruo after a drink. The Ruo River looked deceptively tame now, with several rivulets divided by rocks and tall elephant grass, but during the rainy season, it covered all the rocks and became a big, raging, roaring river. Children, all boys, romped in the water to get relief from the heat. Sankhulani had several villages with a total population of 7,700 people; fifty percent of them were below fifteen years of age and twenty percent below five years, a very young community.[24]

During the night, I tossed and turned, mulling over the problem of the ART clinic in Sankhulani. In the end, I decided to forward a request to build a single shelf for the files and replace the bed with the exam table, as well as donate a small table for the patient consultation room and a bucket with a spigot for hand washing. I would wait to see how long it would take for Sankhulani to have a more functional space.

The long, wide cracks in the walls of the building that housed the maternity unit were the first thing that caught one's eye when one arrived at Masenjere health center. Inside, the ANC, labor and delivery rooms were cordoned off as unsafe, and the postnatal ward was used for ANC, labor and delivery as well. The ominous cracks in the walls and floors, which in some places were buckled, looked like an earthquake had struck. Given the extent and the proximity of the cracks in the postnatal unit, it should really be condemned. The plight of Masenjere had been widely publicized in the news in the past, but no help had been forthcoming.

The ART clinic was in the second building, and unlike Sankhulani, it was spacious. Unfortunately, trash piled up on the floor and on top of the MSF-donated exam table. MSF recently delivered a bookcase, a table, and chairs to the clinic. Apparently, my team visited it last month, addressed the trash issue, and took it upon themselves to clean up. There seemed to be no lasting impact. The TB Clinic was not much better; so much dust covered the surfaces of furniture, it looked as though no one had bothered to clean it in a long while.

A sixteen-year-old girl came with her guardian. Her parents had died when she was a baby, and since then she continued on HIV medications. Until three months ago she and her guardian did not know that she had HIV infection; no one had told her. I found it hard to believe that a sixteen-year-old would continue to take medications without asking

Cracks in the walls of the maternity ward at Mesenjere Health Center, Muona, Nsanje.

the reasons. There were disclosure procedures formulated by the HIV/AIDs unit, and only trained counselors could disclose an HIV status to minors. This patient was retested and confirmed positive. She learned for the first time that she was HIV positive and was so distraught that she refused to resume her medications.

As we left the East Bank, I felt like we were swimming upstream against a whole slew of obstacles that seemed quite insurmountable. Only the simple problem of outfitting the ART clinic in Sankulani seemed within reach, but even that I was holding my breath to see if it could be easily and readily accomplished. With the visit of Masenjere, I had now visited all fourteen health centers at least once during the two months I had been here.

On our way home, in the stretch between Nchalo and Bangula, there seemed to be more aggressive tree chopping, and the trees that were left standing were barren. If there were leaves, they appeared shriveled. The land was dry and dusty and without much tree coverings; it appeared desolate and baked. The aggressive deforestation through random cutting, as well as burning was also seen in the mountainous areas on the way to Thyolo, was an environmental disaster. One could only hope that some programs of replanting and education would slow down this devastating process. I chanced upon some homegrown publications by expats living in Blantyre in the 1990s; apparently deforestation was quite extensive then, and this continues unabated.

This past weekend was so hot that the prolonged blackout did not help matters. The only time it was a little tolerable was early in the morning and in the evening. One morning dark, thick rain clouds gathered in the sky. This had happened once before, but the clouds soon were blown away. While I was getting ready to go running, big drops of rain began to fall. Kuyvina, the kitten, was outside and she looked heavenward, bewildered. The pitter-patter on the roof became louder; heaven opened up, and a heavy downpour descended on us. This was highly unusual for this time of the year. The wind picked up, and the temperature became cool enough I had to wear a cardigan to work.

I looked forward to going to Lulwe in the mountains for its cool weather. Nsanje had been experiencing a period of withering hot weather interspersed with brief but welcoming torrential rain. The rain flooded the trenches on the sides of the dirt road, forming gushing streams, and children waded in the pools that formed around clogged drains.

Before we arrived at Lulwe, the medical assistant sent a man who had been working in Mozambique for an HIV test. When he returned, he came in with his male relative. The medical assistant shooed the relative away and asked to have his wife sent in. He had tested positive for HIV, and she was advised to be tested; she too was positive. There was no discussion as to how he contracted his infection. They had three children; the middle one had died, and the others were aged two and eight and had never been tested. The couple was sent off for counseling.

When the medical assistant called for her next patient, a woman came in with her sixteen-month-old child, her breasts hanging out of the V of her blouse; she was breastfeeding her fussy child. At once the medical assistant asked her to cover herself. She had seven children; one had died. Having nursed so many children, her breasts looked withered and limp, seemingly sucked dry. She had tested positive for HIV during her antenatal visit but refused to start ARVs. Her husband was working in South Africa, and she had said then that she needed to wait for him to return to make the decision with her. She revealed her fear that she would be sent home if her husband learned that she was taking ARVs. He had not been tested. Since there was no actual result of her HIV test, she was retested, and both she and her baby were positive. There was a high probability that her baby could have been spared being infected with HIV if she had started taking medications during her pregnancy. Over the last few months, the baby's height and weight had fallen off the growth chart. She still faced the dilemma of disclosure of her HIV status to her husband when he returned from South Africa, and persuading him to get an HIV testing if she had not been sent home.

Both Lulwe and Chididi were high up in the hard-to-reach mountains, but Lulwe was close to Mozambique where the men went for long periods to work and brought back HIV to their spouses. A lot more women in Lulwe tested positive for HIV than those in Chididi. Some men from Chididi went to cut sugar canes in Nchalo and stayed away from home for long periods, and they too brought home HIV infection. The tradition of men having to abstain from sex when their wives were six months pregnant till six months post-partum also encouraged them to seek sex elsewhere.

Couple testing was launched in several healthcare facilities in Nsanje district starting in August 2013, with more intense training in the last month. That came to an abrupt stop when healthcare personnel objected to having to undergo training without the usual allowance; providing them drinks and biscuits was not enough.

For the mentoring program, we coached the mentees to always ask about the HIV status of their patients' partners and children and to encourage them to bring them for testing. For a serodiscordant couple, that was when an HIV positive partner had an HIV negative partner, the positive partner was started on treatment regardless of his/her immune status (level of CD 4 counts) to decrease transmission of the infection to the negative partner. So far couple testing was not such a frequent happening, and Malawian men were not easily persuaded to come for HIV testing. As in many clinics I had been to in most Africa countries, men constituted a minority, and many sought help late in their infection. This sero-discordant program assumed a couple consisted of two people, but in Malawi where polygamy was a common practice and helped in the spread of HIV, one had to think of several partners for the men. Most men, however, refused to get themselves tested even when their wives were on HIV treatment.

Agnes, the medical assistant, was not very tall, but she wore a slinky, flamenco-like dress giving her the illusion of being slim and lanky. She looked rather distinctive and attractive with her high cheekbones and cornrows on her head, tapering to form a small bun. When asked if she would share her husband with other women, she smiled shyly and said no way. She knew of a man with six wives and thirty-five children, and the women bore the responsibility of raising them.

In Malawi over fifty percent of the women were married by the age of eighteen.[25] After helping a young woman deliver her baby, a middle-aged midwife in Sankhulani threw her hands up in the air and remarked exasperatingly, "These village women are not interested in education; all they want to do is to get married and have many babies."

The practice of kupita kufa or kuchotsa fumbi, literally "taking away dust after death," a widowhood cleansing ritual prevalent in Malawi,[26] has been one of the reasons for the spread of HIV. When a woman's husband dies, she is expected to have sexual relations to be cleansed so that the evil spirit that caused the death of her husband will not visit her and curse her family. She has to be cleansed by having unsafe sex with a man whom the family chooses; it could be a male relative or paid professional cleanser who is paid cash or given cows to perform the cleansing. This man is often mentally unstable or has been ostracized by the villagers. Professional cleansers could charge as much as $50 for such service for a country like Malawi, which subsists on less than $1 a day.[27] The tradition has been so much a part of the culture that some women ask for it.

Any one of the widow's brothers-in-law could take her as a wife. Her property becomes his. She is sent home when no one takes her as a wife; her matrimonial property is taken from her, and often she has to leave all her children to her in-laws. She has no rights to any one of them. Many of the older widows are left landless and without any earning power; they live in abject poverty. Women in Africa account for seventy percent of food production and nearly half of the farm labor but often lack the rights to own land.[28]

Village women often multitask. They till the land, chop wood, pump water with a baby on their backs, or carry a bundle of firewood to the market to sell while holding a baby on a sling with perhaps two more children in tow, one of whom carrying a plastic bag which probably contains their food. Sometimes they breastfeed their babies while carrying a bundle on their head on their way to the market. The babies often get distracted and let go of the nipple, exposing their mothers. However, this is such a common phenomenon that Malawian women have no qualms about displaying their bare breasts in public.

In the village where I lived, the road crew, composed of almost all women, cleared the dirt roads of weeds and leveled the surfaces. They worked for two hours a day in the early mornings for a week and were paid 4000 kwachas. Similarly, in the early morning before the rain came, a row of women balancing hoes on their heads walked towards their plot of land to prepare it for the growing season, some carrying big loads of fertilizers. The women and their children worked the land with an occasional man dotting the landscape. This was backbreaking work, all done with a hoe, clearing the land of weeds which had taken hold when it lay fallow. Women may work the land, but the men own the property.

A few days ago, right outside the gate of Nsanje District Hospital, an old woman, topless with flabby loose breasts, bent down to pick up a mango pit from the ground and promptly delivered it to her mouth to suck. A few feet away she spotted a brown banana peel, and she picked that up as well. She was like the many goats milling around there scavenging for discarded edibles. A frail, blind, old woman holding a walking stick was guided by a youngster, probably her grandson. She stood at the door of a store at the filling station, hoping to be given something. It was indeed a harsh life for these village women with little education, nebulous social standing, and insecure financial status.

Climbing to the highest peak of Mulange, Sapitwa, had been Erin's and my goal, but it would take three days to do so. We took Friday off, headed towards Chetakali with our backpacks of three-day provisions, warm clothing, and a sleeping bag. However, because it was a working day, we could not hire an MSF vehicle. Erin brought along a friend, Daniel, a young man volunteering in Malawi, and we met at the Limbe market hoping to catch a Mulange minibus. Normally it would take an hour to get to Chetakali, but the minibus, unlike MSF cars, would make numerous stops for passengers, so it might take between two to three hours. The minibus had to be almost full with fourteen passengers before departure. When we did finally depart, the conductor continued to solicit passengers on the way to the highway. It seemed that we were stopped at all the police checkpoints, and at the first one, the driver had to pay a fine for some kind of violation. We were stopped at a second checkpoint because the police at the first checkpoint left his cell phone in our vehicle and had called his colleague at the next checkpoint to look out for our minibus. It turned out the passenger sitting by the driver had picked up the phone, intending to keep it. While trying to leave the van, he was accosted and caught red-handed. As he was led away, we saw the police whacking him on the head. The third stop was for the same violation, but the driver was able to show that he had already paid the fine.

Once out of the city limit, the conductor began to pack his van with impunity, and the number of passengers grew to twenty-two, along with bags and baskets of produce and utensils. We were being squeezed, and women with their babies on their backs had the hardest time. At a busy market, a man and two women with a baby and bags of produce stood near the door wistfully. While I thought it was impossible for the conductor to take in more passengers, he did by asking passengers at the back to make more room and pushing bags of produce under the seats. He then stepped into the van, arching his body, lowering his head, and closing the door behind him with a resounding bang. After two hours of painful loading and unloading, we finally reached Chetakali and the info-office of the Mountain Club of Malawi.

We registered at the Mountain Club, and Christopher outlined our routes on a model. Our hike started at the back of the office towards Lichenya Hut, about a five-and-a-half hour journey for the first day. Then on the second day, we were to hike for four hours to Chisepo Hut and from there a three-and-a-half-hour hike to Sapitwa. The descent was three hours down to Chisepo Hut to rest for the night; that would be our hardest day with a ten-and-a-half-hour hike. On our last day, we would descend to the Forestry Office, about a five-and-a-half-hour trek, stopping at the waterfall for a dip on the way. Christopher had already roused up Pious, our guide, and we gave him some kwachas to buy his food.

Our hike started in the small farms of some villagers which eventually led to a large tea estate with Mulange as a backdrop, a very spectacular and peaceful view. The path became steeper through some bamboo groves and more tea plantations; the Mulange Boma became smaller as we climbed higher. We reached a vast area of burnt forests, charred bushes, and ground; the terrain became steeper and rockier where we had to do some scrambling over the rock surface, and soon our legs and hands were smeared with soot. We were aiming for a plateau which could not be seen immediately, as each time we scaled a steep section of rocky surfaces, more sections appeared. It seemed endless. Finally, we pushed through a narrow path flanked by tall bushes onto the plateau, a vast expense with scattered bouquets of papery yellow everlasting flowers and purple irises. The trek was long, but thankfully it was relatively flat. We caught a glimpse of Lichenya Hut, but to get to it we first had to descend and then ascend a steep path. By the time we reached the hut, it was almost five in the afternoon. A sign pointed to Lichenya Pool, but none of us had the desire to go there; it was already cold. An abandoned bathtub sat serenely in the front yard. I wondered how on earth it found its way up there.

Lichenya hut was grand with a wrapped around veranda, three big rooms, and a loft. The hut keeper set a roaring fire of cedar wood, filling the large room with its pleasant scent. Pious said the keeper could warm up some water for us for a bucket bath, but I just chose to towel myself. We ate a simple meal of bread, cheese, apples, peanut butter, and chocolate. The sky was cloudy, but in the middle of the night it cleared up to reveal numerous stars but no Milky Way.

Around six-thirty in the morning after a quick breakfast, we hiked for three and a half hours to Chisepo, traversing over some steep terrain and crossing a shallow stream over some rocks. There were spectacular views of the mountains enshrined in a mysterious fog. At Chisepo we rested for a brief moment and left most of our things, only carrying water, snacks, and warm clothes. We embarked towards Sapitwa, following a dirt path bordered with ferns which soon gave way to steep rocky steps. We negotiated narrow ledges and precarious perches on rocks, hopping over riotous jumbles of gigantic boulders, stretching our legs to their limits. Then came long stretches of steep, sheer rock surfaces where either we walked if there were cracks to provide some traction or crawled on all fours and squeezed through rock crevices or cave-like tunnels. My sneakers often slipped on the rocky surfaces. Towards the peak it was all rocks. The sun disappeared when thick mists came rolling in, and the temperature dropped. For a brief moment, the peak came into view enticingly above us.

We reached the peak, Sapitwa, around two in the afternoon. Half of the view was obscured by thick mists, and on the other side where the mist was thin, a breathtaking vista of rocky mountain peaks loomed. Sapitwa means "Don't go there" in Chichewa; the locals believe that spirits live up there, and hikers, especially those who trek without a guide, have disappeared. Pious told us that a Brazilian hiker got lost last year and was found dead three weeks later.

On our descent we slid down on our bottoms over the rock surfaces. One false step meant one could tumble out of sight over the steep rocky surface into oblivion. It was hairy at times when my shoes were caught in rock ridges and became entangled among long blades of grass. We reached Chisepo around five p.m. after hiking for ten and a half hours. At the hut which consisted of one large room with a central fireplace, we were joined by four other hikers from the Netherlands, Afghanistan, and UK. We were the only hikers summiting Sapitwa that day.

On day three of our hike, after a long night's sleep, we were ready to roll by seven in the morning for what we were told a five-and-a-half-hour hike, retracing our steps towards Lichenya. At a crossroads, Chambe Mountain sat to our right. We followed an endless slog of steep, slippery, stony paths alternating with gravelly steps, quite difficult to traverse without feeling like falling or slipping off the cliff to our left. We debated about making a detour to the waterfall with rocky pools of refreshingly cold water, and in the final analysis we made the right choice and cooled ourselves there.

At the Forestry Department at the bottom of Mulange, we settled our bill for our accommodation and entry fees and walked towards the main road to catch the bike taxi for the ten-kilometer ride to Chetakali to meet our ride back to Limbe and Blantyre. Apart from scraped and bruised knees and traumatizing the new toenail that grew after my last Boston Marathon, I came out of this hike unscathed. The many enchanting faces and hues of Mulange throughout our hike enthralled us all, and the pictures could not do justice to its beauty.

Mother's Day was celebrated in October in Malawi. I took advantage of a long weekend to go to Cape MaClear in Mangochi on Lake Malawi. Fortuitously, Gillian was heading that way, and I was able to get a ride from her. I had mixed up my dates when I reserved my stay in Mgoza Lodge, so I had to stay at Thumbi View Lodge which did not have an oasis-like lawn as at Mgoza Lodge but served the purpose. It was hot the day we traveled to Mangochi, and I found the terrain very much like Nsanje, dry and arid, and some areas had been so overgrazed that there was just sand with little by way of vegetation. Unlike Nsanje, even the limbs of the baobab were amputated so that they looked oddly and sadly deformed.

It was a four-hour drive, and we arrived in time for a dip in the lake before sunset. The village only had dirt, sandy roads, and the lodges seemed to blend unobtrusively into the rest of the scene, not overwhelmingly touristy. Lining the road were several very old baobabs with leathery and pitted swollen trunks resembling elephantiasis. I got up early in the morning to swim in the lake. Lake Malawi is known to have bilharzia. However, since the water for our shower was piped from the lake, even if one avoided swimming one would still be exposed to the water of the lake. Even at this hour, I noticed many villagers, hundreds of them, mainly women and children, by the lakeside washing dishes, clothes, bathing, brushing their teeth, and fetching water. Despite the fact that there was water from boreholes at various spots by the dirt road built by some NGOs, Malawians used the water from the lake, and some even drank from it. The lake was a big bathtub. Ducks and dogs milled around for leftovers, and children caught small, silvery fish and placed them in shallow sand pits where they struggled for their last breath. Men sat on the edges of dugout canoes people-watching; perhaps they had just returned from their night fishing. Despite all that washing, the lake was crystal clear.

Later in the morning I joined William and Verome from South Africa on a boat trip to Thumbi Island and Otter's Point for some snorkeling. There were many brightly colored chichidis: brilliant blue, purple, and neon yellow; some blue ones had black zebra stripes. There were also chambo, a fish known here in the lake. Several fish eagles perched on treetops were calling; Peter the boatman threw fish into the lake, attracting them to swoop down to catch them.

Heading back, we passed the Lake Malawi National Park. Peter bitterly said that five years ago the government promised to revitalize the park, but nothing had been done. There was no electricity or running water, and the few remaining houses were derelict with neglect. This stretch of the beach was lined with beautiful private homes with manicured gardens and swimming pools; big corporations such as the Illovo Sugar Cane Company and the tea estate owned some of them. Caretakers combed the beaches, but Peter said anyone could use them. However, the villagers did not seem to congregate in these areas. Overnight a strong blustery wind blew, reminding me of Limbe when the wind seemed to pick up in the early hours of the mornings.

I spent the rest of the weekend relaxing on a chaise longue, reading, swimming when it got too hot, and walking on the beach. I also swam in the evening as the moon was almost full. Aiden showed me his rented place: a two-story reed and thatched house with a bedroom and a sitting room overlooking the lake. There were no walls to block the view. It must be just a beautiful dream to wake up to see the turquoise blue lake with the gentle breezes constantly blowing.

On our way home, Gillian took a short detour to Monkey Bay, which was essentially a dusty little town on the beach culminating in a big shipyard where we were forbidden to go further. My visit to a small part of Lake Malawi had been a memorable one.

Three of us expats spent four days in Thyolo for an HIV/TB integration workshop; the goal was to have all healthcare centers to be able to provide TB treatment in the ART clinic and vice versa. TB and HIV pretty much go hand in hand. After the withering heat of Nsanje, Thyolo being at a higher elevation was heaven. One had to wear a sweater or a scarf early in the day. The jacaranda trees were shedding their trumpet flowers, covering the ground with their purple petals. The Thyolo District Hospital was just a few years old, painted a reddish-brown with well-kept grounds grown with flowers. At the back stretched a vast green tea estate. Thyolo was known for its many tea estates. Mahogany and cedar were sacrificed long ago with only a small portion preserved; the indigenous forests had all but vanished. There were also groves of macadamia trees in the Conforzi Plantation.

On our last night in Thyolo, we went to Satemwa, founded in 1923 by Maclean Kay. He was a rubber planter from my neck of the woods, Malaya, an immigrant from Scotland who worked in Malaya in 1910. Once one stepped into Satemwa, one was no longer in Africa. Unfortunately, we arrived at dusk, so its full beauty was not revealed to us. The mansion was built with somewhat of a Spanish flair with wide verandas and arches. The reception area and sitting room with a fireplace were open to the outside veranda through big low windows, seemingly making the outside world as one with the inside. The small library was cozy, and that led to a dining room with a long dining table flanked by high-backed chairs, tall candelabras sitting in the center. It opened into another veranda with terraced steps leading right into the garden with a pond of reeds. In the courtyard was another small marbled pond with a gnarled old tree arching gracefully over it and a table set for dining. One of the guest rooms, which was plainly a master bedroom, had a big bed draped with gossamer netting; a bowed window in one corner was lined with comfortable chairs, and at the end of the bed were stained glass windows. The bedroom had a modernized bathroom with a tub and a shower.

Outside was a huge lawn with two clusters of rattan-cushioned chairs, bordered by an archway of creepers and wisteria. Picking our steps carefully in the semi-darkness of dusk, we were greeted by a strong scent of gardenia. An antique-looking, non-functioning stone fountain with a statue stood in a corner, and next to it a wide field of blue hydrangea.

We dined at Satemwa that night.

At the Thyolo MSF expat house were two cats, Lucifer and Zikomo. Lucifer was slated to go to Shire House in Nsanje, but twice when the cat carrier arrived, Lucifer disappeared for a few days. He never was available to be transferred to Nsanje; perhaps it was not meant to be.

In early October, on the front page of the *Daily News* splashed the headline "Capital Hill Billion Mess"; billions of kwachas had been looted by government officials. The German ambassador warned that the Malawian government could not blame the computer for corruption; people ran computers, and the computers did not commit the fraud. The Malawian people and the donors were entitled to know the truth. The Malawian government used the Integration Financial Management Information Services (Ifmis), a computer software in the government payment system. Since then investigations revealed that at least 90 billion kwachas had been pilfered from the Federal Treasury from 2009 to 2012.[29] The current Vice President, Khumbo Kachali, was linked to the looting, and the past regime was believed to be responsible for the systematic stealing. There were at least seven identifiable schemes, including paying off companies that did not provide any services, cashing checks without vouchers, and large sums dispersed without the signing off by senior authorities. In view of the large amount of money missing from the treasury, IMF was withholding seven billion kwachas from Malawi. Some politicians lamented the fact that programs that had started would not be able to continue because of the withheld money. But what about the harm done by this looting?

The news broke while President Joyce Banda of Malawi was visiting the U.S. She came back and fired her cabinet members, only to convene another with most of them back. However, it had emerged as well that since 2012 while she had been President, 20 billion kwachas were also stolen from the coffer. A week after the news broke, Britain announced it would send a forensic auditor team to help to identify the perpetrators. It also came to light that three commercial banks in Blantyre were authorized by the Malawian Reserve Bank to honor government checks of any amount, which seemed a recipe for fraud. When the previous president, Mutharika, came into power in 2004, he declared his wealth at 150 million kwachas, but when he died of a heart attack in 2012, his wealth had grown to 60 billion kwachas.[30] He had bank accounts in Australia, Singapore, and the Isle of Man. One wondered when he thought he would have time to enjoy all of that with three houses in Singapore and two presidential flats in Australia to boot. He evidently did not count on the fact that despite all the wealth, he was powerless to determine how long he had on this earth.

Corruption is probably rampant in many Africa countries, given the fact that many of them receive huge amount of foreign aid. People at the government level must be tempted to siphon off large sums of money, hoping that their misdeeds would never be discovered. Or do they feel that they are entitled to some of the money?

When Malawians were asked what they thought about the stealing, they were not surprised but expressed disgust that the hard-earned money of the taxpayers and donors, which could be used to improve healthcare conditions and the school systems, had been pocketed by greedy politicians. Foreign donors were equally outraged by the news.

The newspaper enumerated what the 110 billion kwachas could do for the healthcare sector, agriculture, and the school system. For 110 billion kwachas, 40,000 medical doctors could be trained at the Medical College, 16,500 classroom blocks could have been built so children did not have to huddle under trees to study, 44 irrigation schemes could have been completed within a year.[31] This last thing was of utmost importance to Malawi given that it still depended on rain-fed agriculture when it had a vast supply of water: the lake and the Shire River. The irrigation scheme named the Green Belt Initiative stalled because of the lack of funding.[32] This was a concept of the former president Bingu wa Mutharika, referring to a stretch of land along the lakes and perennial rivers, supporting irrigated agriculture and offering social and economic services to a community. The idea was to have a well-developed, sustainable and managed infrastructure for a comprehensive land and water resources to increase irrigated agriculture productivity and assure livelihoods. The food insecurity problem of Malawi could have been solved if indeed this scheme worked.

The budget for the healthcare sector was around 48 billion kwachas per year, just about half of what was stolen from 2009 to 2012.[33] Almost all the healthcare facilities that I visited in Nsanje District were in need of maintenance and repair; ambulances were either non-functioning or in need of fuel for their operation. The DHO of Nsanje District Hospital often had to request fuel aid from MSF. He had been quoted in *The Nation* as to the fact that 20 billion kwachas could provide all the health services in Nsanje district for 80 years and 110 billion for 440 years. After grand ward rounds one day, one of the medical assistants informed the DHO that they were out of bandages and plasters. He lowered his head and said, "I suppose we just have to try very hard to persuade our patients not to get sick."

School started during the first week of September; at least half the children walked to school barefoot, many carried no books, and some had only an exercise book in a plastic bag. In the villages, numerous students gathered around a board under a big tree while their teachers held classes there. In Sankhulani, the crowded primary classrooms had no windows; the bricks bordering the window frames were loosening and falling apart.

If the politicians had a heart and a conscience, they would not have looted the Malawians and endangered their lives because of a half-baked healthcare system or robbed the children, who were the future of Malawi, of their much-needed education. While many NGOs spent time, effort, and money to feed these children at school, the politicians chose to enrich themselves, even at the expense of stealing food from the mouths of these children.

One seldom encountered fat, ordinary Malawians, at least in the villages; the politicians appearing on the newspapers were often rotund, double-chinned, meaty, and certainly were by no means starving. Joyce Banda announced that the country silos were suddenly low or almost emptied of maize, and the people would surely starve.[34] Emergency measures were taken to buy maize from South Africa and Zambia to feed the country. Did someone also siphon off some maize to feed their bellies?

The children here sometimes yelled out to me, "Give me *my* money!"

I replied, "I don't have *your* money."

A kid once ran past me and said, "Give me my money buying shoes."

I learned to say "*Mundipatse ndalama zanga!*" ("Give me my money" in Chichewa). This often surprised them so much that they just stood there staring at me with their mouths wide open.

The politicians behaved as if the public funds were theirs to take and spend. Indeed, one of the front pages of *The Nation* showed the new homes built by the "looters." On the same page, there was an article where the World Bank was quoted as saying that if the U.S. would contribute 4.5 billion dollars to Africa to develop its agriculture and boost its development and productivity, it would solve the hunger problem. Many Africans lamentably survive on 1.25 U.S. dollars per day. Would this amount of money really solve the hunger problem if corruption is rampant? I rather doubt it.

November promised to be hotter than October; we were experiencing heat waves of temperatures over forty degrees Celsius or over one hundred degrees Fahrenheit. Last week it reached 108 degrees F. In the office, the electricity supply was not powerful enough to work the air conditioning in the medical part of the building. While the coordination section enjoyed the coolness of the AC, we struggled with two rotating, standing fans blowing and circulating hot air around us. Sweat trickled down the backs of my legs, and I felt like I was in a sauna. My walks to and from the hospital in this temperature had not been pleasant; even the dogs left me alone, having dug themselves enormous holes in the ground for their long, lazy naps. A Malawian boy in our neighborhood rigged up a small fan using discarded materials and operated it with the use of a solar panel as he and his friends rested on a mat outside his house.

In the hospital when the temperature reached above 100 degrees F, the AC ceased to work. The conference room where we held meetings was usually flooded with sunlight, and Malawians seemed to love long meetings, which did not help. The sweltering heat made one sweat through one's clothes, and one's forehead was soon covered with the wet stuff. Throats were soon parched, and with no safe water source, some staff went out to buy water. My bottle of water was hot, and it could not quench my thirst. After all these years of MSF presence in hot Nsanje, no one thought of providing filtered water for our office in the hospital. As we walked out of the office in the mid-afternoon, hot, sultry air just blasted us in the face and burned our skin, wilting our will to carry on, but carry on we must.

This past weekend, our new expat from Argentina who joined us two weeks ago asked James, one of our drivers, to take us to the base of the mountains to Chididi to start our hike. With the Argentinian in the Shire House, we were no longer an all-women team. We brought plenty of water, for it was a hot day. This route was apparently the short cut used by the people of Chididi to go to the Nsanje Boma, and it traversed three slopes. We met many locals who were wondering why we were trekking to Chididi. The Argentinian off-handedly said, "We are just hiking to Chididi to get a cold Fanta!" The locals did not walk this route for leisure, only the *azungus*. As a matter of fact, the Argentinian, being in logistics, was planning to build a wading pool in the backyard of Shire House for us to cool off. He was hoping to get some timber from Chididi.

It took us three and a half hours to reach cooler Chididi, where the Argentinian negotiated to buy some lumber. The locals had gathered somberly at a funeral service but became distracted by our arrival. A few boys hovered over some ant holes to catch the giant ants for a snack. Patrick waited for us by the Chididi health center to take us back in the cruiser to the withering heat of Nsanje.

It rained heavily for an hour the afternoon when the pool was completed, and it became partly filled with rainwater. The drawback was it blocked the view of the mountains in the backyard. We dipped in it after work, cooling off for the first time and feeling deep gratitude for the Argentinian while watching the sunset.

I traveled to Blantyre for a TB/HIV Integration meeting called by the MOH to discuss rolling out the program in Nsanje. The person who called the meeting was attending a TB conference in Paris, and I was doubtful that this meeting would take place. Since we could not reach him, I left for Blantyre only to learn that indeed, he just landed in Malawi, and the meeting would not take place until later in the week. I could not do any of the fieldwork in Nsanje while in Blantyre, and there was nothing to do but to explore the city. Blantyre, being in the highlands, was at least five degrees Celsius cooler than Nsanje. It is the second largest city in Malawi after the capital, Lilongwe. Founded by the Church of Scotland through missionary work in 1876, it was named after the town in Scotland where Dr. David Livingstone was born. His missionary work led to the building of St. Michael's and All Angels Church in 1891 with arches, domes, and flying buttresses. The church was designed and the construction managed by Rev. David Clement Scott, who had no formal architectural training. He managed this feat with the help of local people who had no knowledge of this kind of architecture.[35] Mandala House was one of the oldest buildings in Malawi. It was built in 1882 with mud, grass, and bricks and was then the first house that had another house sitting on top of it.[36] Locals came to gape at it and crawled up the stairs cautiously. John and Frederick Moir, the two brothers who ran the African Lake Corporations, traded in coffee, clothing, ammunition, and hardware. The house was called Mandala because John Moir wore glasses, and Mandala means light reflecting off pools of water, aptly describing the reflection off of his glasses.[37] Mandala now had a shop, an archive library, and a cafe where one could have a light lunch and drinks.

The National Museum was not much to write home about. There was an exhibition of the life of Dr. Livingstone in the lower section to celebrate the bicentenary of his birth.

Queen Elizabeth Central Hospital in Blantyre had both the paying and non-paying sections; cleanliness, crowding, and privacy marked the difference between the two. Overall it was one of the cleaner hospitals I had seen in Africa. In the non-paying section, the nursery was packed, and mothers sat beside the bassinets where their babies slept. The wards had beds placed close to one another, reminiscent of the old Boston City Hospital where I did my Infectious Disease Fellowship. I chanced upon a neurology ward with six hydrocephalus children; their heads were so huge that some of them were weighed down by them. The first hydrocephalus baby I ever saw was in Cook County Hospital in Chicago when I was a medical student. The teenage mother did not realize that her baby's growing big head was abnormal, instead she presumed that it indicated the degree of intelligence of her child.

I walked across a street to the campus of the College of Medicine of the University of Malawi; it looked very clean and new. Makerere University in Kampala could not compare with this campus. This was probably all built with donation money. One wondered when Malawi would get out of the need for foreign aid.

In Limbe where I stayed when I visited Blantyre, the guesthouse Fargo was on BCA hill, which stood for British Central Africa. A passing Malawian offered this piece of information one evening when I took a walk in the neighborhood. The hill was dominated by nice homes inhabited by expats and rich Malawians including the ex-President, all fenced in by brick walls topped with barbed wires and slivers of broken glass, guarded by twenty-four-hour security guards and *agalu olusa* or dangerous dogs. Down in the valley was where the poor locals lived in tin or tiled roofed houses, haphazardly patched together with tarp, mismatched corrugated sheets or wood as in the houses in the slums of Kampala or Nairobi.

The man waved his hand towards the BCA hill, "That's where our people go to work."

Even years after independence, there was still evidence of colonialism in the hierarchical order of the social system here. All over the slopes of the hill, the land had been furrowed and was ready for the growing season. Men chipped painstakingly at big boulders to form small gravels for sale as building materials to earn a living wage. The disparity between the well-to-do and the poor was stark. However, in my walks I found the locals friendly, and they often broke into a ready smile at my attempt at speaking Chichewa. Around four in the morning, the call to prayer arising from the mosque in the valley invariably elicited a chorus of howling from the dogs.

At the outskirt of Blantyre was the Bvumbwe (Wild Cat) market where I asked the driver to take me one Saturday morning. It was a large, local market selling produce, meat, second-hand clothes, and *chitenje*. This was where we got our vegetables that were grown in the cooler region of Thyolo: cauliflower, cilantro, broccoli, carrots, and many more, which we could not get in Nsanje. They were brought to us via the weekly transport from Limbe to Nsanje. In a corner, a cobbler repaired shoes that had seen their better days, but to the poor, they were still salvageable.

Limbe and Blantyre were full of expats. I realized that when I was invited to go to Hillview School, an international school in BCA hill, for their annual Christmas fair. I was just going to pop in for a little while, being more interested in going hiking in Satemwa Tea Estate that morning. A group of Malawian children stood outside the school fence at the entrance gawking, trying to catch a glimpse of what was going on in the schoolyard, while expat children arrived in cars driven by their parents. I would have been one of those kids outside the fence when I was growing up. Somehow I do not remember having been envious of the kids inside the fence or thinking that life had dealt me an unfair fate. I knew that I had to work hard to change my situation. Wandering around the schoolyard filled with festivities, an abundance of crafts, gifts, food, and drinks, with Christmas music in the air, I could not help feeling a twinge of sadness for the inequality of life, and the disparity between the privileged expats, well-to-do nationals, and the local poor.

The day before I had walked deep into the BCA village to see how the other half lived. I tried once to penetrate it but was deterred by a couple of young men outside a bar from which loud music streamed. They looked at me with glassy eyes, having had a little too much to drink. One of them said it would make him very happy if I could give him some money to buy a drink. I carried no money with me and told him so. Standing right at the edge of the village, prudence told me that I should not venture into it that evening. I turned around and walked right back up the hill. This time I walked into the village, greeting the villagers in Chichewa; somehow that always brought out friendly responses, and I felt safe. Some people called out, "*Mupita kuti?*" (Where are you going?) The houses were small, mainly of bricks with worn-out stucco, topped with tin roofs. Narrow and rugged roads with sharp stones crisscrossed the village. Children, most in ill-fitting, dirty clothes, and some boys with big gaping holes in their shorts revealing their bare bottoms, walked barefoot, unperturbed by the jagged rocks protruding from the road surface. Women and men sat on the roadsides selling produce, secondhand shoes, and clothes. Minibuses arrived at the entrance of the village leaving a trail of choking dust behind them. Most of the land was cleared for planting. The people of the village were just waiting for the first rain to fall before seeding.

I met Ruthie, who took me deep into the village through winding, narrow, dirt paths with haphazardly scattered houses, stagnant pools, and a stream filled with plastic bags, and garbage; ideal homes for mosquitoes. We were soon tailed by a group of children. She passed by her mother's home and finally her own house, which consisted of two dark, dingy rooms with only a very small window for the backroom and her bedroom. There was no back door. The front room was filled with her kitchen utensils; the bedroom had a twin bed with no mattress and a pile of clothes stashed along the wall. She lived there with her three children aged three to eight; her husband passed away three months ago of malaria at the Queen Elizabeth Central Hospital. The house had no latrine, and she shared her mother's. There was no electricity or running water; she had to get her water from a communal tap. She pointed to BCA hill where she cleaned house for a man who paid her 2500 kwachas a week, about $6 U.S. She took me out of the village via a back route, and I shook her rough hand as we parted.

That week the water main broke, and a string of women balancing big buckets on their heads walked up the hill for a few kilometers to the water department to fetch water. The people living on BCA hill had huge water tanks; life went on as usual for them, and they were unperturbed by this incident.

The same evening, we drove to Thyolo in a MSF minibus to the Thyolo Sports Club. At the entrance, a group of locals sat silently at the edge of the road. Expats and well-to-do nationals drove in for the night to celebrate Guy Fawkes Day. The locals must have experienced this in years past and partook of the festivity as observers outside the club. The kids outside the gate sat quietly on the ground in the gathering gloom while the rambunctious, privileged kids inside ran around on the lawn doing what kids did. A bonfire was lit as an effigy of Guy Fawkes was burnt. The evening ended with a display of fireworks. We, the privileged ones, left in our cars, leaving the locals behind. I hoped we did not take this privilege for granted.

On Thanksgiving week my team and I were at the East Bank. The rain, which was expected about now, had not come, and the farmers were growing anxious. We stayed in Thekarani up in the mountains, so the nights were windy and cool. On my evening walk, lo and behold, as my mind was on Thanksgiving, I saw three turkeys pecking away by a churchyard, two black and an ancient white turkey.

On Thanksgiving morning, children in Thekerani were going to school; many were not in uniform, and almost half of the children were barefoot. Two boys were walking slowly and aimlessly to the market; obviously they were not going to school. Another two, about fourteen years of age, walked with a grown man who carried a sack. The boys were in shirts filled with holes and shorts that barely clad their skinny bums. They finally settled rather listlessly on the curb. The man reached into the sack and produced two small loaves of bread. He gave them to the boys who bit into them slowly. There was no beverage to wash them down.

As we drove downhill one day from Thekerani to the East Bank, a father frantically flagged us down and asked for a ride to bring his five-months pregnant daughter to Thekerani Rural Hospital run by MSF. It meant going back up the mountain from where we just came. She looked well, but he was worried that she was anemic. She had not had any prenatal care, having hidden her pregnancy from her father as she became pregnant after staying with a man friend. The father was wearing an oversized pinstriped suit, his forehead beading with sweat. We could bring his daughter and told him MSF restricted us to one accompanying guardian in the van. Backtracking was not recommended, but if we were to go forward, she would have to go to Trinity Hospital, a paying hospital. A few hundred yards later, he yelled out to the driver to stop; apparently another daughter had come from Thekerani to meet them. She then boarded the cruiser and the father got off; we were under the impression that his home was close by. Later we learned that father and daughter had walked all the way from Trinity, about fifteen kilometers, to this village to discuss with the baby's father what he planned to do. As we drove back again, we saw the father climbing the road towards Thekerani Hospital, still wearing his jacket in the heat. I felt really bad that we did not realize how far he had walked, and he still had a distance to walk to the hospital, all uphill.

Later that same day we took a young woman to Trinity who was bleeding in her fifth month of pregnancy. Our visit to the East Bank was always filled with surprises. The bridge that would take us straight to Makhanga in the East Bank within an hour instead of five hours was still being built, and it would require an additional three months for completion, by which time the rain and flood would be in full swing. We drove to see it from the Makhanga side, crossing a solid iron railway bridge over the Shire. This bridge was built years ago by the British and still remained strong.

Thanksgiving is a time when we sit down and count the many blessings bestowed on us: peace in our country, loved ones, family, friends, food, shelter, health, financial security... I feel particularly blessed when I travel and volunteer in many countries where I witness the daily struggles of the local people for their daily bread, people who are caught up in war and conflict, with their lives turned upside down by events beyond their control, by natural disaster, hunger, famine, or people dying because of lack of healthcare.

That weekend Erin invited me to spend a long afternoon and evening with a group of fifteen Americans for a Thanksgiving dinner. I went to Blantyre Market to buy fixings for a salad. We were from all over the U.S. and three of us came from Massachusetts. There were Peace Corps volunteers, medical people, logisticians, teachers, counselors from different organizations, and some had stayed in Malawi from a few months to several years. It was good to feel like being home away from home and among friends.

Nsanje Boma had a very small town center with two tarmac roads running through it and some secondary dirt roads. Love and Peace Supermarket was their biggest market, but almost all the products were displayed on shelves behind bars. One could only view them for afar and point to the products that one wished to purchase. There were a few bars and restaurants: Folly Brothers Shop, True Man Executive Barber, Praise God Shop, Chikondi Restaurant, Miss Call Bar... In front of the Nsanje market, women sat selling beans and rice. In the market, there were tomatoes, onions, potatoes, pumpkin leaves, peppers, lemons, limes, bananas, sweet apples, green beans, eggplants, dried and fresh fish, meat, eggs, hardware, and textiles from Malawi and Tanzania.

Near the entrance, Peter, an African doctor, had a store selling all sorts of roots, bark, animal hides, porcupine spikes, and snake skins. One could either have him brew a concoction right on the spot after the recounting of one's symptoms or take home some herbs, roots, etc., with instructions on how to prepare a brew.

Along the dirt road vendors displayed second-hand clothes, shoes, and Chinese-made plastic products: buckets, basins, clogs, and flip-flops. Wednesday was their market day, and the dirt road was completely filled with vendors. We could not wander around in the market without children following us asking for money. Within minutes one would have gone through the whole town, but we were happy that we could find enough of a variety of food to sustain us.

Purple jacaranda had given way to the bright red flowers of the flame trees. The baobab trees put on leaves and no longer looked bare. The rain was late as it was now December. The villagers in Nsanje had been hoeing their fields, mainly the women, but they had not finished preparing them for planting. Every morning, lines of women with hoes, baskets, and babies on their backs, walked to their fields. In Limbe where there had been some rain, they had already planted their maize seeds, and some of them had already sprouted seedlings. I also saw a family working together to plant the seeds, the man hoeing, the daughter placing the seeds, and the son covering them with soil using a shoe.

Every quarter, MSF and MOH jointly presented findings of their joint HIV/AIDS program: accomplishments and obstacles encountered in the previous quarter. In November I participated in my first quarterly presentation. For the preparation, I was given a copy of the PowerPoint presentation from the second quarter as an example of what to present. No one told me the objectives of this exercise, but I gathered that it was a forum for updating the quarterly data. More importantly, it should also be a place where constructive action plans could be put forth for the fourth quarter, although it was already one month late since the report was scheduled a month into the fourth quarter.

Even before the meeting, MSF staff was busy preparing the data for the presentation. The MSF data persons made several trips to the East Bank to gather the final bits of information. I worked on my mentorship part with my mentors and learned that in the past, MSF prepared the PowerPoint presentation, and the MOH staff presented because this was

Planting, a family affair on the hill of British Central Africa in Limbe, Malawi.

supposed to be a collaborative effort. Already this was sounding all wrong to me. The preparation should be a joint effort, but I was told this could never be accomplished because the MOH staff could not be relied upon to appear to work on a project. Eventually succumbing to time pressure, the following scenario developed: the MSF staff analyzed the data, made them into pretty slides, outlined the challenges, the accomplishments, and the action plans all without the input of the MOH. Was this really a collaboration?

A few days before the presentation, after numerous phone calls, text messages, e-mails, friendly cajoling and reminding, the MOH presenters finally came to go over the slides. What were the reasons behind this MOH staff's inertia? Was it because through experience over the last few years, MOH staff had learned MSF would follow through and not fail to present a finished product even if they themselves did not lift a finger? Was it because of a lack of commitment? Was it a leadership issue? Or the universal issue of ALLOWANCE? Would they come and knock on our door to help prepare the presentation if we said we would offer a handsome allowance? In my long discussion with my staff, it was all the above and perhaps some other unknown reasons.

MSF had always taken the leadership role in this supposedly collaborative effort. My observation of the mentorship program in my first couple of months here gave me the distinct impression that MOH mentors were just as content to let MSF lead and they themselves take the back seat. The mentorship program started in 2011, and I came in at the end of quarter two, 2013. Initially MSH and MOH were supposed to come up jointly with a monthly work plan, but now it had become an MSF originated work plan as waiting for MOH staff to work together to formulate one did not succeed. They either did not show up or assumed that someone else would. Days, weeks, and even months would pass, and nothing concrete would come about, so by default MSF filled in the gap. The HIV coordinator from MOH, also called MOH Mentor of Mentors, had difficulty assembling his mentors, and he himself had been known not to show up for meetings that he arranged. There was a lack of commitment on the parts of the MOH mentors and a lack of leadership on the part of the MOH HIV coordinator; their hearts were simply not in this program. The allure of a big city offering a better position and a more exciting life often played a role in sabotaging a well-intentioned program such as this. In the end, the people MSF trained slowly made their inevitable exit from Nsanje.

When MSF still provided an allowance, which ended at the end of September 2013, MOH staff clamored at the door of the mentors' office for a copy of the work plan which they did not work on, and so had no clue what MSF mentors' objectives were for the month. When allowance ended, MSF mentors now in turn had to ask if the MOH mentors were coming with them to the healthcare centers to mentor and remind them when they were being scheduled. There were often excuses for not being able to come: too busy, sick, not feeling well, just back from Blantyre, and now in the middle of doing laundry. These were all actual excuses that we had heard so far. MSF mentors had even asked point-blank why the MOH mentors were not coming for mentorship. One answered, "I'll come when there is money."

In November, we started a series of training through lecture presentations in the health centers. Again the MSF mentors prepared the materials and slotted MOH mentors as trainers, but every day we had to ask them whether they would come to review the slides and go to the health centers to teach jointly. At the training, we dutifully reminded the personnel at the health centers that this was a joint MSF/MOH effort, but was it really?

As was often the case, the meeting for the third quarter presentation started almost an hour late. All MSF staff was present and MOH mentors except one, whom I later learned that the MOH HIV coordinator forgot to invite. The DHO came in to give the opening remarks but did not stay for any of the presentations. The District Nurse Officer (DNO) excused himself in mid-presentation because of a previous engagement in Blantyre. The DMO did not come until close to the end, asked a few questions, and then made the closing remarks. The important people from MOH who needed to hear the presentation could not make themselves available.

Was this a useful exercise? Did we accomplish what we wanted? What did we want to accomplish anyway? The collaboration here was a good show but not a real one. We as MSF staffers were still trudging along as the bulwark of this mentorship. The handover for this part of the MOH-collaborated mentorship was slated for the end of the year, a month and a half from now. The MOH portion was still taking small tentative baby steps, not ready to walk on its own, let alone run.

After the presentation, we all went out to a local restaurant for lunch. As we finished, the MOH HIV coordinator said to me, "Next time, don't arrange for lunch; just give me money."

My mentorship program would end at the end of the fourth quarter instead of the first quarter of next year, so I decided after discussion with the Field Coordinator that I would not come back after the Christmas holidays. The last few weeks had been a whirlwind of activities: HIV training for the healthcare facilities, TB/HIV integration training for Nsanje District, traveling to the East Bank, finishing up reports, and rounding in the hospital. Sankhulani still did not have a functional clinic space, but my mentor and I managed to find a bucket with a spigot for the HIV clinic for hand washing. The delight shown on the face of the healthcare worker with this simple gift just broke my heart.

I had been itching to leave office work for disaster relief work. While I had been here, I had missed being sent to the Philippines for Typhoon Haiyan victims. After a respite at home with my family for Christmas, as everyone would be home for the first time in two years, it might feel like time for me to go to the Philippines to help the typhoon-affected people or to Lebanon to help the Syrian refugees.

As I neared the end of this mission, I would not miss the many long, tedious meetings which usually did not begin on time and lasted at least three hours, and the numerous reports: monthly, quarterly, or whenever reports. I would not miss the argument about who should have access to the database, the half-hearted contributions from the people who worked for the MOH, or the perpetual problem of their demands for allowances. The entitlement to allowances when they were asked to go for training or to collaborate with MSF disheartened me. I was baffled by the demand by a public servant for the right to travel in a private car with a personal driver, of course, with the entire bill to be paid by MSF, in addition to getting a daily allowance for food, lodging, and a stipend. I would also not miss seeing a flock of chicken strung upside down on bicycle handlebars and goats on bended knees tied onto bicycles in the most uncomfortable position on their way to the market, bleating in the most piteous way.

What would I miss? I would miss greeting the Malawians in Chichewa, which never failed to bring broad and ready smiles on their faces or my runs in the village with the children running after me, whom I taught to "high-fiving" with me. I would miss the Malawians' habits of interchanging "r" with "l" (for example exactry for exactly, and the guard, Alan, asking me, "Doctor, you didn't do you lun (run) this morning?"). I would miss the national staff who take great care of us, my mentors whom I had gotten to know very well and had a great deal of fondness, regard, and respect, and I wished them well. I would miss the various species of birds that chirped their various tunes around Shire House. I would miss Roger, Volcano our office guard dog, and most of all the Shire House cat, Kuyvina Mavuto.

And so I bid farewell to Nsanje. *Tsalani bwino*!

Part II

Medical Care for Internally Displaced People and Refugees in Africa, 2011–2013

7

Back to Uganda

2011, The Nakivale Refugee Camp

"I have many scars, even in my heart, the people who put those scars on me still live freely in Rwanda."

—Leodegard Kagaba, a Hutu refugee
in Nakivale Refugee Camp[1]

At the end of June of 2011, Medical Teams International (MTI) called for volunteers to serve in their clinic at the Nakivale Refugee Camp situated in Isingiro District in southwest Uganda when they had their grant from the Bureau of Population, Refugees, and Migration (BPRM) from the U.S. State Department renewed. This is one of the oldest refugee settlements near the volatile borders of the DRC and Rwanda, with more than 100,000 refugees.[2] The refugee camp was first opened in 1958 and officially established as a settlement in 1960. MTI had been there serving 27,000 plus refugees since December of 2008 in collaboration with a number of organizations including the Ugandan government, World Food Program (WFP), and UNHCR. They had set up a permanent clinic providing primary healthcare to the people living in the Ngarama district. Their goal for the volunteer teams and the national staff was to reduce morbidity and mortality of the Congolese refugees living in the Nakivale Refugee Camp. Besides Congolese, they served refugees from other countries such as Rwanda, Burundi, Sudan, Somalia, Ethiopia, and Eritrea.[3]

Kampala had not changed much since I was here in 2007, still bustling and with its share of slums. Trucks parked neatly in a row on the potholed and crumbling pavements, forcing pedestrians to walk on the hazardous roads where *boda boda* and *matatu* seemed to ignore their existence. I paid a visit to Mulago Hospital for old times' sake; the patients still packed the wards, spilling onto the floors and into the hallways.

From Kampala, we drove westwards for about five hours over uneven bumpy roads to Mbarara, a small, dusty, but busy town, to our temporary home in a quiet village and met Opio and Sheila, our housekeeper and cook.

On Sunday, Opio and I walked to All Saints Church, bearing the name of my church at home. The differences were obvious; I thought my eardrums would burst with the rousing singing over the microphones. There must have been about two hundred people there, and spare chairs continued to be put outside the church. Built fifteen to twenty years ago, it had already outgrown its capacity. The congregation had started fundraising and built a new foundation to the right of the old church. To its left was the tiny tin shed that was the first church; it was now their Sunday school.

Kibengo Health Center II at the Nakivale Refugee Settlement in Uganda, run by Medical Teams International.

On Monday, we traveled over compacted red-earth roads for an hour to visit the Nakivale Refugee Camp and the refugee registration center. These days there were between five to ten new refugees a day, much reduced from years ago. The refugees received food, tent sheets, and a plot of land to grow crops. The camps looked more like semi-permanent settlements; refugees erected houses of sticks and mud with thatched or tarpaulin roofs. Around them, they grew corn, sorghum, and vegetables. Children ran in the compounds marked with the UNHCR logo. The clinics we visited were crowded with waiting patients, mostly women and children.

A heavy downpour greeted us on our first day in the clinic; despite that, the waiting room was teeming with patients. We first made our morning rounds in the makeshift overnight ward, a tented area erected with UNHCR tarpaulins. There were four beds; sometimes two to three small children shared the same bed when it became overwhelmingly crowded. That morning, all the patients who stayed overnight were babies with the exception of one grown man, and everyone had malaria; the sicker ones had a higher burden of the parasites. Intravenous quinine was the treatment of choice; and their fevers were kept down with anti-pyretic and sponging. Parents were responsible for the sponging and ensuring that the kids did not pull out their IVs. The caretakers took care of each other's children and frequently shared a meal on the floor: beans, *matoki* (mashed banana), *ododo* (cooked green vegetables), and rarely meat. We made rounds in the in-patient unit at the beginning and at the end of the day, and the on-call medical officers checked on them at night. During the day the patients were cranky, especially the children. However, after an overnight stay, most

The bustling town of Mbarara, Uganda.

were eating, drinking, and eager to go. What a difference a night of intravenous treatment with quinine and IV fluids made.

The clinic had four examination rooms, a prenatal/maternity section, a laboratory, a pharmacy dispensing area, a stock room for medications, and several waiting areas. Throughout the day, we saw a stream of patients who were quite ill: patients with fever, cough, abdominal pain, diarrhea and vomiting. Many had malaria as mosquitoes here reigned supreme.

At the camp, a woman died giving birth to her twenty-third child, beating the woman in the reality show of "19 Kids and Counting." Unfortunately, this was the reality of life here, not a show. A TV producer would not have chosen to air her tragic story. Why would he? The ratings would likely be low. Who would like to see a bunch of malnourished children in ragged clothing, the older ones with children on their backs emulating their mothers, and the younger ones playing barefoot on the dirt, with snot running from their noses? The audience would prefer to watch the Duggars in their big comfortable home doing happy family stuff and going to educational outings.

The Nakivale Refugee Camp was swarming with children, many wearing clothes as brown as the earth itself. They often trailed behind me in my walk. Why have so many children? These women had lost many of their children in the war, and they were replacing them. The more they had, the greater the food portion they would receive from WFP. Looking at the size of the homes the refugees built, one had to wonder how all these children would fit in them comfortably.

Many girls had their first child at the tender age of seventeen. Their young faces still bore traces of childhood innocence. Their own mothers were still actively having babies, and they had to care for their little siblings while caring for their own baby. But soon they had two or more children, tying one to their back, carrying one in front, with two in tow all a year or two apart. The business of childbearing and child-rearing began to wear them down, and they aged rather quickly. A woman who had lost her husband and a twin child in the war was left to rear four children on her own. Her fourteen-month-old baby was clearly malnourished, looking more like a three-month-old, and the mother was a picture of despair as she waited patiently to receive food for her child. The pair reminded me of the HIV-infected mother, Phoebe, and her child, Zedekiah, in Maseno, Kenya, abandoned by her husband and mother-in-law. Then there was a woman whose husband had fled the Congo and left her to raise their two children, one of them blind in the right eye with a growth behind it. The mother could not afford to take her to Mbarara to see an eye specialist.

Domestic and gender-based violence was common here. Early one morning the village chief requested a report for the police for a sixty-year-old woman, assaulted by a man with a *panga* while she came out of a bar; she sustained several superficial cuts to her left wrist and arm and on her left buttock was an enormous swelling.

Children came in all sizes and with various afflictions. One ten-year-old boy walked for an hour to the clinic by himself, arriving with a raging fever; he turned out to have the ubiquitous infection, malaria. He looked quite well after his fever broke and walked home with his malaria medicines. A father brought his eight-year-old son who had had a thorn embedded in his foot for two weeks, now swollen and draining pus. At the bottom of the foot was a gash, an incision made a week ago at another clinic when a medical officer attempted unsuccessfully to remove the thorn. This boy came to our clinic barefoot and limping. We removed an inch-long thorn, probably from an acacia bush, from his swollen foot and gave him a tetanus shot and antibiotics. He had suffered stoically for two weeks and probably had continued to play barefoot with the long thorn buried in the foot. We could not offer a mother any help for her three-year-old who sustained some traumatic birth injuries; she had not been able to stand or walk. A forty-two-year-old woman could not believe it when I told her she was pregnant for the eleventh time. She already had seven living children.

Everywhere one looked, one saw mothers with children and sometimes grandmothers and babies. Often the mothers passed on, leaving their babies in the care of the grand-mothers who had finished with their child-rearing many years ago. Joshua, my African medical officer with whom I shared an examination room, sighed and said it was the grand-mothers who always took care of the babies, never the fathers or grandfathers.

The groundskeeper was a young woman who swept the ground of the Kibengo Health Center and maneuvered a wheelbarrow in the vegetable garden with her peacefully sleeping baby strapped to her back. She did that with the greatest of ease. There were happy children and sad ones; a few sick ones curled up next to the drains, their frail bodies covered with colorful African fabric.

Malaria continued to be rampant; it rivaled respiratory infections in incidence. It did not discriminate and affected the young, the elderly, pregnant, and non-pregnant women. The symptoms of malaria varied so much that any child with vomiting and abdominal pain, especially when there was a fever, warranted a malaria test. Some weeks we were low on rapid malaria test kits and coartem for treatment of malaria, and had to use oral quinine instead. The lab was overwhelmed with so many requests for malaria testing that we started doing our own tests in our exam room. The downside was children waiting outside began to hear crying coming from our room and became fearful when they approached us. Some of them started crying even before they were seen.

One morning a three-year-old child shuffled in with vomiting and fever. Not a whimper issued from her when Joshua pricked her for the rapid malaria test; perhaps she was too sick to cry. An elegantly dressed woman in her seven-month of pregnancy had malaria and had not been able to hold down anything for two days. She held a Japanese waxed floral paper parasol, looking for all the world like a model. We admitted her into the maternity ward.

The clinic saw between two and three hundred patients a day. At the end of one of our busy weekdays, a youngster had a seizure. We suspected he had cerebral malaria and transferred him to a hospital for treatment after starting a dose of diazepam and intravenous quinine.

In my training as an infectious disease specialist, I had read about such tropical diseases as malaria and cholera. Although I have seen cases of malaria in the U.S. mainly in returning travelers from the third world, I had never seen so many cases of cholera and malaria until I volunteered with MTI in Haiti in its cholera outbreak and now malaria in the Nakivale Refugee Settlement. It was quite a humbling learning experience for me indeed.

Joy, my Congolese translator, had traveled for three days and arrived at the border of Uganda as a teenager, escaping the war in November 2008 and carrying whatever he could. He became separated from his parents, who escaped with his younger siblings. In some way, it was a blessing in disguise. Joy registered separately and received his own refugee card, which entitled him to a plot of his own land, tarp, blankets, and cookware. Fortuitously he found his family in Nakivale. He knew French and learned English in Ugandan school. He translated for Joshua and me, but mostly for me since Joshua could often get by using the local language. Despite all the hardship, Joy had a temperament that befitted his name, always greeting me with his wide, white-toothed, joyful, contagious smile. When I showed him the exuberant lyrics to the refrain of "Joy to the World (Jeremiah Was a Bullfrog)" by Hoyt Axton, that talked of bringing joy even to the fish in the ocean, it brought the biggest grin from him.

He would like to return home but was afraid of the insecure situation in Congo. Two of his siblings elected to stay, and they studied in a university, supporting themselves by selling their family properties. Periodically Joy wired money to them when they were in dire need because he was the oldest. He would go back when it was God's will for him to do so. He was insistent about being able to tell a Rwandan refugee from a Congolese from the way they dressed. However, I was convinced that he was aided by their accent, language, and names. I could not tell a Rwandan from a Congolese just by looking at them, and for that matter, I could not tell a Ugandan national from the refugees. The women here wore clothing with a whole variety of clashing colors and materials; there were no distinct differences that I could discern.

Moses 2, who translated for me one day when Joy was not around, had a similar story except that he was around three when he came here in 1994. He would prefer to stay in Uganda and become a citizen. Uganda was all he knew. He had lived here almost all his life, knew only English, and did not think he would fit well in the Congo. Just like Joy, where he ended up would be up to God.

Mary ran the immunization clinic in one of the open-air buildings. The immunizations offered to the children included polio, measles, diphtheria, tetanus and pertussis (DTP), and tetanus for women in their reproductive age. On Wednesdays, she ran a "Growth Monitoring Clinic" for malnourished children, provided education on nutrition, and in some instances, nutritional supplementation.

Rosette and Amulet were the two midwives who ran the ANC on Mondays and Fridays in addition to HIV testing and counseling. Roughly six percent of the pregnant women were tested positive for HIV. The delivery room was next to the maternity ward with two beds, and one could stretch it to three if one had to use the bed in the consultation room. One of the midwives was always on call at night, and oftentimes she spent the night there with the mothers-to-be. Rosette once proudly showed me a newborn baby, soft, innocent, and vulnerable; he was the mother's first and she seemed exhausted, but grandmother was eager to show off her grandson.

In the injection room, Moses 1 and Jocelyn could place IVs expertly in even the tiniest, wriggling baby. Harriet and Jeffrey ran the laboratory. The injection room and the laboratory were the two places the children feared most. Crying often emitted from these rooms, and they were reluctant dragons when it was their turn to face the music.

Joshua was the medical officer with whom I shared a consultation room. We saw patients simultaneously on each side of a desk; not much privacy for them. If I had to do a gynecological examination, I would take my women to the maternity consultation room. For the men who complained of ailments below the waist, I had to empty our consultation room of patients. Joshua, unlike most African medical people with whom I worked, performed physical examinations. Most African doctors just talked to their patients and prescribed medications without laying their hands on them. Joshua was also in charge of the treatment of TB and kept a record of all the patients who had TB as well as HIV testing. About five percent of the HIV patients were positive for TB, and twenty-five percent of patients suspected of TB had HIV.

The power of physical examination was clear in this instance. A man came in complaining of insomnia; he told me that he became "crazy" last January and was admitted and treated with medicine. I decided to do a complete physical examination on him and sent him home on some diazepam (sleep aid). The following week he brought his wife and insisted that she should see me. She also was hospitalized at roughly the same time for a psychotic problem and came in with insomnia. He told Joy that he had been sleeping well since I examined him; he wanted his wife to get the same physical examination that he received from me, fully convinced of the healing power of the laying of the hands.

Sixteen staff members lived in the quarters behind the clinic, two to a room. Many of them had families far away, and yet I did not hear any mutterings of dissatisfaction among the staff. They had to use the latrines, no flush toilets or running water. There was a thriving vegetable garden in the yard with lots of onions, corn, tomatoes, pumpkins, passion fruit, groundnuts, and *ododo*.

The refugees grew a variety of crops and vegetables: corn, sorghum, sunflowers, beans, cassava, sweet potatoes, and groundnuts; some kept a few goats, chickens, and ducks. Many of their activities happened outside the house; women often worked together while socializing, shucking maize or corn, pounding sorghum into flour, mashing reeds, and then drying them for weaving. Corn, sorghum, cassava, and groundnuts were left drying in the hot sun, and even the animals took shelter in the shade wherever they could find it. What would it be like during the rainy season? Children often played in the dirt, boys kicking a ball made with layers of plastic tied together with elastic bands or rolling an old bicycle tire; there were no ready-made toys. An NGO built a playground close by the clinic, a place where the children could play besides in the dirt. Some refugees opened small stores selling small items and airtime for cell phones. There was even a hotel right outside the health center.

During lunchtime, the children shared a meal of potatoes and beans in the kitchen while their mothers had their meal under the shade of a tree, oblivious to the fact that some of the children were sitting dangerously close to hot coals left after the cooking.

The villagers built a huge structure of mud and sticks in a clearing as their place of worship. The benches were made of thin tree trunks supported by even thinner y-shaped tree branches. One needed to be rather alert or risk falling off the bench.

Life went on for the refugees even if exiled from their homeland. The sharp, bleating cries of the ibises that rudely woke me up in the morning were part of the scene here in Mbarara but not in Nakivale. Marabou storks, ugly gigantic birds that had long, ungainly, skinny legs and a big wingspan, seemed to congregate more in the urban areas than in the settlement. Despite their size, they landed ever so gracefully and effortlessly on the topmost branches of tall trees, hardly swaying or disturbing them, perching on the highest points of buildings, resembling steeples on churches. They appeared forlorn and unloved as they scavenged for leftovers in the dumpsters. Rarely a few grey crowned cranes perched on top of the same pine trees where the marabou storks roosted. Next to the marabou storks, the national birds of Uganda were the epitome of elegance and grace. The most impressive animals of all were the Ankole cows with huge horns so perfectly symmetrical. The evolutionary advantages of these astonishingly and ravishingly beautiful horns escaped me.

As it was the season of the *matoki*, men with heavy loads of up to seven bunches of bananas on their bicycles pushed their burden for many kilometers of the dusty road oftentimes uphill towards the market in Mbarara. A journey that took us in our land cruiser a little over an hour would take several hours for them.

Early one morning a man was brought into the compound on a stretcher. I recognized him as the man who had received stitches for a cut on his head and a tetanus shot a week ago. His face was grimacing in pain. His eyes were tightly closed, teeth clenched, periodically arching his neck and back, while a shrill blood-curdling scream issued from his mouth. Moses l miraculously inserted an IV line and gave him IV fluids and antibiotics. As he was moved into an ambulance to be transferred to the German-run hospital, Joy grabbed his leg and entreated God to save him. Joshua said tetanus was not very common here but more often seen in neonates when the village midwives sometimes used cow dung to coat the umbilicus.

Carrying our sobering thoughts back to our consultation room, a frail forty-year-old woman shuffled and stopped every few steps to catch her breath, nostrils flaring and eyes wide with fright. Her pounding heart emitted such a loud murmur it seemed to be ready to burst out of her thin chest. Rheumatic fever had damaged her heart valves, and now her heart was finally failing. There was nothing else we could do besides giving her some water pills and heart medicine to ease her symptoms.

Then an old man walked in with a handkerchief holding an enormous growth hanging from his jaw, dripping copious amount of pus. He had been sitting in a corner away from the crowd, obviously embarrassed because of the odor. The lump distorted his face, stretching the corner of his mouth to one side and making it look as if it had been frozen into a perpetual scream. He had had the growth for four years and had been treated a few times. The last time was two years ago; he could not tell us what treatment he received. Joshua sent the pus for TB smear, but there were no bacilli. Might he be suffering from actinomycosis (lumpy jaw), a chronic bacterial infection seen usually on the face and neck? He would need surgery and long-term antibiotic treatment.

A putrid odor filled the room when another man crawled in with his wife in attendance. Both of his legs were swollen and black with gangrene, and copious, muddy drainage oozed from the bottom of his left foot. With no sensation in either of the legs, he slowly pulled himself upright with the only pair of crutches we had. He would need an amputation as soon as possible. We shipped these two patients to the referral center for further treatment.

As the sun set over Mbarara, the refugees would be here even as I left. UNHCR has been here in southwest Uganda since 1954 taking care of these displaced people. Worldwide there continues to be conflicts and disasters, and as long as these are around, there will always be refugees. While I was here in Uganda, drought across the Horn of Africa, affecting more than 11 million people in Ethiopia, Djibouti, Kenya, and Somalia, had resulted in waves of refugees coming into Ethiopia and Kenya; many would likely die of starvation if humanitarian aid did not reach them in time.[4]

Red Cross trucks came to the settlement to deliver food to the refugees one morning. A few weeks ago, it was WFP. On food delivery days, we saw fewer patients because many stayed back to receive their food ration.

Sadly, my stay here was quickly ending. I would miss the refugees, the staff, the clinic, my early misty morning run, and my evening walk when the Ugandan children often greeted me and asked me where I was from. I tested their knowledge of geography; most knew where the U.S. was, but Malaysia was another matter.

To the staff of Kibengo Health Center II, a big *asante sana*, thank you for welcoming me here. On my last day, they presented to me a wooden plaque with a picture of a zebra carved on it, with love from Mburo National Park, Uganda.

To the refugees, *maniriho*, God be with you.

In April 2015, when President Pierre Nkurunziza of Burundi announced he was running for a third term, widespread protests and unrest occurred, and more than 50,000 Burundians fled to neighboring countries. As a result, the population of the

Patients waiting to get their medications from the pharmacy at Kibengo Health Center II at the Nakivale Refugee Settlement.

Nakivale Refugee Settlement greatly increased.[5] In 2018, the refugees in this settlement represented 17.5 percent of the population of the Kisoro district.[6]

In the middle of my stay in Mbarara, MTI e-mailed a request for volunteers to go to Libya which was caught up in the middle of an uprising against Ghaddafi.[7] My heart skipped a beat. I had always wanted to experience volunteering in a war-torn country, and this would be my chance. I made up my mind to go. In the ensuing days, I transmitted the documents requested by International Medical Corps (IMC) which was the NGO with which MTI would collaborate.

The Nakivale clinic closed on the weekends. One weekend Robert drove me to Lake Bunyonyi right outside of Kabale, two hours from Mbarara. Kabale was an unattractive, dusty, crowded border town only eight kilometers from Rwanda, filled with noisy *boda bodas*. White Horse Hotel, a venerable old British-style hotel with lovely gardens perched on a small hill, was a world apart from the rest of Kabale. Lake Bunyonyi was formed around 10,000 years ago by lava flow from the Virunga Mountains, which blocked off the Ndego River and dammed the valley. It is a serpentine lake with about twenty islands, above 1800 meters high along the winding border of Rwanda to Kabale. Its name means "a place of little birds"; indeed, there were many varieties of birds with loud, incessant chirps especially in the morning. High terraced hills covered with sweet potatoes, *matoki*, sorghum, and beans surrounded the lake. In the mornings, dense mists often shrouded the islands, and the sun struggled to shine through.

A fifty-minute canoe ride took me from Rutinda Market to Itambara Island. As the boatman and I canoed to Itambara Island, Akampere Island or "Punishment Island" eerily appeared in the distance; in the old days unmarried, pregnant women were sent there and left to die.[8] Men who could not afford a wife could claim one for themselves; otherwise, the women starved to death as no food was provided for them. I wondered why the men who impregnated them went unpunished. We rode past Bwama Island which used to be a lepers' colony run by a British doctor, Leonard Sharp.[9] Leprosy was a serious problem in Kigezi around 1929 to 1959; about a hundred lepers at a time lived on the island. The disease was eradicated in the 1960s, and now the island has a school, a handicraft shop, and a church.

I stayed in a dormitory at Byoona Amagara on Itambara Island, idyllic but a little chilly at night. The stars were difficult to see because of the clouds. During the day, I dipped in the cold deep lake, supposedly free of bilharzia, hippopotami, and crocodiles. A sign seemingly from "The Fish" warned humans about polluting the lake.

PLEASE DO NOT POLLUTE THE LAKE
IT PISSES OFF THE FISH!
THIS MEANS NO BATHING WITH SOAP, NO WASHING CLOTHES, ETC.
TAKE NOTE
BYOONA AMARAGA HAS BEEN AUTHORIZED BY THE CREATURES OF THE LAKE TO
FLOG ON SIGHT ANY PERSON INTRODUCING ANYTHING BUT SKIN TO BUNYONYI FROM
THIS DOCK. IF YOU HAPPEN TO GET FLOGGED FOR WASHING IN THE LAKE, PLEASE
ACCEPT IT QUIETLY SO AS NOT TO DISTURB THE BIRDS. AND TRY NOT TO BLEED IN THE
LAKE, AS THAT WILL ATTRACT OTTERS AND PISS OFF THE FISH EVEN MORE! IF YOU HAP-
PEN TO BE IN SUCH DESPARATE NEED OF WASHING PLEASE USE ONE OF MANY BYOONA
AMARAGA'S MANY EFFECTIVE SHOWER AND LAUNDRY FACILITIES.
KIND THANKS,
—THE FISH—

There was no power for four straight days in Mbarara. Geoffrey told us that the Ugandan government owed the power company billions of shillings; as a result, it ran out of money and stopped producing hydropower. It was difficult to read by the dim light of the solar lamps. Power seemed to be cut off when we needed it most, from seven in the evening, when working people were home, until seven in the morning. When the electricity was off, the mosquitoes swarmed. The only safe place was to retreat into my bed-net.

I spent a weekend at Queen Elizabeth National Park staying at Mweya Hostel. It was spartan but clean and not as expensive as the Mweya Safari Lodge, which boasted well-kept grounds, a big outdoor swimming pool, and overlooking the Kazinga Channel and Lake Edward. In the late afternoon a boat ride along the channel revealed an abundance of wildlife: buffaloes wallowing in the mud, hippopotami swimming with their snouts skimping the surface of the water, languorous crocodiles sun-bathing, kingfishers making holes for their nests along the vertical banks, cormorants, eagles, Egyptian geese, pelicans, yellow-billed ducks, and marabou storks. Elephants and waterbucks came for a drink. On one of the wide beaches, a calf lay among a flock of birds while an old buffalo waded alone in the water, having been expelled from the herd; being old, he became an outcast. The sunset was somewhat subdued with hazy clouds hiding the Rwenzori Mountains. For dinner, I had a whole Kazinga tilapia and it was delicious.

John, our guide, took me for an early morning game drive; immediately we spotted two hippopotami running frantically from us in the dawn light after their night feeding. Behind some trees was a herd of elephants. Hanging from a tall tree was a hammer bird's nest—a big nest with an opening at the bottom—that took them a month to build. Along the leopard loop, neither leopards nor lions appeared. Far away in the distant horizon roamed a herd of buffaloes.

The sun came out, a big red ball above the cactus trees, invasive plants transplanted from Senegal in the 1940s, and they now dominated the landscape. Only the baboons thrived on the flowers of the cacti; the juice from the tree apparently was poisonous to most animals. Leaving the Royal Circuit to go to the Kob Circuit, we saw Ugandan kobs and a male waterbuck. John said the waterbuck was the last animal that the lion would resort to eating because before it died, it emitted a gas that changed the taste of the flesh and made it unpalatable. Here in Queen Elizabeth National Park, there were no giraffes for a lack of acacia trees, and no zebras, wildebeests, or rhinoceroses either. A few warthogs were grazing. John said they were one of the most stupid animals he knew because they would run from a predator like the rest of the animals, but after a while, they would stop running and begin feeding, seemingly to have completely forgotten why they were running in the first place.

We took the rugged circuit road chased by swarms of tsetse flies to reach the Queen's Pavillion by the Equator Gate with Lake George in the distance. From there we drove across the length of the park on our way back to Mbarara.

During our last weekend in Mbarara, Augustus took us to Rwanda to trek the gorillas. The road to Rwanda had numerous switchback turns and wound through Kisoro over the mountains. Far in the distance, the volcanoes loomed.

The next day we hiked up Bisoke to look for the Amahora gorilla group. Our vehicle traveled on bumpy rugged roads for an hour and a half to the base of the mountain. We walked through lush Irish potato fields for another twenty minutes before reaching the edge of the park. After ten minutes of hiking, there they were, first the black back gorilla, then mothers and babies climbing up the long vines, swinging on them as though they were a cradle. A silverback, missing an arm from being caught in a trap set up by poachers, arrived and just as quickly left, as the big boss, a silverback, came purposefully and sat only a meter in front of us for several minutes, facing us and contemplating whether he should welcome us. The mother and babies came down from the trees and played in front of him, easing the tension. The guide made "oom ah" noises to indicate to the silverback that we were friendly. Without warning a baby ran to a trekker and whacked her on the leg. The guide made a "click, click, click" noise, and the baby ran away. Then a siesta seemed to be the order of the day. The gorillas pulled down branches and leaves, made a bed on the soft undergrowth, and lay down to rest. I had trekked gorillas in Bwindi Impenetrable Forest in 2007, but this time around, the experience was far more intimate. That night the moon was almost full. I got up in the middle of the night to admire the magical moonlight on the lawn and soaked in the surrounding stillness deep in Africa.

In the morning, I went trekking to visit the Dian Fossey's gravesite and the research center founded by her, accompanied by Augustus, a guide, and an armed guard. An hour of steep trekking led us to a clearing where several paths converged: one for gorilla trekking, one for Crater Lake and Bisoke Mountain, and a third to Dian Fossey's gravesite. After hiking through a dense jungle of trees covered with moss and nettles and along buffalo tracks covered with gorilla poo, we reached the Karisoke Research Center[10] cloaked in thick mist, while a few dik-diks scampered away. The name Karisoke was derived from the first four letters of Karisimbi Mountains, which overlooked the site from the north, and the last four letters of Bisoke, which loomed in the south.

The research center was looted and trashed in 1998 at the end of the Rwandan genocide. All that remained were foundations of buildings with abundant moss growing on them and pathetic-looking signs indicating the sites of the various buildings. Dian Fossey's cabin was just a mound of moss-covered rubble. Close to it was a watering hole she had created for forest animals, now overgrown with bamboos planted by her. The gravesites of the gorillas and her tomb were not far off, about twenty odd wooden stack grave markers with the names and dates of the dead gorillas, including her favorite, "Digit." Since Dian Fossey lived far away from the rest of the staff and did not socialize much with them, when she was murdered, no one heard anything. It was not until the next day on December 27, 1985, when the houseboy came to give her tea, was her body discovered.[11] It was taken to the airport to be flown to the United States, but someone read in her diary that she wished to be buried in the mountains next to her beloved gorillas. And so it was brought back. She was fifty-three years old. Her tomb sat in a corner of the gravesite with the following engraving on the tombstone:

> "NYIRAMACHABELLI"
> DIAN FOSSEY
> 1932–1985
> NO ONE LOVED GORILLAS MORE
> REST IN PEACE, DEAR FRIEND
> ETERNALLY PROTECTED
> IN THIS SACRED GROUND
> FOR YOU ARE HOME
> WHERE YOU BELONG

Dian spent eighteen years in the mountains, and the locals called her "Nyiramachbelli," loosely translated as "the woman who lives alone in the mountains." On the night she was killed, she might have been drunk. To this day her murderer or murderers have not been caught.

That afternoon after the trekking, we drove to Kigali over mountainous roads. Augustus pointed out a river in the valley where so many bodies were dumped during the genocide that the river flowed red. At the Genocide Museum, the planning and execution of the genocide of the Tutsi were detailed with pictures of the horrific crimes of systematic killings and rapes, people buried alive while tied up or dumped into latrines alive with more bodies dumped on top of them, and mass graves created to bury the dead.[12] Hutu women who married Tutsi men were also killed. It was sickening how low humanity could sink. The memorial also recounted other genocides of the twentieth century and offered ways of preventing future genocides.

Outside was a memorial garden with a mass grave of about a quarter of a million people. One plaque recounted an eleven-year-old boy who tried to carry his friend who had one of his legs hacked off. When he saw a truckload of people armed with weapons coming towards them, he had to make up his mind whether to continue to carry his friend or to save himself. When a man with a machete came running to them, he left his friend behind. The last thing he saw was his friend's face looking at him as he was being hacked to death; he would remember that expression for the rest of his life.

Kigali was clean and orderly; motorbikers had to wear helmets and were limited to two passengers per vehicle. Our long drive to the border wound over mountains and many stretches of tea plantations. The border crossing was swift, and we arrived at Mbarara around nine-thirty in the evening. Augustus still had another four and a half hours' drive to Kampala. Sheila packed him some food and water.

The next day Robert drove me back to Kampala where I wandered along Bomba Road, passing a busy market with several children panhandling while a crawling child sat alone on a dusty pavement at the entrance of a gas station by a busy street. Down in the cavernous drains covered with slippery green moss, three young girls were collecting water flowing from sewage spouts into large jerry cans. I truly hoped that they were just going to use the water for washing and not for drinking.

Robert took me to the National Mosque funded by Gaddafi, a boring brownstone structure with some ornate carvings on the inside of the domes. At the gate, I rented a long skirt and a headscarf before being allowed to climb up the minaret to enjoy a panoramic view of Kampala. From there we could see Makerere University, Mulago Hospital, the Anglican and the Catholic Cathedrals.

Later we drove uphill to visit both cathedrals. The Anglican one was a run-down, massive, red brick structure with severe roof leaks. An altar at the Catholic Cathedral commemorated the martyrdom of Christians in the late nineteenth century when more than forty people were tortured and burned alive because they were Catholics.[13] The leader was hacked before being burnt alive. All twenty-one names on the altar were men; the youngest was a fourteen-year-old boy.

In the early evening, I wandered alone into one of the many slums of Kampala. The residents were firing up their stoves to make chapatti, rice, and corn for sale. I picked my way on a path among the rusty tin sheds haphazardly scattered around, avoiding the streams of sewage water flowing into a stagnant pool. I saw children playing around it and women cooking outdoors. I dared not wander too deeply into the slum, fearing that I would be completely engulfed in it and get hopelessly lost.

I said good-bye to Kampala, but deep down I had a feeling that I would soon return.

8

Libya

2011, Arab Spring

"To our son, his excellency, Mr. Barack Hussein Obama. I have said to you before, that even if Libya and the United States of America enter into a war, god forbid, you will always remain a son. Your picture will not be changed."
—*Col. Muammar Gaddafi*[1]

Three weeks after I returned from a trip to Ethiopia, on September 20, 2011, I boarded a plane to Malta en route to Libya. A day later, I said my farewell in the wee hours of the morning to lovely Malta and boarded the United Nation Humanitarian Air Service (UNHAS) flight 97W with fifty or so members of various NGOs: WHO, MSF, IMC. Some were going to Tripoli, and some were heading towards Benghazi in different capacities, ranging from logistics to medical. As the plane hovered over Malta, the sheer cliffs on the south side of the island loomed into view, white surfaces against the deep blue of the Mediterranean Sea, instilling a deep and fervent belief that all was well with the world.

The revolutionary waves of the Arab Spring, which began in Tunisia in December of 2010, swept through Egypt, Libya, Yemen, Bahrain, and Syria.[2] By the time I arrived in Libya, the rebels had captured Tripoli and fighting intensified in Sirte, the birthplace of Muammar Gaddafi, the long-time dictator.

Before leaving for Libya, I had to take the IMC three-hour online course on security and score a hundred percent on the examination; otherwise I had to review the different security scenarios again and retake the exam. MTI collaborated with IMC in providing medical services for the internally displaced people (IDPs) in Libya. There were only two of us in the team: Sharon, a Canadian nurse, and me.

Tripoli from the plane appeared to be miles upon miles of pale yellow, flat-topped buildings with a moderate array of high rises. As we drove through the streets, graffiti in Arabic and the occasional French and English was scrawled over the walls: Revolution Feb 17; Freedom or Free Libya; Finally, we are free; Game over; Gaddafi go to hell. There were pictures of Gaddafi in various poses of humiliation and indignity, fleeing with bags in hands or being punched in the face. Libyan flags were everywhere, flying from cars, buildings, and painted on walls: red, black, and green with a star and crescent in the center. Remnants of roadblocks of spare tires, concrete blocks, and sandbags were scattered along the road; some were unmanned, and others guarded by rough, menacing men toting AK-47s, a few wearing fatigues but many in civilian clothes. Trucks with anti-aircraft artilleries were abundant. We drove through streets with little evidence of destruction. Our driver did not speak English, so we could not ask him where the battles were fought.

Graffiti about the Arab Spring on the wall in Tripoli, Libya.

At the IMC office, our arrival surprised the staff. No one expected us, and they were at a loss as to where to send us. It was also the day when the old country director was eagerly preparing to leave for the U.S., while the new country director from Croatia was just arriving. He had been on the same plane with us and had yet to be briefed. When we told the IMC personnel in Tripoli that MTI had the notion that we would be sent to Sahba in the desert area, south of Tripoli, one of the Tripoli personnel glibly said, "They want you killed!" Astounded and dumbfounded by her reaction, we did not know that it was still very fluid and dangerous in the field hospital there.

Unfortunately, with the confusion and changing of the guard, we felt somewhat put-off and unwanted. There was to be a security briefing when we got to Tripoli, but that never took place. After some back and forth, they decided to send us to Al Zintan, southwest of Tripoli, to assess the four to five clinics there. Our goal was to establish a comprehensive clinic that would include maternity service. When there was no need for us there, they might consider sending us to other places. Right now, active fighting continued in Bena Wali and Sirte, the birthplace of Gaddafi, to the east of Tripoli.

It would be a three-hour drive to Al Zintan in the Nafusa Mountains. The staff there was made aware of our coming, but we were to call them when we were two-thirds on the way there to warn them of our arrival. A cavalcade of land cruisers with anti-aircraft artilleries blared their horns—a victory parade of sort with men flashing victory signs—and passed us in the opposite direction. We drove by a fortress-like military base where Karim, our driver who spoke English, told us Gaddafi tortured the Libyans. When Tripoli fell, freedom fighters raided the base, but Gaddafi's men had already fled. NATO bombings destroyed one building, reducing it to bent metal and concrete rubble, and partially burnt several buildings, the hideouts of Gaddafi's forces, and riddled them with bullet holes. Shallow holes gouged out by air bombings studded the road surfaces. There were many more roadblocks with men toting AK-47s, stopping us and asking questions. Our land cruisers had a prominent display of IMC logos and signs on its front and on the driver's side, indicating there were no weapons aboard. Civilian life, however, seemed to have returned to Tripoli; some shops were open, and we were able to change money and buy some food.

Karim stopped at a junction to buy some fruits where a tank on which was scrawled "Gaddafi's Killing Machine" was parked. Locals stood on top of the tank posing with victory signs. An enthusiastic young Libyan pulled me up the tank to join them, offering me dates and grapes. Passengers in passing cars honked, smiled, and waved victory signs; all seemed happy and friendly. A young man fired into the dry, vast, desert terrain from an anti-aircraft vehicle; he was training to use it.

We arrived late in the day in Al Zintan. Lotfi, a Tunisian emergency nurse, showed us around the one-story, unassuming hospital—Gaddafi's name had been pulled down from its façade—passing quickly through the emergency room with separate sections for women and men, the CT scanner, pharmacy, x-ray rooms, and an empty, three-bed intensive care unit. He spoke mainly Arabic and French peppered with a little English. Many of the healthcare personnel came from the neighboring country of Tunisia where the first revolutionary wave of the Arab Spring began, sympathetic to the cause of the rebels in Libya. In the evening, we met with the field coordinator, a young, vivacious woman from Lebanon, and the logistician, a burly, young Iranian-American who was also in charge of security. Again, from the exchange of furtive glances between them, we had the distinct feeling that they did not know why we had come to the mountains. They had been either assessing the needs for clinics or closing some of the clinical services which other NGOs were providing.

The locals of Al Zintan defeated Gaddafi's men because they knew the terrain better than his men did. We were told that the citizens prided themselves on their refusal of his offer of 100,000 dinars per person for not fighting against him. The city itself was dusty, all yellow and brown with sparse vegetation. The few women on the streets wore long dark dresses and *hijab* or headscarves. This was a post-war area and things had calmed down, although firearms left over from the fighting continued to cause occasional accidental injuries.

At first, we could not go out without the escort of a man, but this rule was soon relaxed or abandoned because most men were busy; eventually we went out on our own. One morning I even managed to work in a run in the back roads, meeting several curious camels fenced in a back yard.

The Lebanese field coordinator, Sharon, and I were the only women in the guesthouse. Even the cook who prepared lunch and dinner for us was a young wiry man who prepared mainly goat meat and unappetizing entrails mixed with spaghetti. One afternoon I walked into the kitchen and was startled by a sad-looking goat's head left by the sink to be used in a stew. My appetite plummeted.

Throughout the night, we could see and hear artillery fire, lighting up the sky with red orange flares. Some were very close to our building which trembled with reverberating rumbling, making our sleep very fitful. In the morning, the other occupants reassured us that the Libyans were just firing their victory volleys. After a while, the nightly firing became a normal background noise for us.

The next day was Friday, which was a prayer day. Clinics were closed, but the field co-

Graffiti on the wall of Al Zintan announcing that "Al Zintan not 4 sale."

ordinator informed us that we could still visit Jadu Hospital in the morning to do a needs assessment after she consulted with the military council as to the security situation. Currently IMC provided support for four hospitals: Zintan, Jadu, Kabaw, and Nalut. They planned to pull out from the last two because another NGO was providing services there. We waited for her to tell us whether it was safe to go. The morning hours came and went with no sign of the coordinator or the logistician. We were left stranded in the guesthouse and unable to leave without a house key or a male escort; there was no one with whom we could communicate. In the afternoon, they finally returned with no good explanation. Feeling sorry for us, the logistician asked us to wait for another hour for him before he could escort us for a walk outside the house. He later relented, as he was too busy, and allowed us to go out on our own. We wandered into town and saw a bullet-riddled building with graffiti on its walls: Revolution Feb. 17, Zintan Not 4 Sale, evidently referring to Gaddafi's attempt to bribe the citizens of Al Zintan not to put up a fight. On a temporary stage, Al Zintanians posted hundreds of pictures of the freedom fighters who died in the revolution. The poignant fact was that some of them were just kids.

Next to the mosque was a market selling fruits and vegetables: tomatoes, potatoes, onions, pomegranates, grapes, dates, and apples. In our walk, we only saw three women: a very elderly woman and two middle-aged women, all covered from head to toe and wearing *hijab*. They pretended to look down or ahead of themselves, but I could feel their stares burning into my back. The rest were being driven in cars, hidden behind tinted windows.

In the early dawn, through the window, I could see a crescent moon hung just above the minaret of a mosque while a gentle, cool, breeze blew softly. A lone dog sniffed around in the backyard where a few dust-covered fig trees grew. Some of the men in the guesthouse escaped the stifling heat indoors and slept on the rooftop.

On Saturday, we traveled west of Al Zintan to Kabaw to close a program in the hospital, pulling out a Tunisian doctor who had spent two months there and would now be reassigned to Misurata. The hospital desperately argued against the doctor's removal, as that left him with only two doctors, an Egyptian and a Croatian.

The mountains from Kabaw to Tiji were dotted with century-old houses carved into their slopes. Our progress was slowed down by numerous roadblocks and checkpoints staffed by freedom fighters carrying Kalashnikovs. The checkpoints were made of chairs, tires, or mounds of earth strategically placed to create a meandering path to slow down vehicles. Traversing over winding mountain roads, we came upon a huge crater in the center of the road, created deliberately by the freedom fighters to impede the advance of Gaddafi's forces. When they were forced to slow down, the fighters then attacked them.

Over the next few days, we continued to do needs assessment by visiting a few clinics in the towns of the mountain region. The clinic in Awlad Talib was clean but devoid of equipment. They had twenty-eight nurses and three social workers but no doctors. Some nurses were sitting around with no work to do. In peacetime, this facility served six thousand people, but only a few people sauntered in. We bypassed the hospital at Tiji, partially destroyed. Gaddafi's forces had taken its equipment to Nalut Hospital on the western border of Libya near Tunisia.

In Badr, the clinic's daily census used to be a hundred and twenty patients and was now down to twenty-five. Again, the facility was badly in need of repair, equipment, medicines, and personnel, especially doctors. There were seventy nurses. Bullet holes spattered the wall of the front hall with "Fuck Gaddafi" spray-painted over the top in Arabic.

It was well past three in the afternoon when we finally stopped at an IMC guesthouse right across from Jadu Hospital and had a late lunch. There was a generous spread of couscous with some meat, a tomato, onion, and cucumber salad, mounds of pink pomegranates, and delicious dates.

The mountain region in the west seemed to be quiet now, and the people we met on the roads and in the clinics were mighty proud of their new-found freedom. Life seemed to be slowly returning to normal.

Most of the hospitals in the Nafusa Mountain region had their names taken off of the front facade because many of them borne Gaddafi's names and pictures. Like most dictators, he splattered his name liberally, claiming everything for himself. On Sunday, we went to the hospital with Lofti, visiting the wards; like most African hospitals, the patients provided their own sheets. The pregnant women here looked rather old and careworn. A boy, who accidentally shot off his thumb while playing with a gun left over from the revolution, was ready for discharge.

In the hospital at Al Zintan, there were two operating rooms: one for clean cases and the other septic; in the cabinet were anesthetics and antiarrhythmics. Neuza proudly showed us his anesthesia machine and Hassain his pharmacy. Several Libyan women in *hijab* ran the laboratory.

Mondays and Thursdays were circumcision days. Mothers, fathers, and baby boys lined up outside the operating rooms. The baby boys, whose angelic faces were graced with beautiful and innocent smiles, sat patiently on the laps of their mothers who were all covered up in black or floral *abayas*; behind the veils, roving eyes followed me. The babies were blissfully unaware of what awaited them. Then a four-year-old boy screamed his head off as a nurse carted him off for his circumcision; all of a sudden, he seemed to understand that he was in for something unpleasant.

Several orderlies pushed a stretcher bearing a young man with a gunshot wound just below his chest into the emergency room. Immediately almost all healthcare personnel were all over him; his blood pressure was barely palpable, his pulse was thready, he was not breathing, and bright red blood seeped from his back onto the stretcher. Soon they hooked him up to a breathing machine and poured in intravenous fluids. Ashen and pale, several times he lost his blood pressure, and they gave him epinephrine, which boosted his blood pressure transiently. He finally got his blood transfusion, and an ambulance came to transfer him to Jadu Hospital. He did not make it.

Back at Al Zintan, we met with the medical director of the hospital of fifty beds. He was interested in changing the infection control practices of the hospital personnel and showed us his lecture slides in Arabic. From my previous experience as a hospital epidemiologist in infection control, I could not foresee changing behavior in the relatively short period of time we had in Libya. I did not volunteer for this educational endeavor, but my partner volunteer, Sharon, went for it. Being a public health nurse, she had been away from the clinical scene for a while now and was not confident of her clinical skills. In the meantime, I was on the phone and e-mail communicating with Tripoli to send me to Misurata, closer to where I could provide medical services to the IDPs. Misurata and Benghazi were quiet after the fierce fighting earlier in the uprising and were not in dire need of medical help. In Sirte, where fighting was ongoing, they were in great need of surgeons and anesthesiologists; however, the situation remained too dangerous. Tripoli sent news about the IDPs in need of medical treatment, food, water, fuel, and clothes in Wadi Imrah, Twarga, and Washka. The clinic at the field hospital in Sirte, fifty kilometers from the front line, requested a doctor and an obstetrician. It was time for me to bid farewell to the friends I made in the Nafusa Mountains and to Sharon, who had elected to stay at Al Zintan, and for me to go to Misurata.

I took the long trip from Al Zintan to Tripoli and from there to Misurata, with Dr. Fatma, an obstetrician from Nalut. The driver came late, and we did not leave Al Zintan until after three in the afternoon. He stopped halfway, kindly buying us cold soft drinks. It was well past six in the evening when we arrived at Tripoli. Dr. Fatma and I thought we would be spending the night in Tripoli and resuming our journey more safely in broad daylight, since traveling in the dark was ill-advised. However, to our surprise, our logistician, who was also our security person, came out of the headquarters and told us that our new driver had been waiting all afternoon for us and was ready to drive us to Misurata that evening. In the dusk, we spotted him, dark-haired, thin and tall man, leaning at the gate, casually smoking. Fatma and I hurried into the building and had a brief pit stop. As I waited for my turn for the bathroom, I gazed up the glowing staircase to my left, longing for the security of the bedrooms upstairs. At that moment, I caught a fleeting glimpse of the Lebanese field coordinator sticking her head over the banister and then quickly withdrawing it. She did not acknowledge me. Fatma and I left Tripoli without any offer of dinner. Soon our driver fumbled for a cigarette, and I threw a quick glance at Fatma. Before he could light up, I decided that I had to ask him not to smoke. The driver muttered to himself that this would be a very long journey without a cigarette now and then, but he acceded to my request. In the gloomy interior of the back seat of the car, Fatma tossed a look of gratitude in my direction. To add cigarette smoke to hunger, thirst, fatigue, and stress, all triggers for a perfect storm for a fulminant migraine, I would gladly risk the driver's displeasure.

In the lingering evening light, we caught glimpses of the Mediterranean Sea and the beaches to our left. There were quite a number of vehicles on the road; the people who drove at this time of the evening must have compelling reasons to do so. We drove in silence for two and a half hours through at least two dozen checkpoints, all heavily guarded; some had five to ten armed guards and tanks. I was thankful to have a Libyan woman traveling with me. As we got close to Misurata, armed guards pulled our car over to the embankment twice and demanded to see our IDs and passports. Our driver left Dr. Fatma and me in the car in the dark and went with the guards; this was his chance to light up. It seemed like ages before he finally returned with our documents while the guards checked the trunk. It was dark by the time we reached Misurata. We were in some sense violating the IMC security guidelines since we were strictly forbidden to travel after dark.

Our driver took us to the IMC office. Ignoring the fact that we were tired and hungry, the IMC officials kept us in the office for a security briefing and updates on the possibility of setting up a mobile clinic for the IDPs. After an hour, the driver drove us to the guest-house. Since we had not eaten in a while, we asked him to take us to a store to buy food. The storekeeper refused to take my ten-dinar bill calling it "Big Money," "Gaddafi's money" and looked at it with disdain. I had changed my dollars to dinars in Tripoli, which supported Gaddafi during the uprising. Evidently, the people in Misurata did not accept the currency; Misurata had received one of the worst and most brutal attacks from Gaddafi's forces. The ten-dinar bill in Tripoli was much bigger than that in Misurata in size, perhaps as big as Gaddafi's ego. Fatma loaned me some dinars. There was not much food to choose from, but we had to cook something to eat for the night and for days afterward. I settled for some pasta, rice, onions, eggs, tomato paste, bread, grapes, canned tuna; the latter seemed to be in abundance. In Misurata we had to be our own cook.

Back at the guesthouse, the sheets were unwashed; I was glad to have my travel towel and large shawls that I could wrap myself in bed for the night. Tomorrow I would contrive to wash the sheets. Because of the war situation, we were to pack lightly for Libya so we could pick up and leave at the spur of a moment if the need arose. I had not packed sheets.

In the early morning, I took a walk outside the guesthouse. Many of the stores remained closed, some with screens riddled with bullet holes; now and then, a few cars roamed the streets. Pictures of Gaddafi and his strong men wearing hideous make-up and colorful *hijab* adorned the door and walls of an office. Long lines of men queued up in front of a bank. On the ground floor of our guesthouse was a man who could change some money for me so I could have the dinars that Misurata would accept. Through the kitchen window, I could see a huge "Free Libya" sign across the street and several significant dates scrawled over the walls.

One tends to forget that Libya is in North Africa, and as such, it is still part of Africa. Therefore "African time" still applies. Fatma left early in the morning via helicopter for the field hospital. My driver did not show up for at least two hours. A kind orthopedic physician working for another NGO let me use his cell phone to make several phone calls to the logistician, but he could not be reached. The field coordinator of Misurata had turned off her phone. Despite a promise from MTI for the use of a cell phone at least for security reasons, I did not get one; just like Sharon and I did not get the security overview when we first arrived at Tripoli. Closer to the field hospital, communication could only be done via a satellite phone.

Walid, our driver, a young man in his twenties, finally appeared with Falid Abood and Ikrimah, two young, enthusiastic male Jordanian nurses, and drove us to Twarga, a town

20 miles southwest of Misurata. These nurses had been in Misurata for the last five months volunteering in the pediatric hospital and were ready to go out into the field. Wide trenches dug by the freedom fighters to trip up the tanks of Gaddafi during the fighting remained gaping on the highways. A line of cars came up from the opposite direction carrying people fleeing Sirte, some with furniture and mattresses strapped on their rooftops, and they stopped at several checkpoints. Along the roadsides were strewn mangled war machines, spent shells, and burnt tires. Miraculously many of the date palms stood intact with a few charred ones; one had sustained a hole in its trunk but still stood tall and erect. The dates were in season, and many goats were busy feasting on the fallen fruits. The landscape was one of arid, dusty, and hot semi-desert.

Walid fought in Misurata and knew many of the freedom fighters staffing the checkpoints; we had no trouble passing through them. He lost three uncles in the fierce fight for Misurata in April and May. Like many young Libyans, it was the first time he ever held and fired a gun. Freedom fighters used cats as decoys at night by tying lights on them and letting them free. Gaddafi's snipers fired at the lights, thinking these were the freedom fighters revealing their positions.

We visited the committee center that oversaw the IDPs who left Sirte to stay in the abandoned apartment complex in Twarga. In contrast to other refugee camps I have been to, there were no tents here. The IDPs lived in the relative comfort of an apartment minus the amenities. Apparently, ten families lived in this complex, each with between ten and fifteen members. Water was supplied via a tank, and the IDPs also received ready-to-eat food as there was no electricity. A pharmacy had just been set up on the day of our visit. Amjad, our logistician, received the wrong pallet of supplies so we could not deliver the needed medicines. Food, trash, kitchen supplies, and boxes of medicines, which had just arrived, piled up in the committee quarter. Sorting through the medicines, we found oral rehydration solutions but no medicines for diabetes, hypertension, analgesics, cough medicines, and antibiotics. In this same room, a row of menacing-looking Kalashnikovs lined the walls, seemingly following our every move.

One of the freedom fighters in his traditional clothes, a long, white cloak or *jarid* worn over a shirt or *jalabiya*, long trousers or *sirwal*, and a white knitted cap, with an AK-47 slung over his shoulder, and the pharmacist, Abdul Rahman, accompanied us to visit several families. Women stayed out of sight inside the apartment while the men lounged on carpets lining the veranda outside. Inside the apartment, mattresses were all over the floor. As we climbed up the stairs, a fierce wind whipped up sand as high up the third floor, coating the steps. The women were just as curious about me as I was about them, and they brought my attention to a few pregnant women. Hypertension, diabetes, diarrhea, and headache were some of the complaints. The apartments reeked of human waste. There were large pits to bury some of the trash, but these did not seem to have kept up with the trash generated daily. Garbage and plastic bottles littered the grounds. Children were the ones suffering from diarrhea; they played around the water tank with buckets of water to cool off and inevitably drank the contaminated water as well. Posters on the walls and plastered on the water tanks showed the danger of firearms and spent shells; the latter were scattered on the sandy soil next to where the children were playing.

Despite the fact that we were told medicines were ready for us to start the mobile clinic for the IDPs in Twarga, we did not find them after going through all the boxes of the International Emergency Health Kits (IEHK) in the basement of the IMC office. Fearing that we would lose another day, Falid Abood and I requested permission to buy medicines. Hassan drove us to an unmarked pharmacy where the owner graciously donated a few boxes of medicines. Then he went to the Polyclinic Hospital and obtained some more free medicines for us. He even discounted our total bill. Hassan stopped at a makeshift roadside stall for me to stock up on vegetables and fruits with my new Misurata dinars: onions, cucumber, tomatoes, apples, and pomegranates.

Twarga was one of Gaddafi's strongholds. When fighting reached this area, the occupants who supported Gaddafi fled. Now the rebels used it as a transit camp for the IDPs. At one of the checkpoints were enormous pipes on which the Misurata rebels scrawled in English and Arabic: *We fight for freedom and justice. We will not surrender, we win or we die.*

At Twarga, the committee swept a room clean for our clinic. There were no tables, so we sat on chairs to see our patients. Our very first patient was a seven-year-old girl with a gunshot wound in the left thigh. According to her father, the bullet came through her bedroom in Sirte, ricocheted off a wall and hit her in the thigh. The bullet did not go through the thigh, and the father had to cut it out. An x-ray later showed that it just grazed the bone. A young boy who looked healthy came in with diarrhea but seemed quite happy showing off his victory sign.

In the back of the complex was a room with an examination table where we saw women who were pregnant, almost all of them near term or past their due dates, and often accompanied by their protective husbands and mothers-in-law. We transferred them to Misurata after writing them an official pass to enable them to get through the checkpoints where the soldiers checked the passengers and the trunks for possible infiltrated persons from Sirte.

A message on a drainpipe by a checkpoint to the south of Misurata: "We Will not surrender we win or we die (Misurata Rebels)."

A doting husband brought in his pregnant wife, who covered herself from head to toe with a black veil and black *abaya*. When I was ready to see her, the men left the room, including my translator who stayed right outside the door, refusing to come in. She remained with her veil covering her face and only lifted it up when I closed the door. After I finished examining her, she gestured whether she could put her veil back. When she got out of the room, her uxorious husband immediately took her to the back, away from the prying eyes of the public, to wait for her transfer paper. Most women were reluctant to come out and often asked the men to come asking for medicines. As opposed to other African countries, here in Libya, fathers not mothers brought their children to see us.

Muhammad, my translator, told me that there was a wide variation of how a woman should cover herself. Universally all Muslim Libyan women covered their bodies down to their ankles, only exposing their faces and hands. However, there were groups that required the women to cover every part of their body except the eyes. At home, they could be uncovered, but men and women remained in separate quarters. Mothers and sisters arranged marriages for the men, and the chosen woman then met the man in the presence of her father or brother for a few minutes. The men and the women could say "no" to the match, but sometimes fathers insisted, and the women had no choice.

In the evenings when we left Twarga for Misurata, we saw wispy smoke rising languidly from burning buildings in the distance. When I asked Walid why the building complex was burning, he turned around, looked at Muhammad, and laughed, but refused to answer me. After a pause, he jokingly muttered that Zoro was at it again. From what I could piece together from the translator, the Misuratans displayed their vengefulness towards the people of Twarga by burning their houses so that they had no place to return to when the war ended.

Curious about Tripoli Street where fierce fighting took place in the spring in Misurata, I found my way there by foot one evening. There were many destroyed buildings; some were riddled with bullet holes and others with enormous gaping holes from the bombs. Gaddafi sent more than twenty tanks there and fired indiscriminately. On one side of the street, the victors displayed missiles, warheads, and tanks captured from Gaddafi's forces. Many Libyan families gathered there, young and old, women and men, to view the spoils. Boys climbed up the tanks, their backdrop the bombed-out and burnt buildings. At one point, an elderly man called out slogans in Arabic. When he finished, a soldier who stood by him fired, "Tat, rat-tat-tat…" into the evening sky. Now things were quiet in Misurata with occasional shots of celebratory gunfire. Outside our accommodation was a sign declaring, "Misurata is Misurata, we have broken the dictator."

I checked with Amjab whether it would be safe to run in the streets of Misurata; he said it would be all right to run on the back roads. One morning I was not sure whether I heard some gunshots when I ran by the hospital, so I avoided that area. Another morning I ran by the heliport, a few blocks from the guesthouse; this time I distinctly heard gunshots. I quickly turned around and just ran on the street by the front of the guesthouse; this led straight up to Tripoli Street. It being Friday, all the streets were eerily quiet. I had run in Haiti after the earthquake, dodging rubble, live wires, gaping cracks in the roads, scavenging pigs, and goats, and now in the early mornings I ran in the streets of Libya and on Tripoli Street, where some of the fiercest fightings in Misurata took place. It was quite surreal.

East of where we lived, destruction was much less with the remains of only a few burned buildings. School had started, and school vans were busy fetching the children. Hordes of young girls and boys carrying school bags walked to school, the boys putting up

Boys climbing up onto the top of a tank, their backdrop the bombed-out and burnt buildings of Misurata, Libya.

their thumbs when they saw me. Numerous tanks with slogans in Arabic were parked in a big plaza; rust had already begun to set in.

This morning we drove for about two hours through a flat, monotonous, arid landscape to the Field Hospital and Clinic in the beach resort of Gaddafi, fifty kilometers from Sirte where active fighting took place. Signs for camel crossings were posted at regular intervals along the road. Occasional camel carcasses lay on the roadsides. At night when the temperature of the desert dipped, the camels, loving the warmth of the tarmac, often settled on the roads and were hit by vehicles. Packs of camels walked slowly and patiently across this unchanging landscape, feeding on scattered, short clumps of brush. Their breakfast, lunch, and dinner were the same, scanty and unappetizing. Like the decoy cats, the camels must be wondering about the unrelenting bombings. There seemed to be perpetual smiles on their faces. On our way to Sirte, I was shocked to see the head of a camel hanging in front of a butcher shop; it still wore a patient smile despite its demise.

Freedom fighters converted one of Gaddafi's beach houses within the walled compound into a field hospital. It had ten beds, two of which were resuscitative beds. An annex room served as a storage room for medicines and equipment. There was only one patient when we arrived. Later in the afternoon, Red Crescent ambulances brought in four casualties from Sirte; evidently fighting had heated up. The latest news from *Al Jazeera* was that the freedom fighters had reached the roundabout of the city center of Sirte where the fighters from the west and east flanks converged.[3] They had also captured the port, thus cutting off the possible retreat route for Gaddafi and his forces which were fighting back, refusing to surrender. Unfortunately, many civilians were caught in the crossfire. One of the patients brought in by the Red Crescent was seriously injured; he was unconscious and intubated, blood pouring out of his mouth and nose. The Chinook that landed this morning at the beach would likely transport these casualties to the Polyclinic Hospital in Misurata, right across from the guesthouse. Two additional tents were set up right outside the field hospital for patients who were stable. Several of the beach houses became dormitories for the volunteers who had to stay overnight, and one was converted to a labor and delivery room where I found my Misurata companion, Dr. Fatma. Whirring helicopters and Chinooks arrived and took off at intervals, bringing healthcare personnel and patients.

Muhammad and I were sent to the field clinic right outside the compound by the checkpoint. It was a container with three rooms, one of which was really a room for storing medicines. Several doctors and medical students were seeing people who had fled Sirte. Outside, freedom fighters stopped cars and searched them thoroughly. The fleeing people were waiting outside their cars patiently in the heat with their suitcases while the fighters flipped through their belongings and the folds of their blankets. One freedom fighter approached me to look at a veiled woman to make sure she was not a man in disguise. She did not wish to have a man peer at her. In the clinic, I saw a young woman with a cut on her arm. I cleaned and dressed it, and she and her father went on their way. Because there were so many volunteers in this crowded and airless container, Muhammad and I retreated into the compound. We had a lunch of couscous and some meat, which I later found out was camel meat! It tasted like beef but was as tough as mutton.

The beach was beautiful save for the trash discarded carelessly by the current occupants; it must have been pristine before the field hospital was set up. In the afternoon lull, I borrowed a long shirt and pants and dipped in the crashing but refreshing waves of the Mediterranean Sea. I swam in a quiet corner behind some rocks, far away from the eyes of the Muslims in order not to be conspicuous or offensive. I wondered how many people could say they swam in Gaddafi's private resort.

The next day we drove to Gate 50 where the field hospital was, then changed vehicle and drove with security to Gate 30, where we delivered many boxes of medicines and supplies. We then spent a couple of hours seeing patients, mostly children with diarrhea. Intermittently the windowpanes rattled with the blasts of bombing. Gate 30, which was thirty kilometers from Sirte, brought us a lot closer to the frontline. After we finished seeing the patients, we went on to Wadi Inffra, passing a checkpoint before we entered the village to deliver medicines to another clinic. Almost all the patients came early in the morning and had left because they feared that the fighting, which usually was more intense in the afternoon, would pick up again. A father came in with his crying and distraught boy, traumatized by the constant shelling. The father spread his arms simulating a plane flying, and then he made the sound of bombing.

At the field hospital, there were no patients in the morning, but in the afternoon, there were three. All of them were being transferred out of Sirte Hospital after the Red Crescent received safe passage to bring out the injured. One of them was an elderly man with a punctured lung and a chest tube hanging; another was a young girl with fractured pelvis and shoulder. A third, a woman who had recently delivered a baby, had sustained many shrapnel injuries from a bomb blast and was paralyzed from the waist down. Because she was a woman, I helped the nurse to wash and dress her wounds as best we could before all three patients were transferred to Misurata in a helicopter. The man with the punctured

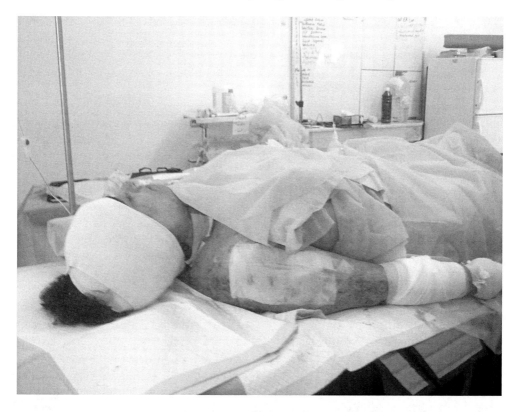

A postpartum woman who sustained many shrapnel injuries from a bomb blast and was paralyzed from the waist down—Field Hospital in Gaddafi's beach resort near Sirte, Libya.

lung told me that his family was evacuated from Sirte two days ago, but he was not able to leave because of his injury.

Although there was supposed to be a truce during one weekend to allow civilians to leave Sirte, shootings continued, so many people were afraid to leave. The hospital in Sirte was within hostile territory close to Gaddafi's stronghold and so there were few doctors; most of them had left to volunteer outside of Sirte. As if between Scylla and Charybdis, patients and staff alike had to run through the gauntlet of gunfire and snipers while getting in and out of the hospital. The hospital had since run out of diesel and there was no electricity or oxygen and little medicines. Many patients who came to the hospital died. There was a plan to move the current field hospital closer to Sirte to shorten the distance of transport of the injured.

In the evening, I took the Chinook along with a fighter with a broken arm and many other healthcare personnel. We stuffed our ears with cotton wool to save our eardrums from the noise. The pilot announced that he had to fly far out over the Mediterranean to be away from the line of fire; almost all of the pilots had defected from Gaddafi's air force. The sun was setting over Libya; its rays pierced through the gathering dark clouds. The Chinook hovered slowly and laboriously for what seemed like a long time before finally landing. When we arrived at the Misurata Airport forty minutes later, there was no cruiser from IMC to receive me, so I rode in the ambulance carrying the fighter with the broken arm to the Polyclinic Hospital. The ambulance driver worked in information technology in Tripoli at peacetime but became an ambulance driver in Misurata during the war. The contributions towards the war efforts of the people of Libya had been tremendous.

A few days ago, a group of military police moved into the same building where we held clinic in Twarga. All morning police carrying guns trouped in and out; it was not a particularly comforting situation to work in. That same day, Refugee International came to see the conditions of the IDPs. A *Time* magazine journalist and a freelance photographer came to interview me about our work at the clinic. Because we were not to work alongside the military, we closed the clinic to move to Kararim, a town closer to Misurata. The committee moved all the Twarga IDPs to the apartment complex, and the grounds were cleaner; there were electricity and running water. The diabetic patients now could keep their insulin in a refrigerator if they could find one. The girl with the gunshot wound came for dressing change; her wound had become considerably smaller.

One of the guestrooms of an apartment on the ground floor became our new clinic in Kararim. This apartment had three bedrooms, a sitting room for the women, a kitchen, two bathrooms, and three balconies. Furniture, cushions, and pillows were strewn on the carpeted floor, and some flour was sprinkled on it as though the owners in their hurry spilled it. Clothes were scattered on the floor of one of the bedrooms, and two open suitcases packed with clothes were abandoned; perhaps there was not enough room in the vehicle. Another bedroom had a photograph of a baby next to an ID card of a young woman, perhaps the mother, and numerous stuffed animals in a corner. A bin in the kitchen held a collection of moldy bread, packed but not taken, and another filled with pots and pans left on the floor. The scene all seemed very chaotic. I could only imagine the turmoil and the heart-wrenching decisions that the family had to make. War had a way of tearing people apart and bringing misery to the lives of ordinary people who only wished to have a better life for their children and themselves.

Muhammad and I went to another apartment complex to make a house call. The patient was a big, seventy-five-year-old woman, diabetic, and hypertensive. Children and grandchildren hovered over her. Her blood sugar was low, and we gave her some juice. Then one of her daughters asked me to change her Foley catheter. The last time I did that was when I was a medical student, although I had recently watched a nurse insert a Foley at the field hospital. I had to do this without the help of my translator, for men could not go into the women's apartment.

One day a freedom fighter with an obvious limp walked in to get his dressings changed. Bullets still lodged in a wound in the left shoulder and the right thigh. He faced a long period of recuperation ahead of him.

Many more people were leaving the apartment complex; long lines of cars waited by the checkpoint to be processed. A big lorry parked by the complex with two children and their mother sitting in front with the driver. In the back of the lorry, out in the open, several grown women dressed in their ubiquitous black *abayas* sat patiently with a mound of blankets in the center. In one of the pick-up trucks, a lamb stood among furniture and blankets, looking lost. Apparently, there had been a forty-eight-hour truce to allow the people from Sirte to leave before fighting began again.

Hani, a Palestinian who spoke some English, was my new driver. His father had moved to Libya forty-four years ago. Hani was thirty-eight years old and a school teacher before the war. However, because he earned 200 dinars a month, which he said was only sufficient for him to buy food for himself, he could not save enough money to get married. IMC had hired him as a driver just five days ago. Although the pay was much better, in his heart, he still wanted to be a teacher. He fought in Misurata in April and May, and during that time he did not know the whereabouts of his two brothers. Only later, he found them alive, but their home right across from the display of arms in Tripoli Street was all but destroyed. All he said was "*Alḥamdulillāh.*"

Since the weekend truce there had been talks about a big push to topple Sirte. Each day was supposed to be the day of reckoning, but it did not happen until this Friday—their prayer Friday which was destined to be their "Bloody Friday." All day casualties poured into the field hospital. The same afternoon on my way home from Kararim, the road to our guesthouse, which was also the road to the Polytechnic Hospital, was blocked to enable easy passage for ambulances from the heliport. Hani told the police he was bringing a doctor through, and they allowed us to pass.

It was as though Mother Nature was sympathetic to the situation. Unexpectedly a fierce wind blew sand, dust, debris, and palm leaves along the streets. Dark, ominous clouds gathered over the heliport. A helicopter took off, having dropped off the injured fighters. The rain came pelting down, and almost immediately, the streets became flooded. A stream of ambulances came roaring by. Men and boys packed the hospital grounds and the entrance of the emergency room. Cars of relatives anxiously looking for their loved ones among the injured clogged the streets. Then all of a sudden, the whole place was plunged into darkness except for the hospital. The fierce wind blew the window shutters wildly, and rain came flooding into our apartment. I was the only one back in the guesthouse and ran around frantically closing the windows.

As each fighter was unloaded from the ambulance, the crowd chanted "*Allahu Akbar.*" I was able to get into the emergency room with my badge to see if I could be of help. Surprisingly it was not full, and the fighters there were not seriously injured. The intensive care unit, however, had five fighters; all seemed mortally wounded. The splinted and dressed fighters filled another room waiting for x-rays. As I left the emergency room, it was filling up quickly.

The helicopters that took off a couple of hours ago returned, and the Chinook was busy transporting patients. There must have been at least twenty ambulances coming into the emergency room. All night long, they continued to come, and the chanting of "*Allahu Akbar*" persisted late into the night. By some reports, there were over two hundred injured, and twenty-two people died on this "Bloody Friday."

Throughout my stay in Libya, the Libyans were very friendly and welcomed foreigners with open arms. Theirs had been a closed society, and under the long, oppressive regime of Gaddafi, they had very little contact with the outside world. The Misuratans whom I met were optimistic about gaining control over Sirte and Bani Walid, and they longed to gain their freedom from the grip of the dictator. Even before their full liberation, they felt free to express themselves. In the days of old, they could not even trust their neighbors; Gaddafi's name could not pass their lips for fear of being reported and arrested.

In my last run in Misurata, I walked into a building that suffered quite a bit of destruction and did a little bit of exploring. It looked like an old battleground. The ceilings were down, shattered glass covered the floor, and papers strewn all over the place. Here and there were spent shells and cartridges. On the second floor was more of the same except up here were windows through which shooting and firing must have occurred. Through one of them, I could see the school that Walid said Gaddafi attended. On the gate to a garden were scrawled the words "Fuck Gaddafi."

A few days ago, I ran past the makeshift war memorial that displayed weapons captured from Gaddafi's soldiers. A father was looking over the display with his daughter and son. When he saw me, he enthusiastically opened the gate to the display. In his broken English he narrated to me what he knew of the various kinds of weapons Gaddafi had used to kill his own people and how Libyans captured them and used them against him. He was so into the narration that his daughter had to remind him she was late for school.

In Twarga and Kararim, I worked with Dr. Muhammad, a Libyan from Tripoli who spent his free time volunteering all over Libya. Volunteering made him happy and helping people touched a chord in his heart. He showed up one day at the clinic, rolled up his sleeves, and worked alongside me. Quiet, gentle, and reflective, he spoke with a calm demeanor and without a trace of bitterness about the situation of Libya then and now. He expressed his hopes and desires for his country and the people of Libya, that they would respect their new-found freedom and the rights of their neighbors, that they would not harbor malice or ill-will towards pro or anti–Gaddafi factions, that they would look past all that and work together to build a new Libya.

Muhammad was also opposed to big families, which he thought was one of Libya's problems. Each family had between eight to ten members, and some men had multiple wives. He recalled the biggest family he knew was a fifty-year-old man with four wives and thirty-five children. One day the man called a boy over and asked him, "Who is your father?"

The boy replied, "You!"

Angrily he said, "Go to your mother." He had so many children that he could not recognize one of his own.

It rained heavily one afternoon for about twenty minutes, at the end of which a rainbow appeared—a rainbow of hope for the people of Libya. The cool breeze was welcoming. A tabby cat lurked at the gate of our clinic. I offered her my spaghetti lunch, but by this time she had run and hidden under a car; she did not care for it. I peeled three pieces of Laughing Cow cheese and that she ate heartily. Even a wartime cat became rather fussy, unlike the undiscerning camels.

In my last few days in Libya before its liberation, I felt in my bones that the war was nearing its end. I wished very much to remain for a few more weeks to witness the victory, the joy, and the relief of the Libyans. In any case, I was glad to be here to watch history unfold. The freedom fighters and the medics were tremendously brave people, fighting for freedom for their country and saving lives on the front lines.

I left Libya on October 12, 2011. Eight days later Muammar Gaddafi was captured and killed.[4] I watched on television the indescribable jubilation of the Libyans. The people, forced to flee the cities, suffered tremendously. *Inshallah*, that peace would prevail and all of them could return to their homes to rebuild their lives and to enjoy their freshly minted freedom.

Unfortunately, since the downfall of Gaddafi, Libya has been labeled a failed state.[5] It has been embroiled in constant unrest and conflict between rival governments, various armed factions loyal to their home cities, ethnic militias with various political or religious ideology, and a renegade general, Khalifa Haftar. There has also been involvement from various foreign powers, including neighboring countries such as Egypt and the United Arab Emirates. Different factions take control over the oil wells, the economic lifeline of Libya, thus destabilizing revenue generation. The security issues have also slowed down economic growth, as foreign investors are reluctant to return. There is no longer a united government or rebel front in the country, for a period enabling the Islamic State of Iraq and the Levant (ISIL) to occupy part of it. The future of Libya remains uncertain; the thousands of freedom fighters and civilians who lost their lives to achieve the downfall of Gaddafi hopefully did not die in vain.

9

Kenya

2011, The Drought and Famine of the Horn of Africa

*"It's a matter of life and death. There was drought; we have been walking for
22 days drinking only water. Since I delivered, I haven't eaten a thing. I now
need food, life, water and shelter—everything that a human being needs."*
—*Weheleey Osman Haji, a day after giving
birth near the Kenyan border town of Liboi
to her baby Iisha, which means "life."*[1]

While I was volunteering in the Nakivale Refugee Camp in July 2011, the nightly
news broadcast by CNN and BBC covered one of the worst droughts that had struck East
Africa in sixty years.[2] This was the sort of news that hardly made the radar of American
news, but night after night in Africa the television showed droves of refugees fleeing the
drought-stricken areas of Somalia to neighboring Ethiopia and parts of Kenya. The rain
had failed for two seasons, and there was no possibility of a rainfall before September. Because of the lack of rainfall, essential crops failed, leading to a severe shortage of food and
no pasturelands for livestock. Farmers had to sell off part of their livestock to buy grain to
feed the rest of the herd.

On July 20, 2011, the UN officially declared two regions in Somalia, southern Bakool
and Lower Shabelle, as having a famine emergency.[3] An estimated eleven million people
were hungry, and hundreds and hundreds of people were on the move in search of food.
In the more severely affected areas, between thirty-five to forty percent of the children
were suffering from malnutrition. The UN reported that a quarter of the Somalians were
either internally displaced or living outside the country. The insecurity of the situation in
Somalia, especially with the unpredictable activities of Al-Shabaab, the terrorist group,
made the delivery of humanitarian relief extremely complex and dangerous. The lack of
funding from the international community made it impossible to implement the desired
aid fully.[4]

MTI collaborated with World Concern (WC), which had an established presence in
the Kenya/Somalia border with its mission to provide healthcare. Because of the strict border security measures, very few NGOs had been able to gain access to these areas. WC's
main project centered on Dhobley, a small border town in Somalia located just across the
border of Kenya and Somalia.

Volunteer teams would stay in Dadaab in Kenya, the location of one of the largest
refugee camps; the security situation there fluctuated daily. The teams would not be
working in the refugee camps in Dadaab where larger NGOs had been working for a number of years. There, 1,500 new drought refugees arrived daily, adding to the 450,000 refugees

already there.[5] We would have a security escort in all our travels around the Kenya/Somalia region.

I had signed up with MTI to volunteer in the Horn of Africa after my time in Libya. I arrived in Nairobi, Kenya, on November 15, 2011, via London after a long layover in Heathrow Airport. A huge traffic jam discombobulated Nairobi. The driver took me to ACK guesthouse, and immediately the receptionist gave me a message to meet with Jim and Andrew. Andrew was an MTI local coordinator in Nairobi, and Jim was our team leader, a physician assistant from Cape Cod, Massachusetts. I was exhausted, having only slept for two hours in more than twenty-four hours of travel.

There had been bad news about the security situation at the Kenya and Somalia border. A couple of weeks ago there were incidents of explosions from improvised explosive devices on the way to the border of Somalia, in addition to banditry. There were increased concerns after the recent abduction of a tourist in Lamu Island near Somalia[6] and the kidnapping of two MSF aid workers at the border near Dadaab.[7] As a result, the Kenyan government sent troops across the Somalia border in the hope of establishing security at least 50 to 100 kilometers from the Kenyan border. Because of the border incursion, Al-Shabaab warned the Kenyan government of retaliation. However, by the time we arrived, the Kenyan police deemed that security had improved, even though they had recently detected some land mines.

The previous team, to which MTI originally assigned me, was in a lock-down situation for two of the three weeks they were there in Dadaab. This meant they were more or less imprisoned in the WC compound, unable to go out to provide any clinical services. In retrospect, I felt lucky not to be included in that team. On Bishop Road close to where we were staying in Nairobi, there were roadblocks with military men toting AK-47s. Security seemed tight, even compared to November 2008 when I visited Nairobi for the first time, and that was almost eleven months after the riots following the ill-fated election.

It rained overnight. The next day I ran around the neighborhood; heaven knows when I could run again in Dadaab. Yvonne the midwife arrived. We spent almost a day at the WC's office going through essential medicines and supplies.

On November 17th, we got up early to go to Wilson Airport to catch the Mission Aviation Fellowship (MAF) plane for an hour and a half flight to Dadaab, about 100 kilometers from the border of Somalia. The MAF has been carrying people for humanitarian missions in Africa since 1948 with Mathew 25:40 as their guiding principle: "Assuredly, I say to you, in as much as you did it to one of the least of these My brethren, you did it to Me." Our plane was a twelve-passenger plane, and there were nine passengers. Each person could bring in fifteen kilograms of luggage, and they weighed us as well.

It rained heavily overnight, and this morning threatening rain clouds hung low in the sky. Finally, we took off and flew over Nairobi with its red-tiled English cottages intermingled with huge areas of shantytowns and slums with tin roofing. Soon this gave way to forests with red-earth paths, and as we approached Dadaab, scattered areas of refugee camps and the UN compound; instead of dry, brown, arid land, there were lush green trees, grass, and animals grazing. For the past four weeks or so, the rain finally came and transformed the arid land into a green miracle, swelling the rivers, and flooding the roads.

David picked us up and drove through the town of Dadaab, a town with thriving commerce of its own. The guesthouse had several rooms, and the women shared a quarter with two bunk beds and a double bed. Krista gave Yvonne and me a little spiel of the dos and don'ts of dressing in Somalia. We had to wear skirts down to our ankles, of which I only brought one; blouses with long or three-quarter length sleeves, and a headscarf in order to respect the local customs We were not to look at the eyes of the men directly and not to shake their hands unless they offered to. The weather here was hot and humid and already in my short-sleeved shirt, below-knee skirt, and without a headscarf, and no searing sun above, I was sweating profusely. I just hoped I would not faint under all these layers of garments.

Sakuda gave us a briefing on the current security situation, which he readily admitted changed every day. They were planning to go to Liboi that morning, but because of an incident there, they had to abort their plan.

Dadaab town was surrounded by three refugee camps: Ifo, Dugahaley, and Hagadera, all run by UNHCR with security provided by the Kenyan police. There were over 400,000 displaced people. There was active commerce, and one could get new cars and guns easily. In the last two weeks, there had been explosions of land mines. Whereas previously there was banditry along the road from Dadaab to the border of Somalia, now there was the additional danger of land mines and improvised explosive devices (IEDs) on the road. In the back of our minds, we had to remember that there was always the possibility of kidnapping for ransom, especially for light-skin folks, crossfire from insurgents, and vehicular accidents.

WC served six communities: Amuna, Damajale, Diif, Liboi, Hamey, and Dhobley. Our focus was on Dhobley, a community in Somalia twenty-five kilometers from the border if security allowed us to go there. The plan was for us to travel in two vehicles accompanied by the Kenyan security police. At the Somalia border, we would change vehicles, and then the Somalia police would take over the escort. The trip would take about two and a half hours each way. UN had deemed this northeastern part of Kenya at level IV security risk, which we understood as being high.

Hundreds of annoying flies, which had come with the rain, besieged us. They disappeared promptly when dusk fell and reappeared at dawn. With the rain, the arrival of the mosquitoes was inevitable. Given that we could not venture out without a male escort and with the question of landmines, it would be hard to run. I eyed the bigger UN compound across from us with envy.

The generator went off around half-past ten at night, and with that went our ceiling fan. It promised to be a sweaty night until the heavy rain came, cooling down the air somewhat. If there were going to be a field day tomorrow, it would have to be canceled because of the slick, muddy road condition. However, it being a Friday, WC's usual planning day, we would not be going anywhere. I dozed off, but soon the five AM call to prayer by the muezzin woke me up. The other day the guard heard a persistent loud banging on the gate and when he hurried to open it, he found three goats waiting to come in. Angrily he shooed them away.

The flies returned with a vengeance in the morning, swarming over my bowl of maize porridge. David had gone to Garrisa yesterday, about one hundred kilometers away, and treated us with bananas, mangoes, and watermelon, warning us not to expect this as a usual daily fare.

We spent part of the morning sorting through medicines and supplies in the storeroom and prepared three bags for midwifery, pediatric, and adult medical care. The medicines that we ordered in Nairobi had not arrived. A village chief and his deputy came to the compound wishing to discuss the possibility of WC going to their village to provide medical care and build more toilets. They wore western garb and had no beards. Speaking in fluent but heavily accented English, they told us that they had about 10,000 inhabitants, and rather than telling us the details, they would prefer we paid them a visit. To get the villagers' cooperation and trust, one had to go through the village elders first and solicit their prioritized needs.

When at last five o'clock rolled around and we were to go to the UN compound to have a short run, it poured; the heavens opened up, and sheets of rain came down. Since the ground had been so dry for so long, it quickly became flooded. Despite our good intentions, we did not think it was a good idea to get soaking wet. I at least had limited clothing to spare, as I had to wrap myself up with all the paraphernalia of a long skirt and long-sleeved shirt with my gym clothes underneath. If my skirt and scarf got wet, I would not have any spare to use for my clinic the next day. So Yvonne and I made do with some indoor exercises.

The next day we heard from security that we would not be going to Dhobley because of some administrative issues; instead, we would visit Damajale where the elders wished us to run a clinic set up by the MOH with a nurse and two community workers. The protean nature of the security situation cast a net of unpredictability over our daily schedule. We loaded up our land cruiser with seven people and medical supplies and drove to the center of Dadaab. Krista made sure that our headscarves covered our hair, and we wore long skirts and long-sleeved blouses. The village square was a large dirt patch with groups of goats resting comfortably here and there. A few police officers were congregating in a shelter, and we the *azungus* were left by ourselves. There we waited for security reports to see if it was safe to travel.

Leaving Dadaab, we took the only dirt road to Liboi near the border of Somalia, accompanied by four armed police officers in a separate land cruiser. Since it had been pouring, big, deep pools of muddy water collected in the center of the road. At one point, the road became just a river of muddy water, and half of our cruiser was submerged. Our driver drove this road so many times that he was familiar with it, even if it was under water. The driver that drove the police officers was more cautious, and many times we lost sight of their cruiser and had to pull over and wait for it. If we were ambushed, I could not imagine how they could help us; since we led the way, we would be the first to hit a landmine. Many goats, cattle, donkeys, and even camels grazed in the green pastures with small yellow flowers and acacia trees with tender new leaves recently replacing the once parched and brown land from just a few weeks ago. Somali women led the tall, handsome camels loaded with firewood. During the drought, livestock died for lack of food, and water and carcasses lay by the side of the road. Halfway through our two-and-a-half-hour journey, the road gave way to red clay-like earth. A lone, handsome, colorful duck was swimming in one of the pools. It was still there when we returned in the afternoon after our clinic and two days later swimming in the same "pond."

At a town called Kulan, a WFP truck came to distribute food. The villages were made up of mud and stick houses, some with UNHCR tarpaulin while others were covered haphazardly with whatever plastic coverings the owners could find, hardly materials to stave off a heavy downpour. We swerved off the road that led to the Somalia border with the border guards a few meters from us; Kenyan and Somalian flags fluttered in the wind.

After two and a half hours of a jostling ride, we had reached our destination. To our surprise, the clinic was closed, but a few hopeful villagers sat on the benches outside. Upon seeing us, they ran to rouse up the community workers to open the clinic. It was a small structure with four rooms, two of which became our consultation rooms; a third marked "Store" was the dispensary, and the fourth was locked. Someone was using the first consultation room as a bedroom, with the telltale signs of a mattress on the floor and many personal belongings. Trash, medicines, empty containers, cold chain packaging, and safety boxes cluttered the second room from floor to ceiling, and the sink had all but disappeared. Mouse droppings peppered the dispensary, and stalactites of termite nests hung from the ceiling. It was grotesquely filthy. A youngster gave this room a quick sweep so we could deposit our three bags of medical supplies.

Krista took two of the armed guards with her to the village to teach sanitation, leaving two other armed guards for the clinic, while Samuel, the water engineer, being a Kenyan, was able to move around freely to access the water situation, the borehole, and the latrines. Girls usually missed one week out of a month of school because of their periods, and the latrines had been built in the school to reduce absenteeism.

Soon word spread to the village that the clinic was open, and the cluttered consultation room became my space. Yvonne used the other consultation room while Jim and Andrew saw patients in the porch using a screen. I wiped down the table thoroughly with disinfectant before seeing my first patient, a young man with a swollen hand caused by a scorpion bite the night before. My translator was Abdirizack, a primary school teacher, a loud gruff man seemingly more interested in seeing the patients quickly rather than taking time to explain things to them. An elder with a henna-colored beard had a classic case of angina; I only had aspirin to offer him. Many children and young women were anemic with worm infestations and pica (the practice of eating soil). Women complained of chest, back, and joint pain from heavy chores and walking long distances. The black headscarves and long dresses that draped all the way down to their ankles hid their malnourished bodies. When they pulled up their long scarves, their clothes stuck to their bodies, drenched in sweat. Soon Jim told us to hurry up to get ready to leave before it turned dark, as the road was difficult, and it had started to rain. We saw a total of 120 patients, more women than men, and a number of children. I realized with relief that I had survived my first day with a headscarf, long sleeves, and long skirt in this inferno.

On our way home, a brief altercation erupted among the police who were supposed to provide us security. Muhammad, our driver, went quickly to defuse the situation. We reached Dadaab just before five PM without any further incidents.

The rain came pouring down; the rainy season was finally here. At night, the frogs croaked enthusiastically, louder when the generator was turned off. The call to prayer happened twice, once at four and again at five in the morning with a string of what I thought to be the donkeys' desperate "hee-haws" interspersed between the calls. Someone informed me that they were actually ecstatic cries of lovemaking.

Hamey was a community about forty-five minutes from Damajale. We took the same road that continued to be a big river, driving through three pools, and it took us three and a half hours to get there. A van was stuck right in the middle of a big pool close to Dadaab. A man driving a donkey cart called out to us in Somali, "White men, help us!" We passed Damajale on our way to Hamey; the government clinic there was again tightly closed.

Before a medium-sized tent was erected as a clinic at Hamey, the community health workers provided medical care under an umbrella shade of an acacia tree. Thorny branches used as a fence surrounded the tent to prevent trespassing. Donkeys grazed and roamed the area. By the time we arrived at Hamey, the four community workers had been busy seeing a number of patients, many of whom were crowding around a table filled with medicines. Medicine was still practiced as the dispensing of pills to treat symptoms; physical examination played little role. Jim and I set ourselves up in the deeper recesses of the tent while Yvonne had her clinic at the back of the tent, away from the prying eyes of the crowd to get some privacy for the pregnant women, not an ideal arrangement by any means.

The temperature in the tent quickly rose; the heat was intolerable, and we were sweating profusely. We sat on low chairs, and the patients only had a mat to sit on while we tried our very best to tend to them. Several youngsters came with high fever, but as our malaria kit did not have the test reagent, we treated them for presumed malaria. A one-year-old baby had had a badly infected sore on the scalp for four months; we cleaned and dressed it, and the community workers would continue to follow this youngster's progress. The women here wore colorful headscarves strikingly different from the stark, depressing black ones in Damajale. We left around three-thirty in the afternoon, and it took us a good three hours to get back. The sun was setting and glowing red and orange through the acacia trees as we approached Dadaab.

Before supper we heard the good news that there might be a helicopter available in a few days that could take us to Liboi at the Somalia border, and also to the various clinics in a far shorter time than our current one a total of six and a half hours each day on the road.

As it had always been the case, we abandoned our schedule planned the night before. We were supposed to go to Damajale, but instead, we went to Kokar to explore the possibility of running a clinic there. We dropped off the water and sanitation people at Damajale en route to Kokar, and again we noticed that the government clinic in Damajale was closed. A desperate woman thrust her sick baby through the window of the cruiser, begging us to see him. Apparently the clinical officer only opened clinic when our team came. At Damajale the four security police refused to split into two groups as had been planned; one to guard the staff in Damajale, and the other to follow us to Kokar to do clinic. Instead, we had to hire additional local police to provide security for the people remaining in Damajale. Precious

Hamey clinic, a tent under an acacia tree.

Somalians and Kenyans crowding the entrance of the Hamey clinic to be seen.

time was wasted. We then had to backtrack forty-five minutes to Kokar. The only constant for us had been the same beautiful duck swimming at the same "pond" for the last few days that we had been traveling on this same road. I did not question why security had contradicted its own dictum, "Never keep a routine and never use the same route." They certainly did not keep the same routine, but they did keep the same route. As far as I could see, there were no other routes.

At Kokar the elders, all men gathered under a tin-roofed open car park, waited to meet with the WC people. Women could not participate, and they loitered around the periphery. The chief sat on a chair; the rest of the elders sat on a mat placed on the dirt by his feet and we on long benches. The village chief gave us his blessings to run a clinic at Kokar; there had not been one for a while. Because we had to trace our way back to Damajale to fetch the water and the sanitation folks and then try to get home before dark, we could only promise an hour of clinic at Kokar after meeting with the chief.

The car park where we held our clinic, however, did not afford good crowd control. We were warned that Somalis refused to queue up, and in fact, they were bearing down on us so much so that it was very difficult to provide any kind of care. Our security person did not speak Somali and was unable to control them. The police did not offer any help and just sat under the shade of the acacia trees, resting comfortably. A number of children clearly had anemia, pica, and worm infestations, but the promised medicines still had not come from Nairobi after a week into our mission, so there were no worm medicines, liquid iron, or vitamins to offer. There were also a whole slew of babies with diarrhea. The WC water sanitation person had not been able to assess the water situation here. With all the pushing

A mother and her sick child on the mat in the tent of the Hamey clinic.

and shoving, we ended up seeing only a few people. The hour went by so quickly that the translator stopped translating, and the medication bags were loaded onto the cruiser. A woman who had been waiting in my line desperately shoved her feverish baby at me, but I could not help her without a translator, and our leader urged me to leave. As I boarded the cruiser, someone in the crowd threw a stone at him; he was stunned but not hurt.

It was rather a long day for such a short clinic. Our total driving time must have been about seven hours that day. Another large truck was stuck in the flooded road right in Dadaab. We had been lucky so far.

The helicopter did come, but we were not the chosen ones to fly to Liboi to do a clinic; instead, the helicopter took some of WC's people to Liboi to concentrate on the water and toilet projects, and then it ferried staff from Garrisa to Dadaab. Since they could only do two trips a day, they did not factor the medical people into the helicopter flight. The rain came and went. At the end of the day, a rainbow appeared in the sky, arching over the tin roof of our bedroom.

The next day we finally boarded the helicopter to go to Hamey, a village that took us about three and a half hours to get to on the flooded road and now took thirty to forty minutes. It was a four-passenger chopper, in addition to the two pilots, and it took off from the Dadaab Airport. The German humanitarian organization, Humedica, provided the helicopter and would serve WC for two weeks before heading to some other humanitarian missions. It could not have come at a better time as the road journey had been arduous and long.

Our plan to go to Dhobley was scratched again. It seemed that WC did not think that the MTI coordinator had enough experience there to run a clinic, so we headed to Hamey. From the helicopter, we could see areas of brown earth still not covered with vegetation. It took us about twenty minutes to arrive at a village. According to the coordinates it was supposed to be Hamey, but in fact, it was Damajale. Droves of villagers, young and old, came running to see the big bird. The pilot asked Andrew to go and ask for directions to Hamey but he was not able to as he did not speak Somali. We took off and flew around looking for Hamey, heading towards Liboi. In the end, we decided to land at Damajale and ran our clinic there. The government clinic again was not open; the two community health workers did not seem to run their clinic consistently.

The store and the consultation room that I used last Saturday were just as filthy as we had left them. I decided to talk to the community health worker about taking responsibility to clean the room. He gave the excuse that the cleaner was away for the day, but I argued that we were there last Saturday; he should have had ample time to clean up. Thereupon he asked me whether we would pay to clean the place. I told him that his community was lucky to have a proper building for a clinic while Hamey had a tent, and Kokar had none; he should take great pride in keeping it clean for the community and neither WC nor MTI would pay for the cleanup. Previous MTI teams had taken upon themselves to clean up the place before starting clinic; however, soon after they left, it quickly reverted to the current filthy condition.

After wiping the table and chairs with alcohol, I set up a clean area for my patient, translator, and myself. For crowd control, we cordoned off the corridor with duct tape, only allowing some patients to wait on the benches while the police stood guard at either end.

Again, malnourished children with anemia, pica, worm infestations, and fungal skin infections seemed quite rampant. I drained a foot abscess of a youngster who fell off a tree and poked his foot with a thorn, and cleaned a *panga* wound on the hand of a man. A cute baby had a bad case of impetigo, but she was still smiling despite all those uncomfortable sores. Women, young and old, complained of chest pain, low back pain, knee pain, and poor appetite; many were anemic. By age twenty, many of them already had at least four babies and looked aged. The amount of clothes they had on made me feel hot and uncomfortable.

We had a date with the chopper and had to finish clinic on time. However, it did not come at the appointed time as ominous storm clouds gathered. Via satellite phone, Andrew learned that the chopper had to travel to Garrisa to refuel and would be late. We waited for an hour and a half with our armed guards while surreptitiously snacking on peanuts and eggs that we saved from breakfast to eat as our late lunch; it felt unseemly to eat in front of hungry children. We flew home in fifteen minutes. What a treat.

We spent our Thanksgiving in the bush of Africa, grateful that we were not beset by famine and hunger, and that we had the good fortune of the arrival of the helicopter to take us quickly to these rural villages at least for the rest of the time we were in Dadaab.

The day when we were supposed to go to Hamey, we ended up in Damajale. Apparently, the coordinates given to the pilot by logistics were incorrect. To ensure that we reached Hamey, we had a human GPS in the form of Samuel, the water engineer, who had the coordinates for the water tank in Hamey, to accompany us. However, early in the morning of our departure, he left with Sakuda, our security person, for Garissa. Fortunately, the flooded road to Garissa was impassable, and he returned in time to go with us in the helicopter. Up in the air, the three groups of refugee camps of Dadaab seemed to huddle together.

We found the small village of Hamey all right; I could even see the tent under the acacia tree from the air and the helicopter landed right next to it. Unlike Damajale clinic, which seemed to be closed most of the time, the tent clinic was open even on a Friday, and when we arrived the healthcare workers were already busy seeing patients.

We took some time to organize some space for ourselves and cordoned off the area for the purpose of crowd control with the help of the police officers. We opened the back flap and all the window flaps of the tent to let in some air, making the condition in the tent tolerable. We were busy seeing children with malnutrition, worm infestations, anemia, pica, diarrhea, fever, and dehydration, and a woman who had suffered from elephantiasis for three years. The very sick child who came to see Jim the other day turned up today all better, smiling and walking on her own two feet. The mosquitoes had returned with the rain; it would be a matter of time before malaria would come back with a vengeance.

The pilots called to say they would be coming to get us a little early because of an impending thunderstorm. The community healthcare workers invited me to join their lunch of rice and meat, which they shared from a big communal pot, scooping up lumps of food hungrily with their hands while squatting behind the tent. The villagers fed them in appreciation for their work. It was not much, a lot of rice and a few pieces of goat meat on bones, but it was very generous of them to share with me.

On our flight back to Dadaab, the rain came, not heavy. Far away towards the direction of Somalia, a faint rainbow arched over the sky.

Our medicines came by truck but not the essential ones we were hoping for. We continued to have to borrow albendazole, the worm medication, from Dadaab District Hospital; we also lacked multivitamins and iron pills for the kids.

Dhobley is in Somalia about twenty-five kilometers from the Kenyan border, one of the communities that WC was involved in the distribution of food vouchers for about 1800 families twice a week and the distribution of non-food items (mosquito nets, sheeting, pots, etc.) for about 800 families in addition to sanitation and water projects. The previous MTI teams were also involved in providing medical care. It had been on our schedule at least three times, but we had been unable to go there for a variety of reasons: the rainy weather, the muddy condition of the roads, and the concern of the WC that our medical coordinator was not familiar with Dhobley. The Kenyan military was going for a sweep of the Kenyan/Somalian border because of recent attacks on the military in Garissa that had resulted in several casualties who had to be flown to Nairobi. Additionally, there was fresh fighting in Dhobley itself. AFREC, Africa Emergency Committee, a partner of WC in Somalia, deemed it unsafe for us to travel into Somalia. Instead, they traveled from Dhobley to Liboi in Kenya to meet with the WC people to receive the food vouchers for distribution. This meant that we would not be going to Dhobley any time soon. Perhaps in our short stay here, it would never be secure enough for us to visit at all.

On our way to Damajale one day, the pilots said since we were such frequent flyers, perhaps they would take us to some place nice. We hinted that we would not mind them doing some aerobatics. Just as soon as we took off the pilots did just that, eliciting whoops and screams from us. Before we reached Damajale, they flew the chopper really low, almost scraping the tops of acacia trees "Did you enjoy your safari?" one of the pilots asked.

"But we did not see any animals."

"That was only for the premier class, not for the business class," he explained.

"Ah, since we have been flying almost daily, we should be upgraded to the premier class."

"The steward would be by to serve you drinks in a little bit, but you have to excuse him for not shaving this morning."

We did see the camels gazing up at us from their browsing. The goats were rather skittish and scrambled for cover just as soon as they heard the noise of the chopper. We landed close to our clinic in Damajale. The healthcare worker did not open the clinic again; he only ran quickly to unlock the doors as soon as he heard the chopper. His record book showed that indeed for the last two weeks, he only opened the clinic on the days we came to Damajale.

That day I was quite busy. I personally saw about fifty-four patients with Abdinasir Mohammad, a strapping hard-working young man, as my translator. After seeing thirty-odd patients, he sat back, sighed, and looked tired; so was I. Many elderly men and women had poor vision with cataracts. Almost all the women, young and old, complained of pain in their chest, low back, and knees, mostly from walking a long way and carrying water. Jokingly I asked if their husbands helped them with the water; their reply was men did not carry heavy things.

Close to the end of my clinic, an eighty-four-year-old man, blind in one eye, walked in slowly with a walking stick fashioned from a tree branch, complaining of joint pain. He loved to walk with his camels and wished to continue to do so. He left happy with the few ibuprofens I gave him.

As we approached Dadaab, the pilots flew over the enormous Dadaab Refugee Camps, partially flooded. Each camp held about 80,000 refugees; the oldest camp had been around for about twenty years, and structures that were more permanent had replaced the tents. Officially, there were three camps in Dadaab, but unofficially, there were six camps holding over half a million refugees. This was an amazing and unfathomable number of people displaced from their homes.

It took the cruiser about three and a half hours to get to Damajale and then perhaps a couple of more hours to reach the border of Somalia. The refugees who fled the drought or conflict in Somalia had to travel by foot with their children and some worldly belongings, in the intense heat, without security of food and water, to reach the Dadaab Refugee Camp. They probably endured many weeks of traveling, with children and animals dying on the way. We have a great deal to be thankful for when we live in parts of the world free of conflict and disasters.

Previous volunteers stayed in Liboi in a WC compound right in the center of town, close to the police station and a military base. From there it was about twenty minutes by car to the Somalia border, and Damajale and Hamey were more easily accessible. However, because of the recent military sweep and the rain that made the road to Liboi impassable, we had to stay in Dadaab.

Dhobley was still a no-go because of the security situation, and we would not be visiting it at all since we would be leaving for Nairobi even earlier than planned because of the current flight situation out of Dadaab. Yvonne fell ill and flew back to Nairobi accompanied by Jim, leaving the MTI coordinator, Andrew, and me in Dadaab to finish the rest of our time here.

Because we had recently run clinics at Damajale and Hamey, we decided to go to Liboi to see if there might be a future collaboration with the MOH or MSF. As we approached Liboi, the roads were just rivers of water; it was difficult to imagine how one could reach it by land vehicles. The helicopter landed in the muddy field close to the military base. Four military officers descended on us after we walked through a muddy path, at one point clinging onto a chain-link fence, slowly inching our way along. They wanted to know why the helicopter did not stop but just dropped us off and took off immediately. They queried about the reason for our visit; I thought logistics or security would have communicated with them beforehand.

After walking through the police ground, the WC vehicle came to meet us, only to be stuck in the mud a few hundred meters down the village; we got off and walked. At the WC compound, the staff had been busy giving out food vouchers.

At the Liboi healthcare center, MSF set up two tents for the treatment of cholera. In October, Somalis crossed the border to be treated, but since the Kenyan incursion, there had been no patients. The inpatient wards were completely empty; the sole patient had just been discharged. The outpatient clinic closed for lunch. We met briefly with two MSF staff, and they were not opposed to having other healthcare volunteers to come to Liboi. Andrew took me to a hut he called Liboi Hilton Hotel for a lunch of *ugali,* cabbage, and goat meat.

We were down to two people and two possible places to go for medical relief, with the third potential place being Kokar. After our disorganized one-hour clinic at Kokar when someone threw stones at Jim, WC wanted to discuss it with the elders to mend fences and make sure such incidents did not recur. It turned out that it was a woman who threw the stones, and according to the elders, they could only do something if it were a man who committed the act.

By the time we arrived at Hamey, the community healthcare workers had seen forty patients. The day was rather hot, but they had now learned to open the flaps of the tent, allowing an occasional breeze to come through. Aden, my translator, was the oldest of nine children, and his parents were both in their forties. I saw close to fifty patients, but towards the end of the clinic, many of the people who were seen in the morning by the community healthcare workers came again in an effort to get more medicines.

The sickest patient, wearing a belt with the name "Obama" embroidered on it, came on a donkey cart, lying prostrate on a UNHCR blanket with a high fever and parched lips. He had been having bloody diarrhea. Suspecting typhoid fever, we gave him an injection of antipyretics, antibiotics, and oral rehydration fluids, of which he was able to take about 250 ml. At the end of the clinic, his fever broke, and he was able to walk home. It was hot; the confounding headscarf got in the way of my stethoscope and so eventually, I let it slip down my head. I did not think the villagers cared.

With the rainy season, the frogs had been croaking, more like honking, all night, and I presumed they had been doing so since the rain started. It was just that the loudness of the generator obscured their noises. When I got up in the middle of the night to see the stars, I heard them very clearly. By then the generator had long since been silenced.

On Sundays, some of us went to church at the Dadaab International Worship Center, a small, long concrete hall. They were a very rowdy, English-speaking group of around a hundred; the Swahili service followed suit. Unlike the Muslims, their attire was more modern, no long skirts, long sleeves or headscarves. In fact, they walked into the town of Dadaab dressed as they were for church. WC chose the more conservative attire in order to win the people they were helping over to their side.

A large pool of brown water collected just outside the compound where some local children used as a swimming pool. Two hotels stood on each side of the compound; one of them was the New Alzazeera Hotel, a tin-roofed structure with two sheds of sticks. Andrew took us down the main street of Dadaab for a walk one evening. With all the hype concerning dress, I felt conspicuous and uncomfortable even wearing my long skirt, long-sleeved shirt, and with my head covered.

WC decided the night before that Kokar was to be our last destination. However, in the morning when the Chief of Kokar came with his councilor, the fourth seat, which was supposed to be for me on the helicopter, was quickly relinquished to the councilor. We were hoping to do a clinic there while the Chief met with the villagers and WC staff, but Andrew explained to me that the Chief did not feel safe for a "white person" to do her clinic, and they could not promise security. I had heard many strange excuses, and this one did not surprise me at all.

So my last day of doing clinic was scratched. Instead, I went with Krista, Tracy, and Samuel to Damajale to inspect the water situation and to see Krista do her sanitation demonstration for the women there. Again, the clinic in Damajale was closed tightly. The community healthcare worker ran hurriedly to open the consultation room, thinking that we came to do clinic; however, he was disappointed when we did not stop. Later as we left Damajale, we observed that the clinic was still closed. There were rumors that the community healthcare workers had not been paid in a while, which might have accounted for their unwillingness to work.

Krista was an enthusiastic teacher. Her translator, Fadum, a tall Kenyan Somali, had gathered a number of women, and she was sitting on a mat under a tree going over pictures of sanitation, with handwashing being foremost for the prevention of the spread of diseases. The women took tea and their lunch break after washing their hands, and Krista gave everyone a washbasin for attending.

Samuel, the water engineer, took me to a borehole where the villagers obtained their water. There was plenty of water now since it had been raining. During the drought, the stench from the animal carcasses was unbearable, and an NGO came to remove them. Some villagers walked up to six hours to the next village to get water when the water pump in their own village did not work. Camel owners had to pay seven shillings a camel for water, and the camels came once every four days to drink.

In the town square, animals were drinking from the water troughs. A few stalls away a woman sold *khat* while caring for her baby. A group of men sat or reclined, chewing *khat* with a glazed look, temporarily transporting themselves into a better imaginary world.

During my last helicopter ride, the pilot swooped up, then nose-dived close to the main road and then to the tops of acacia trees, scaring some camels. We circled around Dadaab, the UN, and our compounds. Ianz, one of the pilots, had been flying humanitarian missions for close to ten years in Pakistan, Sierra Leone, and Sudan.

Kenya gained its independence in 1962, and various NGOs fanned out into the countryside providing heavy relief work. WC concentrated their efforts on the delivery of food and non-food items in the form of vouchers for many families affected by the famine, water in the form of boreholes, water trucks, the construction of latrines, and the provision of sanitation education for the communities. They instilled their philosophy of educating the communities that they, and not the NGOs, owned their problems, and they had to come up with the solutions, even if jointly with WC. The hope was when all NGOs left, if they ever did, the communities would know how to maintain and improve on what had been built. The health portion was a collaboration of MTI with WC, which at this point was not as well coordinated. I hope with time, the medications available would be more in line with the needs of the communities, and that WC could help address the nutritional status of the children.

I was sad to leave this medical relief with the feeling that I really did not accomplish all that I came here to do. The security situation prevented us from crossing the border to Somalia. Having said that, we did provide crucial medical needs of the communities that we visited. Some like Hamey had good hardworking healthcare persons, but others such as Damajale, despite the presence of a facility, received only sporadic care, and Kokar enjoyed none of the above. The upside was the helicopter that saved us many hours of difficult road traveling. God had his own way of arranging things for us. Perhaps someday for me helping in Somalia might still be a reality.

The last night there was a whole lot of planning for WC to go to many places, including Dhobley, which was back on the schedule; there was no talk about security or road conditions. I was not sure whether the fighting in Dhobley had ceased or what happened to the Kenyan military sweep of the border. Security in the person of Omar did not offer any insights.

WC was able to ascertain from their visit to Kokar the lack of sanitation facilities and inadequate water supply, but Andrew, who represented MTI, did not ask for a physical place for medical care or about ensuring security for future MTI teams, questions that were crucial for the provision of medical relief there. Then we learned that the next two MTI teams had been canceled. and there would not be any medical relief for the month of December. No one would be in the compound from December 22 to January 2 because of the holiday break, but that still did not account for the first few weeks of December. The team due to arrive two days from now must have been sorely disappointed. The villagers who had looked to us to provide medical care would not understand why we stopped coming. Each time when we went there, they seemed to welcome us and were extremely happy to see us. Perhaps Andrew, the only MTI Kenyan representative, would continue to go to the various villagers in December to do clinic.

While at the Dadaab compound, I had tried to befriend a cat with beautiful blue eyes, feeding him chewy goat meat. I thought he should be named *Yanburu* or *Parka*; it means cat in Somali and Swahili respectively. Sucri, the day guard, promised to take care of him. I went to tell him goodbye and found him sleeping soundly by the huge water drum. I crept up and touched him on the back, which sent him flying off in a fright.

In the morning, we went to Dadaab Airport to board the MAF plane to Nairobi. It was completely full, and one of the passengers sat in the co-pilot seat. I had to leave a day early because there was no guarantee of a seat on the European Commission Humanitarian Aid (ECHO) flight the next day. As we went down the runway and up in the air, the plane made a sharp turn in the opposite direction of the flight of our usual helicopter ride heading towards Nairobi.

My sick teammate, Yvonne, left for home, having recovered quickly from her brief illness. Jim, our leader who had accompanied her, heard that the next team would not be coming, so he changed his flight and left as well. I chose to remain in Nairobi for a couple of days before flying home.

As I took walks around the neighborhood, I saw signs offered by "doctors" to solve various life troubles. A wizard doctor by the name of Dr. Gujo claimed to be able to help in broken love, lost properties, business matters, jobs, man power (by that he probably meant virility), infertility, and other life hazards. If these doctors had such powers, they would have been very rich by now and would not have to advertise to attract new patients.

Moi Avenue in downtown Nairobi was busy, and the temperature soared quickly as the day wore on. I perused the wares at the Masai Market looking for bargains before walking through Uhuru Park, which was busy with families on outings while a concert was taking place.

I joined Rosalind from Australia for a game drive at Nairobi National Park. Very early on, we spotted a lioness by the roadside; her two cubs stared at us with curiosity while their mother nonchalantly sat several feet from them. We saw rhinoceroses, a white one and a black one, ostriches looking like ballerinas with their elegant tutus, giraffes, buffaloes, impalas, Thomson and Grant's gazelles, zebras, a lone wildebeest, a crocodile from afar, two regal crowned cranes, and many other species of birds that we knew nothing about. The skyscape of Nairobi and the Ngong Hill, or Knuckles Hill in Maasai, stood in the distance. Planes flying by at the periphery of the park broke the silence, as the airport was close by.

The migration corridor of the wildebeests has been blocked off by urban development, and the poor wildebeests are prevented from migrating south through the Rift Valley. Like many of the refugees in Dadaab, they are trapped permanently.

Global Acute Malnutrition (GAM) is a measure of acute malnutrition in refugee children aged between 6 and 59 months. When GAM is 10 percent or more, the severity of the malnutrition becomes a situation of high public health concern, and immediate actions must be mobilized.[8] In 2011, the GAM in southern and central Somalia increased from 16.4 percent to 36.4 percent. The dire warning was loud and clear, but the delayed international response turned the food crisis caused by the drought into an utter humanitarian disaster.[9]

In 2012, the Department for International Development (DfID) estimated that between 50,000 and 100,000 people, more than half of them children under five, died in the 2011 Horn of Africa crisis that affected Somalia, Ethiopia, and Kenya.[10] In the span of three months just before the UN declared famine in Somalia on July 20, 2011, the U.S. estimated that 29,000 children under the age of five died there.[11] By 2013, BBC reported that nearly 260,000 people died during the famine that hit Somalia from 2010 to 2012.[12] The famine further affected 13 million people because of the destruction of livelihoods, livestock, and the local market systems and hundreds of thousands of people would continue to be at risk of malnutrition in the Horn of Africa.

10

Uganda

2012, The Nyakabande Transit Refugee Camp
for the Democratic Republic of Congo

"My neighbors came running to rescue me and my daughters and we all fled and didn't stop until we reached Bunagana, near the Ugandan border. All I think about is my husband, we were married for seven years, I just really miss him."

—*Colletta*[1]

Since I went to Africa for medical relief missions three times in 2011, I decided to take a respite during 2012. However, in July of that year, fresh fighting erupted in the DRC between government forces and M23 militia particularly in the eastern part of the DRC.[2] MTI immediately responded by sending their local national team in Uganda to Kisoro, a border town near the DRC where UNHCR set up the Nyakabande Transit Camp to care for the daily influx of hundreds of refugees arriving on hired trucks or on foot. Most of them were fleeing Bunagana, Jomba, Chengerero, Ntamugenga, Rutshuru, and Rwanguba in the DRC, confirmed by the UN to be under the control of the rebels. As of July 2012, the Uganda Red Cross registered over 16,000 Congolese refugees at the transit camp.[3]

Since independence in 1960, the DRC has not had a peaceful period because of ongoing conflicts over the control of mineral wealth, with coups and corruption under Mbutu Sese Seko when the DRC was called Zaire, conflict supported by neighboring countries either taking the government's side or that of the rebels. In March 23, 2009, the National Congress for the Defense of the People (CNDP), a political armed militia in the DRC, and the government signed a peace treaty, and the soldiers of the CNDP integrated into the armed forces of the DRC.[4] In April of 2012, around 300 soldiers, most of them former CNDP members formed M23, taking their name from the March 23 Peace Treaty and turned against the government, accusing it of not implementing the peace treaty agreements and citing poor conditions of the army. The fighting in April through July of 2012 in the North Kivu area resulted in many displaced people fleeing to the neighboring countries of Uganda and Rwanda.[5]

On July 9, 2012, the situation report showed that a significant number of refugees arrived at the Nyakabande transit center throughout the day, with 895 registered by the Uganda Red Cross, bringing the total number of registered individuals to 14,569. There were late arrivals who had not decided to register.[6] Communal shelters, two-family tents, distribution and administration tents, and kitchens were stretched to capacity. Eventually refugees occupied every inch of sheltered floor, and hundreds had to sleep out in the open.

At the Nyakabande Transit Camp in Kisoro district, Uganda, near the border of the Democratic Republic of Congo (DRC).

It was of great concern because of the cold conditions in Kisoro and the great number of children and pregnant women in the camp. The Nyakabande police outpost enforced security, facilitated by UNHCR with fourteen of the police in the camp. Water had to be trucked into the camp and treated with chlorine; toilets and their disinfection, hand washing facilities, bath shelters, and water tanks were set up. UNHCR tried to ease the crowding condition in the transit camp by moving refugees to Rwamwanja settlement camp in Kamwenge district in Uganda.

MTI and the Kisoro District Health Office with the support of UNHCR were responsible for the provision of health service delivery at Nyakabande Health Center II including immunization, malnutrition screening, health education, antenatal care, and management of common illnesses. With this crisis, I ended my hiatus and headed to the transit camp in Nyakabande in Kisoro, Uganda, in August 2012.

After about twenty-four hours of flight and a layover in Amsterdam and Kigali, we arrived at Entebbe, Uganda. We then had another ten hours of bumpy, overland travel from Kampala before we finally arrived at Kisoro, situated at the southwestern tip of Uganda bordering the DRC and Rwanda. It would have been more expedient to sleep over in Kigali, Rwanda, and drive over from there across the border to Kisoro. It would then have been a two-hour ride instead of the ten that we took traveling overland in Uganda. On our way to Kisoro from Kampala, we stopped briefly at Mbarara, near where I volunteered last summer in the Nakivale Refugee Camp and had a late lunch. From there it was another five hours to Kisoro, passing through Kabale. I probably traveled through this region last year when I

Tents set up by UNHCR at the Nyakabande Transit Camp for the refugees fleeing conflict in the DRC, with the Mufumbiro Mountains looming in the background.

went to the Parcs des Volcans in Rwanda to trek the mountain gorillas, as I recalled having taken the same winding road up and down the volcanic mountains when new roads were being constructed. It being dark this time when we traveled to Kisoro, we did not see much of the mountains.

In the morning, dense fog shrouded Kisoro and the surrounding regions, with only the peak of one of the three volcanic mountains of the Mufumbiro Mountains peeking through. I ran through the village area and on the jagged paths of volcanic rocks. The inhabitants here wore heavy winter garments and wrapped themselves with shawls and blankets, but many remained barefoot.

These days the number of newly arrived refugees at the Nyakabande transit center had slowed down considerably. M23 rebels had succeeded in seizing control of the towns near the border of Uganda, and the fighting had temporarily stopped. However, it remained uncertain whether there might be renewed conflict when the DRC government decided to recoup their losses. A spattering of refugees lined up in front of the administrative tent to register for a UNHCR refugee card that enabled them to stay in a tent, get two hot meals a day, and if available, mats, blankets, plates, cups, and basic staples.

Within the enclosure of the transit center were numerous temporary, caterpillar-like UNHCR tents with two separate dwellings housing two families. There used to be five communal tents that accommodated many people, over four hundred smaller tents that housed at least two families each, and five kitchen tents.[7] Many of the refugees had been moved to a resettlement area, such as Rwamwanja, and the number of tents had decreased. Rainstorms had also taken down a few of them. Food was cooked in enormous cauldrons big enough to fit at least five to six children and served twice a day in the tented kitchen. WFP determined the amount of food given to individuals. Whether that was enough, only the children's bellies could tell. At the evening meals, several children hovered over one of these cauldrons scraping leftovers with their tiny, bare hands and licking them clean. In the nutrition screening program for children under five, thirty-eight percent of the children that reported to the camp were malnourished, with seven percent severely.[8]

The Nyakabande Health Center II set up by MTI was just minutes away from the transit center, and this was where the refugees and Ugandan nationals came for medical care. Daser, the clinical officer, told me that the number of people seen had also decreased. In days past, she had her hands full just giving medications away after hearing the symptoms; there was no time to do careful evaluations. Nowadays with fewer refugees arriving and more of them resettled, fewer people came. The clinic was actually seeing more Ugandan nationals than refugees.

Most refugees had run away with few belongings, and some only had the clothes on their back. In the course of fleeing from the conflict, many became separated from loved ones. A twelve-year-old boy was separated from his parents when the conflict broke out in his village. In the confusion of running away, he had followed other refugees boarding vehicles heading for the border of Uganda. The whereabouts of his family remained unknown.

A grandmother had run away with her two-year-old granddaughter. Her daughter, who was then three months pregnant, had left the child with the grandmother when she was seven months old, declaring herself unable to care for her. This grandmother had raised five of her own children, all grown and all fled to Uganda during this last conflict, leaving her to fend for herself and the little grandchild. At the age of fifty, she started nursing her granddaughter and continued to do so at the camp. Indeed, she showed us that she could still express milk from her breasts.

A quiet mother brought her three-month-old child with diarrhea, and the baby was suckling vigorously at her breast. She had fled the DRC with all five of her children under her care, her husband having fled first on his own and apparently resettled in Uganda. Most men escaped first for fear the rebels would forcibly recruit them, leaving their families to fend for themselves.

It being the rainy season in Uganda, the fields were being prepared for cultivation. It was backbreaking work with only hand implements to dig in land filled with volcanic rocks. Not a single man worked in the fields. Through my clinic window, I could see the women working for hours, patiently and relentlessly, while a couple of cows lay lazily under the sun chewing their cud, and a swaddled baby slept under the shade. Where, oh where, were the men?

All day long refugees and Ugandan nationals came traipsing into the clinic. An old man came in with a bad cut on his left ring finger, having sliced off part of the nail and nail pad with a machete. He had wrapped it up with a strip of plastic; blood simply pooled in the non-absorbent material. We washed the wound copiously, dressed it up, gave him a tetanus shot, instructed him to return for dressing change, and sent him home.

In the afternoon, the kitchen crews in the camp were busy cooking the evening meal in three large cauldrons black with soot in their tented kitchen. Fumes filled the tent, women and men appearing and disappearing through the smoke, stirring the contents with a long stick. The children followed me around the campsite wanting the *mzungu* to take their pictures and were exhilarated to see themselves magically appear on the digital screen. Two

The author with the children of the Nyakabande Transit Camp.

girls, dressed in their best, led me to their tent. The boys with their filthy clothes and shoe-less condition, one holding a precious bicycle tire as a toy, were shyer and followed silently and at a respectable distance. Despite their shabbiness, they carried themselves with a certain quiet dignity, heads held high, shoulders erect, and chests thrust forward,.

Some of the women built cooking fires near their campsite and did their own cooking. A woman proudly showed me her tent and all that she owned, which was not much: two suitcases, some blankets, and a plate of peas, which she had been shelling while cuddling her baby in her arms.

Many more refugees arrived to be registered. There were tales of new eruptions of fighting, looting, and the rebels rounding up new recruits. A hired *boda* deposited a petite woman and her three exhausted small ones at the entrance of the transit center with only a small bag of belongings. They must have just crossed the border a half-hour ago. A family of five hired a motorcycle to help them escape the DRC almost stared death in the face. Six people including the driver and two bags were loaded on the motorcycle. All passengers fell off, and the driver scooted away. They came away with friction burns, except the baby tied upon his mother's back; as the last passenger, he escaped with barely a scratch. The mother had an inch-long gash above her right eyebrow, which required four stitches. A narrow escape indeed.

On Thursday mornings, the convoy of buses took the refugees to Rwamwanja resettle-ment camp, an eight-hour journey with a lunch stop at Mbarara. The first Thursday morn-ing we were there, there were eight buses, and one was only partially filled. A couple of UNHCR trucks with supplies of mats, tents, blankets, and containers for water parked at the transit center. Each refugee bound for resettlement wore a yellow wristband and was given a mat and a blanket. At the peak of the refugee registration, there were two convoys of twenty buses leaving the transit camp for Rwamwanja twice a week. This morning's convoy seemed small in comparison. Soldiers offering security led the convoy, a security police sat next to the bus driver, and bringing up the rear was the MTI ambulance. A little boy held up the departure of this morning convoy. Later he scampered hurriedly to his bus; whether he went off to say his last good-byes to his friends was anybody's guess.

A few weeks ago, one of the buses was negotiating one of the hairpin loops over the mountains when it overturned, killing two refugees, one of whom was a little boy who happened to stick his head out of the bus window. It was as though leaving one's homeland was not enough of a tragedy; these refugees had to endure more unforeseen ones lurking around every corner.

As the convoy with its four hundred and eighty souls rolled out slowly towards the east, engulfed slowly by the cold, morning mist, there seemed to be a lingering sadness about the whole scene. The refugees were leaving all that was familiar, their homes, friends, schools, and heading towards some unknown foreign land to set up a temporary life for themselves, all the while never knowing if they would ever be able to return home again.

The campsite was quiet again; a small number of new arrivals stood in line to be registered, and some had rolled-up mattresses next to them. Women refugees who remained behind swept the floor of their tents with makeshift brooms of cut branches. Tent floors were wet and muddy because of the daily afternoon downpours. The empty tents smelled of sweat reminiscent of the stench of barn animals in a farm. As the transit center only provided two meals a day, some lucky families cooked their own breakfast of cornmeal and beans, huddling in front of the tent entrances sharing a common bowl, while the less fortunate ones had to go hungry.

The clinic was busy again with the arrival of many new refugees. Children ran wildly in the camp, careful to avoid the many dangerous, makeshift stoves made from lava rocks scattered all over the campsite. Women cooked supplementary food for their families, and it was not long before some little ones got too close to such open stoves and pots. A little girl was burned four days ago when she ran over a pot of hot porridge. Her grandmother did her level best and applied "Colgate" on the burn. Her young mother had abandoned her to the care of her grandmother two years ago so she could begin a new life with another man.

Unfortunately, my next patient, who had been stung by a wasp and had big swollen eyes, heard cries emanating from my room made by a young boy who was petrified simply by the sight of the *mzungu*. Even though I did not inflict any physical pain on him, he never dared set his eyes on me. When it was his turn to see me, my wasp-stung boy became frightened and cried heartily.

A young mother was worried about her baby's frequent urination. As I examined him, he immediately sent a stream of urine all over the floor, narrowly missing my face. The lab did not detect any signs of urinary tract infection, and the mother was reassured. It was common for many of these children to run barefoot here despite the cold weather and puddles galore; as a result, cuts and sores were plentiful.

I saw my first case of malaria in the transit camp. Kisoro is over 6,000 feet above sea level, and it could be quite chilly at night and in the early morning. Despite that, the mosquitoes still thrived. Older boys and men did not usually show up in clinics unless they were quite ill. A robust, well-nourished sixteen-year-old boy, not stunted like most adolescents in this part of the world, took time from his job herding cattle all day to come here because of fever and feeling unwell. He reminded me not to forget to put down my bed net at night, even in the cold nights of Kisoro.

The local entrepreneurs of Kisoro came to the campsite to set up daily markets selling food and clothes to the refugees. Where there were people, there was bound to be commerce.

No one seemed to be able to tell us how many refugees were in the transit camp. In the morning there were a few stragglers coming to be registered. The intention of the Red Cross, UNHCR, and the Uganda Office of the Prime Minister (OPM) was to resettle the refugees as quickly as they could so that Nyakabande Transit Camp remained truly a transit camp, ready to absorb a sudden influx of refugees. The flags representing the Red Cross, Uganda, UNHCR, WFP, and MTI flew here. As the fog burned off early in the morning, refugees and Ugandans trooped in. The new arrivals found us and brought in their babies with diarrhea. I loathed giving them oral rehydration packets that they had to mix with contaminated water if they had no means to boil their own. Breast-feeding remained the most efficient way to hydrate the babies.

The mother who sustained a cut over her eyebrow returned and managed to bring with her a piece of jagged broken mirror, wanting to have a look at her face once the dressing was taken down. I was glad she had not seen the original gash. Looking at her reflection, she was happy with the result.

At the end of the day, we went back to the camp in search of a newborn. The kitchen fires were burning as evening meals were being prepared in three giant pots; huge logs burned, creating fumes everywhere. The penetrating, cold afternoon rain was falling steadily. Skirting muddy puddles, two tents away from the kitchen we found a one-day-old swaddled baby, left alone in a bundle in a corner on a folded mat. When he was uncovered, his eyes remained closed. His fists swiped his face aimlessly, and he started to root. Half of the floor in the tent was wet and muddy, and in a dry corner was a lone bundle of clothes with no blanket in sight. The mother returned and quietly picked him up. She did not strike me as a mother who just gave birth, rather she moved around with ease and with no signs of trauma. The baby looked peaceful, oblivious to the seemingly insurmountable problems of this world, least of all the wet floor and the cold night to come.

The full moon shone over the row of eucalyptus trees in front of the Bam Rest House. It provided some semblance of lighting for the camp, which had no electricity, but the threatening clouds were floating close by like the conflict in the homeland of the refugees, weighing over them with no hope of a light at the end of a long dark tunnel.

Early one morning, we drove to the border of Rwanda with the majestic mountains to our right. It took us barely twenty minutes. I recognized the border from my trip to Parcs des Volcans last year trekking the gorillas. It took us another three hours over winding roads to reach Kigali, the capital of Rwanda, hot and crowded. We took our lodging in the guesthouse in the Masson Place of the Episcopal Diocese. Abdullah, our driver, had not been to Kigali, and he was not of much help because he did not speak the local language.

Hotel Des Milles Collins, where the manager hid thousands of Rwandans from the slaughter of the 1994 genocide, was a rather modern hotel situated on a hill overlooking Kigali.[9] We sat by the hotel pool, which had supplied water for the people seeking refuge during the genocide, and had a passionfruit drink. The next day we headed to Bigesera District and stopped by the Nyamza Memorial Site, where over six hundred and thirty people were killed on April 11th, 1994, and their remains buried there. Then it was a long way before we reached the Hamada Memorial Site, a big church with cement pews piled with clothes, bones, coffins, and the belongings of those killed while hiding in it on April 20th, 1994. The victims who were identified had their names carved in stones. A burnt hut stood on one side of the church, witnessing the death of all the people sleeping inside. On the wall of a school house were bloodstains where the assailants had banged the heads of the victims. Further south was Nyamata Genocide Memorial—another church, pews filled with deep piles of bloodstained clothes, stairs leading to glass cases displaying numerous skulls and bones. At the back of the church were underground tunnels filled with coffins and shelves of thousands of bones and skulls. Speechless and sad, we could not fathom how humanity could descend so low as to kill its own, in such numbers, and with such horrific cruelty.

The Colplaki craft shops were competing with one another, selling almost the same things: beads, bags, scarves, carvings, clothes… Abdullah wanted to make it to the border before nightfall. It rained as we approached Kisoro. While Kigali was hot, in Kisoro we needed our sweaters and raincoats again.

Fearing for their lives and those of their children, many refugees fled with only the clothes on their back. An eighteen-year-old woman ran away from her village because thugs not belonging to any rebel group came with guns and *pangas* to kill and loot. She was one of the lucky ones because her husband came with her and her only baby; they did not have time to collect their belongings. They walked for four days to reach the border of Uganda, where UN trucks picked them up and brought them to the transit camp.

When my consultation door opened to let in the next patient, I was bombarded by a thirty-three-year-old woman with five children aged five months to twelve years; all of them were hanging onto one another, wide-eyed and anxious, and the baby clinging to his mother actually looking much better than expected. The exception was a droopy seven-year-old girl who could barely hold herself up. In the course of examining the baby, who had abdominal pain but no diarrhea, the seven-year-old slowly slumped onto the floor, looking listless. Somewhere along the way, the baby must have made a puddle of urine on the floor, and this little girl had curled herself next to it, fast asleep. Their story was a heart-breaking one. The father left them to fend for themselves when the last baby was three months old. Many Congolese men ran away to save themselves from being captured by the rebels and forced to be a soldier; many more were killed. Those who escaped went to Uganda or Rwanda for resettlement, and their wives only hoped to reunite with them once they crossed the borders. They had to be sure that they themselves resettled in the same camp. It took this woman one month to walk to the border with her five barefoot children, with nothing but the clothes on their backs, begging for food and seeking shelter in churches or in the bushes. She said, "Thank God we have finally reached Uganda." Her trouble was not over as she reached the camp late in the day; she received no food, mats or blankets, and the night was cold. Evening meals were over, and breakfast was not a planned meal at the camp. They were all thinly clad and had not eaten. It turned out the droopy girl, her eight-year-old sister, and the baby had malaria. It was hard for me to fathom trudging along with five little ones for a month without the security of food and shelter. This woman did it, like many women in the camp who had similar stories to tell. They survived and endured all the hardship because of their children. They were the true heroes of the refugee stories.

On my way out of the clinic, I saw three of the children sharing a meal of maize and beans from a plastic bag. The droopy girl seemed more energetic and awake as she ravenously scooped handful of beans into her mouth. As we drove by the transit center, two women, each with a bundle of clothes balanced on their heads, made their way slowly to the entrance; some semblance of safety and shelter awaited them at last.

Overnight many more refugees arrived. Some estimates put the number at around five hundred. They slept in communal tents, or when those were full, wherever they could find sheltered, dry, floor space. Many more men were in the group lining up to be registered. They had very few belongings: a bedroll here and there, plastic plates, cups, clothes, and suitcases. There were two very well-fed chickens, pecking away. They probably would become someone's dinner in the not so distant future. Some refugees arrived in trucks provided by the Uganda government and police but funded by UNHCR, as the UN evacuated them from the DRC at the Ugandan border when fighting was intense; many more arrived on foot or by *boda*.

In the month of August, there were three newborns who died of cold exposure at the camp. Congolese women were opposed to going to the hospital and giving birth lying on a bed; they preferred the squatting position at home. Women refugees were unwilling to leave their small children unattended while they were in the hospital. Apparently, multiparous women delivered their own babies, managing to cut the umbilical cord and delivering the placenta. Unfortunately, there were fatalities. The midwife in the camp met a twenty-year-old woman who had six children and a woman with her seventeenth pregnancy; all sixteen of her children were alive. Family planning was not generally accepted, and the men had the final say. It was common to have five to six children by the time the women reached their late twenties.

Refugees from the DRC lined up at the UNHCR administrative tent with their meager belongings to register for a refugee card.

Children, thinly clad, in the Nyakabande Transit Camp.

It took a long time for us to convince a full-term pregnant woman to go to the hospital for her delivery, as the position of the baby made home or tent delivery dangerous. Her husband had left the DRC about two months ago, and she thought he was at the Rwamwanja Camp. This woman wore a "Kids Running America—Going the Distance" T-shirt. She and her children had certainly done that. A few days later I spotted her in her tent, proudly holding her newborn dressed in army fatigue; she was still wearing her "Going the Distance" T-shirt.

Another convoy of seven buses carrying about five hundred refugees left the transit camp heading to Rwangmangi Camp. The boarding seemed to go quite smoothly, and mats and blankets were distributed. A chicken also boarded with its owner, making some complaining clucking noises. It was one well-traveled chicken. I surreptitiously gave the omelet that I saved from my breakfast to a woman holding a baby with another hanging onto her wrapper. Abdullah, our driver, drove the ambulance bringing up the rear of the convoy. In the ambulance was seated a Congolese woman whose husband had been killed by the rebels; she was gang-raped by twenty of them. When she arrived at the camp, she was still bleeding. The psychological trauma inflicted on her was unfathomable. Red Cross had been training some of the Ugandan nurses on gender-based violence and the issue of rape, as many women preferred to remain silent, especially the young ones.

Women always seemed to carry their babies on their backs whenever they worked, tilling the fields, selling or buying in the market, collecting or chopping firewood in the camp. The babies seemed to sleep through it all. One afternoon I dropped in Kisoro District Hospital; the maternity ward was full, and some women were lying on bare mattresses placed on the floor, with four other women in labor. There was a conspicuous absence of bed nets in the ward. A midwife started her mid-day shift with her six-month-old strapped to her back, and she had just delivered a baby in the maternity ward. She would work her shift that way, stopping only to breast-feed her baby. There was no one to care for the baby at home while she was at work. It was usual to see a woman carry a baby on her back, balance a load on her head, and carry two heavy bags in each hand while walking with a man who remained empty-handed.

In the children's ward many beds with old, filthy, beat-up foam mattresses were lined up helter-skelter; only a few of them had patients, and there were no healthcare personnel in sight. The rest of the space was a dumping ground for defunct and unused old equipment, not a place of healing. A mother nursed her baby on a bare mattress placed on the floor, and another woman covered herself and her baby with a wrapper and slept. Outside many women gathered on the lawn, some sitting, socializing, or sharing a meal under the shade of a tree. Hospital scrubs were drying on the grass. Dark clouds gathered and threatened imminent rain; I quickly hurried home before the deluge descended.

We drove to the border town of Bunagana, Uganda, about ten kilometers away to pay a short visit to the rebel-controlled region of the DRC. Ugandans and Congolese seemed to walk across the border freely. The tarmac road ended abruptly at the border of Uganda. A metal barrier with Uganda and DRC written on it spanned the road, followed by a rocky brown earth road on the DRC side. As one stepped onto no man's land lined with old tall eucalyptus trees, there were signs in French, English, Swahili, and Bufumira: *"Bienvenue, Welcomes You, Karibuni, Murakaza-Neza"* greeting us. At the border, we checked into the spartan immigration office now controlled by the rebels, lit by spiral energy-efficient light bulbs hung from the ceiling with wires sticking out. A tall border guard who spoke both French and Swahili took our passports and leafed through them slowly, paying particular attention to mine. He went through it twice, intrigued by the stamps and the countries I had been to. Abdullah had warned us beforehand not to mention the DRC government or the rebels. There was no official stamp, just an entrance fee of 50,000 shillings ($20 USD), which Abdullah negotiated on our behalf in Swahili. We paid and they held our passports in the office; I felt a little uneasy about it. A plain-clothes rebel guided us through the village where a few uniformed men toting AK-47s milled around. The village itself was not different from many other African villages, with littering on the roads and around the houses. A few houses started on a grand scale stood half-completed. In one short block, there were at least five to six pharmacies, but the nearest health center was in the next village. Bunagana in the DRC was nestled in a valley, and every inch of the slopes had been terraced for planting, with women tilling and planting beans, potatoes, and corn. Children began to follow us, yelling out *mzungu*. Children and women congregated around a communal tap to fill their jerry cans with water. Next to it was a small market selling charcoal, potatoes, onions, *matoki*, oil, and sugar cane. The Congolese used a sort of a wooden bike for transportation. Bullet holes in the roofs and walls glared in concrete buildings, and some had been hastily patched up. A few Congolese gathered in a big tin-roofed church practicing on their guitars. The sky peeked through a number of bullet holes in the roof. We spent roughly an hour in the DRC, tipped our rebel guide, and then crossed back the border to Uganda. The sign from the DRC side wished us *"Bon Voyage, Wish you Safe Journey, Safari Njema, Urugendo Ruhire"* in French, English, Swahili, and Bufumira.

One Sunday morning we walked along the main road of Kisoro looking for a church. Within the span of two to three blocks, there were around four churches: Baptist, Seventh Day Adventist, Catholic, and Anglican. We chose to attend All Saints of Bashamba. While waiting, they played "Jingle Bells" several times from their repertoire of recorded music, quite hilarious in September, followed by "Yankee Doodle." The priest arrived and apologized that this would be a small service. There were nine of us; the church could easily accommodate two hundred congregants. We sang "What a Friend We Have in Jesus," "I Surrender All," and "Amazing Grace." The boy playing the synthesizer was quite tone deaf, and together with the loud crackling and creaking over the loudspeaker, the singing sounded rather funereal. Slowly he improved and was able to modulate the volume.

Looking at the empty pews, I let my mind wander. I thought about the piles of blood-stained clothing on the pews of the church at Nyamata Genocide Memorial, where some of the atrocities of the Rwanda genocide took place, and the thousands of bones and skulls found there, the voices forever silenced and innocent lives ended prematurely. The Rwanda genocide hauntingly brought me back to the Killing Fields in Cambodia, and the Terezin Concentration Camp in the Czech Republic. The same eerie feeling surrounded these places, the unspeakable horrors that humankind inflicted on its own, and the senselessness of it all.

When the service ended, there were more people waiting outside for another service, which would be in Bufumira, the local language.

Monday was market day in Kisoro, and that afternoon Abdullah had to bring back a patient from another transit center. Without our vehicle, we were left stranded. We wandered the town milling with the locals; women with baskets selling tobacco and coffee shells, and men selling ropes, clothes, shoes, wooden handles for hoes or other digging implements, and many more. There were shops selling beans, corn, and sorghum; the locals brought corn and sorghum to the mills to grind.

The three mountains overlooking Kisoro were extinct volcanoes, seen as a backdrop for the transit camp. The Muhabura, the tallest, often shrouded in clouds especially during the rainy and thundering season, could look menacing with its dark cloud covers.

I was tempted to hike the highest one but was unable to contact the park office. Instead, I hiked up a small hill in the local area. It was an easy hike and afforded a panoramic view of Kisoro and the mountains. There was hardly any trail in sight, with some of the slopes cultivated and planted with crops. High above a lone woman tilled the land; boys and young men herded cattle on the distant, idyllic slopes. Far away, there were hues of mountains upon mountains; the Rwenzori Mountains or the Mountain of the Moon must be way out there in the northerly direction. At the top, Lake Mutanda suddenly loomed into view, peaceful and tranquil. Every inch of the earth on the islands in the lake was cultivated. I had the peak all to myself, with the lake on one side and the mountains on the other, indulging in my reverie. A plume of smoke trailed from one of the peninsulas in the lake; amplified children's cries and cockcrow rose from the valley. The sun was shining, and a gentle breeze was blowing from the lake. It was not until I descended close to Kisoro that I encountered a few children gathering kindling; a chorus of "*Mzungu*, how are you?" greeted me. I answered, "*Masutay*?"

Over the weekend the OPM estimated about two hundred refugees came to the camp, bringing the total to slightly less than four hundred. The refugees tended to come on Tuesday and Wednesday so they could proceed to the resettlement camp on Thursday, making their stay in the transit camp as short as possible. They lined up at midday to get their supplies of soap, cups, plates, blankets, and mats. One morning, the officials in the camp rounded up the refugees around the flags for a meeting. The gist was they should register at the transit camp in order to get food and prepare for resettlement. They would receive a piece of land to grow food to get some semblance of normalcy back into their lives.

In the clinic, we saw mainly Ugandan nationals with a small number of refugees, many of whom brought in their children because of diarrhea. The clinical officer and I had been seeing patients together. I walked out of the office momentarily, and she saw a patient on her own. When she was done with her and sent her to fetch her medicines at the dispensary, the old woman said, "I want to see the white doctor." She refused to budge until I returned, gave her some attention, and wrote an additional prescription for her. Satisfied, she walked out. I hoped Daser did not feel slighted by her behavior.

A sixty-year-old Congolese woman came in the maternity room at the clinic. Two rebels beat and raped her at the end of August. When they returned the second night, she knew it was no longer safe to stay in the village, and she ran to Uganda with her youngest child. Subdued and quiet when examined, a faint smile appeared fleetingly on her distraught face when she saw me imitating the wobbly walk of a nine-month-old baby who burst out into a peel of happy laughter. A young mother and her three young boys were waiting for the dispensing of their medicines; one of her children wore a shirt and a sweater and nothing below the waist, but he was running around happily, often landing on his bare bottom. It had been raining all day, chilly and damp, and the boys were not properly clad. She walked back to the camp carrying her two young ones in her arms with the oldest trailing behind her in the rain.

A Red Cross man told me of rapes occurring in the camp when it was inundated with thousands of refugees. Many more were cramped into communal camps, and in an unlit campground where the latrines were situated at the fringes, rapes occurred. Different families crammed into the same smaller tents. Occasionally, there were some rebels with weapons in the midst. I caught sight of the sixty-year-old woman who was raped, walking with a cane, visibly limping; her son who looked quite aged was by her side.

A young man came in asking for pain medication. The rebels beat him up to force him to join them. He gave them a lot of money and his car before they let him go. He escaped with his wife and two children. We treated another man who ran away with his friends, leaving his wife and six children behind. When asked why he left them behind, he said his wife wanted to check on her corn crop, and he could not wait for her. He hoped to reunite with his family in Uganda. A fifty-year-old man told us all four of his wives had run away to Uganda with twenty-two of his children, and he was here now to try to locate at least one of them.

A woman came to Uganda with her six children; her husband fled to Uganda and was already in Rwangmangi Camp. She brought three of her children wearing khakis with OBAMA embroidered on their oversized shirts to the clinic, all fearful and frightened. She was lucky; she had had contact with her husband since both of them owned cell phones.

The sun shone brightly this morning. It was a great laundry day for the refugees, who washed and dried their clothes on the grass. A few malnourished children ran around eating plumpy nut, distributed by the nutritional program of MTI; they needed extra calories and protein for their growth and development. Other children learned about this and came asking for "biscuits." I had none to offer them.

The call to prayer woke me up around five in the morning, "*Allah Akbar.*" It was too dark to have an early morning run, and the paths were treacherous with sharp, jagged, volcanic rocks. I had been running after work occasionally, with a string of children running beside me or trailing after me, and chorus of "*Mzungu*, how are you?" I answered back,

"*Amakooru?*" In the beginning of my stay here in Kisoro, the first two hundred meters of my run were the hardest; I felt tightness in my chest and a feeling of weightlessness in my biceps. These feelings all went away with time.

One morning I took an early walk and went by the slope where a small group of Batwas (pygmies) lived. According to Abdullah, years ago the government had built houses for them after they were displaced from the Mhinga National Park, but they were not used to living in houses. They built their own dwellings of sticks, plastic bags, sheets, and gunny sacks, all haphazardly put together. An old woman wrapped in a dirty shawl emerged from a dwelling that looked like a teepee. She mumbled to herself and walked away with a few containers in her hands, stopping periodically to wipe her muddy feet on the grass. From the opening of a tent glinted three pairs of eyes belonging to three children huddled around a briskly burning fire, for the morning was chilly. A sibilant sound emitted from within as an arm shot out toward me with its palm up. The children did not seem to be concerned about the potential of the fire burning down their hut. Not too far away sat an outhouse built by the Dutch in 2010.

At the transit camp, the refugees boarded the seven buses of the convoy very efficiently. This time there were five hundred and nineteen of them. It was a sunny day and the morning mist shrouding the camp and the mountains quickly dissipated. The OPM announced that from now on, no refugees would be allowed to stay longer than two weeks in the transit camp; if they did, their food allowance would be cut off. This was going to create a problem for a forty-year-old woman in her eighth month of pregnancy who came to the transit camp on May 13 with her three-year-old daughter. While she was working in the field with her daughter, the rebels came to the village, and her husband ran away with their five children and headed for Rwanda. When she came back home, no one was left. She fled to Uganda only to find out later that her husband and five children were in a Rwandan refugee camp. She told us that her husband had since contacted her. He was furious that she went to Uganda and accused her of wanting to find another man. Her baby, born in the camp and now three months old, was a result of a rape. Since May, she had sought help from various officials in the camp hoping to reunite with her family but had not been able to get help. She had also gone to the Rwandan border, but the border guards did not allow her to cross from Uganda into Rwanda. The clinical officer suggested to her that she might want to go back to the Congo and then cross over to Rwanda from there; however, the route to Rwanda from the Congo was full of rebels and was fraught with danger. She cried sadly while telling us her story. When asked what she would do when the OPM enforced the rule of a maximum of a two-week stay in the camp, she simply stated that she would beg for food; she did not want resettlement but rather relocation to the refugee camp where her family was.

Outside the registration area, more refugees arrived with suitcases and mattresses, but they arrived too late to leave with the convoy. I took my last walk around the campsite and greeted the refugees in Bufumira, "*ahmakuroo*" and "*nemasutay*," variations of "How are you?" which seemed to delight them. One woman gestured to me that she was hungry, and I heard an infant cry from the tent. She immediately got up, and I walked into her tent to find a baby wrapped up in a blanket, probably only days old. I then recognized her as the woman we had to convince to go to the hospital for her delivery. Although she was not wearing her headcover, I remembered her by her "Going the Distance" T-shirt.

One of my last patients was a woman with a nasty splinter buried deep in her ankle. I could feel it, but it was not visible. After some poking, an inch-long, bamboo-like splinter was pulled out. Her last name was "*Dushimimana*" which means "Thank God."

In the newspaper that morning, there was a piece about a plan in the Great Lakes Region Summit to send a neutral force to the DRC in ninety days; the President of Uganda, Yoweri Museveni, and that of the DRC, Joseph Kabila, were pictured in this article.[10] It was not entirely clear what this neutral force was going to do, providing security for the people or for some other political goals yet to be defined.

A fierce wind blew that evening. It was cold and cut one like a knife. Some refugees who arrived at the transit camp actually did not receive blankets as there was a shortage; some received one when they boarded the bus for resettlement. Those who arrived with only the clothes on their back would be cold; no wonder some newborns died from exposure. This was our last day at the camp, and tomorrow we would leave Kisoro for Kampala. However, the plight of these refugees would remain. We should all count our blessings and "*dushimimana*" for what we have.

Until now, there have been recurrent conflicts in the DRC and the Nyakabande Transit Camp in Kisoro remains open. Uganda is home to 251,730 refugees from the DRC in several resettlement camps of which 48,105 arrived in Uganda since January 1, 2018, with a daily average influx of 681 refugees, comprised mainly of women and children.[11] Similar to 2012, the refugees stayed two to three nights before their transfer to Kyaka II Refugee Settlement in Kyegegwa District, a seven-hour drive. Since the beginning of January 2018, 14,399 refugees have been relocated to Kyaka II, with 60 percent being children.

At the transit camp, UNICEF provides screening for malnutrition and appropriate care, measles vaccination for children, Vitamin A, and deworming. Collaborating with Save the Children, they also provide psychosocial support through the establishment of integrated child-friendly spaces.

RapidFTR (Rapid Family Tracing and Reunification),[12] an open source mobile application, collects data on missing children's identities, photographs, and information about their separation. The data are then shared securely on a central database for family members looking for their missing ones. RapidFTR was first piloted in the Nyakabande Transit Camp and had been a useful tool to help humanitarian workers to more efficiently unite children with their caregivers in disasters. Since then it has been used in 2013 in helping IDPs in South Sudan after the civil wars to reunite families with missing loved ones, in the Philippines after Typhoon Yolanda, and in the current crisis in South Sudan.

Unity State, South Sudan

2013, Providing Medical Care after the Civil War

"Tribalism in South Sudan is an infectious deadly disease that charred and burns the nation to ashes."
—Lul Gatkuoth Gatluak[1]

"The Republic of South Sudan does not belong to a particular tribe—it belongs to all tribes of South Sudan; those who think so should think coherently. The truth is, tribalism kills and destroys."
—Duop Chak Wuol[2]

South Sudan had been on the radar of MTI for quite some time now, and I had expressed a keen interest in going there to provide medical relief. Sometime in January of 2013, our hope of going to South Sudan was raised, only to be dashed soon after, apparently because of security reasons. World Relief (WR) was the partner that has an established presence in South Sudan, and MTI needed a partner that had logistical connections there.

In South Sudan, especially in Unity State, WR provided teacher training and supported the need for primary education especially for girls. Without the support, they might very well be kept out of school to tend cattle or help with chores. It provided nutrition and supplementary feeding programs for the most vulnerable children as South Sudan had one of the highest malnutrition rates in Africa. To address the issue of food insecurity, it also had several agricultural training programs for some lead farmers.

MTI collaborated with WR to provide the delivery of health services. There was a great need because the twenty-odd years of civil war had left South Sudan with few functioning healthcare facilities. The overall immunization rate was poor, and healthcare facilities were ill equipped and lacking in medicines and medical supplies.[3] MTI and WR would concentrate their effort in Unity State, providing mobile medical clinics as most of the communities were agro-pastoral.

In 2005 a peace deal was struck with Khartoum to end the two decades of conflict that resulted in an estimated two million people killed and many more displaced.[4] South Sudan became the newest nation in Africa in July 9, 2011.[5] However, tension still prevailed between Sudan and South Sudan over the shares of oil revenue and disputed land along the shared border.[6] Sudan had the oil refineries and the pipelines to the port in the Red Sea, while landlocked South Sudan had three quarters of the oil reserves. The Khartoum government had spent precious little revenue to develop the southern parts of the old country. As a result, South Sudan had poor infrastructure, and not that long ago it had only sixty kilometers of paved road in the entire country. Electricity and running water were scarce, and most people depended on subsistence farming that was almost all done by hand with the use of hoes. Due to the continued dispute with its neighbors over oil revenues that constituted over eighty-five percent of its economy, together with the unpredictable rebel and tribal violence, South Sudan faced a tremendous challenge in rebuilding a nation from scratch.

As my trip to South Sudan was on and off again, I decided to bandit run the 117th Boston Marathon to raise funds for MSF. Finally, MTI received clearance from WR for us to leave on April 15, a date that coincided with the Boston Marathon. I asked to delay my departure for two days so I could still fulfill my pledge of running. On that fateful day, the bombings at the finish line of the Boston Marathon[7] shook us to the core, and I left Boston two days later still jangled by the tragic event. The whole experience had been quite surreal. I started the marathon running with two of my children, Cara and Charles, full of hopes, anxiety, and excitement, only to be stopped two miles and half a mile from the finish line for me and for my children respectively because of the bombings. What followed was a tragedy that was overwhelmed and overshadowed by countless heroic acts of courage, kindness, self-lessness, and love that bespeak the ever-present humanity that continues to assure us that in the end we will overcome evil with good. I left Boston emotionally in turmoil because of the unresolved issues of the bombings as well as concern for my family, whom I treasure a great deal. Tragedy has its way of making one feel how precious your loved ones are.

Bonnie, a midwife volunteer from Oregon, and I spent a night in Entebbe, Uganda, and boarded a plane the next day to Juba, South Sudan. We flew over vast stretches of stagnated marshlands, then sparsely forested areas due to deforestation. Before landing, the glinting of the galvanized zinc roofs of houses blinded me with their flashes of light. At the Juba International Airport, CNN brought the live broadcast of news that one of the suspects of the bombings had died, and the other was at large in Watertown, the epicenter, next to where I live. My thoughts went to all the thousands of people, including my family, who were hunkered down in their homes. The arrest of one of the perpetrators was good news, but it was also tainted with the sad news of another life lost during the manhunt; a police officer from the Massachusetts Institute of Technology (MIT) was shot dead, in addition to the people who lost their lives, limbs, and were injured at the finish line.[8]

Juba was a chaotic sprawling "big village city." The big tarmac road ran to Juba Town and branching from it were dry red-earth dirt roads. There were no road names here. Juba consisted of single-story buildings, and it was only recently that multi-story constructions sprang up all over town. The multi-story buildings did not inspire confidence; the columns looked tenuous, flimsy, and askew. Like many African towns, Juba had stores lining the streets with haphazard sidewalks, appearing and disappearing at random, and *matatus* attempting to run pedestrians down on non-existent sidewalks. Dirt roads with muddy puddles from the rain the night before were strewn with tons of empty plastic bottles, cans, and garbage. High fences topped with barbed wire stood guard around the buildings of government agencies, NGOs, hotels, and nice private dwellings. Plastic bottles, largely ignored by the children wading in the river here but hungrily collected in Uganda for sale, choked the small tributaries of the White Nile. Shanties and slums lined part of the tributaries, the source of water for the city dwellers. The White Nile flowed through Juba northwards to join the Blue Nile in Khartoum.

Since the UN Humanitarian Air Services did not operate on the weekend, we would fly out after the weekend to Bentiu in Unity State in the northern part of South Sudan. Our work would concentrate in Boaw Payam in Koch County, a one to three-hour drive south of Bentiu, depending on the road conditions. During the pre-independence era, NGOs supported nearly half of South Sudan's 800 health facilities.[9] Koch County had a population of 83,061 (2012) with eight health facilities, four being supported by NGOs and the rest by the Ministry of Health (MOH) of South Sudan.[10]

Amidst our wandering in Juba, we saw a young man lying on the dirt road right outside a market, next to a row of squatting women and children selling mangoes. He was breathing but barely, with dry blood caked on one of his palms and blood stains on his trousers. Flies were swarming on his lips and eyes, and beads of sweat were collecting on his forehead. Passers-by skirted around him, seemingly unaware or chosing to ignore that there was someone lying there. Eventually we were able to get some attention from a couple of young men who asked the vendors about him. A police on a motorbike happened to come along, incongruously wearing a pair of flip-flops. The young men stopped him, but the police told them to report to the police station a few blocks away. We walked with the two young men to the police station, only to find out that the police officer on the motorbike had already reported the incident. We returned to the young man. By then he had woken up and was taking big gulps of water. His family lived close by, and the police would notify them. The local vendors were used to him being drunk and passed out on the road, so it was not anything alarming to them. Bystanders pulled him to the side of the road, and he slumped down in a drunken stupor. We walked on and met four young girls eating chocolate on a veranda. One of them offered Bonnie a one-pound note, unlike children from other countries who often reached out their hands asking for a handout from foreigners.

We had dinner in a restaurant with Tashian, the country director of WR, and I overheard conversations in Malay. At the table next to us sat a group of my fellow Malaysians. Indeed, like China, Petronas, the oil company of Malaysia, had long benefited from the oil wells here in South Sudan. On our way home from dinner, the moon seemed to follow us. I thought about my family who would see the same moon, connecting me to them. I was missing them.

Torrential rain, strong winds, and African time combined to delay our flight to Rubkona. It was utter chaos at the Juba International Airport with luggage check, boarding passes, and security check all congregating in one tight area. We boarded a WFP/UN Humanitarian Airways plane to Malakal where we disembarked for refueling. Hot sultry air greeted us. The terrain was dry and parched.

By the time we reached Rubkona, we were at least an hour and a half late. There was no airport, just a dirt runway. While all the other passengers sped away into the dusty landscape in their respective land cruisers, we remained standing alone like orphans, looking lost next to the chain-link fence of the runway. A kind Sudanese man asked us whether we were looking for WR and pointed to Juma, our driver, who was too preoccupied with his phone call to acknowledge us.

Bentiu was just a ten-minute ride from the airport; *tukuls*, conical houses made of sticks, straw, and mud, occasionally fenced in by reeds, lined the roads. Here and there were abandoned, bombed-out, rusty buses, vans, trucks, and cars devoid of tires, probably legacies of the civil war. Occasional indigenous green acacia trees, interspersed with shriveled brown grass, graced the cracked earth and dry, dusty, red dirt of the parched landscape. Gallant attempts to grow trees along the main dirt road could be seen; all were protected with reed fences from scavenging animals such as cattle and goats, which seemed to be able to forage for food in the meager pickings afforded by nature in this dry land. Tired, long-suffering donkeys pulled heavy water tanks on carts, longing for rest or food at the end of the workday. April was the end of a five-month long dry season; the rainy season would

The dusty road in the town of Bentiu, Unity State, South Sudan.

start in May, and the flooded roads would soon become impassable because of the clay-like soil, transforming the whole landscape into a green "paradise."

We met with James Kuok, the project director, who briefed us on the health center in Boaw, and Mirmir, where we would be the following week for mobile clinic. Johnson, the medical coordinator, would travel with us. It was imperative to meet with the director of the MOH, and Michael Kuong, the country health director of Koch, came with us. The office of the director was in a modest building baked under the hot sun. He sat behind a desk surrounded by dust-covered computers. It was hard to avoid the dust in this dry and sultry weather.

We then paid a quick visit to Bentiu District Hospital. The new tarmac road stopped abruptly after we passed the hospital. The pediatric ward was filled with patients spilling out to the porch at the entrance. There were beds with two to three babies, most of them suffering from complications of malaria, with their anxious mothers hovering nearby. A neonate suffering from sepsis languished in a corner lying beside her mother, with an intravenous line hanging. She would be in a neonatal intensive care unit in the U.S., but there was no such unit in Bentiu. There were a few cases of kala-azar, or visceral leishmaniasis, a parasitic disease transmitted by the sand fly. This was a referral hospital that had the medications to treat this potentially fatal disease if left untreated. Many patients showed signs of malnutrition: light hair, skeletal limbs, and big potbellies. Enormous swarms of flies settled everywhere—floors, beds, walls, patients—and competed with the debilitating crowding and wilting heat. The medical officer, nurse, and clerk looked overwhelmed with the patient load, and their office was filled with the overflow beds for the patients. There were no screens on the windows, fans, or mosquito nets. The patients' families provided sheets and nets. By custom, we also met with the medical director of the hospital to get his goodwill when we had to refer patients. Outside the fence were three abandoned buildings that were to be the new nursing school, but lack of funding stopped it from functioning. Already the buildings showed signs of rampant vandalism.

South Sudan had a population of 10 million in 2018 with slightly over half living under the poverty level. Child mortality was estimated to be 90.4 deaths/1,000 live births in 2018, and maternity mortality was 789 deaths/100,000 live births (estimate for 2015).[11] In April 2013, after over two decades of war, refugees were returning to South Sudan. The Office of Coordination of Human Affairs (OCHA) reported that for one week in April 2013, over 6,000 refugees headed towards their final destination, over 9,000 arrived at their final destination, and another 21,000 were stranded in transit, unable to reach their homes.[12] Jonglei State remained volatile with its cattle raiding in February 2013 leaving thousands of people affected, 85 reported dead, and 33 missing.

In the evening, I took a walk into the village behind the WR Office. A warm breeze picked up; villagers greeted me and waved. The lazy hazy sun was slowly setting. Here in Unity, the two major tribes were the Nuer and the Dinka. Two tall Nuer boys wanted to have their picture taken, and they told me that the Dinkas were taller, "Like mosquitoes," they said. I believed them for I had seen them in Juba; their legs seemed to grow from their chests.

The nights in Bentiu were steamy. The ceiling fans had not been working for a while, and probably no one would fix them any time soon. We wished we could sleep outside for there was a very nice breeze, some twinkling stars, and a patch of the Milky Way if one were to wait patiently to allow the eyes to adjust to the lights. In the morning, I ran down the main dirt road to the next village where a few people were setting up an early market. A couple of enterprising boys set up their shoe polishing business by the dusty roadside, a few cans of Kiwi shoe polish lined up on a towel placed directly on the dirt road. It was baffling to have one's shoes shined, only to get dusty again in a few seconds unless one were to travel in a private vehicle. There were infrequent *matatus* and land cruisers belonging to various NGOs; people here probably were too poor to afford private vehicles. Each passing vehicle churned up clouds of dust for several meters behind it. Johnson, our local medical coordinator, said the inhabitants here often walked hundreds of kilometers a day carrying whatever on their heads to and from the markets. Their means of transportation was their own two feet, or as they said here "footing."

Breakfast, at least for me, was just some sips of water with a few cookies and half a precious orange I bought in Juba. The kitchen staff came just when we were leaving for Koch County.

Our journey consisted of almost three hours of bone rattling, concussive brain jolting on bumpy dirt roads through parched countryside with scattered compounds of *tukuls*. We passed cattle and goats grazing on brown dry grass or gathering around muddy water holes, many of which were completely dry. The road went through landscape with more profuse growth of short acacia trees and brought us finally to Koch County. The Relief Rehabilitation Commissioner was sick and had left for Leer that morning, two hours from Koch, so we could not see him. Colonel John Chuol Wang, the Koch Resident Commissioner, met with us in his stifling, airless cramped office. The seats of the chairs and sofas were worn through the imitation vinyl leather down to the bare fabric. A vase with unattractive shocking pink artificial flowers, probably made in China, sat on one of the three long coffee tables. The droning voices of the colonel, his secretary, and Johnson put me in a soporific mood; I caught myself falling asleep several times, jet lag lurking with its alluring, tantalizing drowsy head at me. Just when I thought we were finally through, the colonel had us wait for water. Here it was customary to serve guests some drinks, and it was rude to refuse. Someone had gone off somewhere to get us bottled water and sodas; he must have made a behemoth effort to get them, and they were deliciously cold. I ventured to ask the colonel about his last name, "Wang," and noted many Chinese sounding names in this area: Kuong, Kuok, Puok, Tang, Deng, Wei… I did not really get a satisfactory answer to my question. Instead, he told us that he once met a Chinese man whose last name was "Wang," and the colonel told him that the Chinese man could be his father. Outside his office were a few men and a woman squatting on the floor, waiting to see him before we arrived, but we had jumped the queue; it made me feel bad.

Koch County Hospital, which was our next stop, was barely functioning with some outpatient activities and a female ward with four beds all crowded in a single room. A nurse was caring for the patients. Boxes of supplies from the government were stacked up to the ceilings in the hallway and reception areas. A bed with a black mattress stood next to the boxes. I almost missed a patient lying on it; she had a black dress that made her blend into the sheetless black mattress. Healthcare personnel from functioning primary care units in Koch County got their supplies from here, but there was no system of inventory, and the pharmacy had meager offerings. As we stepped out of the hospital, all over the walls and doors were old, sun-bleached signs and posters encouraging the populace to vote for a new Sudan in 2011. No one had bothered to take them down.

The hospital had been fully functioning about fourteen months ago and stopped abruptly at the same time the oil stopped flowing. Almost all the economy of South Sudan was dependent on the oil revenue. South Sudan had the oil, and Sudan had the refineries and the pipelines to the Red Sea port. Khartoum of Sudan wanted fifty percent of the oil revenue, but South Sudan was only willing to give a smaller percentage. Thus, when negotiation came to a halt, the oil stopped flowing. Paychecks for the personnel stopped coming too; the whole hospital plunged into disarray and finally ceased to open altogether. The month of April of 2013 when we arrived, the oil started flowing again; the hospital had a few hired personnel offering limited services. It would take a lot of cleaning up and organization before it could fully function, but more importantly, South Sudan had to train more healthcare personnel. At this time, NGOs provided eighty-five percent of the healthcare in South Sudan.[13]

We plodded along to Boaw through lunchtime. There was no place here where one could stop to eat. This was indeed the bush. The soda from the colonel tasted especially good now. A couple of young women with sacks of food on their heads, but no water in hand, walked through the dust our vehicle churned up; miles and miles ahead and behind them, not a living soul. Johnson was trying to handle a pre-eclamptic pregnant woman in Boaw on the phone, triaging her to Leer three hours away by a land cruiser. There was no magnesium sulfate where she was to treat her eclampsia, but there was diazepam.

On the way, Johnson recounted his kidnapping about a year ago in the Upper Nile State while he was working with Tearfund. The militia kidnapped the Liberian country director, the driver, and him, robbed them of the salary money that they had brought along to pay the field workers, took their vehicle, and forced them to walk for two weeks towards Khartoum with little offer of food or water. Once they threatened to kill the Liberian, but the driver, a Sudanese, told them they had to kill him first. The rebels warned him that the next time they saw him they would kill him. Eventually the Red Cross was able to negotiate their release, and they were brought to Khartoum and then to Nairobi. Undeterred by his kidnapping experience, Johnson was back to working with another NGO.

The Sudanese deliberately burned vast stretches of land to encourage new growth of grass for the grazing animals. After about six hours of driving, we arrived at the fenced compound filled with a number of shady Neem trees and graced with a gentle breeze. Many curious children were clinging on to the high chain-linked fence to gawk at us. Our sleeping quarters were in a galvanized tin house, likely a hot oven at night. In the corner of the compound were two latrines, and next to them was a bathroom for bucket bath. The kitchen was a tin shed with a three-stoned stove sitting right outside; the stoned floor inside had bloodstains of previously slain creatures. There was a spacious screened common area for working and relaxing. No lunch waited for us when we arrived shortly after three in the afternoon. Several free-ranging chickens were foraging in the yard; the cook let a few neighboring children into the compound to catch one of them. It was difficult to listen to the squawking, protesting cries of the chicken; one minute it was happy and free, and the next it lost its life, never to enjoy its freedom again. I would have been just as content with rice and beans.

Andrew Walhok, a community health nurse (CHN), told me cows and girls were highly valued in Nuer and Dinka countries. Herders used spears, but often AK-47s left over from the war, to guard a few precious cows they owned. While others used pounds, Euros, USDs, yens, yuans, etc., they traded in "cows." For the Dinka, a girl brought in a highly priced dowry of a hundred cows or so, and the girl's legs must not be seen from any direction while she was being surrounded by the "cash cows," otherwise the dowry would be considered inadequate. The groom-to-be had to bring in more cows to cover the long legs. For the Nuer, thirty to forty cows would be enough. A girl who could read brought in more cows then one who could not. Because of the enormity of the burdensome dowry, cattle raids occurred frequently, especially in Jonglei. Only older men could afford to marry repeatedly and most often took girls as young as thirteen for a wife. Young men without the requisite number of cows would just have to pine away or marry other tribes with much lower demand of the "cash cows," such as the tribes in the Equatorial states; they only required two cows, four goats, twenty-five chickens, and two bags of termites. HOLY COWS!

Last night a couple of bats hovered in our room, driving us batty. I was not sure why, but it drove one of them crazy when I tried to read with the headlamp. It hovered and then stuck itself on top of my mosquito net, peering in. Could it really see, since bats were supposed to be blind? I was not too thrilled about the rabies carrier so close to me. As I tried to open the door to let it out, it flapped around me, threatening to fly right into my face. I left the door open all night. The bats flew around and flapped noisily in the rafters just outside the room. Our sleeping area was quite pleasant with the door open letting in a cool breeze. In the bathroom for our bucket bath, there were three different kinds of toads greeting me as I walked in. They were lurking there probably for a feast of insects.

In the morning, I ran on the road away from Koch. After running past a few compounds, the road petered out. A cow path meandered through this endless flat land. On one side was a big man-made water hole, completely dried up. The area where I ran seemed to be a wetland in the rainy season. Soon I saw a number of curious looking mud craters of various sizes surrounding a borehole. Looking into the hole, I could see water about twenty to thirty feet below. Far away, a group of girls and women were drawing water from another borehole. Indeed, there was about a dozen of them here; some were dry, and all were surrounded by these craters. I was not sure if the craters were made to contain water for the cattle or for other purposes. Later James, the nutritionist, told me the craters contained the mud so it did not block the borehole. Last month two young boys went down one of the boreholes to retrieve a lost item, only to be trapped and suffocated in the hole. Rescue came too late for them. Wandering around this area in the dark, one could really fall into one of the boreholes. The water that was drawn by the women was tinted a light brown.

I ran back to the village, passing a water pump surrounded by a group of village girls drawing water into their jerry cans. The children probably had no schools to go to; some were herding cattle, and the girls were doing chores. A boy had a collection of cow dung stacked up on his palm as he waved at me. In 2013, literacy was around 27 percent among adults, and only 1.6 percent of the children were enrolled in secondary education. Over here in the bush, I had yet to see a school.[14]

After a breakfast of tea and chapatti with locally made peanut butter, we walked to the hut across the road from our compound to meet the director of the Boaw Payam (township), an unsmiling man looking rather stern. Johnson reminded him that Daniel from MTI came and met with him a few weeks ago to do an assessment of the healthcare need of this area. We were the first team to arrive, and others would follow for a period of six months. Again, the meeting with the various heads was all very necessary for a community to accept and support a project. We hoped that being the first team, we could pave the road and make it easier for the teams that followed.

The sun was getting hotter. I was wishing that I had brought my hat and Bonnie her sunscreen as we walked to the Boaw Primary Health Care Center (PHCC) next to our compound. Already there were many patients waiting under a Neem tree right in front of the clinic, sitting on a dead Neem log. In this small block of building, there were six rooms and a small waiting area: two consultation rooms, a laboratory, an injection room, a pharmacy, and an immunization room. The pharmacy had several bottles of amoxicillin, co-trim, and paracetamol, but most of the shelves were empty. Outside there were workers in bright yellow vests; UNICEF was launching a big project to immunize children five years and younger against polio.

The nutrition clinic next to the PHCC had been demolished because of issues of structural safety, and so the community healthcare workers held clinic under a Neem tree, mothers bringing their children to be weighed, fed plumpy nut, and to be given more plumpy nut to bring home to supplement their diet.

Boxes filled the nutrition administrative room in a corner building. Right next to it was the maternity ward run by Scavio, the midwife. It had two labor and delivery rooms and a ward of eight beds. It was quite full later in the day, and a baby was born. Next to this was the mixed medical ward of about fourteen beds run by the CHN and the clinical house officer. This morning it had three patients; several discharges had happened earlier. There were no sheets on the beds because the patients would take them home; they would take the mosquito nets as well if the CHN was not vigilant.

Andrew saw patients with me in the same room, acting as my translator. He was a Nuer but a short one. There were several pregnant women with abdominal pain; some were quite young but already had several pregnancies. Many of the children had diarrhea, and as I feared, there were no oral rehydration solutions; Andrew had to give them instructions on how to make their own. An old woman with scarification on her face was blind, very likely from an untreated trachoma infection of her eyes when she was small. There were several cases of conjunctivitis among the children, troubled by swarming flies around their eyes.

Women and children attending the nutrition clinic gathered on the ground at Boaw primary health care clinic, Koch County, Unity State, South Sudan.

There was no tetracycline eye ointment. And of course we saw many cases of malaria; thank goodness they did have coartem, medication for its treatment.

A fierce wind picked up at mid-morning, whipping up a sandstorm. Women and men covered their faces with their dresses and shirts, but others seemed to be unaffected by it. The *tukuls* in the distance all but disappeared. Later the pharmacist brought in boxes of amoxicillin, which must be lying among the boxes I saw at the nutrition office, or perhaps even in Koch Hospital where we saw all those boxes. At the bottom were mouse droppings; they had been lying around long enough for the mice to feel comfortable and at home.

The afternoon sun actually was so hot that it burned my skin as I walked back to the compound, wishing for an ice bath. It was well past two. Lunch consisted of rice, *posha* (mashed maize), goat stew, and curry. I had heard the pleading bleat of a young goat in the morning while we were having tea. As we left the dining area, I glimpsed the carcass of the goat hung limply from a young Neem tree. I only ate some rice and drank almost three liters of water in the course of the afternoon. After our late lunch, we finished sending off the rest of the patients who were waiting for their lab results before calling it a day.

It was not the end of a workday for Scavio, the midwife, and Bonnie. They delivered a healthy baby during the day. In the evening, they delivered a post-term baby who might have swallowed some meconium, and they had to resuscitate him for twenty minutes. The third baby was not so lucky; it was about twenty-five weeks premature. The mother was quite distraught and took the baby home. Scavio did not think it would survive. Under the best circumstances in a developed country, its survival was not completely assured, and the neonate would be in the intensive care unit for a long period.

The moon was almost full that night. The cows were mooing in somewhat of a contented moan.

The next morning, I explored the village by running in the other direction, but there were only scattered compounds of *tukuls* and nothing more. On my way back, I met two women with yellow vests and UNICEF caps, walking towards a village to begin their work of polio vaccination. The bucket bath was especially refreshing, and I wished I could douse the cold water on my hot body for a long time.

The maternity unit was our first place to visit. The healthy baby that was born yesterday looked just fine with the proud mother. The post-term baby had not attempted to suckle; hopefully it would soon. I later rounded with Michael in the ward. There was only one in-patient, a young man who had been coughing for six months, with weight loss and fever. Admitted three days ago with malaria and a presumed respiratory infection, he continued to do poorly with antibiotic treatment. I slapped a mask on him, but he was not able to tolerate it, saying it was making it hard for him to breath. After examining him, I discussed transferring him to the nearest referral hospital, two hours away, to get a chest x-ray and to get him tested for TB and HIV. Michael informed me that at Boaw where we were, there was no TB or HIV testing. The patient was a very tall Nuer, and Michael told me he was not one of the tallest; there were yet taller Nuer than him. He attended to several patients who returned daily to get their injections for the treatment of *kala-azar*, a combination of intramuscular injections of sodium stibolgluconate and paramomycin.

A team of expats and nationals accompanied by WR manager, Rose, arrived to tour the facility. I met with them briefly; I was not sure if the expats represented the donors. After seeing patients with diarrhea, malaria, conjunctivitis, and various aches and pains, Michael came to fetch me. He told me the BIG MAN, the director of the Boaw Payam, Philip, would like to see me. He was the stern man we met yesterday. The first thing that came to my mind was did I do anything wrong that offended the director or the community? I was thinking in terms of my running (although I checked with Johnson beforehand about dress code, running, etc.) or my interactions with the people. It was past noon, the sun was hot, and I was thankful to have my hat. During the several hundred meters of walking to the director's hut, I felt like I was being summoned to the principal's office or my boss's.

Michael and I stooped down at the door to enter the thatched hut. As my eyes adjusted to the darkness inside, I saw three people: the director of the Payam behind his desk, his secretary, David, and another man. In front of them were two empty chairs. They all stood up and shook Michael's and my hands. What amazed me was the Payam pronounced my name correctly, told me it was an honor to have me in his Payam, and they would honor me with a gift. Oh no! I thought to myself, not a goat! Sure enough, almost on cue, in came a man guiding a handsome horned creature into the hut. He was white with light brown patches of hair. The man handed him over to Michael; the creature promptly sniffed at his pants and then proceeded to nuzzle my hand, looking for food. I petted him and planted a kiss on his forehead. A broad smile spread across the face of the director. My next fear was would they expect me to kill it right there and then. I had heard of such stories in which the recipient of such gift was expected to slaughter the creature in front of everyone in the village. I thanked the director the best I knew how but wished that Johnson were there to help me as to the proper way to respond, remembering the other day he told us it would be very bad to refuse water when it was offered. In my mind, I wondered whether it would be rude to return the gift to the community, which this creature would serve best. I stood up and thanked him from the bottom of my heart for the goat and murmured something to the effect that I did not eat meat. Then I wondered aloud whether the community could use it. He did not take the offer but corrected me that the creature was a ram. Yes, now that I took a good look, it did have a pair of ram-like horns. He wanted to know what I would call such a creature in America. I told him we would call it a ram. He then suggested that I take him back to America on the plane and said if I had stayed two months or longer, there would be more great gifts. I thought to myself, the CASH COWS? A marriage proposal and a dowry? I was running wild with my imagination.

As we walked away with my gift, the villagers passing by were smiling. We led the ram to our compound, and I immediately sought out Elizabeth, the cook. I told her through a combination of gesture and speech that she was not to kill the ram but to allow it to roam in the compound. And so he was tied to a tree by the gatekeeper but managed to release himself soon enough and roamed around scavenging for whatever bits of scant grass in the yard. Later Bonnie commented that his fate was sealed no matter what I did.

When Johnson heard about the ram, he told me the director of the Payam had come to visit the PHCC in the morning before he summoned me. He thought it was a great thing that he offered me a gift but added with some regrets, "Too bad, we cannot roast him."

On my last day at Boaw, I picked up a few words of Nuer: *marlay* (How are you?), *mamuagar* or *mamadli* (I'm fine), *chigualong* (thank you). In the evening, we took a walk into the village to see the market with stalls that seemed to be selling almost the same thing: salt, sugar, rice, some dried fish, eggs, onions… Interspersed among the stalls were tea and

A gift of a ram from the director of the Boaw Payam to the author.

water pipe houses, frequented by men. One middle-aged man approached me and said he would like to go home with me.

Bonnie asked, "How many cows?"

Here in Boaw, our morning wake-up call was the mournful mooing of the cows. Around the boreholes, a number of egrets, cranes, and other birds gathered. They must be longing for the wet season to come. The most comforting noise in the compound was the coo-cooing of the turtledoves. Just by the gate, there were many couples of them; the male could be seen sidestepping on the branch, inching ever closer to its beloved, coo-cooing with a lilting trill at the end of each coo-coo. The children shouted what sounded like *kha-wadiya*, the equivalent of *mzungu* or white person. In the compound the pair of chickens, a black and a white, had been roaming in and out of the dining area and our room looking for food. Occasionally we threw some rice and pieces of chapatti for them. Once there were twelve of them, but eagles snatched them from the compound until there were now two of them left. In the chicken coop, more chicks hatched. These two survivors learned to hide indoors, especially in the afternoon when the eagles were active. They swooped down swiftly into the yard, picking up things that looked edible. The ram roamed about looking for bits of green grass to eat; there was not much in the compound. Andrew, the CHN, was the second person to suggest that I take the ram home on the plane.

The next day Johnson and the rest of the clinic crew were busy packing up chairs, tables, stretcher, screens, medicines, and water for our mobile clinic in Latabang, a village seven kilometers away. In the compound was a building where medicines and supplies were kept, and it had also become a home for bats and mice. As my eyes adjusted to the dim interior, I began to discern many shadowy creatures hanging from the rafters.

When the vaccination team and we arrived at Latabang, there was already a large group of villagers gathering. The village elders were sitting comfortably on chairs next to a wall while women and children sat on mats under a big spreading tree. One of the elders in particular was flouncing around with a stick wearing satin pajamas whose bottom was well-nigh smudged, evidently very proud of his "official attire." A naked Nuer teenage boy greeted us, laughing as he danced and ran wildly around us. While we set up, William spoke to the villagers using a bullhorn. Then each and every one of the elders spoke until one elder in a business suit took the stand. He spoke first in the Nuer dialect, then turned around and spoke to us in English, thanking us for coming. He then proceeded to tell us that there were two things most needed by the village: water and a clinic as the Boaw PHCC was too far away. Apparently, the boreholes here had stopped working, and the villagers had to walk to Boaw to get water. In fact, as the day wore on, our jerry can of water quickly became empty, as the villagers' thirst was tremendous. Johnson had to send for more water, which also quickly disappeared.

When all the elders had their say, they were the first to be seen. Very quickly, the registration cards piled up, and I warned Johnson to cap the registration, as we could not possibly see everyone. However, as in the African way, he hated to turn people down and insisted we could manage. Diarrhea was prominent, and there were some cases of malaria. Johnson undid a homemade splint placed by a villager on the arm of a boy with a broken bone while Bonnie provided prenatal care.

The registration kept on coming, and soon we were inundated with a pile of cards a few inches thick. As the time ticked away, I was afraid that the villagers who were not seen would be angry, having waited for several hours. It reminded me of when we were at Kokar, Kenya, near the Somalian border. The villagers threw stones at one of the volunteers as we beat a hasty retreat, worrying about being ambushed by Al-Shabaab, the militant group of Somalia, while traveling back to Dadaab in the dark.

Miraculously we saw them all, we estimated close to 150, starting some time past eleven in the morning and finishing at four-thirty in the afternoon with no lunch break, just sips of hot water from my Nalgene bottle that baked in the sun; my thirst was not quenched. I was thankful for my hat as the sun moved, and the shade disappeared from our table. We were hoping to stop before three as we had to leave for Bentiu, three hours away. When the rain came, big drops of rain, we hastily packed up. The naked boy danced in the rain, opening his mouth wide to catch the raindrops and flirting dangerously in front of the cruiser, getting thoroughly drenched.

We went back to Boaw camp to pack up, had a late meal, and said our good-byes. My frustrated ram was tied up. I let him loose, and he immediately went to a patch of green to graze. I said my last good-bye and hoped he lived a long life. On our way past a village, a topless, voluptuous woman ran right to the front of the cruiser and flounced her breasts. Young Juma swerved to the side down the trench, undeterred by it all.

Bentiu was hot and wretchedly humid. We moved all the beds to the back yard and slept outside. There was hardly any breeze, but it was less stifling than inside. As I lay there on my bed, I remembered nostalgically the night when I abandoned the Berber tent and went outside, sleeping in four layers of blankets under the inky blue sky of the Sahara Desert in Morocco with a purring desert cat curled snugly by my side. The moon peered down on the giant sand dunes silhouetted in the background, the cold wind blowing, and our pack of camels chewing their cud contentedly and moaning softly in their sleep fifty meters from me.

Here through the night in Bentiu, the moon coursed its way slowly as the dogs barked, howled, and quarreled all night.

We had maize porridge and tea for breakfast, and it was quite good. The sun was fierce even before nine o'clock. On our trip to the town center, we saw a herd of pigs, caked with dried mud, seeking what precious little shade there was to take a mid-morning nap. This semi-desert area was no place for pigs, especially as the mosque, the only landmark here that seemed a permanent structure, was close by. The rest of the structures were of straw, mud, reeds, tarp, plastic, and metal sheeting. Scavio had some banking to do, and it took over an hour just to accomplish that as the queue was long while an armed security man stood guard. I stayed inside taking advantage of the air conditioning while Bonnie was content to sit outside on a chair offered by the guard. A sidewalk vendor was selling used clothes shipped from the western world: pants, shirts, winter jackets, and various sleepers for children, such warm garments for the heat here. Pedicabs weaved their way through the crowd. In the market, some vendors without a stall or shelter simply baked in the noon sun, sitting on the sand selling bags of rice, salt, sugar, or packets of consommé displayed on a mat. Many had a shed selling clothes, shoes, flip-flops, clogs, belts, and bags. The heat really deflated us, and all we wanted was to get back to our home at WR. There, although it was stifling, at least we were shielded from the direct sun.

The "resident cat" meowed loudly, demanding lunch. We surreptitiously fed her some meat which she refused, but she was content with some lentils and rice. Although she was young, she looked like she could be pregnant. Later in the day some drops of rain fell; for a while I was hopeful it would rain but it was just a tease. It did cool off somewhat. We had a meeting with Rose, the manager and director of health and nutrition for WR, to discuss the medicines and supplies that we should get in preparation for the volunteers who would

The mosque in Bentiu, seemingly the only permanent fixture in the town.

follow us. We found a job for our resident cat, to be the resident cat for Boaw Camp taking care of the creatures living in the supply room, especially the mice.

Later in the evening, a cool breeze blew gently. Somewhere close by it must have rained.

In the morning, I saw another runner on the only tarmac road in town. We greeted each other as runners always do. To reach the tarmac road, I had to run on the main, dusty road, crossing frequently to the far side to avoid the dust whenever a *matatu* came by. There was not much beauty in Bentiu; the condition was harsh and dry with few permanent structures, and even those were of a utilitarian nature. The alternative, the rainy season, might not be any better with muddy and slippery roads prolonging traveling time and the breeding of mosquitoes. However, the rain would be needed here for the crops and the sustenance of life.

The next day we went into town in search of heavy-duty gloves for Scavio and Jik, the cleaning agent for her maternity ward. In the market in Rubkona, Rose and Scovia half-heartedly looked for them, but they soon led us to the "5th Avenue of Bentiu" with shops for women's clothes and shoes where they shopped the African way, trying on clothes without the benefit of a fitting room or even a mirror. Bonnie took a picture and showed Rose how she looked in the digital camera. We waited patiently, having no desire to shop for ourselves. Driving to another market, we saw donkeys being herded to the Nile River where water was pumped to the tanks on the carts. The sad, scrawny donkeys must walk this path hauling water several times a day. There were no gloves at the grain market. Back to the busy town of Bentiu, finally gloves, brooms, scrubbers, and hoses.

In the afternoon, we packed chairs, tables, a cooler, and our luggage into the back of the land cruiser and filled up the gas tank, ready to tackle our journey to Leer, our next destination south of Bentiu. For four hours, we rode on uneven, bone-breaking dirt roads, passing an empty transit refugee camp, an oil field in the distance, and many, many villages and cows. The landscape changed from grassland dotted with tall termite hills and green acacia trees to lush palm trees growing around villages. Rusty road signs had the illegible names of the villages, bleached by the sun and neglected during the long years of conflict.

Compared to the Upper Nile Initiative and Development Organization (UNIDO) compound, the Boaw Camp was like the Ritz. Here we had electricity from a loud, obnoxious generator, no plugs for any form of charging, no meeting hall to gather, no fridge to keep the water cold or even semi-cold, for the fridges here in Unity State only seemed to put in a half-hearted effort to keep things cold. There was no cooler to refill our water bottle for purification and only one shower and one latrine for a compound of over twenty people. Many slept in tents, and in our crowded bedroom there was unfinished dirt floor.

Peter, one of the UNIDO people in charge, quickly made it clear to Johnson that the staff at Mirmir PHCC expected to be paid for translating for us, even though we would be there to help them run the clinic. We were thirsty, tired, and hungry after hours of rough driving, and no one showed us where we would settle or asked us whether we needed to freshen up. In the gathering gloom, it was difficult to discuss anything of importance when one could not see the expressions of the speaker. Johnson listened patiently, remained sagacious enough to avoid any confrontation, and said nothing; I let my mind wander.

Tonight the sky was absolutely over the top. The moon had not risen, and the millions of stars and the splash of Milky Way bowled me over. It was good the generator had not been turned on. Throughout the early part of the night, the noisy ibises seemed to be especially active; one ibis took the lead, "Ah, ah, ah…" and the rest joined in a merry chorus, cawing raucously as they flew away from the compound.

In the middle of the night, I got up. The compound was flooded by the light of the waning moon; only a few stars twinkled in the sky. The Milky Way had disappeared. I felt like ET, and I phoned home.

For breakfast, we stood around a table making tea from some powder and had a greasy bun with the busy flies swarming over the table. Then off we drove north to Mirmir, forty minutes away, a dusty and desolate village with its main road lined with stores selling staples of oil, salt, sugar, and rice.

The Mirmir PHCC was run by the MOH; its name in Arabic on a rusty metal board standing just behind a broken chain-link fence was barely discernible. The gate remained standing, seemingly in defiance. Off to one side was a particularly big, shady tree sending buttress-like roots into the earth, reminiscent of a Banyan tree. William, the community health worker, called it the Bieh tree.

A few patients sat on broken benches outside the clinic waiting to be seen. The Mirmir PHCC was a U-shaped structure in a state of disrepair with two wards, a defunct solar room, a pharmacy, a storage room, and an OPD. William was the only health worker. Ward 1 had two beds lined with cardboard as mattresses; a thin woman curled up on one of them, receiving IV fluid. The floor had been doused with brown povidone iodine and purple chlorhexidine, and it bore the stain of the cleansing agents. The solar room was going to be used by Bonnie to examine the pregnant women, but it reeked of urine and the big fridge there had not been working for a while. The shelves in the pharmacy were ninety-five percent empty, and it lacked important medicines: oral rehydration solutions (ORS) for diarrhea, coartem (artemether-lumefantrine) for malaria, paracetamol for fever and pain, and antibiotics. The storage room was locked; later we found that it contained a lot of magnesium trisilicate for acid reflux, gloves, water for injection, and not much more. The OPD was swept recently, and its non-functioning autoclave contained a few rusty clamps clinging onto a wreck. Ward 2 was used to do rapid detection test or Paracheck for malaria, and it was stacked with a combination of trash, boxes of supplies, a bed lined with cardboard, and a used IV hanging from one of the blades of a broken ceiling fan.

Confronted with this sad state of affairs, Johnson took a long thoughtful look at the shady Bieh tree and decided that we would set our mobile clinic there. There followed a flutter of activity to move tables, chairs, benches, an exam table, and some screens. The threatening clouds gathered, but it did not rain; there was a brisk, cool breeze. The children were barely clothed in dirty rags, and the Bieh tree, which became our clinic, was also their playground, the aerial roots hanging from the branches their swing sets. Many climbed up

The stark deteriorating Mimir PHCC run by the Ministry of Health of South Sudan.

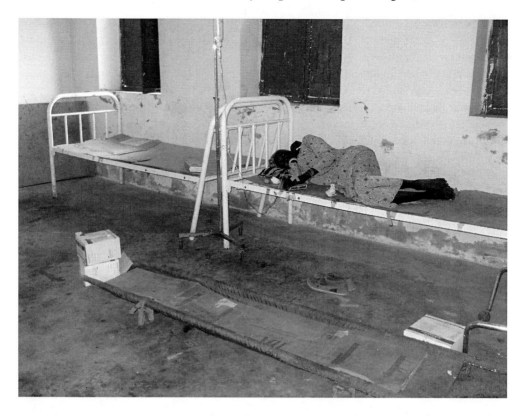

A woman receiving intravenous fluid while lying on a bed at the Mirmir PHCC with a piece of cardboard as a mattress.

the tree like monkeys, picking small, grape-like fruits to eat while the goats foraged for food under and around the tree; children and goats alike were hungry.

With the lack of useful medicines, Johnson sent Juma to Koch County Hospital, an hour away, to get them. However, when he arrived, the boxes were so chaotically stashed that no one could find the needed medicines in a reasonable amount of time to bring to our clinic. Instead, he brought the recently appointed county health director, Michael Kuoak, and his entourage to tour the Mirmir PHCC for the first time. Despite requests to the government for certain medications, the staff at Mirmir kept on receiving tons of magnesium trisilicate. They had been running the clinic without a salary for "a long time"—since the oil stopped flowing. Recently the oil started flowing again, but they were still not factored into the budget of the government. That also explained why they wanted to be paid for translating for us. Johnson said he could only give them payment-in-kind, such as salt, sugar, and maize flour. However, considering their hardship, he was thinking of giving them a small amount of cash. What the new county director could do was beyond me. He had no vehicle to travel around and visit the PHCC that he was to oversee and no budget to pay the staff. Fuel remained very expensive despite this being an oil-rich country. WR hoped to take over the Mirmir PHCC to revive this place and to make it sustainable; the government of South Sudan would eventually have to take the responsibility of running all their clinics.

Children continued to show up with diarrhea, but we could only teach the mothers to make homemade ORS. Bonnie did her childbirth education for the mothers-to-be and some young women. As we ended our clinic, the wind picked up, whipped up a sandstorm,

The author taking care of a sick child under the Bieh tree.

and almost carried the screens away with its gusts. Loose papers flew wildly, and we could feel the sting of the sand on our faces.

Back in the compound in Leer in the evening, I took a walk into the village as the day became cooler. Two children with tops made from plastic bags greeted me, but their shirts were not breathable and must be tremendously hot to wear. I gestured to a woman to ask if I could get inside her *tukul*. There were hardly any belongings: some dry corn and sorghum, a health card attached to one of the stalks of the roof, and bits of clothes hanging. The bed was outside under a tree, and in the yard was a fenced structure for the animals. The woman sat on the dirt mending her fence with thorny fronds from a palm. Children played in a pool of muddy water, and a group of iron forgers fashioned spoons and ladles under a Neem tree while goats and rams foraged on the dry stumps of grass as they headed home. Two children sat on the dirt molding realistic looking mud animal figurines and even a fenced structure with houses and animals. The sun was slowly setting; I sauntered back to the compound before the whole place was engulfed in darkness.

Tonight was cloudy, no spectacular display of stars. The moon shone brightly later in the night. The breeze finally came as the crickets, which lodged themselves on my bed net, chirped most of the night while a firefly blinked on the dirt floor. The ibises were silent until dawn when they made a tremendous raucous cawing to wake us all up.

The next day I ran through the village, trying hard to memorize landmarks, which were not many, so I would not get lost. Many women were already on their way to the market carrying heavy loads of reeds and hay. Breakfast was "milk-tea" and two small pieces of fried dough.

When we arrived at the Mirmir PHCC, the unpaid staff had set up tables and chairs for us under the Bieh tree, and the patients were already waiting. Despite not being paid, they apparently continued to open the clinic even when there were no foreign volunteers. Rose came to visit five months ago and told us that the whole place was even trashier than it was now. She warned them that she would not come back again if they did not clean up. In January, she called to tell them she was coming, and when she arrived, they had made a great effort to clean up. This was her third visit. The place was trashy again, but not as bad as when she first visited it.

Johnson found out that the dispensers in the pharmacy were not giving out the correct amount of medications, so he spent some time with them. Bonnie continued to teach the pregnant women about the birth of low-weight babies, hemorrhaging, and resuscitation. One woman decided to take it upon herself to teach the other village women what she had learned, holding the baby mannequin proudly as we left. One of my last patients was a young boy who had been bitten by a neighbor's dog a day ago, apparently unprovoked. The dog was killed. Mother and child rode on the cruiser with us back to Leer to get the rabies immune globulin and vaccine at a hospital there. He would have to come back for a few more shots. How they were to get there was a huge problem as there was no public transportation here; they would have to rely on their own two feet, probably a three- to four-hour walk under the hot sun one way.

Along the back roads behind the compound, many women eased themselves out in the open field in the morning, now totally devoid of vegetation except for dry stalks of grass and cut sorghum. Most families still did not have latrines; personal hygiene was difficult to maintain, and there were no private bathrooms, at least from what I could see.

We had to fetch our mobile clinic paraphernalia from the Mirmir PHCC as well as the staff to help us run our mobile clinic at Padier, about fifteen minutes away from Mirmir. William remained behind to see the patients who had already gathered there. The sun was getting searing hot, and there was precious little shade in this village. The day before we stopped by on our way home to Leer to ask the Chief to help us set up a clinic, but apparently he did not. Johnson picked the best shade afforded by two Neem trees. Soon the villagers appeared. The flies were fierce and aggressive, swarming around the women's coverings, their children, eyes, noses, mouths, and any open wounds. Roaming cows and goats left dung and droppings, which disintegrated in this dry weather, providing great feeding grounds for the flies; it would be impossible to get rid of them totally. The people here were impoverished, children wearing tattered and filthy clothes, and there were plenty of bare feet. I had not seen them eat anything yet except what they could find from the fruit trees. The boy we took to Leer for his rabies shot was fed some glucose biscuits and a bottle of cow's milk, and the flies competed mightily with him, swarming around the bottle cap and his mouth for the bits of crumbs mingled with milk.

The clouds became dark and threatening around noon, and it seemed that the rain was coming our way. Johnson was optimistic that we could beat it, but we did not. We made a hasty retreat into our cruiser while the local staff ran to some *tukuls* to have some cow's milk or yogurt. It was a torrential rain with heavy winds and lasted for an hour. Big pools of water quickly collected in the clay soil. Finally, it stopped, and we set up the clinic again and spent another hour and a half seeing the rest of the patients. By the time we finished packing up and heading towards Leer, it was almost five. The roads were slick, and the potholes were pools of muddy water. A convoy of trucks from Juba lined up as workers filled the mud and pools with some sandy soil. Our land cruiser was able to weave around them and moved on.

We had the second meal of the day, our lunch, at six in the evening, some fried fish caught in the Nile.

Women were always the fetchers of water here and everywhere in Africa. They did it first thing in the morning and throughout the day, carrying a five-gallon jerry can on their heads. I saw a tall Nuer women carrying one on her head and another in her hand. Men were never seen at the borehole or the water pump; in Bentiu they hauled water on donkey carts to sell it to the merchants in town. Women were the mules here, carrying large loads of logs, reeds, straw, bags of maize, or sorghum all on their heads, walking long distances, as well as hauling water, caring for the children, cooking, and repairing their compounds. Children, mostly girls, would help and walked beside their mothers. I did not see men doing these chores; if they did at all, they would do them with the help of the donkeys or wheelbarrows.

On our way to Mirmir, some UNIDO personnel who traveled with us told us the appalling newsbreak of a seventy-nine-year-old commissioner in one of the Equatorial States marrying a seventeen-year-old girl. It was said that the relatives were very happy, but did anyone bother to interview the poor young lady, who very likely was not given a choice.

Johnson wanted to show us the Nile in Leer, so we left a little earlier in the morning traveling south, joined by Peter who came down to Leer a few days ago. The terrain became greener and marshier. Papyrus with its delicate tufts grew along the marshes. We arrived at a small port, but to Johnson's disappointment, there were no fresh fish. He loved eating his fish dinner so much that he intended to get some fish to cook in Bentiu.

We turned around and drove back to Leer, picking up Thomas. All four of us were crammed in the back of the cruiser, half of which was packed with suitcases and the cooler, and off to Mirmir we traveled. There we left our suitcases behind for the day to make room for our equipment, medicines, and whatnots for the mobile clinic, and a fifth passenger, Andrew, who was to show us to Buok, a Boma in Mirmir. After an hour, we found ourselves at the back of a string of heavy trucks from Juba lumbering very slowly over the potholes. There was no way to overtake them. We slowed to a crawl. Eventually Juma had a break, drove into a flat plain, and overtook three of them. Andrew must have directed him down a secondary road which suddenly appeared, and this road was even bumpier than the main road. For a long, long time there was not a single soul, animal, or *tukul* in sight. We drove for what seemed like ages, and the road just disappeared one hundred meters from a cluster of *tukuls*.

A villager informed us that Buok was not far off, but the cruiser had to traverse over grassland to reach it, as though we were in a safari at a game drive. It took us over two hours to get from Mirmir to Buok. It did not make sense for Juma to go back to Mirmir to fetch the other staff. Unfortunately, the Chief of Buok did not inform the populace of three hundred of our coming, not knowing exactly what we would be offering. We walked in the hot sun and met him under an acacia tree. Johnson took inventories of the kinds of illness the people had here for future reference. A middle-aged man, naked from the waist down, wobbled towards us using two long sticks. The Chief said he became ill three years ago and had not recovered since. He complained of weakness, heaviness, and numbness of his legs from the hips down. I suspected schistosomiasis or bilharzia with transverse myelitis, but there was no way to prove it. In the wet season, there were pools of water here, and snails were plentiful. In fact, snail shells bleached by the sun dotted the parched water holes. He had frequently waded in the water before he came down with the illness. Although this was after the fact, we gave him praziquantel but warned him that it was not a cure. With Thomas translating for us, we advocated a regimen of exercise and muscle strengthening.

In the end, we saw some pregnant women for their prenatal care and the villagers who gathered around us, including the Chief. We had no idea how to get back to the main road, so the Chief hopped on the back seat, wedging himself between Thomas and me; now we had a total of six passengers along with our furniture, buckets, cooler, and medicines. I felt like I was in an overcrowded *matatu* where the conductor continued to take more passengers despite a lack of breathing space in the bus. Bonnie reigned supreme in the spacious front seat next to Juma, unperturbed by the overcrowding. There was no GPS; the Chief just told Juma to go hither and yon, and we saw no paths or recognizable landmarks. Juma simply mowed down short bushes carelessly. Several times the engine stalled. He got out and did something to it, and it started again. It did cross my mind that if indeed the engine failed, we might have to spend a night out in the open plain. After about half an hour we finally reached a dirt road; the Chief jumped off and went trekking the grassland back to his abode. This was indeed a shortcut; it took us an hour, half the time, to get back to Mirmir. By this time Johnson had second thoughts about going back to this elusive Buok.

It was past three-thirty in the afternoon. Juma had to change oil for the car and transfer a fuel tank, all done in the heat of the day. There was a pot full of liver in the village eatery, but nothing else to choose from, so we sat drinking cold drinks instead, dreading the three to four hours more of rough ride. I held my breath using the local latrine, but it was not as bad as I envisioned it to be. However, if I were given a choice I would have preferred the bush. On our way back to Bentiu, well past seven in the evening, we caught up with the three trucks that we passed on our way to Buok. They were still crawling at snail's pace. At eight in the evening, we finally arrived; all my bones felt like they were shattered, and my body ached. Dinner was *posha*, pasta with goat meat, and beans, but in such meager proportion, it was not enough to feed all of us.

We pushed our beds outside and slept under the stars. I got rid of my mosquito net to catch the breeze. Waking up in the middle of the night, I was surprised to see the stars above me. For a brief moment, I forgot where I was. The crescent moon

A *tukul* in Buok, Koch County, Unity State.

shone brightly in a corner. The cat came meowing for food; in the middle of the night she had jumped onto the table and found an open can of tuna fish. I dished her some remnants of pasta with a piece of goat meat, but she showed no interest. I picked her up, and that was what she wanted, some cuddling and petting. Her purring soon dominated the cool night air. At dawn, the cat came again and demanded to be fed. I climbed up to the roof to get a view of the sleeping town under the waning moon, but she did not follow. Far away the donkeys brayed very mournfully, probably not looking forward to another day of arduous labor.

My run took me away from the center of town in the morning. There was not much more to be seen; stretches of dusty flat lands with isolated *tukuls* and buildings with the slight breeze carrying whiffs of the smell of human waste. Only about seven percent of the people here had any kind of sanitary facilities. Since there was no breakfast today, Johnson went into town and bought us each a big bottle of cold mango juice.

We were to leave for Juba in the morning, but the flight had been delayed to the late afternoon because of heavy rainstorms in Juba. This being Friday, this flight would be the last one of the week, for the UN Humanitarian plane did not operate on the weekends. We had time for a quick lunch and drove to the airport, essentially a fenced-in dirt patch with no airport building to speak of. The waiting area was just a big truck tire parked under a young acacia tree whose feathery leaves provided thin patchy shades; many expats crowded underneath it while their land cruisers waited for them. Johnson and Robson, who brought us to the airport, had other things to do in Pairang, north of Bentiu, and they left us there by the tree. So we waited with the rest of the people from WFP, MSF, UNHCR…seeking whatever shade we could find. Blue-helmeted UN soldiers stood guard. I wondered what would happen during the rainy season; the lonely acacia tree and the three-foot tall palm tree in one corner could not shield anyone from the elements. The sun seemed to get hotter, and many expats ran out of water. An enterprising South Sudanese would have made a small fortune selling cold water at this "airport lounge." Our plane was delayed for an hour, but it was a blessing that it came. The storm in Juba had ceased momentarily, giving us a window to fly in and land.

The Nuer are a very friendly tribe, and they make a point to say *"marlay"* and shake your hands when they meet you. Some Nuer men have their foreheads cut with six horizontal lines with a sharp knife when they are about fifteen to initiate them into manhood. If they cry at all, it is a sign of weakness, and they bring shame to their families. Cows are slaughtered to celebrate the occasion. While Westerners have Botox to reduce wrinkles, the Nuer induce more wrinkles early on in their lives. Women do not have such ceremonies; some do have their faces scarified, but no cows are slaughtered. Most of the Nuer display a gap between their front teeth, and women and men alike spit through the gap with practiced ease; the spittle arcs in the air before it hits the dirt. Their skill of spitting through the gap between their front teeth must be the envy of many of our baseball players in the U.S.

Our time here in Koch County in Unity State had come to a very quick end. I mulled over my experience, pondering the human issues and needs of South Sudan that were vast and innumerable. Many of the Nuer here were born into abject poverty with little to call their own. They were destined to repeat many manual and mundane chores and did not enjoy much respite from them. Their recreation was to thump on the jerry can rhythmically in the evening as they gathered around the open cooking fire to share their evening meal. They had scant belongings and little food, and the children probably wore their filthy rags every day. For those who suffer much on earth, it is only fitting that a piece of heaven awaits them. We who are given many blessings on this earth should give back much more during our lifetime. I am often reminded of this verse in the Bible: "For unto whomsoever much is given, of him shall be much required…" (Luke 12:48, King James Version).

The dependence on oil for their sole source of revenue could be the Achilles' heel of South Sudan. The vast distances between the villages and the nearest healthcare center were mind-boggling, and this would be made even more inaccessible with the rains and floods. South Sudan would surely need more long years to improve the situation here ever so slightly, a very sobering thought indeed.

On my run one morning in Juba, I saw a family living under a tarp slung over a horizontal tree trunk by the side of a road. Clothes were drying on the tree branches and on the fences, and the children were sitting on mats looking kind of lost and forlorn. One called out "*khawadiya!*" It made me wonder whether life in one of the isolated rural areas might be better than being homeless in the middle of a bustling city.

Anthony, our driver, failed to show up, and this was a second broken promise. He had said that he would come at nine in the morning to show us Juba town, but right at the outset, I did not believe him. It seemed to be difficult for Africans to say "no," so they resorted to telling you in so many words that "they are coming;" when would they come was a matter of great conjecture. After over two hours of waiting in vain for him, we took the *matatu* to Custom and drove by the burial ground of John Garang, the leader of the Sudanese People's Liberation Army/Movement (SPLA/M).[15] The car park or terminal was situated in a busy sprawling market with people selling produce; this was surrounded by small concrete stalls selling clothes, belts, shoes, boom boxes, cell phones, radios… Men plying the area offered pedicures and manicures; a young lady sat on a low stool having a pedicure. Later we took another *matatu* to Konyokonyo Market where there was another busy car park. The other Sunday we wandered to Juba University. It was closed, but viewing it through the brick fence, many buildings looked run-down, making me wonder whether it was still functioning. This time we drove by the other parts of Juba University; the grounds seemed to be well tended, but we could only view it from afar from the *matatu*. The Konyokonyo Market was enormous and sprawling with many men selling meat and livestock, and women selling fresh produce and spices in addition to the usual wares: clothes, shoes, electronics, and millions of cell phones. There was definitely a glut of Chinese-made goods.

This being one of our last days in South Sudan, we checked out a few places and chose what we thought a more sanitary eatery serving piping hot food. We threw caution to the wind and had the local fare of fish gravy, salad, and *kissera,* which was like *injera* in Ethiopia but made from maize rather than teff flour. Then we walked back to the compound of WR in the hot sun without Anthony's help, aided only by the memory of my running routes.

My last run in South Sudan brought me towards the Nile, where many squatters lived in the midst of the construction of multi-story buildings and some hotels. They were brushing their teeth or hunching in groups having their morning tea. Their homes were patches of reeds, tarp, plastic coverings, and cloth materials all mashed together higgledy-piggledy. It would not be long before they would have to evacuate to some other place when this prime piece of real estate would be gobbled up for more development.

Before we left Juba, the elusive Anthony finally showed up at the request of Tashian to show us the town. He drove to Jebel, where there was a market selling many imports from Uganda. On the way, we passed a military base, which used to be the headquarters of the Sudan People's Liberation Movement (SPLM), where Anthony said many Sudanese were killed. Like many people in the southern part of Sudan during the war, he and his family fled to Uganda. Jebel had a cluster of hills, which looked quite out of place in this very flat area. There were many boulders on these hills, and workers scoured and attacked them. They broke them into tiny pieces, all manually, and sold them as materials for the construction of multi-story buildings cropping up all over Juba. Boulders loosened by the workers had been known to roll down the hills, killing both workers and inhabitants.

We passed by Custom again and had a closer look from the cruiser at the burial place of John Garang, heavily guarded by soldiers. Tashian once commented that he never understood why the dead needed to be guarded. The series of neatly kept ministry buildings near this area were a great contrast to the clumps of ramshackle homes in a small shantytown not too far away.

Not too long after my return from South Sudan, I came down with a mysterious illness. At that time no doctor could say what it was that afflicted me. I was sick enough to be hospitalized. Whatever bug or virus afflicted me was mightier than us mere mortals. Centuries ago, the plague wiped out hundreds and thousands of people, and HIV similarly has done its fair share of devastation. However, I had confidence then that I would recover, and I did. The cause of my affliction was revealed two months later when Dr. Cam Ashbaugh, my infectious disease doctor, wrote to tell me that my blood test at the Centers for Disease Control and Prevention (CDC) showed I had dengue. I was glad it was not chikungunya. By then I was already doing my first mission with MSF in Malawi. I was also told that that was my second episode of dengue. I recalled having a three-day illness with similar symptoms a few weeks after I returned from Haiti after volunteering there during the cholera outbreak in 2010. I surmised it must be then that I came down with dengue for the first time. There, as in South Sudan, I was overwhelmed with mosquito bites.

It was exactly two months after the Boston Marathon that my two children, Cara and Charles, and I ran together through Brookline to Boston to complete the finishing length of the marathon that the bombings had prevented us from completing. My legs carried me well, but I could still feel the effect of the low red blood cell counts from my recent illness, causing my lungs to complain of the lack of oxygen. Cara wore her beat-up T-shirt that she bought after I ran my very first marathon in 2007. It proudly proclaimed "My Mom Ran the Boston Marathon!" At the end, my daughter and I left our old running shoes at the makeshift memorial at Copley Plaza.

South Sudan became a new country in July 9, 2011. The war that had lasted over twenty years had made consistent educational opportunities virtually impossible except for the lucky few who escaped to other countries. The country faced many challenges, not the least of which was raising the next generation of educated citizens to would be its future.

Johnson from WR dropped me a line to tell me that my ram was still alive and thriving. He had plenty to eat now as the rainy season had arrived. The guard at Boaw camp was taking good care of him. He was as equally amazed as I was that the ram had survived this long without being eaten. Because of the rainy season, MTI stopped sending teams to South Sudan temporarily while the local WR continued to provide medical care there. Like the ram which was enjoying a brief reprieve, the future of the South Sudanese remained uncertain and precarious. But I dreamed that one day I could be back there again.

On December 15, 2013, seven months after I left South Sudan, another long, drawn-out civil war was sparked by violence erupting in the headquarters of the South Sudan Army's Presidential Guard in Juba. President Salva Kiir accused former Vice President Riek Machar of an attempted coup, while Mr. Machar accused President Kiir of having instigated the violence in order to remove his opposition to the President's Government.[16] The preexisting ethnic tension between the two main tribes, the Dinka and the Neur, escalated, with the President being Dinka and the Vice President, Neur. In April 15, 2014, a massacre of over 400 people, mainly civilians taking refuge in mosques and churches, occurred in the town of Bentiu.[17]

A report from the London School of Hygiene and Tropical Medicine in 2018 estimated that since the civil war of 2013, over 400,000 people had died, about half of them from violence.[18] As of early 2018, the war had caused the displacement of about two million people within South Sudan and a further 2.5 million as refugees to neighboring countries, bringing a total of 4.5 million people displaced.[19] In August 5, 2018, after nearly five years of civil war, Mr. Kiir signed a power-sharing and cease fire agreement with the rebel leader Mr. Machar in Khartum, Sudan, in an attempt to end the brutal fighting.[20] The final chapter for a prolonged peace in South Sudan has yet to be written.

Afterword

Non Ministrari sed Ministrare

I fell asleep on my way home back from Logan International Airport in Boston. The bumpy ride woke me up. For a brief moment, I thought I was still in Africa, traveling on the road riddled with potholes. No, the houses out of the car window were different, and the trees were bare, for fall had arrived in this part of the world. I was back in Belmont, my town whose roads were just as potholed as those in Africa.

Back at work, I looked at my list of patients spreading over several floors and two buildings of the West Campus of the Beth Israel Deaconess Medical Center and strategized how best to efficiently round on them. I was no longer in the bush of Africa. Here in the U.S., I have access to state-of-the-art medical technologies and treatment modalities. I only have to discuss the care plan with the house-staff, and the wheel will be turning to get things done.

I no longer have to wait for the patients' relatives to raise money to buy medicines or lumbar puncture trays to perform a spinal tap. Antibiotics are given thirty minutes after the patient's arrival in the emergency room if meningitis is suspected. They will not go hungry because they have no relatives to cook for them. Their dressings are changed regardless of whether they can afford to buy them. Their relatives do not have to provide nursing care, as the ratio of nurses to patients is one to three or four patients, whereas it may be one to twenty in Africa.

More importantly, one does not have to wait helplessly for a patient with kidney failure to die because there is no dialysis machine to remove the toxins from the body or decide who is more deserving of oxygen when there is only one oxygen tank for the entire hospital.

On the first day of my return to the ward, my very first patient was a large woman half reclining in her bed with her tray table pushed close to her chest; her protruding belly was wedged below. It was breakfast time. After the niceties of a brief introduction, I asked her how she was doing.

"The breakfast was horrible. The egg was not cooked right. I asked for a soft-boiled egg; it came as hard as a rock."

The poor egg looked like it had been insulted, stabbed several times, and laid in the egg-holder, utterly injured.

"Did you eat the rest of your breakfast?" I picked up the plate cover as I asked her this question. The pancakes had been consumed, and the plate was licked clean. She must have liked them despite her complaints

"Nah, the food here is bad!"

One tended to lose perspective on what was important in life in the setting of plenty.

I held my tongue.

Pictures of my patients in Africa who had little to eat, who would be extremely happy to get eggs or the food that this woman was given, came flooding into my mind. This would be a sumptuous meal for them. I had never seen patients in Africa refusing food except when they lost their appetite, as in the case of Phoebe in Maseno, Kenya, the woman who had wasting disease from HIV. As I rounded in the morning, I took note of the fact that many of the patients I saw had medical problems because of their bad lifestyle habits and choices, more food ingested than needed to sustain life. Many had become so morbidly obese they were unable to move their heavy bodies to do any kind of meaningful exercises.

In the afternoon, a middle-aged lawyer who worked in a high-powered firm came in with new-onset atrial fibrillation (an irregular heart rhythm). All he cared about was that his problem should be solved quickly and expediently so he could return to work without missing much time. I felt very pressured and stressed. Although I did get frustrated with the slow African time, sometimes I wondered whether at times like this we could learn something from them, relish what we had in the moment, and be thankful. In the end, the cardiologist was able to cardiovert (change the heart rhythm by electrical means) him, and he was discharged the same day to return to his busy and demanding world.

I took a deep breath. I was home. The stresses of life were slowly creeping in, threatening the inner peace and tranquility that I often acquired during my sojourn in Africa. I hoped I would not let them win.

In Africa, patients wait and wait for almost a whole day to see a healthcare person with no complaints or arguments. It is not the greatest system, but the lack of healthcare personnel to care for the numerous patients that present every day makes the waiting inevitable.

Friends and my family back in Malaysia have always wondered why I spend time going to difficult, remote, and dangerous places to do medical relief work. Most say they could never do what I do. Always after that comment, there seems to be a pause, and then they wish me a safe trip.

For one thing, when I was little I had the idea of doing something to help people live a better life, and how that was to be accomplished was something that I had to figure out for myself when I grew older. Sure, I could very well enjoy my life here caring for my garden, reading a good book, painting a picture, and sitting on my comfortable couch. I could dig my feet into the fur of my dog, Cosmo, who was my footstool, and pet my cat, Marshmallow, who tried at all costs to dethrone my laptop so she could be my lap cat. However, deep down inside I always know that I have to do something in my life that is more meaningful to me. And so I have a hard time formulating an answer to their question.

In 2013, when I returned from South Sudan, the spring issue of the *Wellesley Alumnae Magazine* had an article on "Exits and Entrances: Women's Career in Transition"[1] to which I eventually wrote my comments expressing some of my sentiments.

"Dear Editors: Many of us probably have occasions to face transition in our careers which could be scary because of the inherent uncertainties. In 2005 after I volunteered as a medical doctor in India in the aftermath of the tsunami, I left my position as a full-time professor of medicine and slowly carved out a part-time position in clinical medicine to enable me to continue to volunteer for several months out of a year. Over the last eight years, I volunteered as a mentor in the HIV/AIDS epidemic in Vietnam, Tanzania, South Africa and Nigeria, in Haiti after the earthquake and during the cholera outbreak, in Libya during the war, the drought and famine of Kenya/Somalia, the Nakivale Refugee Camp in Uganda, the Nyakabande Transit Refugee Camp for the DRC, and most recently in the northern regions of South Sudan where the nearly twenty years of civil war left it with very little functional healthcare system.

When I gazed into the eyes of a twelve-year-old refugee from the DRC who lost all his loved ones, or took care of a woman with her brood of five children who walked for a month running away from the conflict in the DRC to the border of Uganda, half of her children were feverish with malaria, and all of them exhausted and hungry, or a Zimbabwean refugee who swam across the Limpopo River to South Africa, the promised land, risking loss of life and limb to the crocodiles; I struggled to understand the fierce driving force behind their desire to live, to survive, their resilience and patience in the setting of unrelenting waves of violence, harsh circumstances, inadequate food, and shelters... One cannot help but be inspired by the courage displayed by these people who have so little in their transient existence in this world. The transition they face makes mine very insignificant indeed."[2]

Africa continues to tug at my heart, and I feel a great connection to its people. More than a decade ago, I had not stepped foot in that continent, but years later I had visited more than twenty countries and continue to be in awe of its beauty. Most of all, I am in awe at the resilience of its people; they deserve better than what their leaders have been able to offer them so far.

After my stays in Africa, I often have a renewed appreciation for my patients. I pay close attention to their problems, listen to their stories, and often try to get to know them a little bit better and more intimately. I examine them with care and reverence and strive to treat them with compassion. Many of them entrust their fears, wishes, bodies, and lives to me at their most vulnerable moments. I will never forget that caring for my patients is a privilege.

The motto of my alma mater, Wellesley College, *Non Ministrari sed Ministrare* (Not to be ministered unto, but to minister), speaks volumes to what we should strive to be while living on this earth. In my next life, if there is one, I would choose to be a doctor again.

Chapter Notes

Preface

1. Charles River Editors, *The 2004 Indian Ocean Earthquake and Tsunami: The Story of the Deadliest Natural Disaster of the 21st Century* (CreateSpace Independent Publishing Platform, 2014); "Indian Ocean Earthquake & Tsunami, 2004," DirectRelief, https://www.directrelief.org/emergency/south-asian-earthquake-and-tsunami-2004/.

2. U.S. Congress, "Public Law 108–25, 108th Congress," May 27, 2003, the U.S. Senate and House of Representatives passed the President's Emergency Plan for AIDS Relief (PEPFAR), and also Tuberculosis and Malaria Act of 2003, https://www.congress.gov/108/plaws/publ25/PLAW-108publ25.pdf.

3. Centers for Disease and Prevention, "2014–2016 Ebola Outbreak in West Africa," https://www.cdc.gov/vhf/ebola/history/2014-2016-outbreak/index.html.

4. Kwan Kew Lai, *Lest We Forget: A Doctor's Experience with Life and Death During the Ebola Outbreak* (Jersey City: Viva Editions, 2018).

5. Kathryn Reid, "2013 Typhoon Haiyan: Facts, FAQs, and how to help," World Vision, November 9, 2018, https://www.worldvision.org/disaster-relief-news-stories/typhoon-haiyan-facts.

6. Kathryn Reid, "2015 Nepal earthquake: Facts, FAQs, and how to help," World Vision, April 3, 2018, https://www.worldvision.org/disaster-relief-news-stories/2015-nepal-earthquake-facts.

7. Amanda Holpuch, Norbert Figueroa, and Carmen Fishwick, "Puerto Rico battered by Hurricane Maria: 'Devastation—it's everywhere,'" *The Guardian*, September 21, 2017, https://www.theguardian.com/world/2017/sep/21/puerto-rico-hurricane-maria-storm-floods.

8. Patrick Kingsley, "'Better to Drown': A Greek Refugee Camp's Epidemic of Misery," *New York Times*, October. 2, 2018, https://www.nytimes.com/2018/10/02/world/europe/greece-lesbos-moria-refugees.html.

9. "Rohingya emergency," UNHCR, August 15, 2018, https://www.unhcr.org/rohingya-emergency.html; Kristine Kolstad, "Cox's Bazar: The world's largest refugee settlement." Norwegian Refugee Council (NRC), August 24, 2018, https://www.nrc.no/news/2018/august/coxs-bazar-the-worlds-largest-refugee-settlement/.

Introduction

1. David Brooks, "It's not about you," *New York Times*, May 30, 2011, https://www.nytimes.com/2011/05/31/opinion/31brooks.html.

2. Anita Powell, "Hunger spreads to Ethiopia's adults as food crisis worsens," *Associated Press*, June 10, 2008, http://archive.boston.com/news/world/africa/articles/2008/06/10/hunger_spreads_to_ethiopias_adults_as_food_crisis_worsens/; Kaye Milner, "Flashback 1984: Portrait of a famine," BBC, April 6, 2000, http://news.bbc.co.uk/2/hi/africa/703958.stm; Andy Jackson, "October 23, 1984: BBC report on Ethiopian famine sparks global fundraising campaign," BBC, October 17, 2018, https://home.bt.com/news/on-this-day/october-23-1984-bbc-report-on-ethiopian-famine-shakes-the-world-into-action-11364012387968. The famine that raged in Ethiopia during the early 1980s was estimated to have killed over one million people. Drought and the refugee crisis created by war and government policies were the main causes.

3. "2004 Indian Ocean Tsunami: A disaster that devastated 14 countries," CNN, December 26, 2014, https://www.cnn.com/2014/12/23/world/gallery/2004-indian-ocean-tsunami/index.html.

4. Information on Singarathopu provided to us from the Cooperative Baptist Fellowship.

5. Thomas A. Dooley, *The Night They Burned the Mountain* (New York: Farrar Straus & Giroux, 1960).

6. Albert Schweitzer, *Out of My Life and Thought: An Autobiography* (New York: The New American Library, 1964).

Chapter 1

1. "AIDS is a Menace to Democracy, Says Clinton," AllAfrica, February 12, 2003, https://allafrica.com/stories/200302120202.html.

2. "The Genocide," UNICTR, IRMCT, December 31, 2015, http://unictr.irmct.org/en/genocide.

3. John Iliffe. *A Modern History of Tanganyika (African Studies)* (Cambridge: Cambridge University Press, 1979).

4. Alan Wood. *The Groundnut Affair* (London: The Bodley Head, 1950).

5. "United Republic of Tanzania," WHO, Decem-

ber 2005, https://www.who.int/hiv/HIVCP_TZA.
pdf.

6. "AIDS Epidemic Update," WHO, December
2005, pp. 3, 4, 17 and 28), https://www.who.int/hiv/
epi-update2005_en.pdf?ua=1.

7. CHAI provided these data.

8. Geoffrey Popplewell, "The British Empire, In the
wake of the Germans, Tanganyika in the Inter-War
Years," Britishempire, https://www.britishempire.
co.uk/article/inthewakeofthegermans.htm.

9. João M. Cabrita, *Mozambique: A Tortuous Road
to Democracy* (New York: Macmillan, 2001).

10. Felix Chami, et al., Odunga, *Historical Archaeology of Bagamoyo Excavations at the Caravan Serai
(Dar es Salaam: Dar es Salaam University Press,
2000).*

11. Charles River Editors, *The Slave Trade in
Africa: The History and Legacy of the Transatlantic
Slave Trade and East African Slave Trade across the
Indian Ocean,* (CreateSpace Independent Publishing
Platform, *2017*).

12. Martin Dugard, *Into Africa: The Epic Adventures of Stanley and Livingstone* (New York: Doubleday, 2003).

13. "90–90–90 An ambitious treatment target
to help end the AIDS epidemic," UNAIDS, October 2014, http://www.unaids.org/sites/default/files/
media_asset/90-90-90_en.pdf.

14. "HIV and AIDS in Tanzania," Avert, February 2, 2019, https://www.avert.org/professionals/hiv-
around-world/sub-saharan-africa/tanzania.

15. Martin Dugard, *Into Africa: The Epic Adventures of Stanley and Livingstone* (New York: Doubleday, 2003).

Chapter 2

1. Ramola T. Badam, "Ralph Fiennes visits
India HIV patients," *Washington Post,* originally
appeared in *Associated Press*, January 31, 2007,
https://www.washingtonpost.com/wp-dyn/content/
article/2007/01/31/AR2007013100838.html.

2. Allan Ronald, Moses Kamya, Elly Katabira, et
al. "The Infectious Diseases Institute at Makerere
University at Kampala, Uganda." *Clinical Infectious
Diseases* 25; 2 (June, 2011):369–383, https://doi.
org/10.1016/j.idc.2011.02.007.

3. Information provided by IDI

4. Neil MacFarquhar, "8 Tourists Slain in
Uganda, Including U.S. Couple in Uganda," *New
York Times*, March 3, 1999, https://www.nytimes.
com/1999/03/03/world/8-tourists-slain-in-uganda-
including-us-couple.html.

5. "Mulago National Referral Hospital," Ministry
of Health, Republic of Uganda, accessed January 19,
2019, https://health.go.ug/content/mulago-national-
referral-hospital.

6. "Mildmay Uganda," Mildmay, accessed January
21, 2019, https://mildmay.org/our-overseas-work/
mildmay-uganda/.

7. Reach Out Mbuya, accessed January 21, 2019,
http://www.reachoutmbuya.org/.

8. The AIDS Support Organization (TASO),
accessed January 21, 2019, http://www.tasouganda.
org/.

9. Uganda Cares, accessed January 21, 2019,
https://www.aidshealth.org/global/uganda/.

10. *Ibid.*

11. "Africa's Orphaned and Vulnerable Generations, Children Affected by AIDS," UNICEF, June,
2006, p. 8, https://www.unicef.org/publications/files/
Africas_Orphaned_and_Vulnerable_Generations_
Children_Affected_by_AIDS.pdf.

12. "HIV and AIDS in Uganda," Avert,
accessed February 2, 2019, https://www.avert.org/
professionals/hiv-around-world/sub-saharan-africa/
uganda.

13. "Toward an AIDS-free Uganda: Scaling up 90–
90–90 targets," accessed February 2, 2019, https://static1.
squarespace.com/static/5a57ffe52aeba57afe10b243/t/5
ae7a29f8a922d40d2a8185b/1525129893034/ABH_
aids_free_uganda_br.pdf.

14. Peter Bridges, "A Prince of Climbers," *Virginia Quarterly Review* 76, no. 1 (2000). https://www.
vqronline.org/essay/prince-climbers.

Chapter 3

1. Chris Bohjalian, https://www.azquotes.com/
quote/1419099.

2. Maseno Mission Hospital, accessed January 21,
2019, http://web.archive.org/web/20120422041417/
masenomissions.org/hospital.htm.

3. Wangui Kanina, "Kenya's election seen as
badly flawed," *Reuters*, September 18, 2008, https://
uk.reuters.com/article/uk-kenya-election/kenyas-
election-seen-as-badly-flawed-idUKLI387861200
80918.

4. Mark Trans and agencies, "Kenya's leaders
agree power-sharing deal," *The Guardian,* February
28, 2008, https://www.theguardian.com/world/2008/
feb/28/kenya.

5. Maseno Mission Hospital.

6. Information provided by the Comprehensive
Care Center for HIV/AIDS.

7. Hermann Feldmeier, Jorg Heukelbach, Uade
Samuel Ugbomoiko, et al., "Tungiasis—A Neglected
Disease with Many Challenges for Global Public
Health." *PLoS Neglected Tropical Diseases.* 8 (10)
(October 3, 2014): e3133.

8. Loren Eiseley. *The Star Thrower* (New York:
Harvest Books, 1979), pp.169–184.

9. Dianne Smith. "Sophie's Choice—and Ours,"
HEART TO GOD: MISSION TO MASENO, December 1, 2008, http://heart-to-god.blogspot.com, permission granted by Sophie to reprint her poem,
January 28, 2005. Sadly, she died of AIDS in 2018.

10. Avert, "HIV and AIDS in Kenya," accessed February 4, 2019, https://www.avert.org/professionals/
hiv-around-world/sub-saharan-africa/kenya,

11. Briana Duggan, "Kenya's top court considers
case to legalize homosexuality," CNN, February 23,
2018, https://edition.cnn.com/2018/02/23/africa/
case-legalize-homosexuality-kenya/index.html.

12. Bertran Auvert, Dirk Taljaard, Emmanuel Lagarde, *et al.*, "Randomized, controlled intervention trial of male circumcision for reduction of HIV infection risk: The ANRS 1265 Trial," *PLoS Med.* 2(11): e298 (2005), https://doi.org/10.1371/journal.pmed.0020298; R. C. Bailey, S. Moses, C. B. Parker, *et al.* "Male circumcision for HIV prevention in young men in Kisumu, Kenya: a randomized controlled trial," *Lancet* 24;369(9562) (2007): 643–56.

13. Mike Mswati, "Sex tourism: 'Mzungu' women who travel to Kenya to get laid by local men," 2018, https://www.sde.co.ke/article/2001252790/sex-tourism-mzungu-women-who-travel-to-kenya-to-get-laid-by-local-men.

Chapter 4

1. Nelson Mandela, "Address by Nelson Mandela at 46664 Concert, Cape Town," 46664 Concert, Cape Town, South Africa, November 23, 2003, http://www.mandela.gov.za/mandela_speeches/2003/031129_46664.htm.

2. "Global Task Force on Cholera Control, Cholera Country Profile: Zimbabwe," WHO, October 31, 2009, https://www.who.int/cholera/countries/ZimbabweCountryProfileOct2009.pdf?ua=1.

3. "Cholera outbreak in South Africa: preliminary descriptive epidemiology on laboratory-confirmed cases, 15 November 2008 to April 2009." Communicable Diseases Surveillance Bulletin, 7:2 (May 2009): 3, 4, http://www.nicd.ac.za/assets/files/CommDisBullMay09_Vol0702.pdf.

4. "Land Reform in the Twenty Years After Independence in Zimbabwe," Human Rights Watch, 2002. https://www.hrw.org/reports/2002/zimbabwe/ZimLand0302-02.htm#TopOfPage.

5. Constitutional Hill Foundation, *Number 4: The Making of Constitution Hill* (South Africa: Penguin Global, 2006).

6. Noor Nieftagodien, *The Soweto Uprising (Ohio Short Histories of Africa)* (Ohio: Ohio University Press, 2014).

7. "King of Swaziland changes his country's name to eSwatini," Sky News, 2018, https://news.sky.com/story/king-of-swaziland-changes-his-countrys-name-to-eswatini-11338333.

8. "Global Health—Swaziland," CDC, 2015, accessed February 4, 2019, https://www.cdc.gov/globalhealth/countries/swaziland/.

9. "Eswatini at-a-glance," World Bank, 2018, accessed February 4, 2019, https://www.worldbank.org/en/country/eswatini.

10. "2008 Report on the global AIDS epidemic," UNAIDS, 2008, 214, 218, http://www.unaids.org/sites/default/files/media_asset/jc1510_2008globalreport_en_0.pdf.

11. Leigh Johnson and Rob E. Dorrington, "Modelling the impact of HIV in South Africa's provinces: 2017 update," September 2017, 34, 37, https://www.thembisa.org/content/filedl/Provinces2017.

12. "Republic of South Africa country progress report on the declaration of commitment on

HIV/AIDS 2010 report," UNAIDS, 2010, pp.10, 22–24, http://data.unaids.org/pub/report/2010/southafrica_2010_country_progress_report_en.pdf.

13. Sarah Boseley, "Mbeki Aids denial 'caused 300,000 deaths," *The Guardian*, November. 26, 2008, https://www.theguardian.com/world/2008/nov/26/aids-south-africa.

14. "SA's Zuma 'showered to avoid HIV,'" BBC, April 5, 2006, http://news.bbc.co.uk/2/hi/africa/4879822.stm.

15. Kerry Cullinan, "Health officials promote untested uBhejane," *South African Health News Service*, March 22, 2006, https://www.health-e.org.za/2006/03/22/health-officials-promote-untested-ubhejane/.

16. S. S. Abdool Karim, G. J. Churchyard, Q. A. Karim, *et al.*, "HIV infection and tuberculosis in South Africa: an urgent need to escalate the public health response, "*Lancet*, 374 (9693) (August 25, 2009): 921–933. https://doi:10.1016/S0140-6736(09)60916-8.

17. Nelson Mandela, "Confronting the Joint HIV/TB Epidemics," Presentation at XV International AIDS Conference, Bangkok, Thailand, July 15, 2004. https://www.who.int/3by5/news21/en/.

18. Data provided by the Fountain of Hope Clinic

19. Alex Ogle, "Zimbabwe cholera outbreak spreads to SA," *Mail & Guardian*, December 5, 2008, https://mg.co.za/article/2008-12-05-zimbabwe-cholera-outbreak-spreads-to-sa.

20. Janet Koech, "Hyperinflation in Zimbabwe," *Federal Reserve Bank of Dallas*- 2011 Annual Report, Globalization and Monetary Policy Institute, 2011, 4, https://www.dallasfed.org/~/media/documents/institute/annual/2011/annual11b.pdf.

21. Gerry Simpson and Joe Amon, "Neighbors in need: Zimbabweans seeking refuge in South Africa," Human Rights Watch, June 19, 2008, https://www.hrw.org/report/2008/06/19/neighbors-need/zimbabweans-seeking-refuge-south-africa.

22. Andrew Meldrum, "Zimbabwe's health-care system struggles on," *Lancet* 371:9618 (March 29, 2008):1059–1060, https://doi.org/10.1016/S0140-6736(08)60468-7.

23. Rhodri Davies, "Braving peril to reach South Africa," *Al Jazeera*, July 18, 2008, https://www.aljazeera.com/focus/2008/07/20087188353663376.html.

24. Lee Rondganger, "Musina at breaking point as refugees pour in," *IOL*, December 23, 2008, https://www.iol.co.za/news/politics/musina-at-breaking-point-as-refugees-pour-in-429590.

25. "South Africa: More Zimbabwean migrants expected in Musina," Reliefweb, April 30, 2009, https://reliefweb.int/report/south-africa/south-africa-more-zimbabwean-migrants-expected-musina.

26. *Ibid.*

27. "Forced closure of 'Refugee Reception Office' further endangers health of vulnerable Zimbabweans in South Africa," Médecins Sans Frontières, March 4, 2009, https://www.msf.org/forced-closure-refugee-reception-office-further-endangers-health-

vulnerable-zimbabweans-south; Refworld, "World Refugee Survey 2009—South Africa," accessed January 23, 2019, https://www.refworld.org/docid/4a40d2b22.html.

28. Barry Bearak and Celia W. Duggar, "South Africans Take Out Rage on Immigrants," *New York Times*, May 20, 2008, https://www.nytimes.com/2008/05/20/world/africa/20safrica.html.

29. Rudyard Kipling, *Just So Stories—Illustrated* (SMK Books, 2018): 32.

30. "HIV and AIDS in South Africa," Avert, accessed February 10, 2019, https://www.avert.org/professionals/hiv-around-world/sub-saharan-africa/south-africa.

31. "PrEP," CDC, accessed February 19, 2019, https://www.cdc.gov/hiv/basics/prep.html.

32. Médecins Sans Frontières (March 4, 2009)

33. Sumayya Ismail, "Ahmed Kathrada: The Robben Island diaries," *Al Jazeera*, March 28, 2017, https://www.aljazeera.com/indepth/features/2013/12/ahmed-kathrada-robben-island-diaries-201312883340753376.html.

34. Langston Hughes, *The Dream Keeper and Other Poems* (New York: Knopf Books for Young Readers; 1st edition, 1996), 3.

35. Jan Greshoff. *The Last Days of District Six* (South Africa, Cape Town: District Six Museum, 1996).

36. Noor Ebrahim. *Noor's Story: My Life in District Six* (South Africa, Cape Town: District Six Museum. 2nd Edition, 1999).

Chapter 5

1. Sola Ogundipe and Chioma Obinna, "HIV & AIDS: If you're not infected, you're affected," Vanguard, December 4, 2010, https://www.vanguardngr.com/2010/12/hiv-aids-if-youre-not-infected-youre-affected/.

2. "About Institute of Human Virology Nigeria (IHVN)," accessed February 19, 2019, http://www.ihvnigeria.org/index.php/about-ihvn/introduction.html.

3. "HIV/AIDS UNICEF Nigeria," June 2007, https://www.unicef.org/wcaro/english/WCARO_Nigeria_Factsheets_HIV-AIDS.pdf,

4. Awoyemi A. Awofala and Olusegun Emmanuel Ogundele, "HIV epidemiology in Nigeria," *Saudi J Biol Sci.* 25 (4) (May 9, 2018): 697–703, https://doi.org/10.1016/j.sjbs.2016.03.006.

5. Data provided by IHV-N

6. *Ibid.*

7. "HIV and AIDS in Nigeria," Avert, accessed February 6, 2019, https://www.avert.org/professionals/hiv-around-world/sub-saharan-africa/nigeria#footnote117_unw55a3.Avert.

8. *Ibid.*

9. Sophie Barton-Knott and Ibon Villelabeitia, "UNAIDS and the Global Fund express deep concern about the impact of a new law affecting the AIDS response and human rights of LGBT people in Nigeria," 2014 http://www.unaids.org/en/resources/presscentre/pressreleaseandstatementarchive/2014/january/20140114nigeria/.

10. "HIV and AIDS in Nigeria," Avert, accessed February 6, 2019.

11. "Profile: Boko Haram," describing the profile of the group called Boko Haram in Nigeria calling for Islamic law to be implemented throughout the country," Al Jazeera, December 31, 2010, https://www.aljazeera.com/news/africa/2010/12/2010123115425609851.html.

12. Sonia F. Graham, *Government and mission education in northern Nigeria, 1900–1919; with special reference to the work of Hanns Vischer* (Ibadan, Nigeria: Ibadan University press, 1966).

13. The Editors of Encyclopedia Britannica, "Kano, Historical Kingdom, Nigeria," accessed January 23, 2019, https://www.britannica.com/place/Kano-historical-kingdom-Nigeria#ref151151.

14. Kingsley Igwe, "Eight killed by Nigeria Independence day bombs," October 1, 2010, https://www.reuters.com/article/us-nigeria-eight-killed-by-nigeria-independence-day-bombs-idUSTRE6901Y320101001.

15. "Nigerian capital Abuja hit by barracks bomb," BBC, January 1, 2011, https://www.bbc.com/news/world-africa-12099176.

Chapter 6

1. Gabriel Byrne, "Gabriel Byrne Quotes," accessed March 1, 2014, https://www.azquotes.com/author/2292-Gabriel_Byrne.

2. Xan Rice, "Two aid workers kidnapped from Kenyan refugee camp," *The Guardian*, October 13, 2011, https://www.theguardian.com/world/2011/oct/13/aid-workers-kidnapped-kenyan-camp; "Spanish aid workers kidnapped in Kenya freed, "AL Jazeera, July 18, 2013, https://www.aljazeera.com/news/africa/2013/07/2013718184232912671.html.

3. Paul Theroux, *The Lower River* (New York: Mariner Books, 2012).

4. Paul Theroux, *Dark Star Safari: Overland from Cairo to Capetown* (New York: Houghton Mifflin, 2003): 331.

5. Sanya Khetani. "This landlocked African state's dreams of an inland port are turning into a $6 billion debacle," May 12, 2012, https://www.businessinsider.com/malawi-nsanje-port-2012-5.

6. "Comprehensive Analytical Profile: Malawi,," accessed January 24, 2019, http://www.aho.afro.who.int/profiles_information/index.php/Malawi:Index.

7. *Ibid.*

8. Daniel Chris Khomba and Alex Trew, "Aid and growth in Malawi," accessed February 1, 2019: 6, 7, https://www.st-andrews.ac.uk/~wwwecon/repecfiles/4/1612.pdf.

9. "Malawi Life Expectancy," 2018, https://www.worldlifeexpectancy.com/malawi-life-expectancy.

10. Owen Nyaka, "Malawi faces shortage of healthcare workers as it battles AIDS epidemic," January 21, 2014, http://www.aidspan.org/gfo_

article/malawi-faces-shortage-healthcare-workers-it-battles-aids-epidemic.

11. "Malawi Demographic and Health Survey 2010." September 2011: 166, 196–199, https://dhsprogram.com/pubs/pdf/FR247/FR247.pdf.

12. "Malawi National HIV and AIDS Strategic Plan 2011–2016." December 21, 2011: 13, http://www.nationalplanningcycles.org/sites/default/files/country_docs/Malawi/malawi_national_hiv_and_aids_plan_2011-2016.pdf.

13. *Ibid.* (p.13).

14. "HIV and AIDS in Malawi," accessed February 7, 2019, https://www.avert.org/professionals/hiv-around-world/sub-saharan-africa/malawi.

15. "Malawi: Constitution no longer allows child marriage," April 26, 2017, https://www.girlsnotbrides.org/malawi-constitution-no-longer-allows-child-marriage/.

16. "HIV and AIDS in Malawi," accessed February 7, 2019.

17. Information supplied by MSF.

18. Emmanuel Muwamba, "Food insecurity to rise in Malawi," July 31, 2013, https://mwnation.com/food-insecurity-to-rise-in-malawi/.

19. "Kenya's MPs ordered to pay higher taxes." June 21, 2011, https://www.bbc.com/news/world-africa-13857480.

20. João M. Cabrita, *Mozambique: A Tortuous Road to Democracy* (New York: Macmillan, 2001).

21. Andrew Hankey and Marc Stern, "Vachellia xanthophloea (Benth.) P.J.H.Hurter," March 2002, http://pza.sanbi.org/vachellia-xanthophloea.

22. Rudyard Kipling, *Just So Stories—Illustrated* (SMK Books, 2018): 32.

23. "Guidelines on when to start antiretroviral therapy and pre-exposure prophylaxis for HIV," WHO, September 2015: 3–34, https://apps.who.int/iris/bitstream/handle/10665/186275/9789241509565_eng.pdf;jsessionid=11DF1DFC06EC38B571679C9F40871236?seq.

24. Information provided by MSF.

25. "HIV and AIDS in Malawi," Avert, December 10, 2018.

26. Gertrude Aopesyaga Kapuma. "Widowhood: a story of pain, a need for healing," 2011, 3, http://academic.sun.ac.za/teologie/netact/genderequality2011/new/Ch5-Widowhood%20story%20of%20pain%20and%20healing-Kapuma.pdf.

27. Philo Lomba, "Widow Cleansing in Malawi," *American International Journal of Contemporary Research* 4, no. 1 (January 2014): 34–40.

28. Mary Kimani, "Women struggle to secure land rights," 2012, https://www.un.org/africarenewal/magazine/special-edition-women-2012/women-struggle-secure-land-rights.

29. "Malawi cash-gate: The truth is on holiday!" November 27, 2013, https://www.nyasatimes.com/malawi-cash-gate-the-truth-is-on-holiday/; Z. Allan Ntata, "License to loot, A report on the Cashgate corruption scandal in Malawi," November 2013, https://www.whatdotheyknow.com/request/202520/response/524932/attach/html/5/MALAWI%20CASHGATE%20SCANDAL%20REPORT.pdf.html.

30. Archibald Kasakura, "Bingu's wealth under probe," March 11, 2017, https://mwnation.com/bingus-wealth-under-probe/.

31. Dumbani Mzale, "Cashgate darkened the economy in 2013," December 16, 2013, https://mwnation.com/cashgate-darkened-the-economy-in-2013/.

32. "Insufficient Funding Suffocates Green Belt Initiative." CISANET (Civil Society Agriculture Network, accessed February 7, 2019, http://www.cisanetmw.org/index.php/45-insufficient-funding-suffocates-green-belt-initiative.

33. "Health budget below recommended targets." March 5, 2013, https://mwnation.com/health-budget-below-recommended-targets/.

34. "Kapito claims Malawi Pres. Banda has created hunger: 'She emptied maize silos,'" March 8, 2013, http://www.nyasatimes.com/kapito-claims-malawi-pres-banda-has-created-hunger-she-emptied-maize-silos/.

35. Todd Statham, *Dictionary of African Christian Biography*, "Scott, David Clement," 2014, https://dacb.org/stories/malawi/scott-davidc/.

36. Wilfrid Robertson, *Mandala trail: A tale of early days in Nyasaland* (Oxford University Press, 1956).

37. The Mandala House, accessed March 27, 2019, https://societyofmalawi.org/the-mandala-house/

Chapter 7

1. Rodney Muhumuza, "Hutu refugees fear forced return to Rwanda," *Omaha World-Herald*, April 19, 2013, https://www.omaha.com/news/hutu-refugees-fear-forced-return-to-rwanda/article_1a2b6775-98fe-5927-88f3-cea2ce081e8f.html.

2. "Uganda Refugee Response Monitoring Settlement Fact Sheet: Nakivale (June 2018)," June 3. 30, 2018, https://reliefweb.int/report/uganda/uganda-refugee-response-monitoring-settlement-fact-sheet-nakivale-june-2018.

3. Information provided by Medical Teams International.

4. "Horn of Africa sees 'worst drought in 60 years.'" BBC, June 28, 2011, https://www.bbc.com/news/world-africa-13944550.

5. Sarah Steffen, "Crisis in Burundi—a timeline," December 5, 2015, https://www.dw.com/en/crisis-in-burundi-a-timeline/a-18446677.

6. "Uganda Refugee Response Monitoring Settlement Fact Sheet: Nakivale (June 2018)." (June 30, 2018).

7. "Arab uprising: Country by country—Libya," December 16, 2013, https://www.bbc.com/news/world-12482311.

8. Uganda's Punishment Island: 'I was left to die on an island for getting pregnant.'" April 27, 2017, https://www.bbc.com/news/world-africa-39576510.

9. Leonard E. S. Sharp, *Island of miracles ~ the story of the Lake Bunyoni leprosy settlement, Uganda* (Rwanda: Ruanda General and Medical Mission, C.M.S, 1951).

10. Dian Fossey, *Gorillas in the Mist* (New York: Mariner Books, 2000).

11. Harold T. P. Hayes, *The Dark Romance of Dian Fossey* (New York: Simon & Schuster, 1990).

12. Susan Thomson, *Rwanda: From Genocide to Precarious Peace* (New Haven: Yale University Press, 2018).

13. Gloria Lotha, *Martyrs of Uganda,* March 10, 2016, https://www.britannica.com/event/Martyrs-of-Uganda.

Chapter 8

1. Michael Tomasky, "Gaddafi's letter to Obama," May 19, 2011, https://www.theguardian.com/commentisfree/michaeltomasky/2011/mar/19/barack-obama-muammar-gaddafi-answer-the-letter.

2. Mark L. Haas and David W. Lesch, *The Arab Spring: The Hope and Reality of the Uprisings* (New York: Westview Press, 2016).

3. "Libya fighting rages in 'final push' on Sirte." October 8, 2011, https://www.aljazeera.com/news/africa/2011/10/201110783935223881.html; "Libya conflict: Pro-Gaddafi troops 'cornered' in Sirte," October 10, 2011, https://www.bbc.com/news/world-africa-15242235.

4. "Libyan forces 'capture Gaddafi," October 20, 2011, https://www.bbc.com/news/world-middle-east-15385955.

5. Zaineb Abdessadok, "Libya Today: From Arab Spring to failed state," *Al Jazeera,* May 30, 2017, https://www.aljazeera.com/indepth/features/2017/04/happening-libya-today-170418083223563.html; Shafik Mandhai, "Libya six years on: No regrets over Gaddafi's demise," *Al Jazeera,* Oct 20, 2017, https://www.aljazeera.com/news/2017/10/years-regrets-libya-gaddafi-demise-171019073901622.html.

Chapter 9

1. Anne Mawathe, "Horn of Africa drought: Survival of the fittest," July 9, 2011, https://www.bbc.com/news/world-africa-14084670.

2. "Horn of Africa sees 'worst drought in 60 years,'" BBC, June 28, 2011, https://www.bbc.com/news/world-africa-13944550.

3. "UN declares Somalia famine in Bakool and Lower Shabelle," July 20, 2011, https://www.bbc.com/news/world-africa-14211905.

4. "Horn of Africa • Drought Crisis, Updates & Developments," Office for the Coordination of Humanitarian Affairs (OCHA), August 9, 2011, https://reliefweb.int/sites/reliefweb.int/files/resources/HoA_Updates%20and%20Developments_09%20Aug%202011.pdf; Somalia• Famine & Drought, Situation Report No. 8," OCHA, August 10, 2011, https://reliefweb.int/sites/reliefweb.int/files/resources/OCHA%20Somalia%20Situation%20Report%20No.%208%2010%20August%202011.pdf.

5. Osman Dar and Mishal Khan, "The Dadaab camps—Mitigating the effects of drought in the Horn (perspective)," *PLoS Curr.* 15, 3 (2011), https//doi: 10.1371/currents.RRN1289 (2011).

6. Andrew Meldrum, "Kenya: Lamu island hit by new kidnapping," October 1, 2011, https://www.pri.org/stories/2011-10-01/kenya-lamu-island-hit-new-kidnapping.

7. Xan Rice, "Two aid workers kidnapped from Kenyan refugee camp," *The Guardian* (2011), https://www.theguardian.com/world/2011/oct/13/aid-workers-kidnapped-kenyan-camp.

8. UNHCR, "Acute malnutrition threshold," accessed February 7, 2019, https://emergency.unhcr.org/entry/249075/acute-malnutrition-threshold.

9. Debbie Hillier, *A Dangerous Delay: The cost of late response to early warnings in the 2011 drought in the Horn of Africa* (Oxford: Oxfam GB, Oxfam House, 2012): 13.

10. Simon Tisdall, "East Africa's drought: the avoidable disaster," *The Guardian,* January 17, 2012, https://www.theguardian.com/world/2012/jan/18/east-africa-drought-disaster-report.

11. "U.S.: 29,000 Somali kids have died in the last 90 days." August 8, 2011, https://www.cbsnews.com/news/us-29000-somali-kids-have-died-in-last-90-days/.

12. "Somalia famine 'killed 260,000 people.'" May 2, 2013, https://www.bbc.com/news/world-africa-22380352.

Chapter 10

1. Oxfam International, ""I miss my husband"—DRC refugees seek safety in Uganda," Conflict and Emergencies blog channel, September 3, 2012, https://blogs.oxfam.org/en/blogs/12-09-03-drc-refugees-seek-safety-uganda.

2. "Q&A: DR Congo's M23 rebels," November 5, 2013, https://www.bbc.com/news/world-africa-20438531.

3. Catherine Ntabadde, "Uganda Red Cross to manage Congolese refugees camp in Kisoro," July 16, 2012, https://reliefweb.int/report/uganda/uganda-red-cross-manage-congolese-refugees-camp-kisoro.

4. UN Peacemaker, "Peace Agreement between the Government and the CNDP," March 23, 2009, https://peacemaker.un.org/sites/peacemaker.un.org/files/CD_090323_Peace%20Agreement%20between%20the%20Government%20and%20the%20CNDP.pdf.

5. "Q&A: DR Congo's M23 rebels," BBC (November 5, 2013).

6. Situation Report provided by MTI for the Nyakabande Transit Center (July 9, 2012).

7. *Ibid.*

8. *Ibid.*

9. Edouard Kayihura and Kerry Zukus, *Inside the Hotel Rwanda: The Surprising True Story ... and Why It Matters Today* (Dallas: BenBella Books; First Edition, 2014).

10. Hilary Heuler, "African Summit Fails to Agree on DRC Force Details," August 8, 2012, https://www.voanews.com/a/1476390.html.

11. UNHCR Uganda, UN Uganda Bulletin Vol 25 (March 23, 2018) http://ug.one.un.org/sites/default/files/newsletters/UN%20Uganda%20Bulletin%20Vol%2025%20%2023%20March%202018.pdf.

12. "RapidFTR (Family tracing and reunification)," UNICEF, May 20, 2014, http://unicefstories.org/2014/05/20/rapidftr-2/.

Chapter 11

1. Lul Gatkuoth Gatluak, "Tribalism in South Sudan is an infectious deadly disease that charred and burns the nation to ashes," November 21, 2018, https://www.nyamile.com/2018/11/21/tribalism-in-south-sudan-is-an-infectious-deadly-disease-that-charred-and-burns-the-nation-to-ashes/.

2. South Sudan Quotes, accessed December, 21, 2016, Duop Chak Wuol left Sudan for Ethiopia as a refugee before coming to the U.S. He is a graduate of the University of Colorado, https://www.goodreads.com/quotes/tag/south-sudan.

3. Jan Grevendonk, Anuph Akkihal, and Morris Gargar. "Optimize South Sudan Report." Accessed February 7, 2019, 1, https://www.who.int/immunization/programmes_systems/supply_chain/optimize/south_sudan_optimize_report.pdf?ua=1.

4. "The Comprehensive Peace Agreement between the government of the Republic of South Sudan and the Sudan's People Liberation Movement/Sudan People's Liberation Army," accessed January 27, 2019, https://peacemaker.un.org/sites/peacemaker.un.org/files/SD_060000_The%20Comprehensive%20Peace%20Agreement.pdf; "Sudan peace agreement signed 9 January historic opportunity, Security Council told," February 8, 2005, https://www.un.org/press/en/2005/sc8306.doc.htm; Gladys Njorge, and Tumi Makgabo,"Historic Sudan peace accord signed," January 9, 2005, http://www.cnn.com/2005/WORLD/africa/01/09/sudan.signing/.

5. "South Sudan's flag raised at independence ceremony," July 9, 2011, https://www.bbc.com/news/world-africa-14092375.

6. "World Report 2013: South Sudan." 2013. Accessed January 27, 2019 https://www.hrw.org/world-report/2013/country-chapters/south-sudan#; "Situation overview," OCHA. *Humanitarian Bulletin South Sudan,* April 1–7, 2013, https://reliefweb.int/sites/reliefweb.int/files/resources/OCHA%20South%20Sudan%20Weekly%20Humanitarian%20Bulletin%201-7%20April%202013.pdf.

7. John Eligon and Michael Cooper, "Blasts at Boston Marathon Kill 3 and Injure 100," *New York Times,* April 15, 2013, https://www.nytimes.com/2013/04/16/us/explosions-reported-at-site-of-boston-marathon.htm.

8. History.com Editors, "Boston Marathon Bombing," accessed January 28, 2019, https://www.history.com/topics/21st-century/boston-marathon-bombings.

9. "Repositioning primary health care in South Sudan: Transitioning From NGO-Managed to MOH-Directed Primary Health Care Service Delivery," accessed January 28, 2019, https://imaworldhealth.org/wp-content/uploads/2016/07/Repositioning-Primary-Health-Care-in-South-Sudan.pdf.

10. "Village Assessment Survey 2013 County Atlas," accessed January 27, 2019, 1, 10, https://iomsouthsudan.org/tracking/sites/default/publicfiles/documents/Unity_Koch_Atlas.pdf.

11. Central Intelligence Agency, "The World Factbook," accessed January 29, 2019, https://www.cia.gov/library/publications/the-world-factbook/geos/od.html.

12. "Situation overview," OCHA, *Humanitarian Bulletin South Sudan* (April 1–7, 2013).

13. Richard Downie, "The state of public health in South Sudan," CSIS, November 2012: 2, 3, 8, https://csis-prod.s3.amazonaws.com/s3fs-public/legacy_files/files/publication/121114_Downie_HealthSudan_Web.pdf.

14. "Situation overview," OCHA, Humanitarian Bulletin South Sudan (April 1–7, 2013).

15. Roba Gibia, *John Garang: And the Vision of New Sudan.* (Toronto: Key Publishing House Inc., 2008).

16. "UNHCR position on returns to South Sudan," accessed February 9, 2019, https://www.refworld.org/pdfid/52fa1ecd4.pdf.

17. "South Sudan, A new depth of horror." *Economist,* April 26, 2014, https://www.economist.com/middle-east-and-africa/2014/04/26/a-new-depth-of-horror.

18. F. Checchi, A. Testa, A. Warsame, L. Quach, et al., "Estimates of crisis-attributable mortality in South Sudan, December 2013–April 2018: A statistical analysis," accessed February 9, 2019, https://crises.lshtm.ac.uk/2018/09/26/south-sudan-2/.

19. "South Sudan 2018 Humanitarian Needs Overview." Accessed February 9, 2019, 7, https://reliefweb.int/sites/reliefweb.int/files/resources/South_Sudan_2018_Humanitarian_Needs_Overview.pdf.

20. "South Sudan's rival leaders sign power-sharing agreement." August 5, 2018, https://www.aljazeera.com/news/2018/08/south-sudan-rival-leaders-sign-power-sharing-agreement-180805172347086.html; "South Sudan country profile." August 6, 2018, https://www.bbc.com/news/world-africa-14069082.

Afterword

1. Melissa Ludtke, "Exits and Entrances: Women's Careers in Transition," *Wellesley Magazine,* April 1, 2013, 19–24, https://repository.wellesley.edu/wellesleymagazine/2/.

2. Kwan Kew Lai, "Letters to the Editor: Courage in transition," *Wellesley Magazine,* October 1, 2013, 76, https://repository.wellesley.edu/cgi/viewcontent.cgi?article=1004&context=wellesleymagazine.

Bibliography

Abdessadok, Zaineb. "Libya Today: From Arab Spring to failed state." *Al Jazeera.* May 30, 2017. Accessed February 24, 2019. https://www.aljazeera.com/indepth/features/2017/04/happening-libya-today-170418083223563.html.

Abdool Karim Salim. S., G. J. Churchyard, Q. A. Karim, S. D. Lawn. "HIV infection and tuberculosis in South Africa: an urgent need to escalate the public health response. "*Lancet,* 374 (9693) (August 25, 2009): 921–933. https://doi.org/10.1016/S0140-6736(09)60916-8. Accessed January 22, 2019.

The AIDS Support Organization (TASO). Accessed January 21, 2019. http://www.tasouganda.org/.

Al Jazeera. "Libya fighting rages in 'final push' on Sirte." October 8, 2011. Accessed January 25, 2019. https://www.aljazeera.com/news/africa/2011/10/201110783935223881.html.

Al Jazeera. "Profile: Boko Haram." December 31, 2010. https://www.aljazeera.com/news/africa/2010/12/2010123115425609851.html.

Al Jazeera. "South Sudan's rival leaders sign power-sharing agreement." August 5, 2018. Accessed January 23, 2019. https://www.aljazeera.com/news/2018/08/south-sudan-rival-leaders-sign-power-sharing-agreement-180805172347086.html.

Al Jazeera. "Spanish aid workers kidnapped in Kenya freed." July 18, 2013. Accessed January 25, 2019. https://www.aljazeera.com/news/africa/2013/07/2013718184232912671.html.

AllAfrica. "AIDS is a Menace to Democracy, Says Clinton." February 12, 2003. Accessed January 19, 2019. https://allafrica.com/stories/200302120202.html.

Auvert, Bertrand, Dirk Taljaard, Emmanuel Lagarde, Joëlle Sobngwi-Tambekou, Rémi Sitta, and Adrian Puren. "Randomized, controlled intervention trial of male circumcision for reduction of HIV infection risk: The ANRS 1265 Trial." *PLoS Med.* 2(11): e298 (2005). https://doi.org/10.1371/journal.pmed.0020298. Accessed February 7, 2019.

Avert. "HIV and AIDS in Kenya." May 21, 2018. Last updated December 10, 2018. Accessed February 4, 2019. https://www.avert.org/professionals/hiv-around-world/sub-saharan-africa/kenya.

Avert. "HIV and AIDS in Malawi." April 23, 2018. Updated December 10, 2018. Accessed February 7, 2019. https://www.avert.org/professionals/hiv-around-world/sub-saharan-africa/malawi.

Avert. "HIV and AIDS in Nigeria." May 25, 2018. Last updated December 10, 2018. Accessed February 6, 2019. https://www.avert.org/professionals/hiv-around-world/sub-saharan-africa/nigeria#footnote117_unw55a3.

Avert. "HIV and AIDS in South Africa." January 3, 2018. Last updated January 18, 2019. Accessed February 10, 2019. https://www.avert.org/professionals/hiv-around-world/sub-saharan-africa/south-africa.

Avert. "HIV and AIDS in Tanzania." June 20, 2018. Last updated January 8, 2019. Accessed February 2, 2019. https://www.avert.org/professionals/hiv-around-world/sub-saharan-africa/tanzania.

Avert. "HIV and AIDS in Uganda." January 24, 2018. Last updated January 2, 2019. Accessed February 2, 2019. https://www.avert.org/professionals/hiv-around-world/sub-saharan-africa/uganda.

Awofala, Awoyemi A., and Olusegun Emmanuel Ogundele. (2016) "HIV epidemiology in Nigeria." *Saudi J Biol Sci.* 25 (4) (May 9, 2018): 697–703. https://doi.org/10.1016/j.sjbs.2016.03.006. Accessed January 23, 2019.

Badam, Ramola T. "Ralph Fiennes visits India HIV patients." *Washington Post,* originally appeared in Associated Press, January 31, 2007. Accessed January 20, 2019. http://www.washingtonpost.com/wp-dyn/content/article/2007/01/31/AR2007013100838.html.

Bailey, R. C., S. Moses, C. B. Parker, K. Agot, I. Maclean, J. N. Krieger, C. F. Williams, R. T.

Barton-Knott, Sophie and Ibon Villelabeitia. "UNAIDS and the Global Fund express deep concern about the impact of a new law affecting the AIDS response and human rights of LGBT people in Nigeria." UNAIDS. 2014. Accessed February 6, 2019. http://www.unaids.org/en/resources/presscentre/pressreleaseandstatementarchive/2014/january/20140114nigeria/.

BBC. "Arab uprising: Country by country—Libya." December 16, 2013. Accessed January 24, 2019. https://www.bbc.com/news/world-12482311.

BBC. "Horn of Africa sees 'worst drought in 60 years.'" June 28, 2011. Accessed January 24, 2019. https://www.bbc.com/news/world-africa-13944550.

BBC. "Kenya's MPs ordered to pay higher taxes." June 21, 2011. Accessed January 24, 2019. https://www.bbc.com/news/world-africa-13857480.

BBC. "Libya conflict: Pro-Gaddafi troops 'cornered' in Sirte." October 10, 2011. Accessed January 25, 2019. https://www.bbc.com/news/world-africa-15242235.

BBC. "Libyan forces 'capture Gaddafi.'" October 20, 2011. Accessed January 25, 2019. https://www.bbc.com/news/world-middle-east-15385955.

BBC. "Nigerian capital Abuja hit by barracks bomb." January 1, 2011. Accessed January 23, 2019. https://www.bbc.com/news/world-africa-12099176.

BBC. "Q&A: DR Congo's M23 rebels." November 5, 2013. Accessed January 25, 2019. https://www.bbc.com/news/world-africa-20438531.

BBC. "SA's Zuma 'showered to avoid HIV.'" April 5, 2006. Accessed January 22, 2019. http://news.bbc.co.uk/2/hi/africa/4879822.stm.

BBC. "Somalia famine 'killed 260,000 people.'" May 2, 2013. February 1, 2019. https://www.bbc.com/news/world-africa-22380352.

BBC. "South Sudan country profile." August 6, 2018. Accessed February 9, 2019. https://www.bbc.com/news/world-africa-14069082.

BBC. "South Sudan's flag raised at independence ceremony." July 9, 2011. Accessed January 27, 2019. https://www.bbc.com/news/world-africa-14092375.

BBC. "Uganda's Punishment Island: 'I was left to die on an island for getting pregnant.'" April 27, 2017. Accessed January 24, 2019. https://www.bbc.com/news/world-africa-39576510.

BBC. "UN declares Somalia famine in Bakool and Lower Shabelle." July 20, 2011. Accessed February 17, 2019. https://www.bbc.com/news/world-africa-14211905.

Bearak, Barry, and Celia W. Duggar. "South Africans Take Out Rage on Immigrants." *New York Times,* May 20, 2008. Accessed January 23, 2019. https://www.nytimes.com/2008/05/20/world/africa/20safrica.html.

Boseley, Sarah. "Mbeki Aids denial 'caused 300,000 deaths." *The Guardian,* November 26, 2008. Accessed January 22, 2019. https://www.theguardian.com/world/2008/nov/26/aids-south-africa.

Bridges, Peter. "A Prince of Climbers." *Virginia Quarterly Review* 76, no. 1 (2000). Accessed January 21, 2019. https://www.vqronline.org/essay/prince-climbers.

Brooks, David. "It's not about you." *New York Times,* May 30, 2011. Accessed January 13, 2019. https://www.nytimes.com/2011/05/31/opinion/31brooks.html.

Byrne, Gabriel. "Gabriel Byrne Quotes." Accessed March 1, 2014. https://www.azquotes.com/author/2292-Gabriel_Byrne.

Cabrita, João M. *Mozambique: A Tortuous Road to Democracy,* New York: Macmillan, 2001.

Campbell, J. O. Ndinya-Achola. "Male circumcision for HIV prevention in young men in Kisumu, Kenya: A randomized controlled trial." *Lancet* 24;369(9562) (February 4, 2007): 643–656. Accessed February 7, 2019.

CBS. "US: 29,000 Somali kids have died in the last 90 days." cbsnews.com. August 8, 2011. Accessed February 7, 2019. https://www.cbsnews.com/news/us-29000-somali-kids-have-died-in-last-90-days/.

Centers for Disease Control and Prevention. "Global Health—Swaziland." 2015. Accessed February 4, 2019. https://www.cdc.gov/globalhealth/countries/swaziland/.

Centers for Disease Control and Prevention. "PrEP." Accessed February 10, 2019. https://www.cdc.gov/hiv/basics/prep.html.

Centers for Disease Control and Prevention. "2014–2016 Ebola Outbreak in West Africa." December 17, 2017. Accessed February 1, 2019. https://www.cdc.gov/vhf/ebola/history/2014-2016-outbreak/index.html.

Central Intelligence Agency. "The World Factbook." 2019. Accessed January 29, 2019. https://www.cia.gov/library/publications/the-world-factbook/geos/od.html.

Chami, Felix, Eliwasa Mato, Jane Kessy and Simon Odunga. *Historical Archaeology of Bagamoyo: Excavations at the Caravan Serai.* Dar es Salaam: Dar es Salaam University Press, 2000.

Charles River Editors. *The Slave Trade in Africa: The History and Legacy of the Transatlantic Slave Trade and East African Slave Trade Across the Indian Ocean.* CreateSpace Independent Publishing Platform, 2017.

Charles River Editors. *The 2004 Indian Ocean Earthquake and Tsunami: The Story of the Deadliest Natural Disaster of the 21st Century.* CreateSpace Independent Publishing Platform, 2014.

Checchi, F., A. Testa, A. Warsame, L. Quach, and R. Burns. "Estimates of crisis-attributable mortality in South Sudan, December 2013- April 2018: A statistical analysis." Health in Humanitarian Crises Centre. September 26, 2018. Accessed February 9, 2019. https://crises.lshtm.ac.uk/2018/09/26/south-sudan-2/.

CNN. "2004 Indian Ocean Tsunami: A disaster that devastated 14 countries." December 26, 2014. Accessed January 19, 2019. https://www.cnn.com/2014/12/23/world/gallery/2004-indian-ocean-tsunami/index.html.

"Comprehensive Analytical Profile: Malawi." African Health Observatory. 2018. Accessed January 24, 2019. http://www.aho.afro.who.int/profiles_information/index.php/Malawi:Index.

Constitutional Hill Foundation. *Number 4: The Making of Constitution Hill.* South Africa: Penguin Global, 2006.

Cullinan, Kerry. "Health officials promote untested uBhejane." The South African Health News Service, March 22, 2006. Accessed January 22, 2019. https://www.health-e.org.za/2006/03/22/health-officials-promote-untested-ubhejane/.

Dar, Osman and Mishal Khan. "The Dadaab camps—Mitigating the effects of drought in the Horn (perspective)." *PLoS Curr.* 15, 3 (2011). https://doi.org/10.1371/currents.RRN1289.

Davies, Rhodri. "Braving peril to reach South Africa." Al Jazeera, July 18, 2008. Accessed January 22, 2019. https://www.aljazeera.com/focus/2008/07/20087188353663376.html.

Direct Relief. "Indian Ocean Earthquake & Tsunami, 2004." Accessed February 1, 2019. https://www.directrelief.org/emergency/south-asian-earthquake-and-tsunami-2004/.

Dooley, Thomas A. *The Night They Burned the Mountain*. New York: Farrar Straus & Giroux, 1960.

Downie, Richard. "The state of public health in South Sudan." Center for Strategic and International Study (CSIS). November 2012. Accessed January 28, 2019. https://csis-prod.s3.amazonaws.com/s3fs-public/legacy_files/files/publication/121114_Downie_HealthSudan_Web.pdf.

Dugard, Martin. *Into Africa: The Epic Adventures of Stanley and Livingstone*, New York: Doubleday, 2003.

Duggan, Briana. "Kenya's top court considers case to legalize homosexuality." CNN. February 23, 2018. Accessed February 4, 2019. https://edition.cnn.com/2018/02/23/africa/case-legalize-homosexuality-kenya/index.html.

Ebrahim, Noor. *Noor's Story: My Life in District Six*. South Africa, Cape Town: District Six Museum. 2nd Edition, 1999.

The Editors of Encyclopedia Britannica. "Kano, Historical Kingdom, Nigeria." britannica.com. July 20,1998. Accessed January 23, 2019. https://www.britannica.com/place/Kano-historical-kingdom-Nigeria#ref151151.

Eiseley, Loren. *The Star Thrower*. New York: Harvest Books, 1979.

Eligon, John, and Michael Cooper. "Blasts at Boston Marathon Kill 3 and Injure 100." *New York Times*, April 15, 2013. Accessed January 28, 2019. https://www.nytimes.com/2013/04/16/us/explosions-reported-at-site-of-boston-marathon.htm.

Feldmeier, Hermann, Jorg Heukelbach, Uade Samuel Ugbomoiko, Elizabeth Sentongo, Pamela Mbabazi, Georg von Samson-Himmelstjerna, Ingela Krantz, The International Expert Group for Tungiasis. "Tungiasis—A Neglected Disease with Many Challenges for Global Public Health." *PLoS Neglected Tropical Diseases*. 8 (10) (October 3, 2014): e3133. https://doi.org/10.1371/journal.pntd.0003133.

Fossey, Dian. *Gorillas in the Mist*. New York: Mariner Books, 2000.

Gatluak, Lul Gatkuoth. "Tribalism in South Sudan is an infectious deadly disease that charred and burns the nation to ashes." Nyamilepedia. November 21, 2018. Accessed February 2, 2019. https://www.nyamile.com/2018/11/21/tribalism-in-south-sudan-is-an-infectious-deadly-disease-that-charred-and-burns-the-nation-to-ashes/.

Gibia, Roba. *John Garang: And the Vision of New Sudan*. Toronto: Key Publishing House Inc., 2008.

Graham, Sonia F. *Government and mission education in northern Nigeria, 1900–1919; with special reference to the work of Hanns Vischer*. Ibadan, Nigeria: Ibadan University press, 1966.

Greshoff, Jan. *The Last Days of District Six*. South Africa, Cape Town: District Six Museum, 1996.

Grevendonk, Jan, Anuph Akkihal, and Morris Gargar. "Optimize South Sudan Report." WHO. September 2013. Accessed February 7, 2019. https://www.who.int/immunization/programmes_systems/supply_chain/optimize/south_sudan_optimize_report.pdf?ua=1.

Haas, Mark L., and David W. Lesch. *The Arab Spring: The Hope and Reality of the Uprisings*. New York: Westview Press, 2016.

Hankey, Andrew, and Marc Stern. "Vachellia xanthophloea (Benth.) P.J.H.Hurter." March 2002. Accessed February 6, 2019. http://pza.sanbi.org/vachellia-xanthophloea.

Hayes, Harold T. P. *The Dark Romance of Dian Fossey*. New York: Simon & Schuster, 1990.

Heuler, Hilary. "African Summit Fails to Agree on DRC Force Details." Voice of America. August 8, 2012. Accessed January 25, 2019. https://www.voanews.com/a/1476390.html.

Hillier, Debbie. *A Dangerous Delay: The Cost of Late Response to Early Warnings in the 2011 Drought in the Horn of Africa*. Oxford: Oxfam GB, Oxfam House, 2012.

History.com Editors. "Boston Marathon Bombing." March 28, 2014. Last updated August 21, 2018. Accessed January 28, 2019. https://www.history.com/topics/21st-century/boston-marathon-bombings.

Holpuch, Amanda, Norbert Figueroa, and Carmen Fishwick. "Puerto Rico battered by Hurricane Maria: 'Devastation—it's everywhere.'" *The Guardian,* September 21, 2017. Accessed February 1, 2019. https://www.theguardian.com/world/2017/sep/21/puerto-rico-hurricane-maria-storm-floods.

Hughes, Langston. *The Dream Keeper and Other Poems*. New York: Knopf Books for Young Readers; 1st edition, 1996.

Human Rights Watch. "Land Reform in the Twenty Years After Independence in Zimbabwe." 2002. Accessed January 22, 2019. https://www.hrw.org/reports/2002/zimbabwe/ZimLand0302-02.htm#TopOfPage.

Human Rights Watch. "World Report 2013: South Sudan." 2013. Accessed January 27, 2019. https://www.hrw.org/world-report/2013/country-chapters/south-sudan#.

Igwe, Kingsley. "Eight killed by Nigeria Independence day bombs." Reuters. October 1, 2010. Accessed January 23, 2019. https://www.reuters.com/article/us-nigeria/eight-killed-by-nigeria-independence-day-bombs-idUSTRE6901Y320101001.

Iliffe, John. *A Modern History of Tanganyika (African Studies)*. Cambridge: Cambridge University Press, 1979.

IMA World Health. "Repositioning primary health care in South Sudan: Transitioning From NGO-Managed to MOH-Directed Primary Health Care Service Delivery." July 2016. Accessed January 28, 2019. https://imaworldhealth.org/wp-content/uploads/2016/07/Repositioning-Primary-Health-Care-in-South-Sudan.pdf.

"The Infectious Diseases Institute at Makerere University at Kampala, Uganda." *Clinical Infectious Diseases* 25, 2 (June, 2011): 369–383. https://doi.org/10.1016/j.idc.2011.02.007. Accessed January 21, 2019.

Institute of Human Virology Nigeria (IHVN). "About

Institute of Human Virology Nigeria (IHVN)." Accessed February 16, 2019. http://www.ihvnigeria.org/index.php/about-ihvn/introduction.html.

"Insufficient Funding Suffocates Green Belt Initiative." CISANET (Civil Society Agriculture Network. Accessed February 7, 2019. http://www.cisanetmw.org/index.php/45-insufficient-funding-suffocates-green-belt-initiative.

International Criminal Tribunal for Rwanda (UNICTR), International Residual Mechanism for Criminal Tribunals (IRMCT). "The Genocide." December 31, 2015. Accessed January 19, 2019. http://unictr.irmct.org/en/genocide.

IOM, International Organization of Migration. "Village Assessment Survey 2013 County Atlas 2013." Accessed January 27, 2019. https://iomsouthsudan.org/tracking/sites/default/publicfiles/documents/Unity_Koch_Atlas.pdf.

Ismail, Sumayya. "Ahmed Kathrada: The Robben Island diaries." *Al Jazeera,* March 28, 2017. Accessed February 6, 2019. https://www.aljazeera.com/indepth/features/2013/12/ahmed-kathrada-robben-island-diaries-201312883340753376.html.

Jackson, Andy. "October 23, 1984: BBC report on Ethiopian famine sparks global fundraising campaign." BBC. October 17, 2018. Accessed January 19, 2019. https://home.bt.com/news/on-this-day/october-23-1984-bbc-report-on-ethiopian-famine-shakes-the-world-into-action-11364012387968.

Johnson, Leigh F., and Rob E. Dorrington. "Modelling the impact of HIV in South Africa's provinces: 2017 update." September 2017. Accessed January 22, 2019. https://www.thembisa.org/content/filedl/Provinces2017.

Kanina, Wangui. "Kenya's election seen as badly flawed." *Reuters,* September 18, 2008. Accessed January 21, 2019. https://uk.reuters.com/article/uk-kenya-election/kenyas-election-seen-as-badly-flawed-idUKLI38786120080918.

Kapuma, Gertrude Aopesyaga. "Widowhood: a story of pain, a need for healing." 2011. Accessed January 21, 2019. http://academic.sun.ac.za/teologie/netact/genderequality2011/new/Ch5-Widowhood%20story%20of%20pain%20and%-20healing-Kapuma.pdf.

Kasakura, Archibald. "Bingu's wealth under probe." mwnation.com. March 11, 2017. Accessed January 24, 2019. https://mwnation.com/bingus-wealth-under-probe/.

Kayihura, Edouard, and Kerry Zukus. *Inside the Hotel Rwanda: The Surprising True Story ... and Why It Matters Today.* Dallas: BenBella Books; First Edition, 2014.

Khetani, Sanya. "This landlocked African state's dreams of an inland port are turning into a $6 billion debacle." Business Insider. May 12, 2012. Accessed January 23, 2019. https://www.businessinsider.com/malawi-nsanje-port-2012-5.

Khomba, Daniel Chris, and Alex Trew. "Aid and growth in Malawi." St. Andrew. November 4, 2016. Revised February 1, 2019. Accessed February 16, 2019. https://www.st-andrews.ac.uk/~wwwecon/repecfiles/4/1612.pdf.

Kimani, Mary. "Women struggle to secure land rights." Africa Renewal 2012. Accessed February 6, 2019. https://www.un.org/africarenewal/magazine/special-edition-women-2012/women-struggle-secure-land-rights.

Kingsley, Patrick. "'Better to Drown': A Greek Refugee Camp's Epidemic of Misery." *New York Times,* October. 2, 2018. Accessed February 1, 2019. https://www.nytimes.com/2018/10/02/world/europe/greece-lesbos-moria-refugees.html.

Kipling, Rudyard. *Just So Stories—Illustrated.* SMK Books, 2018.

Koech, Janet. "Hyperinflation in Zimbabwe." Federal Reserve Bank of Dallas - 2011 Annual Report, Globalization and Monetary Policy Institute. Accessed January 22, 2019. https://www.dallasfed.org/~/media/documents/institute/annual/2011/annual11b.pdf.

Kolstad, Kristine. "Cox's Bazar: The world's largest refugee settlement." Norwegian Refuge Council (NRC). August 24, 2018. Accessed February 1, 2019. https://www.nrc.no/news/2018/august/coxs-bazar-the-worlds-largest-refugee-settlement/.

Lai, Kwan Kew. *Lest We Forget: A Doctor's Experience with Life and Death During the Ebola Outbreak.* Jersey City: Viva Editions, 2018.

Lai, Kwan Kew. "Letters to the Editor: Courage in transition." *Wellesley Magazine,* October 1, 2013. accessed December 22, 2013. https://repository.wellesley.edu/cgi/viewcontent.cgi?article=1004&context=wellesleymagazine.

Lomba, Philo. "Widow Cleansing in Malawi." *American International Journal of Contemporary Research* Vol. 4, No. 1 (January 2014): 34–40. Accessed February 6, 2019. http://www.aijcrnet.com/journals/Vol_4_No_1_January_2014/6.pdf.

Lotha, Gloria. Martyrs of Uganda. britannica.com. March 10, 2016. Accessed January 25, 2019. https://www.britannica.com/event/Martyrs-of-Uganda.

Ludtke, Melissa. "Exits and Entrances: Women's Careers in Transition." *Wellesley Magazine,* April 1, 2013. Accessed May 14, 2013. https://repository.wellesley.edu/wellesleymagazine/2/.

MacFarquhar, Neil. "8 Tourists Slain in Uganda, Including US Couple in Uganda." *New York Times,* March 3, 1999. Accessed January 23, 2019. https://www.nytimes.com/1999/03/03/world/8-tourists-slain-in-uganda-including-us-couple.html.

"Malawi: Constitution no longer allows child marriage." girlsnotbrides.org. April 26, 2017. Accessed February 7, 2019. https://www.girlsnotbrides.org/malawi-constitution-no-longer-allows-child-marriage/.

"Malawi Demographic and Health Survey 2010." dhsprogram.com. September 2011. Accessed January 24, 2019. https://dhsprogram.com/pubs/pdf/FR247/FR247.pdf.

"Malawi Life Expectancy." worldlifeexpectancy. 2018. Accessed January 24, 2019. https://www.worldlifeexpectancy.com/malawi-life-expectancy.

Malawi Nation. "Health budget below recommended targets." mwnation.com. March 5, 2013. Accessed February 17, 2019. https://mwnation.com/health-budget-below-recommended-targets/.

Malawi National AIDS Commission. "Malawi National HIV and AIDS Strategic Plan 2011–2016." December 21, 2011. Accessed February 17, 2019. http://www.nationalplanningcycles.org/sites/default/files/country_docs/Malawi/malawi_national_hiv_and_aids_plan_2011-2016.pdf.

The Mandala House. Accessed March 27, 2019. https://societyofmalawi.org/the-mandala-house/.

Mandela, Nelson. "Address by Nelson Mandela at 46664 Concert, Cape Town." 46664 Concert, Cape Town, South Africa, November 23, 2003. Accessed April 2, 2010. http://www.mandela.gov.za/mandela_speeches/2003/031129_46664.htm.

Mandela, Nelson. "Confronting the Joint HIV/TB Epidemics." Presentation at XV International AIDS Conference, Bangkok, Thailand, July 15, 2004. Accessed January 22, 2019. https://www.who.int/3by5/news21/en/.

Mandela, Nelson. *Nelson Mandela by Himself: The Authorized Book of Quotations.* New York: Macmillan, 2011.

Mandhai, Shafik. "Libya six years on: No regrets over Gaddafi's demise." Al Jazeera. Oct 20, 2017. Accessed February 24, 2019. https://www.aljazeera.com/news/2017/10/years-regrets-libya-gaddafi-demise-171019073901622.html.

Maseno Mission Hospital. Accessed January 21, 2019. http://web.archive.org/web/20120422041417/masenomissions.org/hospital.htm.

Mawathe, Anne. "Horn of Africa drought: Survival of the fittest." bbc.com. July 9, 2011. Accessed January 21, 2019. https://www.bbc.com/news/world-africa-14084670.

Médecins Sans Frontières. "Forced closure of 'Refugee Reception Office' further endangers health of vulnerable Zimbabweans in South Africa." March 4, 2009. Accessed January 23, 2019. https://www.msf.org/forced-closure-refugee-reception-office-further-endangers-health-vulnerable-zimbabweans-south.

Meldrum, Andrew. "Kenya: Lamu island hit by new kidnapping." pri.org. October 1, 2011. Accessed January 25, 2019. https://www.pri.org/stories/2011-10-01/kenya-lamu-island-hit-new-kidnapping.

Meldrum, Andrew." Zimbabwe's health-care system struggles on." Lancet 371:9618 (March 29, 2008): 1059–1060. https://doi.org/10.1016/S0140-6736(08)60468-7. Accessed January 22, 2019.

Mildmay. "Milway Uganda." Accessed January 21, 2019. https://mildmay.org/our-overseas-work/mildmay-uganda/.

Milner, Kate. "Flashback 1984: Portrait of a famine." BBC. April 6, 2000. Accessed January 19, 2019. http://news.bbc.co.uk/2/hi/africa/703958.stm.

Ministry of Health, Republic of Uganda. "Mulago National Referral Hospital." Accessed January 21, 2019. https://health.go.ug/content/mulago-national-referral-hospital.

Mswati, Mike. "Sex tourism: 'Mzungu' women who travel to Kenya to get laid by local men." 2018. Accessed February 4, 2019. https://www.sde.co.ke/article/2001252790/sex-tourism-mzungu-women-who-travel-to-kenya-to-get-laid-by-local-men.

Muhumuza, Rodney. "Hutu refugees fear forced return to Rwanda." Omaha World-Herald, April 19, 2013. Accessed January 24, 2019. https://www.omaha.com/news/hutu-refugees-fear-forced-return-to-rwanda/article_1a2b6775-98fe-5927-88f3-cea2ce081e8f.html.

Muwamba, Emmanuel. "Food insecurity to rise in Malawi." mwnation.com. July 31, 2013. Accessed February 7, 2019. https://mwnation.com/food-insecurity-to-rise-in-malawi/.

Mzale, Dumbani. "Cashgate darkened the economy in 2013." mwnations.com. December 16, 2013. Accessed February 7, 2019. https://mwnation.com/cashgate-darkened-the-economy-in-2013/.

National Institute for Communicable Diseases Bulletin (NICD). "Cholera outbreak in South Africa: preliminary descriptive epidemiology on laboratory-confirmed cases, 15 November 2008 to April 2009." *Communicable Diseases Surveillance Bulletin,* 7:2 (May 2009). Accessed January 22, 2019. http://www.nicd.ac.za/assets/files/CommDisBullMay09_Vol0702.pdf.

Nieftagodien, Noor. *The Soweto Uprising (Ohio Short Histories of Africa).* Ohio: Ohio University Press, 2014.

Njoroge, Gladys, and Tumi Makgabo. "Historic Sudan peace accord signed." CNN. January 9, 2005. Accessed January 27, 2019. http://www.cnn.com/2005/WORLD/africa/01/09/sudan.signing/.

Ntabadde Catherine. "Uganda Red Cross to manage Congolese refugees camp in Kisoro." Reliefweb.int. July 16, 2012. Accessed January 25, 2019. https://reliefweb.int/report/uganda/uganda-red-cross-manage-congolese-refugees-camp-kisoro.

Ntata, Z. Allan. "License to loot: A report on the Cashgate corruption scandal in Malawi." whatdotheyknow.com. November 2013. Accessed February7, 2019. https://www.whatdotheyknow.com/request/202520/response/524932/attach/html/5/MALAWI%20CASHGATE%20SCANDAL%20REPORT.pdf.html.

Nyaka, Owen. "Malawi faces shortage of healthcare workers as it battles AIDS epidemic." aidspan.org. January 21, 2014. Accessed January 24, 2019. http://www.aidspan.org/gfo_article/malawi-faces-shortage-healthcare-workers-it-battles-aids-epidemic.

Nyasa Times. "Kapito claims Malawi Pres. Banda has created hunger: 'She emptied maize silos.'" March 8, 2013. Accessed February 7, 2019. http://www.nyasatimes.com/kapito-claims-malawi-pres-banda-has-created-hunger-she-emptied-maize-silos/.

Nyasa Times. "Malawi cash-gate: The truth is on holiday!" November 27, 2013. Accessed January 24, 2019. https://www.nyasatimes.com/malawi-cash-gate-the-truth-is-on-holiday/.

OCHA, Office for the Coordination of Humanitarian Affairs. "Horn of Africa: Drought Crisis, Updates & Developments." Aug. 9, 2011. Accessed September 1, 2011. https://reliefweb.int/sites/reliefweb.int/files/resources/HoA_Updates%20and%20Developments_09%20Aug%202011.pdf.

OCHA. Office for the Coordination of Humanitarian Affairs. "Situation overview." April 1–7,

2013. Accessed April 27, 2013. Humanitarian Bulletin South Sudan. https://reliefweb.int/sites/reliefweb.int/files/resources/OCHA%20South%20Sudan%20Weekly%20Humanitarian%20Bulletin%20I-7%20April%202013.pdf.

OCHA, Office for the Coordination of Humanitarian Affairs. "Somalia• Famine & Drought, Situation Report No. 8." August 10, 2011. Accessed September 1, 2011. https://reliefweb.int/sites/reliefweb.int/files/resources/OCHA%20Somalia%20Situation%20Report%20No.%208%2010%20August%202011.pdf.

Ogle, Alex. "Zimbabwe cholera outbreak spreads to SA." *Mail & Guardian,* December 5, 2008. Accessed January 22, 2019. https://mg.co.za/article/2008-12-05-zimbabwe-cholera-outbreak-spreads-to-sa.

Ogundipe, Sola, and Chioma Obinna. "HIV & AIDS: If you're not infected, you're affected." *Vanguard,* December 4, 2010. Accessed February 6, 2019. https://www.vanguardngr.com/2010/12/hiv-aids-if-youre-not-infected-youre-affected/.

Oxfam International. "'I miss my husband'—DRC refugees seek safety in Uganda." Conflict and Emergencies blog channel, September 3, 2012. Accessed September 30, 2012. https://blogs.oxfam.org/en/blogs/12-09-03-drc-refugees-seek-safety-uganda.

Popplewell, Geoffrey. "The British Empire: In the wake of the Germans, Tanganyika in the Inter-War Years." Britishempire. Accessed February 2, 2019. https://www.britishempire.co.uk/article/inthewakeofthegermans.htm.

Powell, Anita. "Hunger spreads to Ethiopia's adults as food crisis worsens." Associated Press, June 10, 2008. Accessed January 19, 2019. http://archive.boston.com/news/world/africa/articles/2008/06/10/hunger_spreads_to_ethiopias_adults_as_food_crisis_worsens/.

Reach Out Mbuya. Accessed January 21, 2019. http://www.reachoutmbuya.org/.

Refworld. "UNHCR position on returns to South Sudan." February 2014. Accessed February 9, 2019. https://www.refworld.org/pdfid/52fa1ecd4.pdf.

Refworld. "World Refugee Survey 2009—South Africa." June 17, 2009. Last updated February 15, 2019. Accessed January 23, 2019. https://www.refworld.org/docid/4a40d2b22.html.

Reid, Kathryn. "2015 Nepal earthquake: Facts, FAQs, and how to help." World Vision. April 3, 2018. Accessed February 1, 2019. https://www.worldvision.org/disaster-relief-news-stories/2015-nepal-earthquake-facts.

Reid, Kathryn. "2013 Typhoon Haiyan: Facts, FAQs, and how to help." World Vision. November 9, 2018. Accessed February 1, 2019. https://www.worldvision.org/disaster-relief-news-stories/typhoon-haiyan-facts.

Reliefweb. "South Africa: More Zimbabwean migrants expected in Musina." April 30, 2009. Accessed February 5, 2019. https://reliefweb.int/report/south-africa/south-africa-more-zimbabwean-migrants-expected-musina.

Reliefweb. "South Sudan 2018 Humanitarian Needs Overview." November 2017. Accessed February 9, 2019. https://reliefweb.int/sites/reliefweb.int/files/resources/South_Sudan_2018_Humanitarian_Needs_Overview.pdf.

Reliefweb. "Uganda Refugee Response Monitoring Settlement Fact Sheet: Nakivale (June 2018)." June 30, 2018. Accessed January 24, 2019. https://reliefweb.int/report/uganda/uganda-refugee-response-monitoring-settlement-fact-sheet-nakivale-june-2018.

Rice, Xan. "Two aid workers kidnapped from Kenyan refugee camp." *The Guardian.* October 13, 2011. Accessed January 25, 2019. https://www.theguardian.com/world/2011/oct/13/aid-workers-kidnapped-kenyan-camp.

Robertson, Wilfrid. *Mandala Trail: A Tale of Early Days in Nyasaland.* Oxford University Press, 1956.

Ronald, Allan, Moses Kamya, Elly Katabira, W. Michael Scheld, and Nelson Sewankambo. "The Infectious Diseases Institute at Makerere University at Kampala, Uganda." *Clinical Infectious Diseases* 25, 2 (June, 2011): 369–383. https://doi.org/10.1016/j.idc.2011.02.007. Accessed January 21, 2019.

Rondganger, Lee. "Musina at breaking point as refugees pour in." *IOL,* December 23, 2008. Accessed January 23, 2019. https://www.iol.co.za/news/politics/musina-at-breaking-point-as-refugees-pour-in-429590.

Schweitzer, Albert. *Out of My Life and Thought: An Autobiography.* New York: The New American Library, 1964.

Sharp, Leonard E. S. *Island of Miracles: The Story of the Lake Bunyoni Leprosy Settlement.* Uganda. Rwanda: Ruanda General and Medical Mission, C.M.S, 1951.

Simpson, Gerry, and Joe Amon. "Neighbors in need: Zimbabweans seeking refuge in South Africa." Human Rights Watch. June 19, 2008. Accessed January 23, 2019. https://www.hrw.org/report/2008/06/19/neighbors-need-zimbabweans-seeking-refuge-south-africa.

Sky News. "King of Swaziland changes his country's name to eSwatini." 2018. Accessed February 4, 2019. https://news.sky.com/story/king-of-swaziland-changes-his-countrys-name-to-eswatini-11338333.

Smith, Dianne. "Sophie's Choice—and Ours," HEART TO GOD: MISSION TO MASENO, December 1, 2008. Accessed December 11, 2011. http://heart-to-god.blogspot.com.

"South Sudan, A new depth of horror." *Economist,* April 26, 2014. Accessed February 9, 2019. https://www.economist.com/middle-east-and-africa/2014/04/26/a-new-depth-of-horror.

Statham, Todd. "Scott, David Clement." *Dictionary of African Christian Biography,* 2014. Accessed January 24, 2019, https://dacb.org/stories/malawi/scott-davidc/.

Static1. "Toward an AIDS-free Uganda: Scaling up 90–90–90 targets. "Accessed February 2, 2019. https://static1.squarespace.com/static/5a57ffe52aeba57afe10b243/t/5ae7a29f8a922d40d2a8185b/1525129893034/ABH_aids_free_uganda_br.pdf.

Steffen, Sarah. "Crisis in Burundi—a timeline."

December 5, 2015. Accessed February 10, 2019. https://www.dw.com/en/crisis-in-burundi-a-timeline/a-18446677.

Theroux, Paul. *Dark Star Safari: Overland from Cairo to Capetown.* New York: Houghton Mifflin, 2003.

Theroux, Paul. *The Lower River.* New York: Mariner Books, 2012.

Thomson, Susan. *Rwanda: From Genocide to Precarious Peace.* New Haven: Yale University Press, 2018.

Tisdall, Simon. "East Africa's drought: The avoidable disaster." *The Guardian,* January 17, 2012. Accessed February 7, 2019. https://www.theguardian.com/world/2012/jan/18/east-africa-drought-disaster-report.

Tomasky, Michael. "Gaddafi's letter to Obama." *The Guardian,* May 19, 2011. Accessed January 25, 2019. https://www.theguardian.com/commentisfree/michaeltomasky/2011/mar/19/barack-obama-muammar-gaddafi-answer-the-letter.

Trans, Mark, and agencies. "Kenya's leaders agree power-sharing deal." *The Guardian,* February 28, 2008. Accessed March 25, 2019. https://www.theguardian.com/world/2008/feb/28/kenya.

Uganda Cares. Accessed January 21, 2019 https://www.aidshealth.org/global/uganda/.

UN Peacemaker. "The Comprehensive Peace Agreement between the government of the Republic of South Sudan and the Sudan's People Liberation Movement/Sudan People's Liberation Army." May 26, 2004. Accessed January 27, 2019. https://peacemaker.un.org/sites/peacemaker.un.org/files/SD_060000_The%20Comprehensive%20Peace%20Agreement.pdf.

UN Peacemaker. "Peace Agreement between the Government and the CNDP." March 23, 2009. Accessed January 25, 2019. https://peacemaker.un.org/sites/peacemaker.un.org/files/CD_090323_Peace%20Agreement%20between%20the%20Government%20and%20the%20CNDP.pdf.

UNAIDS. Joint United Nations Programme on HIV/AIDS. "90–90–90 An ambitious treatment target to help end the AIDS epidemic." October, 2014. Accessed February 2, 2019. http://www.unaids.org/sites/default/files/media_asset/90-90-90_en.pdf.

UNAIDS. "Republic of South Africa country progress report on the declaration of commitment on HIV/AIDS 2010 report." Accessed January 22, 2019. http://data.unaids.org/pub/report/2010/southafrica_2010_country_progress_report_en.pdf

UNAIDS. "2008 Report on the global AIDS epidemic." 2008. Accessed January 22, 2019. http://www.unaids.org/sites/default/files/media_asset/jc1510_2008globalreport_en_0.pdf.

UNHCR. "Acute malnutrition threshold." Accessed February 7, 2019. https://emergency.unhcr.org/entry/249075/acute-malnutrition-threshold.

UNHCR. "Rohingya emergency." August 15, 2018. Accessed February 1, 2019. https://www.unhcr.org/rohingya-emergency.html.

UNHCR Uganda. UN Uganda Bulletin Vol 25, March 23, 2018. Accessed February 17, 2019. http://ug.one.un.org/sites/default/files/newsletters/UN%20Uganda%20Bulletin%20Vol%2025%20%2023%20March%202018.pdf.

UNICEF. "Africa's Orphaned and Vulnerable Generations, Children Affected by AIDS." August, 2006. Accessed January 21, 2019. https://www.unicef.org/publications/files/Africas_Orphaned_and_Vulnerable_Generations_Children_Affected_by_AIDS.pdf.

UNICEF. "HIV/AIDS UNICEF Nigeria." June 2007. Accessed January 23, 2019. https://www.unicef.org/wcaro/english/WCARO_Nigeria_Factsheets_HIV-AIDS.pdf.

UNICEF. "RapidFTR (Family tracing and reunification)." Unicefstories.org. May 20, 2014. Accessed February 8, 2019. http://unicefstories.org/2014/05/20/rapidftr-2/.

United Nations. "Sudan peace agreement signed 9 January historic opportunity, Security Council told." February 8, 2005. Accessed January 27, 2019. https://www.un.org/press/en/2005/sc8306.doc.htm.

US Congress. "Public Law 108–25,108th Congress." May 27, 2003. Accessed January 15, 2019. https://www.congress.gov/108/plaws/publ25/PLAW-108publ25.pdf.

Wood, Alan. *The Groundnut Affair.* London: The Bodley Head, 1950.

World Bank. "Eswatini at-a-glance." 2018. Accessed February 4, 2019. https://www.worldbank.org/en/country/eswatini.

World Health Organization. "AIDS Epidemic Update." December, 2005. Accessed January 20, 2019. https://www.who.int/hiv/epi-update2005_en.pdf?ua=1.

World Health Organization. "Global Task Force on Cholera Control, Cholera Country Profile: Zimbabwe." October 31, 2009. Accessed January 22, 2019. https://www.who.int/cholera/countries/ZimbabweCountryProfileOct2009.pdf?ua=1.

World Health Organization. "Guidelines on when to start antiretroviral therapy and pre-exposure prophylaxis for HIV." September 2015. Accessed January 24, 2019. https://apps.who.int/iris/bitstream/handle/10665/186275/9789241509565_eng.pdf;jsessionid=11DF1DFC06EC38B571679C9F40871236?seq.

World Health Organization. "United Republic of Tanzania." December, 2005. Accessed January 25, 2019. https://www.who.int/hiv/HIVCP_TZA.pdf.

Wuol, Duop Chak. "South Sudan Quotes." Accessed December 21, 2016. https://www.goodreads.com/quotes/tag/south-sudan.

Index

Numbers in *bold italics* indicate pages with illustrations